LSD
PSYCHOTHERAPY

Stanislav Grof, M.D.

Multidisciplinary Association for Psychedelic Studies

Multidisciplinary Association for Psychedelic Studies (MAPS)
10424 Love Creek Road, Ben Lomond, CA 95005
voice: (831)336-4325 • fax: (831)336-3665
e-mail: askmaps@maps.org • www.maps.prg

Libray of Congress Cataloging-in-Publication Data
Grof, Stanislav, 1931–
LSD Psychotherapy: exploring the frontiers of the hidden mind / by Stanislav Grof

p. cm.
Pbk ed. of:LSD Psychotherapy, 2001, 1980
Includes biographical references and index.
ISBN 0-9798622-0-5 (pbk. 2007)
1. LSD (Drug)—Therapeutic use. 2. Psychotherapy.
I. Grof, Stanislav, 1931– LSD Psychotherapy.
II. Title: {DNLM: 1.Lysergic Acid Diethylamide—therapeutic use.
2. Psychotherapy. WM420 G874f}
RC483.5L9G75 1994
616.89'18—dc20 DNLM/DLC 92-1429

Cover design/build: Mark Plummer
Cover Photo: Razvan Multescu
Printed by: McNaughton & Gunn, Saline MI

9 8 7 6 5 4 3 2 1   Fourth Edition

Dedicated with love
to Christina

THIS NEW EDITION FUNDED BY
GRANTS TO MAPS FROM
KEVIN HERBERT AND
THE HELIOS FOUNDATION.

List of Color Plates

LIST OF CONTENTS

INTRODUCTION to Fourth Edition

By Albert Hofmann

On my 102nd birthday, I feel a profound sense of satisfaction and peace to be able to witness while I am still alive a budding renaissance in legal psychedelic research. The culmination of this quiet renewal, which has been building since about 1990, is the resumption of LSD psychotherapy research, which has now been approved for the first time in about 35 years. LSD is the most stigmatized of all the psychedelics and is the last to reenter the laboratory.

As I reflect on all the LSD and psilocybin research that has been conducted to date, I'm most appreciative of the work of Dr. Stanislav Grof, author of *LSD Psychotherapy.* If I am the father of LSD, Stan Grof is the godfather. Nobody has contributed as much as Stan for the development of my problem child. Not only does Stan have more direct experience than anybody else sitting with patients under the influence LSD, but he also has cultivated a clarity of intellect and a strength of emotion that enabled him to develop a theory and a method of LSD-assisted psychotherapy. In this superb textbook, Stan describes in detail a method of therapy that hasn't been practiced for decades and painstakingly explains how his theories of mind grew out of the empirical observations that he made during his LSD research studies. *LSD Psychotherapy* is a powerful, sustained and persuasive argument for the renewal of psychedelic research.

LSD and psilocybin are not drugs in the usual sense, but are part of the sacred substances, which have been used for thousand of years in ritual settings. The classic psychedelics like LSD, psilocybin and mescaline are characterized by the fact that they are neither toxic nor addictive. It is my great concern to separate psychedelics from the ongoing debates about drugs, and to highlight the tremendous potential inherent to these substances for self-awareness, as an adjunct in therapy, and for fundamental research into the human mind. In all of these areas, Stan has been an outstanding pioneer.

Alienation from nature and the loss of the experience of being part of the living creation is the greatest tragedy of our materialistic era. It is the causative reason for ecological devastation and climate change. Therefore I attribute absolute highest importance to consciousness change. I regard psychedelics as catalyzers for this. They are tools which are guiding our perception toward other deeper areas of our human existence, so that we again become aware of our spiritual essence. Psychedelic experiences in a safe setting can help our consciousness open up to this sensation of connection and of being one with nature. The elegance of Stan's approach to LSD psychotherapy is that it blends psychotherapeutic with existential insights, as in the days of old when therapy and religion were co-mingled.

It is my wish that a modern Eleusis and a modern psychiatry will emerge, in which seeking humans can learn to have transcendent experiences with sacred substances in a safe setting, and in which LSD and other psychedelics become once again tools for psychotherapeutic healing and for discovery of the breadth and depth of the mind. When that day comes, Stan will have laid the cornerstone and his classic work, *LSD Psychotherapy*, will be the jumping off point for further developments and refinements.

Albert Hofmann
Basel, Switzerland
January 11, 2008

FOREWORD

By Andrew Weil, M.D.

It seems astonishing that almost half a century after Stan Grof began using LSD as a tool in psychotherapy, the drug remains off limits for therapeutic purposes and even for medical research. In purely physiological terms, lysergic acid diethylamide is the least toxic drug known to science. It does not kill, even in massive overdose, and despite producing dramatic changes in consciousness, has no adverse or lasting effects on the body. Numerous case reports testify to its positive potential in psychotherapeutic use – for the treatment of addictions, neuroses, and anxiety disorders — and there are suggestions of further usefulness in treating chronic medical illness, including pain syndromes. Nevertheless, at the dawn of the twenty-first century, LSD remains a demonized drug in most societies, officially declared to be both dangerous and devoid of therapeutic value.

The reasons for this irrational state of affairs are several. One is that LSD has kept "bad company" in the past: with hippies, revolutionaries, rock-and-roll fanatics, and other elements of society perceived by the dominant culture as antisocial and subversive. It is also, by law and necessity, now forced to keep company with other "drugs of abuse," including cocaine and heroin, whose dangers are obvious and frightening. Furthermore, LSD has a reputation as a kind of stealth drug, since it produces its effects in amounts so small as to be invisible. The ease of smuggling and concealing it fuels fantasies of its being slipped to unsuspecting victims, even put into water supplies to render whole populations psychotic and helpless. It was this characteristic of LSD that made it attractive to the military and the Central Intelligence Agency in the 1950s as a possible tool for purposes far from therapeutic.

For medical and psychiatric professionals, LSD is problematic in another way. Its effects are highly variable from person to person and exquisitely dependent on set and setting, that is, on expectation and environment. LSD sessions can be trips to heaven or hell, and the apparent unpredictability of the direction they take has scared off both researchers and therapists.

In fact, the chance that an LSD reaction will be hellish is not so unpredictable. It increases with dose, with lack of preparation of the subject, and with lack of attention to environmental factors that promote anxiety or security. In the hands of a skilled and experienced therapist like Stanislav Grof, LSD was quite safe, and the reactions it produced were manageable and useful, even if intense. "Experienced" in this context must include having had personal experience with the drug.

This is not an easy point to explain to the medical community. Doctors value drugs that work as magic bullets – that have precise, predictable actions, relatively consistent from person to person and explainable in terms of specific biochemical mechanisms, not in terms of practitioner experience or patient expectation. Psychiatrists and others who read published reports of early therapeutic successes with LSD and attempted to use it as a magic bullet without attention to set, setting, or their own experience failed to reproduce the desired results. Almost half a century later, with traditional psychotherapy largely replaced by overwhelming prescribing of psychopharmaceutical magic bullets (the selective serotonin reuptake inhibitor antidepressants accounting for a lion's share of the prescriptions), the chances of psychiatrists and others understanding the subtleties and artfulness of LSD psychotherapy seem smaller than ever.

Nonetheless I believe it remains worth the effort to try to increase that understanding, because the therapeutic potential of LSD is undiminished. Perhaps, now that recreational use of the drug has subsided and stabilized and authorities are much more worried about other psychoactive agents, the time is right to reopen the conversation. I can think of no better way to do so than to publish this ground-breaking book in a new edition. *LSD Psychotherapy* is a classic work in both the psychotherapeutic and psychopharmacological traditions, and I very much hope than Stan Grof's experience and wisdom will find a new and wider readership in the new century.

Andrew Weil, MD
Tucson, Arizona
October, 2000

PREFACE

In 1980 when this book first appeared, the timing of its publication could not have been worse. By that time, psychedelic therapy had been practically discontinued in all the countries of the world as a result of extremely stringent legislation. It made scientific research difficult, if not impossible. The image of LSD was not shaped by already existing extensive professional literature; it was dictated by mass media sensationalizing the accidents of unsupervised self-experimentation and spreading scientifically unsubstantiated rumors about chromosome damage and genetic dangers associated with this substance. Under these circumstances, it seemed that *LSD Psychotherapy* was destined to become an esoteric historical document of an exciting, but relatively brief and transient era of psychiatric history.

Considering the situation described above, it seems appropriate to look at some of the recent developments that justify a new edition of this work. The most important reason for making the observations from psychedelic research available to professionals, as well as the general public, is the revolutionary nature of the observations associated with it. I seriously believe that unbiased systematic study of this material would lead to changes in our understanding of the human psyche and of the nature of reality that would be as far-reaching and radical as those that were introduced into physics by the theories of relativity and the quantum theory.

The critical element here is the recognition that LSD and other psychedelics function more or less as nonspecific catalysts and amplifiers of the psyche. This is reflected in the name given by Humphrey Osmond to this group of substances; the Greek word "psychedelic" translates literally as "mind-manifesting." In the dosages used in human experimentation, the classical psychedelics, such as LSD, psilocybin, and mescaline, do not have any specific pharmacological effects. They increase the energetic niveau in the psyche and the body which leads to manifestation of otherwise latent psychological processes.

The content and nature of the experiences that these substances induce are thus not artificial products of their pharmacological interaction with the brain ("toxic psychoses"), but authentic expressions of the psyche revealing its functioning on levels ordinarily not available for observation and study. A person who has taken LSD does not have an "LSD experience," but takes a journey into deep recesses of his or her own psyche. When this substance is given in the same dosage and under comparable circumstances to a large number of individuals, each of them will have a different experience reflecting the specificities of his or her psyche. In addition, serial sessions of the same person will vary in their content and show a characteristic progression.

For this reason, it does not seem to be an exaggeration to say that psychedelics, used responsibly and with proper caution, would be for psychiatry what the microscope is for biology and medicine or the telescope is for astronomy. These tools make it possible to study important processes that under normal circumstances are not available for direct observation. In the first edition if this book, I wrote that the best way of understanding LSD is to see it as an unspecific amplifier of psychological processes. If I had any remaining doubts about this point of view, they have been all but dispelled by our observations from Holotropic Breathwork™. This approach is a powerful method of therapy and self-exploration that my wife Christina and I have developed over the last eighteen years and have used in workshops and seminars all over the world. It combines extremely simple nonpharmacological means, such as accelerated breathing, evocative music, and a system of body interventions aimed at release of pent-up emotions and blocked physical energies. As I have described in *The Adventure of Self-Discovery*, a book specifically discussing the theory and practice of Holotropic Breathwork™, the spectrum of the experiences evoked by this procedure is practically identical with that of psychedelic sessions.

Experiences occurring in psychedelic and holotropic sessions cannot be described in terms of the narrow and superficial conceptual model used in academic psychiatry and psychology, which is limited to biology, postnatal biography, and the Freudian individual unconscious. Deep experiential work requires a vastly extended cartography of the psyche that includes important domains uncharted by traditional science. My own version of such a model described in the present volume includes two additional levels of the psyche, for which I use the terms *perinatal* and *transpersonal*.

The phenomena originating on the perinatal and transpersonal levels of the psyche include sequences of psychological death and rebirth, encounters with archetypal beings, visits to mythological realms of various cultures, past incarnation memories, extrasensory perception, episodes of out-of-body states, experiences of cosmic consciousness research. These have to be considered to be natural and normal manifestations of the deeper dynamics of the human psyche.

They have been repeatedly described in the context of various shamanic procedures, rites of passage, aboriginal healing ceremonies, and mysteries of death and rebirth, as well as Eastern spiritual philosophies and mystical traditions of all ages. For this reason, any serious effort to understand spirituality and religion requires recognition of the perinatal and transpersonal dimensions of the psyche. Attempts to interpret any of these phenomena in the context of the narrow and superficial model of the psyche currently used by Newtonian-Cartesian science necessarily leads to serious distortions and to pathologization of the entire spiritual history of humanity.

From this perspective, the founders of the great religions of the world, as well as their prophets, saints, and eminent teachers, all of whom had visionary experiences, are labeled as psychotics. Shamans are diagnosed as ambulant schizophrenics, hysterics, or epileptics. Religion and spirituality are interpreted as resulting from superstition, lack of education, infantile regression to primitive and material thinking, or mental disease. Similar pathological criteria are applied to the ritual and spiritual life of pre-industrial cultures that cannot be adequately understood and makes no sense to Western scientists with their limited model of the human psyche.

Among additional phenomena that elude the reductionist interpretations of Western materialistic science are the experiences in near-death situations, reports about UFO abductions, various parapsychological occurrences, as well as experiences and behaviors observed in certain forms of hypnosis and various powerful experiential psychotherapies other than Holotropic Breathwork™. Experiences induced by biofeedback training, sensory deprivation and overload, different electronic and kinesthetic devices, and lucid dreaming are additional important examples.

The same can be said about a large subgroup of states that contemporary psychiatry diagnoses and treats as functional psychoses, meaning mental diseases of unknown etiology. The understanding of the psyche that includes the perinatal and transpersonal levels shows these conditions in an entirely new light as psychospiritual crises or "spiritual emergencies." If they are properly understood and the individuals engaged in this process are encouraged to surrender to their experiences, these states can result in emotional and psychosomatic healing, deep personality transformation, and consciousness evolution.

The extended cartography of the psyche described in the present volume, although originally based on the research with LSD and other psychedelics, is equally applicable to all the above situations. It makes it possible to account for many phenomena that traditional psychiatry and psychology have to deny, pathologize, or explain in a superficial and inadequate way. However, the new findings offer much more than a revised and vastly expanded theoretical model of the psyche. Many of the new principles discovered during psychedelic research are of a highly practical nature and are directly applicable to therapeutic situations without the use of psychoactive substances. Here belongs a new and revolutionary understanding of the nature and architecture of emotional and psychosomatic disorders, including certain forms of psychoses, effective mechanisms of healing and transformation, therapeutic techniques, and strategies of self-exploration.

The future implications of psychedelic research thus fall into two different categories. The first of these involves the destiny of psychedelic therapy per se, the other the theoretical and practical importance of the new discoveries about the nature of the psyche and of consciousness. Whether or not psychedelics will return into psychiatry and will again become part of the therapeutic armamentarium is a complex question. Most likely, what will have the decisive influence will not be the results of scientific research, but a variety of political, legal, economic, and mass-psychological factors.

After having personally conducted over the years more than four thousand psychedelic sessions, I have developed great awe and respect for these substances and their enormous positive, as well as negative potential. They are powerful tools and like any tool they can be used skillfully, ineptly, and destructively. The question whether LSD is a phenomenal medicine or a devil's drug makes as little sense as a similar question asked about the positive or negative potential of a knife. Naturally, we will get a very different picture from a surgeon who bases his or her judgment on successful operations and from the police chief who investigates murders with knives. Similarly, the image of LSD will vary whether we focus on the results of responsible clinical or spiritual use, naive and careless mass self-experimentation of the young generation, or deliberately destructive experiments of the army or the CIA.

The results of the administration of psychedelics are critically influenced by the factors of set and setting. Until this is clearly understood, there is no hope for rational decisions in regard to psychedelic drug policies. I believe that psychedelics can be used in such a way that the benefits by far outweigh the possible risks. This has been amply proven by centuries of safe ritual and spiritual use of psychedelics by generations of shamans, individual healers, and entire aboriginal cultures. However, the Western industrial civilization has so far abused all its discoveries and there is not much hope that psychedelics will make an exception, unless we rise as a group to a higher level of consciousness and emotional maturity.

On the positive side, it can be said that Western society is at present much better equipped to assimilate psychedelics than it was in the 1960s. At the time when psychiatrists and psychologists started to experiment with LSD, the official image of psychotherapy was that of civilized face-to-face discussions or disciplined free-associating on the couch. Intense emotions and active behavior were referred to as "acting-out" and were seen as violations of basic therapeutic rules. In contrast, psychedelic sessions were associated with dramatic emotions, psychomotor excitement, and vivid perceptual changes.

They thus seemed to be closer to states that psychiatrists considered to be pathological and tried to suppress by all means than to conditions to which one would attribute therapeutic potential. This was reflected in the terms "hallucinogens" and "experimental psychoses" used initially for psychedelics and the states induced by them. In any case, psychedelic sessions resembled more scenes from anthropological movies about shamanic rituals of "primitive" cultures and wild aboriginal ceremonies than those from a psychoanalyst's office.

In addition, many of the experiences and observations from psychedelic sessions seemed to seriously challenge the image of the human psyche and of the universe developed by Newtonian-Cartesian science and considered to be accurate and definitive descriptions of "objective reality." Psychedelic subjects reported experiential identification with other people, animals, and various aspects of nature during which they gained access to new information about areas about which they previously had no intellectual knowledge. The same was true about experiential excursions into the lives of their human and animal ancestors, as well as racial, collective, and karmic memories.

On occasion, this new information was drawn from experiences involving archetypal beings and mythological realms of different cultures in the world. In out-of-body experiences, experimental subjects often witnessed and accurately described remote events occurring in locations that were outside of the range of their senses. None of these happenings were considered possible in the context of traditional materialistic science and yet, in psychedelic sessions, they were observed on a daily basis. This naturally caused deep conceptual turmoil and confusion in the minds of conventionally trained experimenters. Under these circumstances, many professionals chose to stay away from this area to preserve their scientific world-view and to protect their common sense and sanity.

The last three decades brought many revolutionary changes that have profoundly influenced the climate in the world of psychotherapy. Humanistic and transpersonal psychologies have developed powerful experiential techniques that emphasize deep regression, direct expression of intense emotions, and bodywork leading to release of physical energies. The inner experiences and outer manifestations, as well as therapeutic strategies, in these therapies bear a great similarity to those observed in psychedelic sessions. As I mentioned earlier in relation to Holotropic Breathwork™, these nondrug approaches involve a similar spectrum of experiences, as well as comparable conceptual challenges. As a result of it, for therapists practicing along these lines, the introduction of psychedelics would represent the next logical step rather than dramatic change in their practice.

Moreover, the Newtonian-Cartesian thinking in science that in the 1960s enjoyed great authority and popularity has been progressively undermined by astonishing developments in a variety of disciplines. This has happened to such an extent that an increasing number of scientists feel an urgent need for an entirely different world-view, a new scientific paradigm. Philosophical implications of quantum-relativistic physics, David Bohm's theory of holomovement, Karl Pribram's holographic theory of the brain, Ilya Prigogine's theory of dissipative structures, Rupert Shekdrake's theory of morphogenetic fields, and Gregory Bateson's brilliant anthropology and psychology, are just a few eminent examples of this development. It is very encouraging that all these new developments that are in irreconcilable conflict with traditional science seem to be compatible with the findings of modern consciousness research and with transpersonal psychology.

From a practical point of view, it is important to mention that legal experimentation with psychedelics has been resumed in Switzerland and several new research projects have recently been approved in the United States. In spite of all these encouraging developments, the future of psychedelic therapy as such remains uncertain. However, the situation is very different in regard to its revolutionary findings concerning the nature of the psyche and human consciousness; their relevance for psychiatry and psychology is independent from the fate of this therapeutic modality. Since it has become clear that the phenomena involved represent genuine manifestations of the psyche that occur in many situations where no psychoactive substances are involved, they have to be taken into consideration in any serious attempt to understand the human psyche.

If the experiences observed in psychedelic sessions were toxic artifacts, professionals would have a reasonable excuse for their disinterest in this area. One could be an expert in the field without having knowledge about the pharmacological effects of an exotic group of psychoactive substances. However, ignoring or misinterpreting observations from a large category of situations, including ancient and Oriental spiritual practices, trance states in aboriginal rituals, near-death experiences, various forms of nonpharmacological experiential psychotherapies, and psychospiritual crises is a different matter. Such an approach reflects rigid adherence to a superficial and inadequate model of the psyche and resembles more religious fundamentalism than good science.

The critical issue here is the ontological status of non-ordinary states of consciousness—whether we see them as pathological conditions that should be indiscriminately suppressed or variable alternatives to our everyday states of consciousness that can contribute to our understanding of the psyche and have a great therapeutic potential. Of all the human groups, the Western industrial civilization is the only one that has taken the former position. All the ancient and pre-industrial societies have held non-ordinary states of consciousness in high esteem and used them for a variety of purposes—diagnosing and healing diseases, ritual, spiritual, and religious activity, cultivation of extrasensory perception, and artistic inspiration. These cultures have spent much time and energy developing various techniques of inducing these states, including a wide range of nonpharmacological approaches and psychedelic plants.

Michael Harner, a well-known anthropologist who has also undergone personal shamanic initiation during his field work in the Amazon, describes that from his dual perspective Western psychology and psychiatry are seriously biased in two important ways. They are *ethnocentric*, which means that they consider their own idiosyncratic point of view to be superior to that of any other cultural group and label as pathological any activities that they cannot understand in their own framework. Harner's name for the second serious conceptual distortion is *cognicentric*, although a better term for it might be *pragmacentric*. What he means by it is that theoretical speculations in Western academic psychology and psychiatry are based exclusively on experiences and observations made in the ordinary states of consciousness (with the possible exception of dreams). The evidence from the study of non-ordinary states of any kind are systematically ignored or pathologized.

Herein lies the importance of the material from psychedelic therapy. It is the most extreme and dramatic example of the challenge that the research of non-ordinary states of consciousness presents to traditional Newtonian-Cartesian science. Systematic and open-minded study of the evidence amassed by this work strongly suggests the need for a radical revision of our basic ideas about the human psyche and the nature of consciousness. It would lead to an entirely different understanding of emotional and psychosomatic disorders, as well as the therapeutic process and strategy of self-exploration. Some of the observations from non-ordinary states would require not only revision of our ideas about the human psyche, but of the traditional beliefs about the nature of reality. An extreme example of this kind is the ability of individuals in near-death situations to accurately perceive, without the use of their senses, not only the immediate environment, but also various remote locations. Observations of this kind seriously question the most fundamental metaphysical assumptions of Western philosophy of science.

In view of the above facts, *LSD Psychotherapy* represents much more than a source of information on psychedelics and their use. It certainly is a book that is of interest for therapists who treat casualties of unsupervised self-experimentation or for those who might conduct psychedelic therapy in the future. It can also be useful for those who have already experienced psychedelic states and need more understanding, as well as for lay audiences specifically interested in the subject. However, its significance goes beyond that; it is a book that describes the deepest dynamics and the outer reaches of the human psyche, as they manifest in non-ordinary states of consciousness of many different kinds. The experiences and observations that it describes have far-reaching implications for our understanding of consciousness, human nature, and the nature of reality. For this reason, the material in this book should be available to all those who are interested and open to it.

Stanislav Grof
November, 1993

Numbers in parentheses refer to Bibliography on Page 302.
Notes referred to in the text by superior numbers are
located at the end of each chapter.

ACKNOWLEDGMENTS

Having completed the work on this book, I would like to remember with deep gratitude some friends who have given me important help at various stages of this project. Dr. George Roubíček, former Associate Professor of the Department of Psychiatry at Charles University School of Medicine, was my first preceptor and guide for my first LSD session in 1956. This experience was the beginning of my profound interest in and life-long commitment to the study of unusual states of consciousness. Dr. Miloš Vojtěchovský was the head of an interdisciplinary team with which I started my research of psychedelic drugs. He introduced me to several new psychedelic substances and gave me basic training in scientific research and its methodology.

Much of the work that was of crucial significance for the development of the ideas presented in this book had been conducted at the Psychiatric Research Institute in Prague, Czechoslovakia. Its director, Dr. Lubomír Hanzlíček, through all the years of my clinical research with LSD, showed unusual understanding and support for this unconventional scientific venture. I also feel deep appreciation for the help of my colleagues at the institute and for the dedication and enthusiasm of the nursing team.

My initial work in the United States was made possible by a generous grant from the Foundations' Fund for Research in Psychiatry from New Haven, Connecticut. Dr. Joel Elkes, Professor of the Department of Psychiatry and Behavioral Sciences at Johns Hopkins University School of Medicine in Baltimore, invited me to the Henry Phipps Clinic, first as a clinical and research fellow and later as Assistant Professor; he gave me invaluable help and guidance during the years of my stay there.

The period between 1967 and 1973 that I spent at the Maryland Psychiatric Research Center in Catonsville, Maryland, was a time of exciting team cooperation with a group of enthusiastic and congenial researchers. I would like to thank Dr. A. A. Kurland, former director of the center and Assistant Commissioner for Research of the Maryland State Department of Mental Hygiene, as well as my colleagues and friends from Spring Grove, for their contributions to my work and enhancement of my personal life.

The Esalen Institute in Big Sur, California, has played a very important role in my life. Since my first visit in 1965, it has offered me many opportunities to conduct seminars and workshops and share my material with open-minded and sympathetic audiences. In the last five years it has become my home base and a unique emotional and intellectual resource. In this extraordinary natural laboratory of the human potential movement I met many creative people pioneering in experiential psychotherapies and had the opportunity to relate their work to my own. This made it possible for me to integrate the observations from LSD research into a broader theoretical context. Of particular value have been the experiences from a series of experimental educational programs for professionals, which my wife Christina and I have been conducting at Esalen. These events, which organically combine didactic input, intrapsychic exploration and group work, and have a guest faculty ranging from Mexican and North-American shamans to theoretical physicists, have become an invaluable source of inspiration. I would like to express my deep gratitude to Michael and Dulce Murphy, Richard and Chris Price, Julian Silverman, Janet Lederman, Beverly Silverman, Gregory and Lois Bateson, and all our other friends at Esalen, for all their support and understanding. Of these, Rick Tarnas has been extremely helpful during the preliminary work on the manuscript and Kathleen O'Shaughnessy in the typing of the final version.

Other friends whose interest and support I would like to gratefully acknowledge are Louis and Hazel Valier, Edward Dreesen, and Joseph Chambeau.

My deepest appreciation is reserved for hundreds of patients and LSD subjects who participated in my psychedelic research over the years. Without their trust, dedication and courage, this book could not have been written.

                                    Stanislav Grof
                                    April, 1979

LSD PSYCHOTHERAPY

HISTORY OF LSD THERAPY

1

The Discovery of LSD and its Psychedelic Effects
Early Laboratory and Clinical LSD Research
Therapeutic Experimentation With LSD
Studies of Chemotherapeutic Properties of LSD
LSD–Assisted Psychotherapy
The Need for a Comprehensive Theory
  of LSD Therapy

THE DISCOVERY OF LSD AND ITS PSYCHEDELIC EFFECTS

LSD-25 (or diethylamide of d-lysergic acid) was first synthesized in 1938 by Albert Hofmann in the Sandoz chemical-pharmaceutical laboratories in Basle, Switzerland. As its name indicates, it was the twenty-fifth compound developed in a systematic study of amides of lysergic acid. LSD is a semisynthetic chemical product; its natural component is lysergic acid, which is the basis of all major ergot alkaloids, and the diethylamide group is added in the laboratory. According to Stoll, Hofmann and Troxler(98), it has the following chemical formula:

$$
\begin{array}{l}
\text{H} \quad \text{CON} \diagup^{C_2H_5}_{C_2H_5} \\
\text{C}^* \quad \text{CH}_2 \\
\text{HC} \qquad \text{NCH}_3 \\
\text{C} \qquad \text{CH}^* \\
\text{HC} \quad \text{C} \qquad \text{CH}_2 \\
\text{HC} \qquad \text{C} \quad \text{C} \\
\text{CH} \quad \text{C} \qquad \text{CH} \\
\text{NH}
\end{array}
$$

Various ergot alkaloids have important uses in medicine, primarily as drugs that can induce uterine contractions, stop gynecological bleeding, and relieve migraine headache. The objective in the Sandoz study of ergot derivatives was to obtain compounds with the best therapeutic properties and least side effects. After LSD had been synthesized, it was subjected to pharmacological testing by Professor Ernst Rothlin. (88) It showed a marked uterotonic action and caused excitation in some of the animals; at the time these effects were not considered of sufficient interest to be further explored.

The unique properties of the new substance were brought to the attention of the researchers by a series of events involving a fortuitous accident. In 1943 Albert Hofmann was reviewing the results of early pharmacological tests on LSD and decided to investigate the stimulating effects on the central nervous system indicated in animal experiments. Because of its structural similarity with the circulatory stimulant nikethamide, LSD seemed promising as an analeptic substance. Feeling that it would be worthwhile to carry out more profound studies with this compound, Albert Hofmann decided to synthesize a new sample. However, even the most sophisticated experiments in animals would not have detected the psychedelic effects of LSD, since such specifically human responses cannot be anticipated on the basis of animal data alone. A laboratory accident came to the help of the researchers; by a strange play of destiny Albert Hofmann became an involuntary subject in one of the most exciting and influential experiments in the history of science. Working on the synthesis of a new sample of LSD, he accidentally intoxicated himself during the purification of the condensation products. The following is Albert Hofmann's own description of the perceptual and emotional changes that he experienced as a result: (38)

"Last Friday, April 16, 1943, I was forced to stop my work in the laboratory in the middle of the afternoon and to go home, as I was seized by a peculiar restlessness associated with a sensation of mild dizziness. On arriving home, I lay down and sank into a kind of drunkenness, which was not unpleasant and which was characterized by extreme activity of the imagination. As I lay in a dazed condition with my eyes closed, (I experienced daylight as disagreeably bright) there surged upon me an uninterrupted stream of fantastic images of extraordinary plasticity and vividness, accompanied by an intense kaleidoscope-like play of colors. This condition gradually passed off after two hours."

After he had returned to his usual state of consciousness, Hofmann was able to make the hypothetical link between his extraordinary experiences and the possibility of accidental intoxication by the drug he was working with. However, he could not understand how the LSD had found its way into his body in a sufficient quantity to produce such phenomena. He was also puzzled by the nature of the effects, which were quite different from those associated with ergot poisoning. Three days later he intentionally ingested a known quantity of LSD, to put his suspicions to a solid scientific test. Being a very conservative and cautious person, he decided to take only 250 micrograms,[1] which he considered to be a minute dose judging by the usual dosage level of other related ergot alkaloids. At that time he had no way of knowing that he was experimenting with the most powerful psychoactive drug known to man. The dose he chose and ingested without any special preparation, or any knowledge about psychedelic states, would at present be considered a high dose and has been referred to in the LSD literature as a "single overwhelming dose." If used in clinical practice it is preceded by many hours of preparatory psychotherapy and requires a trained and experienced guide to handle all the complications that might occur.

About forty minutes after the ingestion, Hofmann started experiencing dizziness and unrest; he had difficulties in concentration, disturbances of visual perception, and a strong unmotivated desire to laugh. He found it impossible to keep a written protocol about his experiment as originally planned. The following is an excerpt from his subsequent report written for Professor Stoll: (38)

"At this point, the laboratory notes are discontinued; the last words were written only with great difficulty. I asked my laboratory assistant to accompany me home, as I believed that I should have a repetition of the disturbance of the previous Friday. While we were cycling home, however, it became clear that the symptoms were much stronger than the first time. I had great difficulty in speaking coherently, my field of vision swayed before me, and objects appeared distorted like images in curved mirrors. I had the impression of being unable to move from the spot, although my assistant told me afterwards that we had cycled at a good pace. Once I was at home, the physician was called.

"By the time the doctor arrived, the peak of the crisis had already passed. As far as I remember, the following were the most outstanding symptoms: vertigo; visual disturbances; the faces of those around me appeared as grotesque, colored masks; marked motoric unrest, alternating with paralysis; an intermittent heavy feeling in the head, limbs, and the entire body, as if they were filled with lead; dry, constricted sensation in the throat; feeling of choking; clear recognition of my condition, in which state I sometimes observed, in the manner of an independent, neutral observer, that I shouted half-insanely or babbled incoherent words. Occasionally, I felt as if I were out of my body.

"The doctor found a rather weak pulse, but an otherwise normal circulation. . . . Six hours after ingestion of the LSD, my condition had already improved considerably. Only the visual disturbances were still pronounced. Everything seemed to sway and the proportions were distorted like reflections in the surface of moving water. Moreover, all the objects appeared in unpleasant, constantly changing colors, the predominant shades being sickly green and blue. When I closed my eyes, an unending series of colorful, very realistic and fantastic images surged in upon me. A remarkable feature was the manner in which all acoustic perceptions, (e.g. the noise of a passing car), were transformed into optical effects, every sound evoking a corresponding colored hallucination constantly changing in shape and color like pictures in a kaleidoscope. At about one o'clock, I fell asleep and awoke the next morning feeling perfectly well."

This was the first planned experiment with LSD, and it proved in a dramatic and convincing way Hofmann's hypothesis about the mind-altering effects of

LSD. Subsequent experiments with volunteers from the Sandoz Research Laboratories confirmed the extraordinary influence of this drug on the human mind.

The next important figure in the history of LSD was Walter Stoll, son of Hofmann's superior and psychiatrist at the Psychiatric Clinic in Zürich. He found the new psychoactive substance of great interest and conducted the first scientific study of LSD in normal volunteers and psychiatric patients. His observations of the LSD effects in these two categories of subjects were published in 1947. (97) This report became a sensation in the scientific world and stimulated an unusual amount of laboratory and clinical research in many countries.

EARLY LABORATORY AND CLINICAL LSD RESEARCH

Much of the early LSD research was inspired and strongly influenced by the so-called "model psychosis" approach. The incredible potency of LSD and the fact that infinitesimally small quantities could profoundly alter mental functioning of otherwise healthy volunteers gave a new impetus to speculations about the basically biochemical nature of endogenous psychoses, particularly schizophrenia. It was repeatedly observed that microscopic doses of LSD, in the range of 25 to 100 micrograms, were sufficient to produce changes in perception, emotions, ideation and behavior that resembled those seen in some schizophrenic patients. It was conceivable that the metabolism of the human body could, under certain circumstances, produce such small quantities of an abnormal substance identical with or similar to LSD. According to this tempting hypothesis, endogenous psychoses such as schizophrenia would not be primarily mental disorders, but manifestations of an autointoxication of the organism and the brain caused by a pathological shift in body chemistry. The possibility of simulating schizophrenic symptoms in normal volunteers and of conducting complex laboratory tests and investigations before, during, and after this transient "model psychosis" seemed to offer a promising key to the understanding of psychiatry's most enigmatic disease.

Much research during the years following the discovery of LSD was aimed at proving or disproving the "model psychosis" hypothesis. Its power was such that for many years LSD sessions conducted for any purpose were referred to as "experimental psychoses," and LSD and similar substances were called hallucinogens, psychotomimetics (psychosis-simulating compounds) or psychodysleptics (drugs disrupting the psyche). This situation was not rectified until 1957 when Humphrey Osmond, after mutually stimulating correspondence with Aldous Huxley, coined a much more accurate term, "psychedelics" (mind-manifesting or mind-opening drugs). (74) In these years much effort was directed toward accurate phenomenological description of the LSD experience and assessment of the similarities and differences between the psychedelic states and schizophrenia. These descriptive studies had their counterpart in the research exploring parallels between these two conditions, as reflected in clinical measurements, psychological tests, electro-physiological data, and biochemical findings. The significance attributed to this avenue of research found an expression in the number of studies contributing basic data about the effects of LSD on various physiological and biochemical functions as well as on the behavior of experimental animals, on isolated organs and tissue cultures, and on enzymatic systems. Of special interest from the point of view of the "model psychosis" hypothesis were experiments studying the antagonism between LSD and various other substances. The possibility of blocking the LSD state, by premedication with another drug or by its administration at the time of fully developed LSD effects, was seen as a promising approach to the discovery of new directions in the pharmaco-therapy of psychiatric disorders. Several biochemical hypotheses of schizophrenia were formulated at this time, implicating specific substances or whole metabolic cycles as the primary cause of this disease. The serotonin hypothesis coined by Woolley and Shaw (104) received by far the most attention. According to their model LSD causes abnormal mental functioning by interfering with the neurotransmitter substance serotonin (5-hydroxytryptamine). A similar mechanism was postulated as the biochemical cause of schizophrenia.

This reductionistic and oversimplified approach to schizophrenia was repeatedly criticized by psychoanalytically and phenomenologically oriented clinicians and biochemical investigators, and finally abandoned by most researchers. It became increasingly obvious that the LSD-induced state had many specific characteristics clearly distinguishing it from schizophrenia. In addition, none of the biochemical mechanisms postulated for schizophrenia was unequivocally supported by clinical and laboratory data. Although the "model psychosis" approach did not resolve the problem of the etiology of schizophrenia or provide a miraculous "test-tube" cure for this mysterious disease, it served as a powerful inspiration for many researchers and contributed in a decisive way to the neurophysiological and psychopharmacological revolution of the fifties and early sixties.

Another area in which the extraordinary effects of LSD proved extremely helpful was *self-experimentation by mental health professionals*. In the early years of LSD research, didactic LSD experiences were recommended as an unrivalled tool for the training of psychiatrists, psychologists, medical students, and psychiatric nurses. The LSD sessions were advertised as a short, safe and reversible journey into the world of the schizophrenic. It was repeatedly reported in various books and articles on LSD that a single psychedelic experience could considerably increase the subject's ability to understand psychotic patients, approach them with sensitivity, and treat them effectively. Even though the concept of the LSD experience as "model schizophrenia" was later discarded by a majority of scientists, it remains an unquestionable fact that experiencing the profound psychological changes induced by LSD is a unique and valuable learning experience for all clinicians and theoreticians studying abnormal mental states.

The early experimentation with LSD also brought important new insights into the nature of the creative process and contributed to a deeper understanding of the *psychology and psychopathology of art*. For many experimental subjects, professional artists as well as laymen, the LSD session represented a profound aesthetic experience that gave them a new understanding of modern art movements and art in general. Painters, sculptors and musicians became favorite LSD subjects because they tended to produce most unusual, unconventional and interesting pieces of art under the influence of the drug. Some of them were able to express and convey in their creations the nature and flavor of the psychedelic experience, which defies any adequate verbal description. The day of the LSD experience often became a dramatic and easily discernible landmark in the development of individual artists.

Equally deep was the influence of LSD research on the *psychology and psychopathology of religion*. Even under the complex and often difficult circumstances of early LSD experimentation, some subjects had profound religious and mystical experiences that bore a striking similarity to those described in various sacred texts and in the writings of mystics, saints, religious teachers and prophets of all ages. The possibility of inducing such experiences by chemical means started an involved discussion about the authenticity and value of this "instant mysticism." Despite the fact that many leading scientists, theologians and spiritual teachers have discussed this theme extensively, the controversy about "chemical" versus "spontaneous" mysticism remains unresolved until this day.

Any discussion of the various areas of LSD research and experimentation would remain incomplete without mentioning certain systematic explorations of its negative potential. For obvious reasons, the results of this research, conducted by the secret police and armed forces of many countries of the world, have not been systematically reported and most of the information is considered classified. Some of the areas that have been explored in this context are *eliciting of confessions, gaining of access to withheld secrets and information, brainwashing, disabling of foreign diplomats*, and *"non-violent" warfare*. In working with individuals, the destructive techniques try to exploit the chemically induced breakdown of resistances and defense mechanisms, increased suggestibility and sensitivity to terroristic approaches, and intensification of the transference process. In the mass approaches of chemical warfare, the important variables are the disorganizing effect of LSD on goal-oriented activity, and its uncanny potency. The techniques of dispensation suggested for this warfare have been various kinds of aerosols and contamination of water supplies. For everybody who is even remotely familiar with the effects of LSD, this kind of chemical warfare is much more diabolical than any of the conventional approaches. Calling it non-violent or humane is a gross misrepresentation.

THERAPEUTIC EXPERIMENTATION WITH LSD

From the point of view of our discussion, the most important area of LSD research has been experimental therapy with this substance. Observations of the dramatic and profound effects of minute quantities of LSD on the mental processes of experimental subjects led quite naturally to the conclusion that it might be fruitful to explore the therapeutic potential of this unusual compound.

The possibility of therapeutic use of LSD was first suggested by Condrau (21) in 1949, only two years after Stoll had published the first scientific study of LSD in Switzerland. In the early fifties several researchers independently recommended LSD as an adjunct to psychotherapy, one which could deepen and intensify the therapeutic process. The pioneers of this approach were Busch and Johnson (17) and Abramson (1,2) in the United States; Sandison, Spencer and Whitelaw (91) in England; and Frederking (28) in West Germany.

These reports attracted considerable attention among psychiatrists, and stimulated clinicians in various countries of the world to start therapeutic experimentation with LSD in their own practice and research. Many of the reports published in the following fifteen years confirmed the initial claims that

LSD could expedite the psychotherapeutic process and shorten the time necessary for the treatment of various emotional disorders, which made it a potentially valuable tool in the psychiatric armamentarium. In addition, there appeared an increasing number of studies indicating that LSD-assisted psychotherapy could reach certain categories of psychiatric patients usually considered poor candidates for psychoanalysis or any other type of psychotherapy. Many individual researchers and therapeutic teams reported various degrees of clinical success with alcoholics, narcotic-drug addicts, sociopaths, criminal psychopaths, and subjects with various character disorders and sexual deviations. In the early sixties a new and exciting area was discovered for LSD psychotherapy: the care of patients dying of cancer and other incurable diseases. Studies with dying individuals indicated that LSD psychotherapy could bring not only an alleviation of emotional suffering and relief of the physical pain associated with chronic diseases, it could also dramatically change the concept of death and attitude toward dying.

Since the appearance of the early clinical reports on LSD much time and energy has been invested in research of its therapeutic potential, and hundreds of papers have been published on various types of LSD therapy. Many psychopharmacological, psychiatric, and psychotherapeutic meetings had special sections on LSD treatment. In Europe, the initially isolated efforts of individual LSD researchers resulted in an effort to create a homogeneous organizational structure. LSD therapists from a number of European countries formed the European Medical Society for Psycholytic Therapy, and members held regular meetings dealing with the use of psychedelic drugs in psychotherapy. This organization also formulated the specifications and criteria for selection and training of future LSD therapists. The counterpart of this organization in the United States and Canada was the Association for Psychedelic Therapy. During the decade of most intense interest in LSD research several international conferences were organized for the exchange of experiences, observations and theoretical concepts in this field (Princeton, 1959; Goettingen, 1960; London, 1961; Amityville, 1965; Amsterdam, 1967; and Bad Nauheim, 1968).

The efforts to use LSD in the therapy of mental disorders now span a period of almost three decades. It would be beyond the scope of this presentation to describe all the specific contributions to this unique chapter of the history of psychiatric treatment, as well as give due attention to all the individual scientists who participated in this avenue of research. The history of LSD therapy has been a series of trials and errors. Many different techniques of therapeutic use of LSD have been developed and explored during the past thirty years. Approaches that did not have the expected effect or were not supported by later research were abandoned; those that seemed promising were assimilated by other therapists, or developed further and modified. Instead of following this complicated process through all its stages, I will try to outline certain basic trends and the most important therapeutic ideas and concepts. Three decades of LSD therapy is a sufficiently long period for accumulating clinical observations and verifying research data. We can, therefore, attempt a critical review of the clinical experience in this area, summarize the current knowledge about the value of LSD as a therapeutic tool in psychiatry, and describe the safest and most effective techniques for its use.

Various suggestions concerning the therapeutic use of LSD were based on the specific aspects of its action. The frequent occurrence of euphoria in LSD sessions with normal volunteers seemed to suggest the possibility that this drug could be useful in the treatment of depressive disorders. The profound and often shattering effect of LSD on psychological as well as physiological functions, amounting to an emotional or vegetative shock, seemed to indicate that it could have a therapeutic potential similar to electroshocks, insulin treatment, or other forms of convulsive therapy. This concept was supported by observations of striking and dramatic changes in the clinical symptomatology and personality structure of some subjects after administration of a single dose of LSD. Another aspect of the LSD effect which seemed to be promising from the therapeutic point of view was the unusual ability of this drug to facilitate intensive emotional abreactions. The therapeutic success of abreactive techniques such as hypnoanalysis and narcoanalysis in the treatment of war neuroses and traumatic emotional neuroses encouraged explorations of this property of LSD. One additional interesting possibility of therapeutic use was based on the activating or "provocational" effect of LSD. The drug can mobilize and intensify fixated, chronic and stationary clinical conditions that are characterized by just a few torpid and refractory symptoms, and it was hypothesized that such chemically induced activation might make these so-called oligosymptomatic states more amenable to conventional methods of treatment. By far the most important use of LSD was found in its combination with individual and group psychotherapies of different orientations. Its effectiveness is based on a very advantageous combination of various aspects of its action. LSD psychotherapy seems to intensify all the mechanisms operating in drug-free psychotherapies and involves, in addition, some new and powerful mechanisms of psychological change as yet unacknowledged and unexplained by mainstream psychiatry.

In the following sections, I will describe the most important areas of therapeutic experimentation with LSD, give actual treatment techniques and concepts, and discuss their empirical or theoretical bases. Special attention will be paid to an evaluation of how successfully individual approaches have withstood the test of time.

STUDIES OF CHEMOTHERAPEUTIC PROPERTIES OF LSD

The approaches that will be discussed in this section are based on different clinical observations and different theoretical premises; the common denominator is an exclusive emphasis on LSD as a chemotherapeutic agent that has certain beneficial effects just by virtue of its pharmacological action. The authors of these techniques were either unaware of the significance of extrapharmacological factors or did not specifically utilize them. If psychotherapy was used with these approaches at all, it was only supportive and of the most superficial kind, without any organic link to the LSD experience.

EXPLORATION OF EUPHORIANT AND ANTIDEPRESSIVE EFFECTS OF LSD

When Condrau (21) proposed the use of LSD for depression on the basis of its euphoriant effect on some subjects, he followed the model of opium treatment. He administered small and progressively increasing daily doses of LSD to depressive patients and expected alleviation of depression and positive changes in mood. According to Condrau's statement, the results were not convincing and the observed changes did not exceed the limits of the usual spontaneous variations. He also noticed that LSD medication usually resulted in deepening of the pre-existing mood rather than consistent euphorization.

Similar results were reported by other authors who used either Condrau's model of daily medication with LSD in depressive patients or isolated administrations of medium dosages of LSD with the intention to dispel depression. Negative or inconclusive clinical experiences have been reported by Becker, (8) Anderson and Rawnsley, (3) Roubiček and Srnec, (89) and others.

By and large, the results of this approach to LSD therapy did not justify continuation of research in this direction. Clinical studies clearly indicated that LSD does not *per se* have any consistent pharmacological effects on depression that could be therapeutically exploited, and this approach has been abandoned.

SHOCK-INDUCING PROPERTIES OF LSD AND
ITS EFFECT ON PERSONALITY STRUCTURE

In the early period of LSD research, several authors suggested that the profound and shattering experience induced by LSD could have a positive effect on some patients comparable to the effect of various methods of convulsive treatment such as electroshocks, insulin coma therapy, or cardiazole and acetylcholine shocks. Occasionally, unexpected and dramatic clinical improvements were reported in psychiatric patients after a single LSD session. Observations of this kind have been described in papers by Stoll, (97) Becker, (8) Benedetti, (10) Belsanti, (9) and Giberti, Gregoretti and Boeri. (30)

In addition, an increasing number of reports seemed to suggest that sometimes a single administration of LSD could have a deep influence on the personality structure of the subject, his or her hierarchy of values, basic attitudes, and entire life style. The changes were so dramatic that they were compared with psychological conversions.[2] Many LSD researchers made similar observations and became aware of the potential therapeutic value of these transformative experiences. The major obstacle to their systematic utilization for therapeutic purposes was the fact that they tended to occur in an elemental fashion, without a recognizable pattern, and frequently to the surprise of both the patient and the therapist. Since the variables determining such reactions were not understood, therapeutic transformations of this kind were not readily replicable. However, it was this category of observations and systematic efforts to induce similar experiences in a more predictable and controlled way that finally resulted in the development of an important treatment modality, the so-called psychedelic therapy. The basic principles of this therapeutic approach will be discussed later.

In summary, LSD can undoubtedly produce a profound emotional and vegetative shock in a patient or an experimental subject. The shock-effect tends, however, to be more disorganizing and disruptive than therapeutic, unless it occurs within a special framework, in a situation of complex psychological support, and after careful preparation. The conversion mechanism is too unpredictable, elemental and capricious to be relied upon as a therapeutic mechanism *per se*.

THERAPEUTIC USE OF THE ABREACTIVE EFFECT OF LSD

Many observations from early LSD research clearly indicated that the drug can facilitate reliving of various emotionally relevant episodes from infancy, childhood, or later life. In the case of traumatic memories, this process was preceded and accompanied by powerful emotional abreaction and catharsis. It seemed, therefore, only logical to explore the value of LSD as an agent for abreactive therapy in a way similar to the earlier use of ether, short-acting barbiturates, or amphetamines, in the same indication.

From the historical and theoretical point of view, this mechanism can be traced back to the early concepts of Freud and Breuer. (29) According to them, insufficient emotional and motor reaction by a patient to an original traumatic event results in "jamming" of the effect: the strangulated emotions ("abgeklemmter Affekt") later provide energy for neurotic symptoms. Treatment then consists in reliving the traumatizing memory under circumstances that make possible a belated redirection of this emotional energy to the periphery and its discharge through perceptual, emotional, and motor channels. From the practical point of view, the abreactive method was found especially valuable in the treatment of traumatic emotional neuroses and became popular during the Second World War as a quick and effective remedy for hysterical conversions occurring in various battle situations.

There is hardly a single LSD therapist who would have doubts about the unique abreactive properties of LSD. It would be, however, a great oversimplification to approach and understand LSD treatment only as abreaction therapy. This was clearly demonstrated in a controlled study by Robinson. (86) Present opinion is that abreaction is an important component of LSD psychotherapy, but it represents just one of many therapeutic mechanisms resulting from the complex action of this drug.

USE OF THE ACTIVATING EFFECT OF LSD
ON CHRONIC AND FIXATED SYMPTOMS

This approach was inspired by the clinical experience that LSD has an intensifying and mobilizing effect on manifest and latent psychopathological symptoms. The principle of activation or "provocation" therapy with LSD was theoretically developed and employed in practice by the Austrian researcher Jost. (41) This concept was based on clinical observations of an interesting relationship between the nature and course of the psychotic process and prognosis of the disease. It has been a well-known clinical fact that acute schizophrenic episodes with dramatic, rich and colorful symptoms have a very good prognosis. They frequently result in spontaneous remission, and therapy of these conditions is usually very successful. Conversely, schizophrenic states with an inapparent and insidious onset, a few stagnating and torpid symptoms, and a stationary course have the poorest prognosis and are very unresponsive to conventional treatments.

After analyzing a great number of trajectories of psychotic episodes, Jost came to the conclusion that it is possible to find a certain culmination point in the natural course of psychosis beyond which the disease shows a trend towards spontaneous remission. In schizophrenia, these culmination points are usually characterized by hallucinatory experiences of death or destruction, disintegration of the body, regression and transmutation. These negative sequences are then followed by fantasies or experiences of rebirth.

The assumption of such a culmination point in the spontaneous course of the illness could explain, according to Jost, some puzzling observations made during electroshock therapy. As ECT seems to accelerate the spontaneous development of the disease along the intrinsic trajectory, it makes a great deal of difference at which point it is applied. If the electroshock is administered before the psychosis reaches the culmination point, it produces dramatic manifestations and intensifies the clinical picture. If it is given after the culmination point has been reached, this results in a rapid sedation of the patient and remission of the symptoms.

In their practical approach, Jost and Vicari (42) intended to accelerate the spontaneous development of the disease by a combination of chemical and electrophysiological means to mobilize the autonomous healing forces and processes within the organism. They administered LSD and when the clinical condition was activated by its effect, they applied electroconvulsive therapy. The authors described substantial shortening of the schizophrenic episode, reduction in the number of electroshocks required to reach clinical improvement, and often a deeper remission.

Sandison and Whitelaw, (92) two British researchers and pioneers in LSD research, used a similar principle of applying a conventional treatment technique in patients whose clinical condition was activated by LSD. However, instead of administering ECT, they used the tranquilizing effect of chlorpromazine (Thorazine). In their study, psychotic patients from various diagnostic groups were given LSD and two hours later intramuscular injection of the tranquillizer. Although the results seemed promising, the authors themselves later discarded the idea that the administration of chlorpromazine played a positive role in this procedure.

In general, the idea of provocational therapy with LSD has not found a broader acceptance in clinical practice and has remained limited to the attempts described above. However, Jost's theoretical speculations contain several interesting ideas that can prove very fruitful if used in a more dynamic and creative way. The basic principle of activating fixated symptoms by LSD can be used in the context of intensive psychotherapy; a single LSD session can often help overcome stagnation in a long-term psychotherapeutic process. Also, Jost's concepts of an intrinsic trajectory of the psychotic process and the value of its acceleration are in basic agreement with certain modern approaches to schizophrenia discussed in the writings of R. D. Laing, (52) John Perry, (80) Julian Silverman, (94,95) and Maurice Rappaport. (84) Similarly, the observations regarding Jost's concept of the culmination moment of the schizophrenic process and the specific experiences associated with the breaking point make new sense if they are viewed in the context of dynamic matrices in the unconscious rather than from the point of view of Jost's mechanical model. We will discuss this issue in detail in connection with the perinatal matrices and the therapeutic significance of the ego death and rebirth experience.

LSD-ASSISTED PSYCHOTHERAPY

As indicated in the above survey of therapeutic experimentation with LSD, the efforts to exploit purely pharmacological properties of this drug have failed to bring positive results. The concept of LSD as simply a chemotherapeutic agent has been abandoned by all serious researchers in the field. The use of LSD as an activating substance, in Jost and Vicari's sense, has not found its way into clinical practice, at least not in its original mechanical form. The abreactive action of LSD is valued highly, but it is usually considered to be only one of many effective mechanisms operating in LSD therapy. The shock-effect of LSD cannot in itself be considered therapeutic; unless it occurs in a specifically structured situation, it can have detrimental rather than beneficial consequences. The influence of LSD on the personality structure in the sense of a conversion is a well-established clinical fact; however, the occurrence of this phenomenon during unstructured administrations of LSD is rare, unpredictable and capricious. Special preparation, a trusting therapeutic relationship, psychological support, and a specifically structured set and setting are necessary to make therapeutic use of this aspect of the LSD effect.

There seems to be general agreement at present among LSD therapists that the therapeutic outcome of LSD sessions depends critically on factors of a non-pharmacological nature (extrapharmacological variables). The drug itself is seen as a catalyst that activates the unconscious processes in a rather unspecific way. Whether the emergence of the unconscious material will be therapeutic or destructive is not determined simply by the biochemical and physiological action of LSD. It is a function of a number of non-drug variables, such as the personality structure of the subject, the relationship he or she has with the guide, sitter or persons present in the session, the nature and degree of specific psychological help, and the set and setting of the psychedelic experience. For this reason all the approaches that try to utilize LSD simply as another chemotherapeutic agent are, by and large, bound to fail. This does not mean that it is not possible to benefit from an LSD experience if the drug is taken in an unstructured situation. However, extrapharmacological factors have such a profound influence on the LSD session and its final outcome that one cannot expect a reasonable degree and consistency of therapeutic success unless the non-drug variables are sufficiently understood and controlled. Thus the optimal use of LSD for therapeutic purposes should always involve administration of the drug within the framework of a complex psychotherapeutic program; this approach offers the most therapeutic possibilities. In this respect, the potential of LSD seems to be quite extraordinary and unique. The ability of LSD to deepen, intensify and accelerate the psychotherapeutic process is incomparably greater than that of any other drug used as an adjunct to psychotherapy, with the exception perhaps of some other members of the psychedelic group, such as psilocybin, mescaline, ibogain, MDA, (methylene-dioxy-amphetamine), or DPT (dipropyltryptamine).

In the professional literature, the combination of LSD with various forms of psychotherapy has been referred to by many different names: psycholysis (Sandison), psychedelic therapy (Osmond), symbolysis (van Rhijn), hebesynthesis (Abramson), lyserganalysis (Giberti and Gregoretti), oneiroanalysis (Delay), LSD analysis (Martin and McCririck), transintegrative therapy (MacLean), hypnodelic treatment (Levine and Ludwig), and psychosynthesis (Roquet). Individual therapists using LSD psychotherapy have differed considerably in regard to the dosage used, frequency and total number of psychedelic sessions, the intensity and type of the psychotherapeutic work, and certain specificities of set and setting.

In view of all these differences and variations, any comprehensive discussion of the history of LSD psychotherapy would involve giving separate descriptions of all the individual therapists and therapeutic teams. Yet, it is possible with a degree of over-simplification, to distinguish certain basic ways of using LSD in psychotherapy. These modalities fall into two major categories, which differ in the degree of significance attributed to the role of the drug. The first category involves approaches in which the emphasis is on systematic psychotherapeutic work; LSD is used to enhance the therapeutic process or to overcome resistances, blocks and periods of stagnation. The approaches in the second category are characterized by a much greater emphasis on the specific aspects of the drug experience and the psychotherapy is used to prepare the subjects for the drug sessions, give them support during the experiences, and to help them integrate the material.

FACILITATION OF THE PSYCHOTHERAPEUTIC PROCESS
BY LSD ADMINISTRATION

During the years of therapeutic experimentation, there have been several systematic attempts to use small doses of LSD to enhance the dynamics of individual or group psychotherapy. In general, the disadvantages of this approach seem to outweigh its potential benefits. The use of small dosages does not save much time, since it does not shorten the duration of the drug action so much as decrease its depth and intensity. Similarly, the risks involved in the use of low doses in psychiatric patients are not necessarily lower than those related to high-dose sessions. It is of greater advantage to interpolate occasional LSD sessions using medium or high dosages in the course of systematic long-term psychotherapy at times when there is little therapeutic progress. In the following text we will briefly describe each of the above approaches.

Use of Small Doses of LSD in Intensive Psychotherapy
In this treatment modality the patients participate in a systematic course of long-term psychotherapy, and in all the sessions they are under the influence of small doses of LSD in the range of 25 to 50 micrograms. The emphasis is clearly on psychotherapy and LSD is used to intensify and deepen the usual psychodynamic processes involved. Under these circumstances, the defense mechanisms are weakened, the psychological resistances tend to decrease, and the recall of repressed memories is greatly enhanced. LSD also typically intensifies the transference relationship in all its aspects and makes it easy for the therapist as well as the patient to understand clearly the nature of the processes involved. Under the influence of the drug, patients are usually more ready to face repressed material and accept the existence of deep instinctual tendencies and conflicts within themselves. All the situations in these LSD sessions are approached with appropriate modifications of techniques of dynamic psychotherapy. The content of the drug experience itself is interpreted and used in much the same way as the manifest content of dreams in regular non-drug psychotherapy. In the past this approach has been mostly used

in combination with psychoanalytically oriented psychotherapy, although it is theoretically and practically compatible with many other techniques, such as Jungian analysis, bioenergetics and other neo-Reichian therapies, and Gestalt practice.

Use of Small Doses of LSD in Group Psychotherapy
In this treatment modality all the participants in a session of group psychotherapy, with the exception of the leaders, are under the influence of small doses of LSD. The basic idea is that the activation of individual dynamic processes will result in a deeper and more effective group dynamic. The results of this approach have not been very encouraging. Coordinated and integrated group work is usually possible only with small dosages of LSD which do not have a very profound psychological impact on the group members. If the dosages are increased, the group dynamic tends to disintegrate and it becomes increasingly difficult to get the group to do organized and coordinated work. Each participant experiences the session in his or her unique way, and most of them find it difficult to sacrifice their individual process to the demands of group cohesion.

An alternative approach to the psychedelic group experiences which *may* be very productive is its ritual use, as practiced by certain aboriginal groups: the peyote sessions of the Native American Church or Huichol Indians, yagé ceremonies of the Amahuaca or Jivaro Indians in South America, ingestion of sacred mushrooms (*Psilocybe mexicana*) by the Mazatecs for healing and sacramental purposes, or the ibogain rites of some tribes in Gabon and adjacent parts of the Congo. Here verbal interaction and the cognitive level are typically transcended and group cohesion is achieved by non-verbal means, such as collective rattling, drumming, chanting, or dancing.

After a few initial attempts to conduct traditional group psychotherapy with all the members intoxicated by LSD, this technique was abandoned. However, exposure to a group or contact with co-patients during the termination period of an individual LSD session can be a very useful and productive experience. The assistance of an organized group of drug-free peers can be particularly helpful in working through some residual problems from the drug session. A combination of the new experiential techniques developed for use in encounter groups can also be of great value in this context. Another useful technique is the combination of individually experienced LSD sessions with subsequent analysis and discussion of the material in drug-free group sessions involving all the subjects participating in the LSD program.

Occasional Use of LSD Sessions in Intensive Psychotherapy
This approach involves regular, systematic, long-term psychotherapy, with occasional interpolation of an LSD session. The dosages administered in this context are in the medium or high range, usually between 100 and 300 micrograms. The aim of these psychedelic sessions is to overcome dead points in psychotherapy, intensify and accelerate the therapeutic process, reduce the resistances, and obtain new material for later analysis. A single LSD session interpolated at a critical time can contribute considerably to a deeper understanding of the client's symptoms, the dynamics of his or her personality, and the nature of the transference problems. The revealing confrontation with one's unconscious mind, recall and reliv-

ing of repressed biographical events, manifestation of important symbolic material, and intensification of the therapeutic relationship that results from a single LSD session can frequently provide powerful incentives for further psychotherapy.

TECHNIQUES OF LSD THERAPY

Although psychotherapy is a very important component of the approaches in this category, the primary emphasis is on the specificities of the drug experience. The psychotherapeutic techniques involved are modified and adjusted to the nature of the LSD state to form an integral and organic unit with the psychedelic process.

Psycholytic Therapy With LSD

The term *psycholytic* was coined by the British researcher and pioneer in LSD therapy, Ronald A. Sandison. Its root, *lytic* (from the Greek lysis = dissolution) refers to the process of releasing tensions, dissolving conflicts in the mind. It should not be confused with the term *psychoanalytic* (analyzing the psyche). This treatment method represents in theory as well as in clinical practice an extension and modification of psychoanalytically oriented psychotherapy. It involves administration of LSD at one- to two-week intervals, usually in the dosage range of from 75 to 300 micrograms. The number of drug sessions in a psycholytic series varies depending on the nature of the clinical problem and the therapeutic goals; it oscillates between fifteen and one hundred, the average probably being somewhere around forty. Although there are regular drug-free interviews in the intervals between the sessions, there is a definite emphasis on the events in the LSD sessions.

The drug sessions take place in a darkened, quiet and tastefully furnished room that suggests a homelike atmosphere. The therapist is usually present for several hours at the time when the session culminates, giving support and specific interpretations when necessary. During the remaining hours the patients are alone, but they may ring for the therapist or nurse if they feel the need. Some LSD programs use one or more co-patients as sitters for the termination periods of the sessions, or allow the patient to socialize with the staff and other clients.

All the phenomena that occur in LSD sessions or in connection with LSD therapy are approached and interpreted using the basic principles and techniques of dynamic psychotherapy. Certain specific characteristics of the LSD reaction however, require some modifications of the usual techniques. These involve a greater activity on the part of the therapist, elements of assistance and attendance (for example, in case of vomiting, hypersalivation, hypersecretion of phlegm, coughing, or urination), a more direct approach, occasional physical contact and support, psychodramatic involvement in the patient's experience, and higher tolerance for acting-out behavior. This makes psycholytic procedure similar to the modified psychoanalytic techniques used for psychotherapy with schizophrenic patients. It is necessary to abandon the orthodox analytic situation where the patient reclines on the couch and is expected to share his or her free associations while the detached analyst sits in an armchair and occasionally offers interpretations. In psycholytic therapy, patients are also asked to stay in the reclining position with their eyes closed. However, LSD subjects may on occasion remain silent for long periods of time or, conversely, scream and produce inarticulate sounds; they might toss and turn, sit up, kneel, put their head in one's lap, pace around the room, or even roll on the floor. Much more personal and intimate involvement is necessary, and the treatment frequently requires genuine human support.

In psycholytic therapy, all the usual therapeutic mechanisms are intensified to a much greater degree than in single LSD sessions. A new and specific element is the successive, complex and systematic reliving of traumatic experiences from childhood, which is associated with emotional abreaction, rational integration, and valuable insights.[3] The therapeutic relationship is usually greatly intensified, and analysis of the transference phenomena becomes an essential part of the treatment process.

The toll that psycholytic therapy has had to pay for its theoretical rooting in Freudian psychoanalysis has been confusion and conflict about the spiritual and mystical dimensions of LSD therapy. Those psycholytic therapists who firmly adhere to the Freudian conceptual framework tend to discourage their patients from entering the realms of transcendental experiences, either by interpreting them as an escape from relevant psychodynamic material or by referring to them as schizophrenic. Others have identified the psychoanalytic framework as incomplete and restricting and become more open to an extended model of the human mind. The conflict concerning the interpretation of transpersonal experiences in LSD therapy and the attitude toward them is not only a matter of academic interest. Major therapeutic changes can occur in connection with transcendental states, and so facilitation or obstruction of these experiences can have very concrete practical consequences.

Typical representatives of the psycholytic approach have been Sandison, Spencer and Whitelaw, Buckman, Ling, and Blair in England; Arendsen-Hein and van Rhijn in Holland; Johnsen in Norway; and Hausner, Tauterman, Dytrych and Sobotkiewiczová in Czechoslovakia. This approach was developed in Europe and is more characteristic of European LSD therapists. The only therapist using psycholytic therapy in the United States at this time is Kenneth Godfrey of the Veterans Administration Hospital in Topeka, Kansas. In the past it was practiced by Eisner and Cohen, Chandler and Hartman, Dahlberg and others.

Psychedelic Therapy with LSD
This therapeutic approach differs from the preceding one in many important aspects. It was developed on the basis of dramatic clinical improvements and profound personality changes observed in LSD subjects whose sessions had a very definite religious or mystical emphasis. Historically, it is related to the development of a unique LSD treatment program for alcoholics, conducted in the early fifties by Hoffer and Osmond in Saskatchewan, Canada. These authors were inspired by the alleged similarity between the LSD state and delirium tremens, reported by Ditman and Whittlesey (23) in the United States. Hoffer and Osmond combined this observation with the clinical experience that many chronic alcoholics give up drinking after the shattering experience of delirium tremens. In their program, they initially gave LSD to alcoholic patients with the intention of deterring them from further drinking by the horrors of a simulated delirium tremens. Paradoxically, however, it seemed to be the profound positive experiences in LSD sessions that were correlated with good therapeutic results. On

the basis of this unexpected observation Hoffer and Osmond, in cooperation with Hubbard, laid the foundations of the psychedelic treatment technique.

The main objective of psychedelic therapy is to create optimal conditions for the subject to experience the ego death and the subsequent transcendence into the so-called psychedelic peak experience. It is an ecstatic state, characterized by the loss of boundaries between the subject and the objective world, with ensuing feelings of unity with other people, nature, the entire Universe, and God.[4] In most instances this experience is contentless and is accompanied by visions of brilliant white or golden light, rainbow spectra or elaborate designs resembling peacock feathers. It can, however, be associated with archetypal figurative visions of deities or divine personages from various cultural frameworks. LSD subjects give various descriptions of this condition, based on their educational background and intellectual orientation. They speak about cosmic unity, *unio mystica*, *mysterium tremendum*, cosmic consciousness, union with God, Atman-Brahman union, Samadhi, satori, moksha, or the harmony of the spheres.

Various modifications of psychedelic therapy use different combinations of elements to increase the probability of psychedelic peak experiences occurring in LSD sessions. Before the actual session there is typically a period of drug-free preparation conducted with the aim of facilitating the peak experience. During this time, the therapist explores the patients' life history, helps them to understand their symptoms, and specifically focuses on personality factors that could represent serious obstacles to achieving the psychedelic peak experience. An important part of the preparation is the therapist's explicit and implicit emphasis of the growth potential of the patients, and an encouragement to reach the positive resources of their personalities. Unlike conventional psychotherapy, which usually goes into detailed exploration of psychopathology, psychedelic therapy tries to discourage the patient's preoccupation with pathological phenomena, be they clinical symptoms or maladjustive interpersonal patterns. In general, there is much more concern about transcending psychopathology than interest in its analysis.

Occasionally, patients even receive direct advice and guidance as to how they could function more effectively. This approach is very different from the undisciplined and random advising in life situations against which psychoanalytically oriented therapists so emphatically warn. It does not involve specific suggestions for solving important problems of everyday life, such as marriage or divorce, extramarital affairs, induced abortions, having or not having children, and taking or leaving a job. Psychedelic counseling operates on the very general level of a basic strategy of existence, life philosophy, and hierarchy of values. Some of the issues that might be discussed in this context are, for example, the relative significance of the past, present, and future; the wisdom of drawing one's satisfaction from ordinary things that are always available in life; or the absurdity of exaggerated ambitions and needs to prove something to oneself or to others. From the practical point of view, the general directions in psychedelic counseling are based on observations of specific changes in individuals who have been successfully treated with LSD psychotherapy. They involve an orientation and approach toward life that seem to be associated with the absence of clinical symptoms and with a general feeling of well-being, joy and affirmation of the life process. Although the psychedelic philosophy and life strategy were developed quite independently from the work of Abraham Maslow, (64) some of the principles of this approach are closely related to his description of a self-realizing person and his concept of metavalues and metamotivations. Another important aspect of the discussions in the preparatory period is exploration of the subject's philosophical orientation and religious beliefs. This is particularly relevant in view of the fact that psychedelic sessions frequently revolve around philosophical and spiritual issues.

The last interview before the drug experience usually focuses on technical questions specifically related to the psychedelic session. The therapist describes the nature of the drug effect and the spectrum of experience that it might trigger; special attention is paid to the importance of total yielding to the effect of the drug and psychological surrender to the experience.

In psychedelic therapy there is great emphasis on aesthetically rich settings and a beautiful environment. LSD sessions are conducted in tastefully furnished rooms, decorated with flowers, paintings, sculptures and selected art objects. Wherever possible, natural elements are emphasized. The treatment facility should ideally be located near the ocean, mountain ranges, lakes or wooded areas as exposure of LSD subjects to natural beauty during the termination period of the sessions is an important part of the psychedelic procedure. If this is not possible, examples of nature's creativity are brought into the treatment room: beautiful potted plants and fresh-cut flowers, collections of colorful minerals of interesting shapes, a variety of exotic sea-shells, and photographs of enticing scenery. Fresh and dried fruit, assorted nuts, raw vegetables and other natural foods are characteristic items in the armamentarium of psychedelic therapists, as are fragrant spices and incense; these offer an opportunity to engage both smell and taste in the rediscovery of nature. Music plays a very important role in this treatment modality; a high fidelity stereophonic record player, a tape recorder, several sets of headphones and a good collection of records and tapes are standard equipment in psychedelic treatment suites. The selection of music is of critical importance, in general and in relation to different stages of the sessions or specific experiential sequences.

The dosages used in this approach are very high, ranging from 300 to 1500 micrograms of LSD. In contrast to the use of serial LSD sessions in the psycholytic treatment, psychedelic therapy typically involves only one high-dose session or, at the most, two or three. This procedure has been aptly referred to as a "single overwhelming dose." During the drug experience, patients are encouraged to stay in a reclining position, use eyeshades, and listen to stereophonic music through headphones for the entire period of maximum drug effect. Verbal contact is generally discouraged and various forms of non-verbal communication are preferred whenever it seems necessary to provide support.

The content of psychedelic sessions frequently has a definite archetypal emphasis and draws on the specific symbolism of certain ancient and pre-industrial cultures. Some psychedelic therapists therefore tend to include elements of Oriental and primitive art in the interior decoration of their treatment rooms. The art objects used in this context range from Hindu and Buddhist sculptures, paintings and mandalas, Pre-Columbian ceramics and Egyptian statuettes to African tribal art and Polynesian idols. In extreme instances of this approach, some LSD therapists burn fragrant incense, use ritual objects from specific spiritual traditions and read passages from ancient sacred texts such as the I Ching or the

Tibetan Book of the Dead. (54) Systematic use of universal symbols has also been described as part of the setting for psychedelic sessions. (60)

In the psychedelic approach, not much attention is paid to psychodynamic issues unless they specifically emerge and present a problem in treatment. The development of transference phenomena is generally explicitly or implicitly discouraged; the limitation of visual contact by the use of eyeshades for most of the session helps to considerably decrease the occurrence of severe problems of this nature. The therapeutic mechanism considered of utmost importance is the psychedelic peak experience, which usually takes the form of a death-rebirth sequence with ensuing feelings of cosmic unity. None of the theoreticians of psychedelic therapy has as yet formulated a comprehensive theory of psychedelic treatment that accounts for all the phenomena involved and is supported by clinical and laboratory data. The existing explanations use the framework and terminology of religious and mystical systems or make general references to the mechanisms of religious conversion. Some authors who have tried to offer physiochemical or neurophysiological interpretations have not been able to move in their speculations beyond the most general abstract concepts. These include explanations suggesting that LSD facilitates the process of unlearning and relearning by activation of stress mechanisms in the organism, or that the therapeutic effect of LSD is based on chemical stimulation of the pleasure centers in certain archaic parts of the brain. This lack of a comprehensive theoretical system constitutes an important difference between the psychedelic approach and psycholytic therapy, which leans in theory and practice on the systems of various schools of dynamic psychotherapy.

Psychedelic therapy has never become popular in Europe and with a few exceptions has not even been recognized or accepted by European therapists. Its use has remained by and large limited to the North American continent where it originated. Its most noted representatives in Canada have been Hoffer, Osmond and Hubbard, Smith, Chwelos, Blewett, McLean, and McDonald. In the United States, the beginnings of psychedelic therapy were associated with the names of Sherwood, Harman and Stolaroff; Fadiman, Mogar and Allen; Leary, Alpert, and Metzner; and Ditman, Hayman and Whittlesey. During the last fourteen years, a group of psychiatrists and psychologists working in Catonsville, Maryland, has been systematically exploring the potential of psychedelic therapy in the treatment of various psychiatric problems, in the training of mental health professionals, and in the care of dying cancer patients. This research program, conducted initially at the Research Unit of the Spring Grove State Hospital and, since 1969, at the Maryland Psychiatric Research Center in Catonsville, Maryland, has been headed by Albert A. Kurland, M.D. The basic principles of the kind of psychedelic therapy employed by this group and the methodological approach to its clinical evaluation had been formulated by Sanford Unger. Other professionals who functioned as LSD therapists and researchers in this team were Cimonetti, Bonny, Leihy, DiLeo, Lobell, McCabe, Pahnke, Richards, Rush, Savage, Schiffman, Soskin, Wolf, Yensen, and Grof.

In general, psychedelic therapy seems to be most effective in the treatment of alcoholics, narcotic-drug addicts, depressed patients, and individuals dying of cancer. In patients with psychoneuroses, psychosomatic disorders and character neuroses, major therapeutic changes usually cannot be achieved without systematically working through various levels of problems in serial LSD sessions.

Anaclitic Therapy With LSD (LSD Analysis)

The term *anaclitic (from the Greek anaklinein*—to lean upon) refers to various early infantile needs and tendencies directed toward a pregenital love object. This method was developed by two London psychoanalysts, Joyce Martin (62) and Pauline McCririck. (68) It is based on clinical observations of deep age regression occurring in LSD sessions of psychiatric patients. During these periods many of them relive episodes of early infantile frustration and emotional deprivation. This is typically associated with agonizing cravings for love, physical contact, and other instinctual needs experienced on a very primitive level.

The technique of LSD therapy practiced by Martin and McCririck was based on psychoanalytic understanding and interpretation of all the situations and experiences occurring in drug sessions and in this sense is very close to psycholytic approaches. The critical difference distinguishing this therapy from any other was the element of direct satisfaction of anaclitic needs of the patients. In contrast to the traditional detached attitude characteristic of psychoanalysis and psycholytic treatment, Martin and McCririck assumed an active mothering role and entered into close physical contact with their patients to help them to satisfy primitive infantile needs reactivated by the drug.

More superficial aspects of this approach involve holding the patients and feeding them warm milk from a bottle, caressing and offering reassuring touches, holding their heads in one's lap, or hugging and rocking. The extreme of psychodramatic involvement of the therapist is the so-called "fusion technique," which consists of full body contact with the client. The patient lies on the couch covered with a blanket and the therapist lies beside his or her body, in close embrace, usually simulating the gentle comforting movements of a mother caressing her baby.

The subjective reports of patients about these periods of "fusion" with the therapist are quite remarkable. They describe authentic feelings of symbiotic union with the nourishing mother image, experienced simultaneously on the level of the "good breast" and "good womb." In this state, patients can experience themselves as infants receiving love and nourishment at the breast of the nursing mother and at the same time feel totally identified with a fetus in the oceanic paradise of the womb. This state can simultaneously involve archetypal dimensions and elements of mystical rapture, and the above situations be experienced as contact with the Great Mother or Mother Nature. It is not uncommon that the deepest form of this experience involves feelings of oneness with the entire cosmos and the ultimate creative principle, or God.

The fusion technique seems to provide an important channel between the psychodynamic, biographical level of the LSD experience and the transcendental states of consciousness. Patients in anaclitic therapy relate that during their nourishing exchange with the mother image, the milk seemed to be "coming directly from the Milky Way." In the imaginary re-enactment of the placentary circulation the life-giving blood can be experienced as sacramental communion, not only with the material organism, but with the divine source. Repeatedly, the situations of "fusion" have been described in all their psychological and spiritual ramifications as fulfillment of the deepest needs of human nature, and as extremely healing experiences. Some patients described this technique as offering the possibility of a retroactive intervention in their deprived childhood. When the original traumatic situations from childhood become reenacted in all their relevance and complexity with the help of the "psychedelic time-machine," the therapist's affection and loving care can fill the vacuum caused by deprivation and frustration.

The dosages used in this treatment technique ranged between 100 and 200 micrograms of LSD, sometimes with the addition of Ritalin in later hours of the sessions. Martin and McCririck described good and relatively rapidly achieved results in patients with deep neuroses or borderline psychotic disorders who had experienced severe emotional deprivation in childhood. Their papers, presentations at scientific meetings, and a film documenting the anaclitic technique stirred up an enormous amount of interest among LSD therapists and generated a great deal of fierce controversy. The reactions of colleagues to this treatment modality ranged from admiration and enthusiasm to total condemnation. Since most of the criticism from the psychoanalytically oriented therapists revolved around the violation of the psychoanalytic taboo against touching and the possible detrimental consequences of the fusion technique for transference-countertransference problems, it is interesting to describe the authors' response to this serious objection.

Both Martin and McCririck seemed to concur that they had experienced much more difficulty with transference relationships before they started using the fusion technique. According to them, it is the lack of fulfillment in the conventional therapeutic relationship that foments and perpetuates transference. The original traumatic situations are continuously reenacted in the therapeutic relationship and the patient essentially experiences repetitions of the old painful rejections. When the anaclitic needs are satisfied in the state of deep regression induced by the drug, the patients are capable of detaching themselves emotionally from the therapist and look for more appropriate objects in their real life.

This situation has a parallel in the early developmental history of the individual. Those children whose infantile emotional needs were adequately met and satisfied by their parents find it relatively easy to give up the affective ties to their family and develop independent existence. By comparison, those individuals who experienced emotional deprivation and frustration in childhood tend to get trapped during their adult life in symbiotic patterns of interaction, destructive and self-destructive clinging behavior, and life-long problems with dependence-independence. According to Martin and McCririck, the critical issue in anaclitic therapy is to use the fusion technique only during periods of deep regression, and keep the experience strictly on the pregenital level. It should not be used in the termination periods of the sessions when the anaclitic elements could get easily confused with adult sexual patterns.

The anaclitic technique never achieved wide acceptance; its use seemed to be closely related to unique personality characteristics in its authors. Most other therapists, particularly males, found it emotionally difficult and uncomfortable to enter into the intimate situation of fusion with their clients. However, the importance of physical contact in LSD psychotherapy is unquestionable and many therapists have routinely used various less-intense forms of body contact.

Hypnodelic Therapy

The name of this treatment technique is a composite derived from the words "hypnosis" and "psychedelic." The concept of hypnodelic therapy was developed by Levine and Ludwig (58) in an effort to combine the uncovering effect of LSD into an organic whole with the power of hypnotic suggestion. In their approach the hypnotic technique was used to guide the subject through the drug experiences and modulate the content and course of the LSD session.

The relationship between hypnosis and the LSD reaction is very interesting and deserves a brief mention here. Fogel and Hoffer (27) reported that they were able to counteract the effects of LSD by hypnotic suggestion and, conversely, at a later date evoke typical LSD phenomena in a subject who had not ingested the drug that day. Tart (100) conducted a fascinating experiment of "mutual hypnosis," in which two persons trained both as hypnotists and hypnotic subjects continued to hypnotize each other into an increasingly deep trance. From a certain point on they became unresponsive to Tart's suggestions and shared a complicated inner journey that bore many similarities to psychedelic states.

In Levine and Ludwig's hypnodelic treatment, the first interview focused on the exploration of the patient's clinical symptoms, present life situation, and past history. Subsequently, the patient was trained as a hypnotic subject; high fixation of the eyes was used as the principle method of trance induction. Ten days later the psychiatrist conducted a psychedelic session using 125 to 200 micrograms of LSD. During the latency period, which usually lasts thirty to forty minutes when the drug is administered orally, the patient was exposed to hypnotic induction so that at the time of onset of the LSD effect, he or she was typically in a state of trance. Because of a basic similarity between LSD experiences and the phenomena of hypnosis the transition from hypnotic trance to the LSD state tends to be relatively smooth. During the culmination period of the LSD session, the psychiatrists tried to use the effect of the drug for therapeutic work while also utilizing their hypnotic rapport with the patients. They helped them to work through important areas of problems, encouraged them to overcome resistances and psychological defenses, guided them to relevant childhood memories, and facilitated catharsis and abreaction. Toward the end of the session, the patients wore given posthypnotic suggestions to remember all the details of the session and to continue thinking about the problems that emerged during the session. A special isolated room was provided for them for the rest of the session day.

Levine and Ludwig explored the efficacy of the hypnodelic technique in narcotic-drug addicts and alcoholics. According to their original report, the combination of LSD administration and hypnosis proved to be more effective than either of the components used separately.

Aggregate LSD Psychotherapy

In this form of LSD therapy *en masse*, patients experience their LSD sessions, usually with medium or high dosages, in the company of several co-patients participating in the same psychedelic treatment program. The basic difference between this therapeutic approach and the LSD-assisted group psychotherapy described earlier is the absence of any effort at coordinated work with the group as a whole during the time of the drug action. The most important reason for giving the drug simultaneously to a large number of individuals is to save time for the therapeutic team. Despite the fact that they share the same room, patients essentially experience their sessions individually with only occasional, unstructured encounters and interactions of an elemental nature. A standard program of stereophonic music is usually offered to the entire group, or several alternative channels might be made available on different headphone circuits. Sometimes the projection of slides of emotionally relevant and provocative material or aesthetically stimulating pictures and mandalas can form an integral part of the program for the session day. The therapist and his helpers provide collective supervision; individual attention is given only if absolutely necessary. On the day following the drug session or later on, the individual experiences of the participants are usually shared with other group members.

This approach has its advantages and disadvantages. The possibility of treating a number of patients simultaneously is an important factor from the economic point of view, and could in the future represent the answer to the unfavorable ratio between mental health professionals and psychiatric patients. On the other hand, the lack of sensitive individualized support might make this treatment less effective and less conducive to working through some especially difficult and demanding areas of personal problems. There is also, in such a collective situation, a danger of psychological contagion; panic reactions, aggressive behavior and loud abreactions of individual patients can negatively influence the experiences of their peers. If the group approach is sensitively combined with individual work when necessary, however, its advantages can outweigh its drawbacks.

The best-known treatment program of this kind was a multidimensional approach to psychedelic psychotherapy developed by Salvador Roquet, (87) a Mexican psychiatrist and founder of the Albert Schweitzer Association in Mexico City. Although his therapeutic program utilized other psychedelic drugs and substances of plant origin in addition to LSD, it deserves more detailed discussion in this context. Roquet combined his training as a psychoanalyst with his knowledge of the indigenous healing practices and ceremonies of various Mexican Indian groups and created a new approach to therapy with psychedelic drugs that he called psychosynthesis. This should not be confused with the theory and practice of the original psychotherapeutic system also called psychosynthesis developed in Italy by Roberto Assagioli. The latter approach is strictly a non-drug procedure, although it shares with psychedelic therapy a strong transpersonal emphasis. In Roquet's approach, therapy was conducted with groups of ten to twenty-eight patients of differing ages and sexes. The members of each group were carefully selected to make the group as heterogeneous as possible with respect to age, sex, clinical problems, the psychedelic drug received, and length of time already spent in treatment. Each group included novices just beginning therapeutic work, individuals who were in the main course of treatment, and patients about to terminate therapy. An important goal of the selection process was to offer a broad spectrum of suitable figures for projections and imaginary roles. Various members of such a heterogeneous group could then represent authority figures, maternal and paternal images, sibling substitutes, or objects of sexual interest.

Following the example of Indian rituals, the drug sessions took place at night. All the participants met in a large room for a leaderless group discussion that lasted about two hours. These meetings allowed the patients to meet new members and discuss their fears, hopes and expectations; they also gave the participants ample opportunity for projections and transferences that had an important catalyzing influence on their drug sessions and frequently provided valuable learning experiences. The treatment room was large and decorated with paintings and posters with evocative themes. A wide spectrum of psychedelic substances were administered in these meetings, including LSD, peyote, a variety of psilocybin-containing mushrooms, morning glory seeds, *Datura ceratocaulum*, and ketamine.

The patients spent most of the time in a reclining position on mattresses arranged along the walls, though they were allowed to move around freely if they wanted. Two stereo systems were used and a wide variety of music and sounds was available to influence the depth and intensity of the group's reactions. An important part of the psychedelic sessions was a sensory overload show using slides, movies, stereo effects, and intermittent flashes of colored floodlights. Several themes considered to be of crucial relevance were interwoven in the otherwise erratic and confused barrage of unrelated images and sounds; these included birth, death, violence, sexuality, religion, and childhood. The sensory overload portion of the drug sessions lasted about six hours and was followed by a reflective phase that lasted until sunrise. Following this, the therapists and all participants rested for an hour.

The integrative session involved group discussions and sharing of experiences. The main objective of this phase was to facilitate integration of the material uncovered in the drug session and to apply the insights to the problems of everyday living. Depending on the nature of the interactions this process took from four to twelve hours. The course of therapy consisted of ten to twenty drug sessions, depending on the nature and seriousness of the clinical problems involved. The patient population consisted mostly of neurotic out-patients, although Roquet also described various degrees of success with some antisocial personalities and selected schizophrenics.

THE NEED FOR A COMPREHENSIVE THEORY OF LSD THERAPY

Therapeutic experimentation with LSD, and psychedelic research in general, has been very negatively influenced by the existence of the black market, unsupervised self-experimentation, sensational journalism, and irrational legislative measures. Despite the fact that LSD now has been known for almost three decades, the literature describing its effects and therapeutic potential is controversial and inconclusive. Further developments in this field would require that independent teams in different countries interact and cooperate in collecting experimental data and exchanging information. However, the number of places studying LSD has been cut down considerably and continues to decrease. Although the present prospects for extensive psychedelic research are rather grim, there are indications that systematic exploration will be resumed after the general confusion has been clarified and rationality reintroduced into the study of the problems involved.

Whatever becomes of LSD research in the future, there are good reasons to analyze the observations and results of past psychedelic experimentation and present the most important insights and findings in a simple and comprehensive form. Such an effort seems justified whether this study becomes an epitaph to the LSD era or a manifesto for future psychedelic researchers. If we are witnessing the "swan song" of psychedelic research, it would be interesting in retrospect to be able to throw more light on the controversies and lack of theoretical understanding concerning the nature of the LSD effect. If LSD research continues into the future, clarification of the present confusion and disagreements would be of great practical importance. Additional controlled studies on a large scale are needed to assess the efficacy of LSD as an adjunct to psychotherapy with a satisfactory degree of scientific accuracy. However, unless the critical reasons for past controversies can be clearly identified and taken into consideration in future research, the new studies will probably perpetuate old errors and yield correspondingly inconclusive results.

As indicated above, individual authors and research teams used LSD starting from very different premises. They followed different therapeutic objectives, adhered to different theoretical systems, employed differing technical approaches, and administered the drug in the most disparate frameworks and settings. It is my belief that the main reason for the controversies about LSD therapy is a lack of understanding regarding the nature of the LSD effect, and the absence of a plausible and generally acceptable conceptual framework that would reduce the vast amounts of observed data to certain common denominators. Such a theoretical system would have to provide understanding of the content and course of separate sessions as well as of repeated exposures to LSD in a therapeutic series. And it should be able to explain the paramount importance of extrapharmacological factors—the personalities of the subject and the guide, their mutual relationship, and the elements of the set and setting—in the development of LSD sessions.

Other important problems that should be accounted for within a comprehensive theoretical framework are the occasional prolonged reactions and even psychotic breakdowns that occur after some of the sessions, or the later recurrences of the LSD-like states ("flashbacks"). The general understanding of these phenomena is at present very incomplete and unsatisfactory, a situation that has serious practical consequences. One result of it is that the approach of mental health professionals to complications of the non-medical use of psychedelics is generally ineffective and often harmful.

A comprehensive theory of LSD psychotherapy should also be able to bridge the gap at present existing between psycholytic and psychedelic therapy, the two most relevant and vital approaches to LSD treatment, and some other therapeutic modifications such as anaclitic and hypnodelic therapy. It should be possible to find important common denominators and explanatory principles for these various approaches and understand their indications and contraindications, as well as successes and failures. A conceptual framework correctly reflecting the most important aspects of the LSD effect should be able to provide practical directives concerning the optimal conditions for the use of this substance in psychotherapy. This would involve general treatment strategy, as well as details concerning dosages, effective approaches to various special situations, use of auxiliary techniques, and the specific elements of set and setting. Finally, a useful, comprehensive theory should provide a number of partial working hypotheses of a practical and theoretical nature that could be tested with the use of scientific methodology.

In view of the complex and multileveled nature of the problems involved, it is extremely difficult to formulate at present a conceptual framework that would fully satisfy all the above criteria. For the time being, even a tentative and approximate theoretical structure, organizing most of the important data and providing guidelines for therapeutic practice, would represent distinct progress. In the following chapters an attempt will be made to present a tentative framework for the theory and practice of LSD psychotherapy. It is my belief that a conceptual system that could account for at least the major observations of LSD therapy requires not just a new understanding of the effects of LSD, but a new and expanded model of the human mind and the nature of human beings. The researches on which my speculations are based were a series of exploratory clinical studies, each of which represented an exciting venture into new territories of the mind as yet uncharted by Western science. It would be unrealistic to expect that they would be more than first sketchy maps for future explorers. I am well aware of the fact that, following the example of old geographers, many areas of my cartography would deserve to be designated by the famous inscription: *Hic sunt leones.*[5]

The proposed theoretical and practical framework should be considered as an attempt to organize and categorize innumerable new and puzzling observations from several thousand LSD sessions and present them in a logical and comprehensive way. Even in its present rough form, this conceptual framework has proved useful in understanding the events in psychedelic sessions run in a clinical setting, as well as LSD states experienced in the context of non-medical experimentation; following its basic principles has made it possible to conduct LSD therapy with maximum benefit and minimum risk. I believe that it also offers important guidelines for more effective crisis intervention related to psychedelic drug use and more successful treatment of various complications following unsupervised self-experimentation.

NOTES

1. One microgram or gama is one millionth of a gram, about thirty-five billionths of an ounce.

2. *Conversions* are sudden, very dramatic personality changes occurring unexpectedly in psychologically predisposed individuals in certain specific situations. The direction of these profound transformations is usually contrary to the subject's previous beliefs, emotional reactions, life values, attitudes and behavior patterns. According to the area which they primarily influence, we can distinguish religious, political, moral, sexual, and other conversions. Religious conversions of atheists to true believers or even religious fanatics have been observed in gatherings of ecstatic sects and during sermons of famous charismatic preachers, such as John Wesley. Maya Deren gave in her *Divine Horsemen* (22) a unique description of her conversion to Haitian voodoo, which occurred during her study of aboriginal dances. Victor Hugo's example of the moral conversion of Jean Valjean in *Les Misérables* (39) found its way into psychiatric handbooks and gave its name to a special kind of corrective emo-

tional experience. The most spectacular illustration of political conversion and later reconversion was described by Arthur Koestler in his *Arrow in the Blue* (47) and *The God That Failed*. (46) Biblical examples of moral and sexual conversions of a religious nature are the stories of Barabas and Mary Magdalene.
3. The significance of traumatic memories from childhood for the dynamics of psycholytic therapy has been systematically studied and described by Hanscarl Leuner. (57) See also the discussion of psychodynamic experiences in the first volume of this series, Stanislav Grof, *Realms of the Human Unconscious: Observations from LSD Research*. (32) Subsequent references to this book will be indicated by a shortened title, thus: *Realms of the Human Unconscious*.
4. Walter Pahnke (76) summarized the basic characteristics of spontaneous and psychedelic peak experiences in his nine mystical categories. According to him, the essential features of these states are: (1) feelings of unity, (2) transcendence of time and space, (3) strong positive affect, (4) sense of reality and objectivity of the experience, (5) sacredness, (6) ineffability, (7) paradoxicality, (8) transiency, and (9) subsequent positive changes in attitudes and behavior. The Psychedelic Experience Questionnaire (PEQ) developed by Pahnke and Richards makes it possible to assess whether or not the psychedelic peak experience occurred in an LSD session, and allows for its gross quantification.
5. *Hic sunt leones* literally means "Here are lions"; this expression was used by early geographers in the old charts to denote insufficiently explored territories, possibly abounding in savages, wild animals, and other dangers.

CRITICAL VARIABLES IN LSD THERAPY 2

Pharmacological Effects of LSD
Personality of the Subject
Personality of the Therapist or Guide
Set and Setting of the Sessions

A deep understanding of the nature and course of the LSD experience and the dynamics of LSD psychotherapy is impossible without full awareness of all the factors involved in the LSD reaction. The early simplistic and reductionistic models of the LSD experience as being either "model schizophrenia" or a "toxic psychosis"—basically a result of the drug's interference with the normal physiological and biochemical processes in the brain—have been abandoned a long time ago by all serious researchers. The LSD literature abounds in observations indicating the utmost importance of non-drug factors as determinants of psychedelic experiences and the critical role they play in the therapeutic process. In order to understand the nature of the LSD reaction in all its complexity, we have to discuss not only the actual pharmacological effect of the drug, but also the most important extrapharmacological factors—the role of the personality of the subject, his or her emotional condition and current life situation, the personality of the guide or therapist, the nature of the relationship between the subject and the guide, and an entire complex of additional factors usually referred to as set and setting.

PHARMACOLOGICAL EFFECTS OF LSD

Since administration of LSD is the *conditio sine qua non*, or the absolutely necessary condition for the LSD reaction, it would seem only logical to consider the drug itself as the factor of fundamental importance. Careful analysis of clinical observations from LSD psychotherapy, however, shows this issue to be much more complicated. The phenomena that can occur in the course of LSD sessions cover a very wide range; there are hardly any perceptual, emotional, or psychosomatic manifestations that have not been observed and described as part of the LSD spectrum. If different subjects take the same dosage of the drug under relatively standard circumstances, each will have a distinctly different experience. The extreme multiformity and interindividual variability of the LSD state is complemented by its equally striking intraindividual variability. If the same person takes LSD repeatedly, each consecutive session is usually quite different from the others as to its general character, specific content, and course. This variability certainly is a serious objection to the concept that the LSD reaction has simple biochemical and physiological determinants.

The question whether there exist invariant, repeatable and standard effects of LSD that are purely pharmacological in nature is very interesting and important from both the theoretical and practical point of view. Such effects would have to be unrelated to the personality structure and independent of external circumstances; they would have to occur without exception in every subject who took a sufficient dose of LSD. Conversely, the questions of the extent to which various extrapharmacological factors participate in the LSD experience, and the nature and mechanism of their effect, are equally interesting and theoretically as well as practically relevant. The search for typical and mandatory pharmacological effects of LSD was an important aspect of my analytical work on the LSD data. The result of this quest was rather surprising: after analyzing almost five thousand records from LSD sessions, I did not find a single symptom that was an absolutely constant component in all of them and could thus be considered truly invariant.

Changes in optical perception are usually described as typical manifestations of the LSD state and are thus serious candidates for being pharmacological invariants. Although reports of various abnormal visual phenomena occurred frequently in my records, I have observed a number of high-dose sessions where there were no alterations in optical perception. Some of these LSD reactions where visual changes were absent had the form of intense sexual experiences; others were characterized by massive somatization with feelings of general malaise and physical illness, or experiences of excruciating pain in various parts of the body. Special examples of sessions without optical perceptual changes were observed in advanced stages of psycholytic treatment and in some psychedelic sessions. They involved either a brutal and primitive experiential complex described by various subjects as reliving of their own birth, or transcendental experiences of cosmic unity and the Supracosmic Void which had the paradoxical quality of being "contentless yet all-containing."

Physical manifestations of the LSD state deserve special notice in this context since, in the early reports, they were seen as simple pharmacological effects of the drug and attributed to direct chemical stimulation of the vegetative centers in the brain. Careful observation of a large number of sessions and analysis of the records does not support this explanation. The physical concomitants of the LSD reaction vary considerably from session to session. The spectrum of so-called "vegetative symptoms" is very broad and exceeds that of any other drug known, with the exception of some other psychedelics. Strangely enough, these symptoms include both sympathetic and parasympathetic phenomena, and they appear in clusters involving various combinations thereof. They occur with the same frequency and intensity in low- and high-dose sessions and there is no demonstrable dose–effect relationship. In many high-dose LSD sessions, physical manifestations

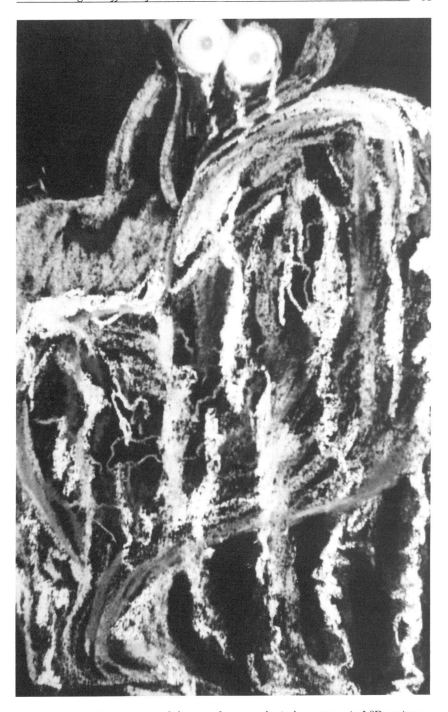

An experience of nausea, one of the most frequent physical symptoms in LSD sessions.

are entirely absent, or they occur intermittently in close connection with difficult and strongly defended unconscious material. Conversely, some low-dose sessions are characterized by massive vegetative symptoms during the entire course of the drug reaction. It is not uncommon that after administration of an additional dose of LSD a subject suffering from severe physical symptoms surrenders to the experience, works through the underlying problem, and gets rid of the somatic distress. Another aspect of these symptoms that is particularly relevant to our discussion is their unusual sensitivity to various psychological factors; they can often be modified or even terminated by specific external influences and psychotherapeutic interventions. The factors that can dramatically affect "vegetative" and other physical manifestations in LSD sessions range from relevant interpretations or arrival of a specific person to the use of physical contact and various bioenergetic exercises.

One of the physical manifestations of the LSD reaction that deserves special mention is the dilation of the pupils (mydriasis). It is so common that its presence has been used by many experimenters and therapists as a relatively reliable indication that a person is still under the influence of the drug. For a long time, mydriasis seemed to be a serious candidate in my investigations for being the invariant manifestation of the LSD effect. Later, I witnessed several LSD sessions, some of them very dramatic, in which the pupils of the subjects appeared constricted or in which they oscillated rapidly between extreme dilation and constriction.

A similar situation exists in the area of gross physical manifestations such as psychomotor excitement or inhibition, muscular tension, tremors, twitches, seizure-like activities, and various twisting movements. None of these symptoms is standard and predictable enough to be considered a specific pharmacological effect of LSD. This does not mean that LSD does not have any specific physiological effects *per se*; these can be clearly demonstrated in animal experiments using incomparably higher dosages. However, my experience indicates that within the dosage range commonly used in human experiments or in psychotherapeutic practice, physical manifestations do not result from direct pharmacological stimulation of the nervous system. They seem to reflect chemical activation of dynamic matrices in the unconscious and have a structure similar to hysterical conversions, organ-neurotic phenomena, or symptoms of psychosomatic disorders.

As unpredictable as the content of the LSD reaction is its intensity, and individual responses to the same dosage level vary considerably. The degree of sensitivity or resistance to LSD seems to depend on complicated psychological factors rather than on variables of a constitutional, biological, or metabolic nature. Subjects who in everyday life manifest a strong need to maintain full self-control, and have difficulties in relaxing and "letting go," can sometimes resist relatively high dosages of LSD (300–500 micrograms) and show no detectable change. Occasionally, individuals can resist considerable doses of LSD if they have set this as a personal task for themselves. They may do it to defy the therapist and compete with him or her, to prove or demonstrate their psychological "strength," to endure more than their fellow patients, to impress their friends, or for many other reasons. However, it is obvious that deeper and more relevant unconscious motives should be looked for behind such superficial rationalizations. Additional causes of high resistance to the effect of the drug may be insufficient preparation,

instruction and reassurance of the subjects, lack of their full agreement and cooperation, or absence of basic trust in the therapeutic relationship. In this case, the
LSD reaction sometimes does not take its full course until the motives for resistance are analyzed and understood. Similar factors seem to be responsible for the
inability of many persons to surrender to the effect of the drug under the circumstances of unsupervised self-experimentation in the presence of strangers and in
unfamiliar environments. Such sessions are conducive to incomplete resolution
and integration, adverse after-effects, and later recurrences ("flashbacks"). Instant
sobering, which can occur at any period of the session and on any dosage level,
typically indicates a sudden mobilization of defenses against the impending
emergence of unpleasant traumatic material.

Among psychiatric patients, severe obsessive-compulsive neurotics are particularly resistant to the effect of LSD. It has been a common observation in my
research that such patients can frequently resist dosages of more than 500 micrograms of LSD and show only slight signs of physical or psychological distress. In
extreme cases it can take several dozen high-dose LSD sessions before the psychological resistances of these individuals are reduced to a level where they start having episodes of regression to childhood and become aware of the unconscious
material that has to be worked through. After observing several situations in
which even a drastic increase of dosage—in one instance to 15000 micrograms given
intramuscularly—did not result in a fully developed LSD experience, it became
obvious that high psychological resistance to LSD cannot be overcome just by an
increase in dosage; it has to be gradually reduced in a series of sessions. There
seems to be a saturation point of LSD somewhere between 400 and 500 micrograms; if the subject does not respond adequately to this dosage, additional LSD
will not change anything in the situation.

There is some evidence, of an anecdotal rather than experimental nature,
suggesting that a lowered response to LSD can occur in spiritually highly-
developed individuals who have extensive experience of unusual states of mind or
live in such a state most of the time. The most famous example of this is Ram Dass'
account, according to which his Indian guru did not respond on two occasions to
extremely high dosages of LSD (900 and 1200 micrograms respectively). (83) This
would indicate the possibility that lack of reaction to the drug can be associated
paradoxically with two opposite conditions, namely excessive rigidity and a strong
psychological defense system or extreme openness and a lack of separating
barriers.

Having reviewed various kinds of evidence suggesting the absence of any
clear, specific and invariant pharmacological effects of LSD at the dosage level
commonly used in experimental and clinical work with human subjects, we can
try to outline what the effects of LSD actually are. According to my experience,
they are very unspecific and can be described only in the most general terms. In a
great majority of sessions there is an overall tendency toward perceptual changes
in various sensory areas. Consciousness is usually qualitatively changed and has a
dream-like character. The access to unconscious material is typically facilitated
and psychological defenses are lowered. Emotional reactivity is almost always
greatly enhanced and affective factors play an important role as determinants of
the LSD reaction. A rather striking aspect of the LSD effect is a marked intensification of mental processes and neural processes in general; this involves
phenomena of differing nature and origin.

Pre-existing and recent psychogenic symptoms, as well as those the individual had suffered from in childhood or at some later period of life, may be amplified and exteriorized. While experiencing them in an exaggerated form the individual frequently develops insights into the network of unconscious processes that underlies them, discovering their specific psychodynamic, perinatal and transpersonal roots. Traumatic or positive memories connected with a strong emotional charge are activated, brought forth from the unconscious, and relived, and the content of various dynamic matrices from different levels of the individual and collective unconscious may emerge into consciousness and be experienced in a complex way. Occasionally, phenomena of a neurological nature can be amplified and manifested in the sessions; this is true for pains associated with arthritis, dislocation of vertebral discs, inflammatory processes, or post-operative and post-traumatic changes. Reliving sensations related to past injuries and operations is particularly common. What is interesting from a theoretical point of view is that LSD subjects even seem to be able to relive pains and other sensations related to past operations conducted under deep general anesthesia. The propensity of LSD and other psychedelics to activate and amplify various neurological processes is so striking that it has been used by several Czech neurologists as a diagnostic tool for the exteriorization of latent paralyses and other subtle organic damage of the central nervous system. (24) The negative side of this interesting property of LSD is the fact that it can activate seizures in patients suffering from manifest epilepsy, or those who have a latent disposition to this disease. A rapid sequence of epileptic seizures that might be difficult to control, the so-called *status epilepticus*, represents one of the few serious physical risks of LSD therapy.

By and large, I have not been able to discover during my analyses of the data any distinct pharmacological effects that are constant and invariant and can therefore be considered drug-specific. At present, I see LSD as a powerful unspecific amplifier or catalyst of the biochemical and neurophysiological processes in the brain. It seems to create a situation of general undifferentiated activation that facilitates the emergence of unconscious material from various levels of the personality. The richness, as well as the unusual inter- and intra-individual variability, can be explained by the participation and determining influence of extrapharmacological factors.

In the following sections we will discuss in detail all the major non-drug variables that seem to have a decisive influence on the process of LSD psychotherapy. They include the personality structure and current life situation of the subject, the personality of the guide, the nature of their mutual relationship, and the set and setting of the sessions.

PERSONALITY OF THE SUBJECT

When we discuss the significance of the subject's personality for the nature, content and course of the LSD experience, it is necessary to distinguish between the role of personality factors in individual sessions using low and medium dosages on the one hand, and in consecutive sessions of a therapeutic series or high-dose psychedelic sessions on the other. We will first cover the more superficial personality variables and later move on to the deeper underlying structures that function as determinants of the LSD experience.

Some interesting personality variables can already be observed in the predrug phase of LSD treatment—during the initial interview and the preparatory period. There is a very typical group of individuals who approach the LSD sessions with multiple anxieties and great apprehension. They raise a number of questions and doubts concerning the effect of the drug and value of the therapeutic procedure, dwell on the horror stories they have read in the newspapers or heard on the radio and TV, and show a tendency to procrastinate and delay the actual session as long as possible. It is not uncommon that these subjects have serious disturbances of sleep or terrible nightmares as a result of the approaching prospect of taking the drug. Such persons usually require much reassurance of a general and specific nature before they agree to have a drug session.

There seems to exist a typical cluster of conflicts and problems that many of these individuals share. In their everyday life they are constantly concerned about maintaining perfect control over their feelings and behavior. They are afraid of temporary or permanent unleashing of instinctual energies, especially those of a sexual and aggressive nature, and of involuntary emotional outbursts. There is frequent preoccupation with the issue of loss of control and fear of social embarrassment, blunder and public scandal resulting from the ensuing behavior. The struggle with forces that threaten to emerge from the unconscious can take much time and energy in the life of these persons, and is often associated with feelings of inferiority, a sense of guilt, and self-reproach in regard to the instinctual drives. In the extreme, the above concerns can take the form of fear of insanity or death. These persons typically dislike and fear all situations such as fatigue, diseases with fever, sleep deprivation, and the hypnagogic period which threaten to reduce the degree of conscious control over the unconscious impulses. In some instances the fear of the transition between waking consciousness and sleep is so intense that these patients take long, fatiguing walks before going to sleep or keep themselves busy until late hours to shorten the hypnagogic period and expedite the process of falling asleep.

Since full sexual orgasm requires a temporary suspension of voluntary control, such problems usually find their most salient expression in the sexual life of these persons. Their problems in this area range from impotence, frigidity or incomplete and superficial orgasms to a tendency to avoid sexual situations altogether. Discussions about their experience of sexual intercourse may reveal a fear of unleashing aggressive impulses in themselves or their partners, and a frightening sense that the situation might get "out of control." On a deeper level the associated fantasies can take the form of intense unconscious fears of devouring the partners or being devoured by them. People with such problems usually instinctively sense or deduce from the reports of others that LSD has a disinhibiting effect, and that its administration can result in loss of control and a powerful upsurge of unconscious material. The prospect of having an LSD session thus feeds directly into the central fears of these individuals. The problems related to sexual intercourse and orgasm that are described here also betray the manifestation of perinatal energies in these persons. (See a detailed discussion of these problems on p 69, ff.)

Another problem related to the negative attitude toward LSD therapy and unwillingness to have a drug session is associated with a lack of trust in oneself, other people, human society, and the world in general. If these feelings are within the neurotic range it is necessary to spend extra time with the patient to develop a sufficient degree of trust before administration of the drug. Openly paranoid attitudes about the procedure, especially when the patient tends to include the therapist among the suspected persecutors, should be considered a contraindication for LSD therapy.

An enthusiastic approach to LSD treatment, vivid interest in the drug, and an eagerness to have psychedelic sessions has been observed in certain types of intellectuals who are dissatisfied with the dullness and monotony of their everyday life and are looking for unusual, exotic and stimulating experiences. In this group, the possibility of exploring hidden recesses of the mind is also frequently seen as a unique learning opportunity, and adds to the special appeal of the experience. Patients with a strong positive component in the transference relationship sometimes see the major attraction of the psychedelic session as the prospect of having the full and undivided attention of the therapist for an entire day. Some of the patients, unconsciously or with various degrees of conscious awareness, use the framework of the drug session as an opportunity to experience, express and act out some of their otherwise unacceptable tendencies.

On occasion, a potentially dangerous eagerness and strong motivation to have a psychedelic session is observed in certain desperate patients with few alternatives left in life. They find themselves in a subjectively unbearable situation of intense conflict associated with great emotional distress and tension. Typical characteristics include serious questioning of the meaning of life, toying with suicidal fantasies, and a careless and risky approach to various life-situations in general. Unable to tolerate the intensity of the conflicting psychological forces, and tired of making painful compromises, they crave instant termination of this agonizing state. In their fantasy LSD becomes the magic tool that will give them instant relief, either by mediating a miraculous cure or by precipitating self-destruction. If the psychedelic sessions with these individuals do not result in elements of ego death and transcendence, they can activate the existing self-destructive tendencies. It is quite important to detect such attitudes in advance, analyze the underlying motives, and discuss the situation with the subject before the administration of the drug.

All the factors discussed above are of primary importance before the first LSD session. When the drug has been repeatedly administered in the context of a therapeutic series, most patients realize the possibilities that psychedelic experiences can offer in terms of deep self-exploration, finding the roots of one's emotional symptoms, and solving life problems. Even those patients who were initially concerned about loss of control usually discover its therapeutic value. Their previous concept of control, that once lost it cannot be regained, is replaced by the insight that suspension of defenses is a liberating experience. They discover a new way of being in the world in which one can exert control without any effort because the urgent forces that required constant anxious attention have been discharged.

By and large, all patients treated with serial LSD sessions tend to develop a positive atittude toward the treatment. Although after particularly difficult sessions some individuals might show fear and a reluctance to continue, they usually do not lose trust in the value of the process. The major exception to this rule are patients with severe obsessive-compulsive neuroses, who can maintain a generally pessimistic attitude all through the procedure. Their pessimism is frequently reinforced and confirmed by uneventful sessions and an apparent lack of therapeutic benefit.

Special mention should be made of subjects with superior intelligence and strong intellectual interests in human culture, psychology, art, philosophy, and religion. Such subjects tend to discover very quickly that the process of serial LSD sessions transcends the framework of traditional depth-psychological analysis and offers unique possibilities for a serious philosophical and spiritual quest. As a result of this insight, they pursue psychedelic self-exploration with great interest and emotional involvement. In this context, LSD sessions can be seen as an opportunity to confront the mysteries of the universe and the riddle of human existence. They thus assume a function comparable to the spiritual practices of ancient and Oriental cultures, or to rites of passage, temple mysteries, and various esoteric procedures of the mystical tradition.

We have also observed interesting connections between the clinical diagnosis or symptomatology of some patients and the nature of their LSD sessions. These are most striking in the case of persons suffering from severe obsessive-compulsive neuroses. These patients usually belong to the group of those who are afraid of the drug session before they have experienced it; they tend to voice a number of concerns and questions, and typically delay the onset of treatment. Their resistance to the effect of LSD is extremely high and even sessions with excessive dosages are frequently uneventful. The phenomenology of their LSD sessions is usually limited to a determined fight against the effect of the drug and an extreme effort to maintain reality-testing and full self-control. There are practically no disturbances of optical perception and the only manifestations of the LSD effect are typically massive somatizations. If they experience any unusual feelings at all, these patients usually present multiple complaints about unpleasant physical symptoms, such as headaches, weakness, fatigue, general malaise, a tendency to collapse or swoon, nausea, profuse sweating, chills and hot flashes. They might be alarmed by their sense of losing touch with reality, concerned about intensification of their sexual and aggressive drives, or preoccupied with conflicts regarding self-esteem and ethical issues. Their sessions are characterized by intense inner struggle and are usually followed by excessive feelings of fatigue. For patients with obsessive-compulsive neuroses of extreme intensity, it can take a considerable number of LSD sessions before their resistances are reduced and the sessions start having a more concrete content.

In individuals with a hysterical personality structure and symptomatology, the nature, content and course of the LSD sessions is usually substantially different; as a matter of fact, they seem to be at the opposite end of the spectrum from the obsessive-compulsives. Excitement, and intense curiosity about the procedure is quite typical of these patients and their attitude toward the drug experience is generally much more positive. They are extremely sensitive to the effects of LSD and frequently display a rather dramatic reaction after a relatively small dose. In this group, the various perceptual changes are extraordinarily rich, with a definite predominance of visual elements and intense body sensations. In agreement with observations from classical psychoanalysis, perceptions of an erotic nature and rich sexual symbolism seem to dominate the experiential world of these patients. Their images tend to have a flowing scenic character; they are usually dramatic, vivid and colorful with visualization of various glamorous daydreams and other wishful elements of fantasy life. This smooth scenic course can be disturbed when patients approach traumatic and pathogenic memory constellations. Like everyone else, hysterical patients are not immune to difficult and painful experiences in psychedelic sessions. However, they seem to have high tolerance of suffering and can appreciate periods of inhuman horror and torture as much as episodes of ecstatic rapture. During LSD psychotherapy, as in systematic drug-free therapy, these patients might present special challenges and problems in regard to transference and countertransference.

Observations from LSD psychotherapy seem to confirm Freud's findings of a close relationship between homosexuality and paranoid behavior. It was repeatedly observed that patients with serious latent or manifest problems concerning homosexuality had a greater disposition toward panic reactions, paranoid perception, use of projection in regard to their LSD experiences, and delusional interpretation of the situation and the session in general. These difficulties usually occurred or were particularly accentuated when a preoccupation with their homosexual problems was the central focus of their experience.

We have not been able to detect any fixed and specific correlations between symptoms of clinical depression and the nature of the psychedelic experiences. Although deepening of pre-existing depression and intensification of suicidal ideation can often be observed in LSD sessions, the clinical condition of depressed persons frequently appears quite labile and prone to dramatic changes and breakthroughs. In neurotic depressions, heightened affective lability sometimes results in a peculiar condition in which depressive affect and crying occurs simultaneously with euphoria and forceful laughing, or alternates with them in a rapid succession. In general, it is not uncommon that a depressed patient experiences most of the session in a thoroughly euphoric or even ecstatic way and that a marked and sometimes lasting improvement can be noted after the session. Several accidental observations have suggested that a single LSD session can cause a complete remission of a serious periodic depression with a very stubborn pattern without, of course, changing the underlying personality structure or preventing recurrence of future depressions at the usual time periods.

Repeated observations of LSD sessions in depressed patients suggest that the drug can be useful in making a differential diagnosis between exogenous and endogenous depressions. Patients whose depression is basically of exogenous origin usually deal in their sessions with rich biographical material which is thematically and dynamically related to their disease. In patients with endogenous depressions, the content of the sessions is usually much more limited and frequently consists of accentuation of the deep and primordial feelings constituting the depression. In these patients there is a definite risk that their clinical symptoms might be temporarily intensified after some LSD sessions. This observation is in agreement with the experiences of Arendsen-Hein (5), a Dutch psychiatrist and pioneer in LSD psychotherapy.

In general, it can be concluded that the relationship between the diagnostic group and the nature of the LSD experience is not sufficiently distinct and constant to be of great clinical value, except in the few extreme cases mentioned above. In this sense, LSD certainly cannot contribute much to the clinical

diagnosis established by psychiatric interviews and conventional diagnostic techniques. The relationship between the original diagnostic category of the patient
and his or her psychedelic experiences becomes even looser and less predictable in
serial LSD sessions. As we will discuss later, repeated exposures to the drug are
associated with major dynamic shifts in the personality structure and frequent
changes of symptoms.

The limited value of LSD as an auxiliary to conventional clinical diagnosis
contrasts sharply with its potential for dynamic diagnosis. It is an unrivalled tool
for the exploration of the forces constituting the basic personality, and for study of
the deep dynamic structures underlying clinical symptoms. In sessions with lower
and medium dosages of LSD, and in the termination periods of high-dose sessions,
one can often observe a marked intensification of pre-existing personality
characteristics and behavior patterns. This is typically accompanied by accentuation of current clinical symptoms or recurrence of emotional and psychosomatic
effects that the patient suffered from at some point in the past. Sometimes this
reenactment involves relatively recent history, at other times very early periods of
childhood or even infancy.

Occasionally, completely new symptoms may emerge during a session which
the patient does not remember ever having experienced before. This offers a
unique opportunity for the researcher to study the psychogenesis and physiogenesis
of clinical symptoms in the process of their origination, *in statu nascendi*. The
general dynamic structure of these newly formed symptoms seems to be identical
with that of the usual neurotic manifestations; it represents a compromise formation between powerful unconscious drives or tendencies and the mechanisms of
defense. Phenomena of this kind seem to be reflected in activation and exteriorization of latent matrices of the unconscious which exist in the dynamic structure of
the personality. The reason why they have not manifested earlier in life is that
they have not been activated by biochemical or psychological forces to a sufficient
degree to influence the patient's ego. The so-called "vegetative" symptoms frequently seem to fall into this category.

The individual characteristics that are amplified in the low-dose range
represent more superficial but practically important aspects of the personality. In
everyday life some of these elements are so inapparent that they are not readily
detected and identified, or the subjects use various techniques to counteract and
hide them. LSD can enhance these subtle features to such a degree that they reach
the point of a caricature. Under the magnifying effect of the drug they become so
obvious that they cannot possibly escape the attention of either the therapist or the
subject. The broad spectrum of phenomena belonging to this group can be divided
into several typical categories.

The first category includes manifestations reflecting *emotional reactivity*
and *general feeling tone*. The subjects can get deeply in touch with their present
emotional condition and explore the experiential dimensions and characteristics of
the various affective states that it entails. Probably the most valuable insights
available in this context are into positive and negative feelings towards certain
persons and situations, especially in the form of ambivalence and conflicting attitudes. Similarly, many patients may fully experience and express their anxieties
and various specific fears, depression and despair, states of aggressive tension, irritability and impulsivity, or emotional lability with alternating depressive and
euphoric moods. An experience that characteristically occurs in neurotic patients

is an agonizing feeling of loneliness and isolation with a sense of uselessness. The feeling of being superfluous in the world and the inability to see the meaning of one's existence are frequently associated with the need to be needed and sought after. Individuals who experienced marked emotional deprivation and rejection in childhood frequently show at this point an intense need for love. Such cravings usually have strong infantile features and involve anaclitical elements. On occasion, experiences of this kind can result in valuable insights into the basically childlike nature of various dependency needs, and lead to an understanding of how this confusion creates conflicts in everyday life.

The second category involves problems related to *self-image* and *self-esteem*. The most frequent phenomena in this area are agonizing inferiority feelings experienced in regard to different dimensions of one's existence. Thus patients quite often express dissatisfaction, unhappiness, or even despair about their physical appearance. They complain about being ugly, misshapen or repulsive, point to imagined or insignificant physical defects, and greatly exaggerate the relevance of some existing handicaps. This preoccupation with self-esteem is as often related to intellectual abilities. Subjects describe themselves as stupid, dull, unimaginative, incapable, primitive and uneducated, often directly contradicting their real qualities and social achievements. It is typical of the neurotic group to compare their own abilities unfavorably with those of significant others, such as parents, siblings, peers, and co-patients. This is frequently projected onto the therapist, who is highly idealized and seen as far superior in every respect. As a result, patients may spend much time and emotional energy ruminating obsessively that they do not deserve the attention being offered to them, and that some other patients could make better use of the therapist's time.

An especially striking manifestation in a great number of subjects is low moral self-evaluation and conflicts between instinctual impulses and ethical or aesthetic principles. They feel that they are bad, evil, disgusting and worthless human beings and see their lives as utterly immoral or sinful. It suddenly appears to them that by their actions in everyday life they are exploiting other people, betraying them, offending or bothering them, imposing upon them, or hurting them. This can reach such proportions that some subjects talk about sensing dirty, perverted, bestial, or even criminal elements in their own personality. In most instances these objectionable traits involve tendencies and activities that are quite trivial, or represent ubiquitous and common human characteristics. Another variation of low self-esteem is the feeling of emotional inferiority. Some subjects complain that while others treat them with love and warmth, they are unable to reciprocate these emotions. They feel incapable of experiencing genuine affection and human concern toward their children, marital partners, lovers, parents, or siblings. Other common manifestations in this area are agonizing guilt feelings, qualms of conscience, and self-accusation.

Less frequently, one may see an activation of self-aggrandizing tendencies, such as unnatural bragging and boasting, condescending and pseudoauthoritative attitudes, exaggerated demonstrations of power, indulgence in caustic attacks and hypercritical comments, or a tendency to cynicism and ridicule. The amplified caricature-like quality of these manifestations makes it easy to recognize them as compensatory maneuvers covering up underlying feelings of basic inferiority and inadequacy. These dynamics quite regularly reflect important pre-existing problems in the subject.

The third important category of phenomena related to personality characteristics involves accentuation of typical patterns in the subject's *social reactivity*. Some individuals show a marked enhancement of sociability, with incessant search for human contact, non-stop talking, and a tendency towards clowning, joking, and entertaining others. Sometimes there is an enormous need for attention and imagined or actual neglect is experienced as very painful. This may be associated with various attention-getting maneuvers, typically those also used to some degree in everyday life. They can range from noisy and theatrical performances to affectionate behavior and seeking gentle physical contact. Sometimes the erotic component can come to the foreground; this results in coquetry, seductiveness, minor sexual aggression, or verbalizations full of sexual undertones or overt obscenities.

Conversely, one may observe a marked accentuation of withdrawal mechanisms which the subject uses habitually in everyday life. Psychological withdrawal and an unwillingness to interact with people in an LSD session can be an expression of a lack of interest in socialization and preference for aesthetically or intellectually more attractive introspection. However, in some instances it can be a manifestation of complicated interpersonal problems and inner conflicts. Avoidance of human contact may reflect the patient's fear of people and his or her low self-esteem. Sometimes this comes from an underlying feeling of being unimportant, uninteresting, unpleasant, or disgusting; in others, it may be associated with a strong fear of rejection. Tendencies to withdraw can also reflect conflicts and problems related to aggression: the presence of other people, their expressions and behavior are experienced as irritating and trigger hostile impulses which are unacceptable and frightening. In this case, withdrawal is used in the service of self-control. A typical problem that an LSD session can amplify is the conflict between the need for the company of others and the tendency to be alone. The patient is afraid to be alone but at the same time cannot stand the company of others; he or she has an intense craving for human contact but is also afraid of it.

Another frequent occurrence is intensification of social and interpersonal patterns related to dominance and submission. This can be reflected in strong tendencies to manipulate, control, criticize, or mentor others. The subject may make determined efforts to create situations involving competition and testing of powers, or the derogation, humiliation and ridicule of others. Similarly, submissive manifestations and deferential behavior patterns can be accentuated to the point of caricature. Some subjects keep apologizing for various trivial or imaginary things and require reassurance that they are not interfering with anything or anyone. Others keep asking if they are offending or hurting anybody, or want to make sure that nobody is angry with them. Irresolution, anxious clinging and passive–dependent maneuvers may also reach extreme dimensions and border on anaclitic behavior.

A remarkable and frequently observed manifestation is the desperate and determined fight for maintenance of full self-control. As already described above, this typically occurs in subjects who have various problems with self-control even in their everyday life. Conversely, individuals with a rich inner world to which they can turn as a protective shelter against traumatizing reality, often complain in an LSD session about their inability to relate fully to either the external world or their inner experience.

While lower dosages of LSD activate and accentuate superficial layers of the subject's personality structure which play an important role in everyday interaction, higher doses exteriorize deep dynamic forces and tendencies. After the LSD dose reaches a certain critical limit, which varies considerably from one person to another, a striking psychological reversal can often be observed. At this point, various powerful tendencies which are contrary to the above superficial elements tend to surface and dominate the experiential world and behavior of the subject. These represent important dynamic undercurrents that are counteracted and controlled under normal circumstances by various defense mechanisms. While the phenomena discussed earlier lead to a better descriptive knowledge of various more-or-less manifest aspects of the subject's personality the emergence of these deep tendencies can contribute significantly to an understanding of the dynamics of the personality structure.

This reversal is most frequently observed in extremely submissive and anxious persons who in their everyday existence are timid, shy and overly polite, and meticulously avoid any interpersonal conflict. After losing the struggle for self-control, these individuals exhibit marked aggressivity with hostile and destructive tendencies. A temporary conversion of a similar kind is quite common in subjects who normally have strong sexual inhibitions, Victorian prejudices, an excessive proneness to shame, and tendencies toward asceticism, puritanism and prudishness. In the LSD sessions of such persons, overt sexual manifestations frequently dominate the experience. These subjects tend towards coquetry, frivolous or seductive behavior, and social exhibitionism with a sexual undertone. They may indulge in obscenities, show signs of sexual aggression, or attempt to masturbate in the presence of the sitters.

Sudden, dramatic changes can take place in persons who normally suffer from intense feelings of inadequacy and inferiority. They tend to become grandiose and overtly self-confident, manifest various dictatorial and domineering tendencies, and express megalomanic ideas and fantasies. Conversely, in markedly authoritarian persons who are excessively autocratic in their normal life and ostentatiously demonstrate their personal strength and power, this phase of LSD therapy frequently brings out the compensatory and defensive character of their stances. Under the influence of LSD, the underlying feelings of abysmal insecurity, low self-esteem, and childlike helplessness surface and dominate the experiential field. Many male patients who in their everyday life demonstrate elements of masculine pride and macho behavior with an emphasis on bodybuilding, who accentuate male supremacy and superiority, and treat women with disrespect and irony, discover in these sessions that they have serious doubts about their masculinity and harbor intense homosexual fears. Similarly, hypersensitivity, emotional frailty and excessive vulnerability frequently appear in sessions of people with a manifestly cynical attitude toward the world, who are otherwise overtly caustic and derisive of human feelings and positive values in life.

It is also quite common that church-oriented persons, who have been brought up in families dominated by religious fanaticism and hypocritical bigoted attitudes, often manifest strong antireligious tendencies and make heretical or blasphemous comments. Conversely, extremely rational and logical persons, whose adherence to pragmatic values and reason has a defensive character, often show on a deeper level intense tendencies towards metaphysical fears, irrational ideation, superstition, and magical thinking.

Various aspects of the personality structure discussed above—the superficial facade, the deep dynamic forces that underly it, and the interplay between the two—can be expressed in LSD sessions in many different ways. These elements may be experienced in the form of emotional feelings, physical sensations, specific thought-processes, and behavior patterns. However, they are more typically associated with a variety of perceptual changes in all the sensory areas. These can result in systematic distortions of the body image, intricate autosymbolic transformation, and experiences of complex symbolic scenes, in which not only self-perception but the perception of the human and even the physical environment is drastically changed.

Instead of attempting to describe the entire spectrum of phenomena that can occur in this context, we will briefly review the animal symbolism that is particularly frequent. During characterological self-exploration, many LSD subjects identify experientially with various animals that traditionally represent certain human personalities, attitudes and behaviors. Thus an autosymbolic experiential stylization into a predator such as a tiger, lion, jaguar or black panther can be used as an expression of the subject's intense aggressive feelings. Identification with a monkey can reflect polymorphously perverted tendencies and uninhibited indulgence in genital as well as pregenital pleasures. A strong sexual drive can be represented by a transformation into a stallion or a bull; if it has a strong component of lust and indiscriminate promiscuity it might be symbolized by a dirty wild boar. A streak of masculine vanity and sexually tainted exhibitionism can be ridiculed by an autosymbolic representation of the subject as a noisy cock on a dunghill. A donkey or an ox may symbolize stupidity, a mule can indicate stubbornness, and a hog usually represents self-neglect, sloppiness, and moral flaws.

In sessions where the subject's eyes are open, the intrapsychic events can get projected onto other persons or even on the physical environment. Therapists, nurses, co-patients, friends or relatives can be illusively transformed into representatives of the subject's instinctual tendencies. They can be perceived as sadists, lechers, perverts, criminals, murderers, or demonic characters. Conversely, they can represent embodiments of the critical attitudes of the Superego and be seen as parental figures, judges, members of a jury, policemen, jailers, or executioners. In the extreme, the entire human and physical situation may be systematically transformed into a complex scene of a bordello, harem, sexual orgy, medieval dungeon, concentration camp, courtroom, or death row.

Detailed analysis of the form and content of all these phenomena, using the method of free account or free association to all their elements, can become the source of additional specific and relevant information about the personality of the subject. If LSD therapy is combined with non-drug experiential approaches, any of these images can be used later for further therapeutic work; for instance, the complex scenes mentioned above are particularly suitable for the gestalt techniques developed by Fritz Perls for dream analysis. (79) Thus it is clearly demonstrated that LSD experiences are highly specific for the personality of the subject; they represent in a condensed and symbolic way his or her most important emotional problems, and are closely related to various relevant situations from past history and the present life situation. A detailed study of the individual elements of the LSD experience on this level, using Freudian technique or the new experiential approaches, reveals far-reaching similarities between their dynamic

A patient expresses how, during a psychedelic session, he saw the situation in his marriage. IIis wife appears as a monstrous predator; he as a helpless mouse hanging from her mouth. This experience was strongly colored by the underlying perinatal elements.

structure and the structure of dreams. Freud once called dreams the "via regia" or "royal road" to the unconscious, and this is even more applicable to LSD experiences. Association to all the elements of the experiential content of an LSD session that appear on the psychodynamic level leads very directly to important emotional problems of the subjects.

The tendency of LSD to selectively activate unconscious material that has the strongest emotional charge makes this drug a unique tool for psychodynamic diagnostics. Even one LSD exposure can frequently identify the areas of most significant conflict, reveal the deep dynamic structure of clinical symptoms, and help differentiate between relevant and irrelevant problems. All LSD experiences of a psychodynamic nature are generally multiply overdetermined, and express in the cryptic shorthand of their symbolic language the key problems of the personality.[1]

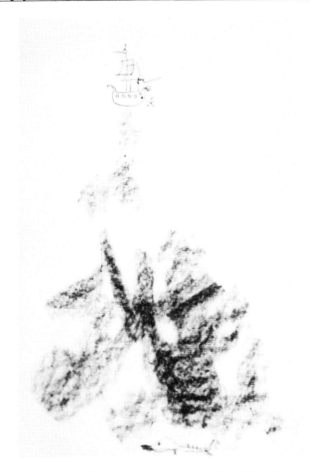

Symbols of a patient's general feelings about his life. The ship of his existence is precariously balanced on the top of a dangerous wave while a shark-like monster waits in the depths ready to devour the ship-wrecked victim.

The significance of personality factors for the nature, content, and course of the LSD experience becomes even more evident when the drug is administered repeatedly in the framework of an entire therapeutic series. Under these circumstances the subject is usually able to trace various emotional and psychosomatic symptoms, interpersonal attitudes and behavior patterns to their deep sources in the unconscious. This occurs quite spontaneously in most instances, without the use of free association or much interpretive help from the therapist. Sequential LSD sessions can be understood as a process of progressive activation and unfolding of the content of dynamic matrices in the unconscious.

The nature of the LSD experience depends on the level of the unconscious that gets activated and becomes the focus of conscious awareness. Although the nature of the unconscious, and thus the nature of LSD phenomena, is holographic, multileveled and multidimensional, it is useful for theoretical and practical purposes to distinguish certain major experiential realms. Each of them has a distinct content, is governed by specific dynamic systems, and has a characteristic significance for mental functioning. The following three categories of LSD phenomena seem to be sufficiently distinct and well-defined to be described as separate types:

    a. Psychodynamic experiences
    b. Perinatal experiences
    c. Transpersonal experiences

We will omit in this context the abstract or aesthetic level of the LSD experience which seems to reflect chemical stimulation of sensory organs and is not relevant from the point of view of a deeper understanding of the personality structure.[2]

PSYCHODYNAMIC EXPERIENCES

The experiences belonging to this category are associated with and derived from biographical material from the subject's life, particularly from emotionally highly-relevant events, situations, and circumstances. They are related to important memories, problems, and unresolved conflicts from various periods of the individual's life since early childhood. Psychodynamic experiences originate in areas of the human personality that are generally accessible in normal states of consciousness, or in the individual unconscious which contains repressed biographical material. The least complicated psychodynamic phenomena have the form of actually reliving events from the past and vivid reenactments of traumatic or unusually pleasant memories from infancy, childhood or later periods of life. More complicated experiences involve creative combinations of various memory elements, pictorial concretizations of fantasies, dramatizations of wishful daydreams, screen memories, and other complex mixtures of fantasy and reality. In addition, the psychodynamic level involves a variety of experiences that contain important unconscious material in the form of symbolic disguises, cryptic defensive distortions, and metaphorical allusions.

The experiences in psychodynamic LSD sessions can be understood to a great extent in terms of basic psychoanalytic concepts. If psychodynamic episodes were the only type of LSD experience, the observations from LSD psychotherapy could be considered laboratory proof of the Freudian theoretical framework. Psychosexual dynamics and the basic conflicts described by Freud are manifested with unusual clarity and vividness even in the sessions of naïve subjects. Under the influence of LSD, such persons experience regression to childhood and early infancy, relive various psychosexual traumas and confront conflicts related to activities in different libidinal zones. They have to face and work through some of the basic psychological problems described by psychoanalysis, such as the Oedipus and Electra complex, early cannibalistic feelings, conflicts about toilet training, castration anxiety, and penis envy.

However, for a more complete understanding of these sessions and of the consequences that they have for the clinical condition of psychiatric patients and their personality structure, a new principle has to be introduced into psychoanalytic thinking. Many LSD phenomena on this level can be comprehended and some of them even predicted if one thinks in terms of specific memory constellations, for which I use the name *COEX systems* (systems of condensed experience).[3]

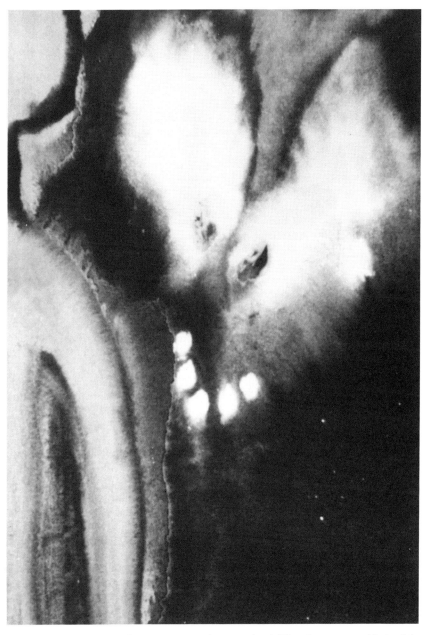

Fear of threat unknown. The patient was reliving early childhood memories of being left alone at home.

This concept emerged from my analysis of the phenomenology of therapeutic LSD sessions conducted in the early phase of my psychedelic research in Prague. It has proved unusually helpful for understanding the dynamics of the initial stages of psycholytic therapy with psychiatric patients.

A *COEX system* can be defined as a specific constellation of memories (and associated fantasies) from different life periods of the individual. The memories belonging to a particular COEX system have a similar basic theme or contain similar elements, and are accompanied by a strong emotional charge of the same quality. The deepest layers of this system are represented by vivid and colorful memories of experiences from the period of infancy and early childhood. More superficial layers involve memories from a later time, leading up to the present life situation. The excessive emotional charge which is attached to COEX systems (as indicated by the powerful abreaction often accompanying the unfolding of these systems in LSD sessions) seems to represent a summation of the emotions belonging to all the constituent memories of a particular kind.

Individual COEX systems involve special defense mechanisms, and are connected with specific clinical symptoms. The detailed interrelations between constitutent parts of the COEX systems are in most instances in basic agreement with Freudian thinking; the new element from the theoretical point of view is the concept of the organizing dynamic system. The personality structure of psychiatric patients usually involves several major COEX systems. Their specific forms, total number, extensity and intensity vary considerably from one individual to another. The psychodynamic level of the unconscious, and thus the role of COEX systems, is much less significant in individuals whose childhood was not particularly traumatic.

According to the basic quality of the emotional charge we can differentiate *negative* COEX systems (condensing unpleasant emotional experiences) from *positive* COEX systems (condensing pleasant emotional experiences and positive aspects of the individual's past). Although there are certain interdependencies and overlaps, individual COEX systems function relatively autonomously. In a complicated interaction with the environment they can selectively influence the subject's perception of himself or herself and of the world, his or her feelings and thoughts, and even somatic processes.

The phenomena observed in LSD sessions that are predominantly psychodynamic in nature can be understood in terms of the successive exteriorization, abreaction, and integration of various levels of negative COEX systems in the subject, and an opening of pathways for the influence of positive ones. When a negative COEX system approaches the experiential field, a specific change takes place in the content and course of the LSD sessions. The system assumes a governing influence on all the aspects of the psychedelic experience. It determines the direction in which the physical and interpersonal environment is illusively transformed, dictates the way the subject sees and experiences himself or herself, and dominates the emotional reactions, thought-processes, and certain physical manifestations. In general, the COEX system plays this governing role until the oldest memory, or core experience, of the system is completely relived and integrated. After this happens, another system takes over and dominates the experiential field. Frequently, several COEX systems alternate in the leading role during a particular session or sequence of sessions, undergoing a parallel process of abreaction and integration.

A very interesting interdependence and interplay can be demonstrated between the dynamics of COEX systems and events in the external world. It has already been mentioned that an activated COEX system determines the subject's perception of the environment and his or her reaction to it. Conversely, certain elements of the setting or specific events during the session can activate a COEX system which has associated features; we will discuss this mechanism again in connection with the significance of the set and setting of LSD sessions. The governing function of an activated COEX system may not be limited to the period of pharmacological action of LSD; it can continue for days, weeks, or months following the session. The principles of COEX dynamics described above are thus important for understanding the therapeutic effect of psychodynamic LSD sessions, as well as their complications. (See chapters 5 and 6 on Complications of LSD Psychotherapy and the Course of LSD Psychotherapy.)

Before concluding this discussion of the psychodynamic and biographical aspects of LSD sessions, it is important to mention a category of experiences that represent a transitional form between the psychodynamic area and the following perinatal level, which focuses on the phenomena of birth and death, or death and rebirth. This transitional group involves the reliving of traumatic memories from the life of an individual that are of a physical rather than a purely psychological nature. Such memories typically deal with situations from the past that represented a threat to survival or body integrity. They cover a wide range, from serious operations, painful and dangerous injuries, severe diseases and instances of near drowning to episodes of cruel psychological and physical abuse. Memories of incarceration in concentration camps, exposures to the brainwashing and interrogation techniques of Nazis or Communists, and maltreatment in childhood could be mentioned as special examples of the latter group.

These memories are clearly biographical in nature, yet thematically they are closely related to perinatal experiences. Not infrequently, the reliving of various physical traumas from one's life occurs simultaneously with the experience of the birth agony as a more superficial apposition. Memories of somatic traumatization are a frequent source of very painful and frightening experiences in LSD sessions. They also seem to play a significant role in the psychogenesis of various emotional disorders that is as yet unrecognized and unacknowledged by the schools of dynamic psychotherapy. This is particularly true in the case of depressions, suicidal behavior, sadomasochism, hypochondriasis, and psychosomatic disorders.

PERINATAL EXPERIENCES

The most important common denominator and focus of the experiences originating in this area of the unconscious is a group of problems related to biological birth, physical pain and agony, disease, aging, decrepitude, dying and death. It is important to emphasize that the encounter with these critical aspects of human life typically takes the form of a profound first-hand experience, rather than just symbolic confrontation. Specific eschatological ideation, and visions of wars, revolutions, concentration camps, accidents, decaying cadavers, coffins, cemeteries and funeral corteges occur as characteristic illustrations and concomitants of perinatal experiences. However, their very essence is an extremely realistic and authentic sense of the ultimate biological crisis which subjects frequently confuse with real dying. It is not uncommon for patients in this situation to lose critical insight and develop a delusional conviction that actual physical demise is imminent.

The shattering confrontation with these alarming aspects of existence and deep realization of the vulnerability and impermanence of humans as biological creatures has two important consequences. The first of these is a profound emotional and philosophical crisis that forces individuals to question seriously the meaning of existence and their values in life. They come to realize through these experiences, not intellectually but on a deep, almost cellular level, that no matter what they do, they cannot escape the inevitable. They will have to leave this world, bereft of everything that they have achieved and accumulated. This process of ontological crisis is usually associated with a definite crystallization of basic values. Worldly ambitions, competitive drives, and cravings for status, power, fame, prestige and possessions tend to fade away when viewed against the background of the mandatory ending of each human drama in biological annihilation.

The other important consequence of this shocking encounter with the phenomenon of death is the opening of areas of religious and spiritual experience that seem to be an intrinsic part of the human personality and are independent of the individual's cultural and religious background and programming. The only way to resolve the existentialist dilemma described above is through transcendence. The individual has to find reference points that are beyond the narrow boundaries of his or her perishable physical shrine and the limitations of the individual life span. It would appear that everybody who experiences these levels develops convincing insights into the utmost relevance of the spiritual dimension in the universal scheme of things. Even positivistically oriented scientists, hard-core materialists, sceptics and cynics, uncompromising atheists and antireligious crusaders such as Marxist philosophers and politicians, suddenly become interested in the spiritual quest after they confront these levels in themselves.

The sequences of dying and being born (or reborn) that are characteristic of the process of perinatal unfolding are frequently very dramatic and have many biological concomitants, apparent even to the outside observer. Subjects may spend hours in agonizing pain, with facial contortions, gasping for breath and discharging enormous amounts of muscular tension in tremors, twitches, violent shaking and complex twisting movements. The face may turn dark purple or dead pale, and the pulse show considerable acceleration. The body temperature usually oscillates in a wide range, sweating may be profuse, and nausea with projectile vomiting is a frequent occurrence.

It is not quite clear at the present stage of research how the above experiences are related to the circumstances of the individual's actual biological birth. Some LSD subjects refer to them as reliving of their birth trauma, others do not make this explicit link and conceptualize their encounter with death and rebirth in purely symbolic, philosophical, and spiritual terms. However, even in this latter group perinatal experiences are quite regularly accompanied by a complex of physical symptoms that can best be interpreted as a derivative of biological birth.

In addition to the seizure-like motor discharges and other conditions described above, there may be cardiac distress and irregularities, and hypersecretion of mucus and saliva. Such subjects also assume various fetal postures and move in sequences that bear a similarity to those of a child during the stages of biological delivery. In addition, they frequently report visions of or identification with fetuses and newborn children. Equally common are several authentic neonatal feelings, postures and behavior, as well as visions of female genitals and breasts.

Most of the rich and complex content of the LSD sessions reflecting this level of the unconscious seems to fall into four typical clusters or experiential patterns. Searching for a simple, logical and natural conceptualization of this observation, I was struck by the astonishing parallels between these patterns and the clinical stages of delivery. It proved very useful for didactic purposes, theoretical considerations, and the practice of LSD psychotherapy, to relate these four categories of phenomena to the four consecutive stages of the biological birth process and to the experiences of the child in the perinatal period. For the sake of brevity I refer to the functional structures in the unconscious which manifest in these four major experiential patterns as *Basic Perinatal Matrices* (BPM I–IV). I see them as hypothetical dynamic governing systems that have a similar function on the perinatal level of the unconscious as the COEX systems have on the psychodynamic level.

Basic perinatal matrices have specific content of their own: concrete, realistic and authentic experiences related to individual stages of the biological birth process and their symbolic and spiritual counterparts (exemplified by the elements of cosmic unity, universal engulfment, no-exit, death-rebirth struggle, and death-rebirth experience). In addition to manifesting specific content, basic perinatal matrices also function as organizing principles for the material from other levels of the unconscious. Perinatal experiences can thus occur in psychedelic sessions in association with specific psychodynamic material related to various COEX systems, and also in association with certain types of transpersonal experiences. Particularly frequent concomitants of the birth experience are memories of diseases, operations and accidents from the individual's life, archetypal phenomena (especially images of the Terrible Mother and the Great Mother), elements of group consciousness, ancestral and phylogenetic experiences, and past-incarnation memories.

Individual perinatal matrices also have fixed associations with activities in the Freudian erotogenic zones and with specific categories of psychiatric disorders. All these complex interrelations are shown in the synoptic paradigm on pages 73–76. They provide clues to the understanding of many otherwise puzzling aspects of LSD experiences, and also have far-reaching implications for psychiatric theory. This paradigm demonstrates, among other things, the close parallels between the stages of biological delivery and the pattern of sexual orgasm. The similarity between these two biological patterns is a fact of fundamental theoretical importance. It makes it possible to shift the etiological emphasis in the psychogenesis of emotional disorders from sexual dynamics to perinatal matrices, without denying or negating the significance and validity of the basic Freudian principles for understanding the psychodynamic phenomena and their mutual interrelations.

In the following text, Basic Perinatal Matrices will be discussed in the sequence in which the corresponding phases of biological delivery follow during childbirth. In serial LSD sessions this chronological order is not maintained, and elements of individual matrices can occur in most variegated sequential patterns. The death-rebirth process does not consist of one single experience of dying and being reborn, no matter how profound and complete this experience might feel. As a rule it takes a great number of death-rebirth sequences and an entire series of high-dose LSD sessions to work through the material on the perinatal level, with all its biological, emotional, philosophical and spiritual manifestations.

In this process the individual has to face the deepest roots of existential despair, metaphysical anxiety and loneliness, murderous aggression, abysmal guilt and inferiority feelings, as well as excruciating physical discomfort and the agony of total annihilation. These experiences open up access to the opposite end of the spectrum—orgiastic feelings of cosmic proportions, spiritual liberation and enlightenment, a sense of ecstatic connection with all of creation, and mystical union with the creative principle in the universe. Psychedelic therapy involving experiences on the perinatal level thus seems to represent a twentieth-century version of a process that has been practiced through millenia in various temple mysteries, rites of passage, secret initiations, and religious meetings of ecstatic sects.

BPM I

Related Psychopathological Syndromes

schizophrenic psychoses (paranoid symptomatology, feelings of mystical union, encounter with metaphysical evil forces, karmic experiences); hypochondriasis (based on strange and bizarre physical sensations); hysterical hallucinosis and confusing daydreams with reality

Corresponding Activities in Freudian Erotogenic Zones

libidinal satisfaction in all erogenic zones; libidinal feelings during rocking and bathing; partial approximation to this condition after oral, anal, urethral, or genital satisfaction and after delivery of a child

Associated Memories from Postnatal Life

situations from later life where important needs are satisfied, such as happy moments from infancy and childhood (good mothering, play with peers, harmonious periods in the family, etc.), fulfilling love, romances; trips or vacations in beautiful natural settings; exposure to artistic creations of high aesthetic value; swimming in the ocean and clear lakes, etc.

Phenomenology in LSD Sessions

undisturbed intrauterine life: realistic recollections of "good womb" experiences; "oceanic" type of ecstasy; experience of cosmic unity; visions of Paradise; *disturbances of intrauterine life:* realistic recollections of "bad womb experiences" (fetal crises, diseases and emotional upheavals of the mother, twin situation, attempted abortions), cosmic engulfment; paranoid ideation; unpleasant physical sensations ("hangover," chills and fine spasms, unpleasant tastes, disgust, feelings of being poisoned); association with various transpersonal experiences (archetypal elements, racial and evolutionary memories, encounter with metaphysical forces, past-incarnation experiences, etc.)

BPM II

Related Psychopathological Syndromes

schizophrenic psychoses (elements of hellish tortures, experience of meaningless "cardboard" world); severe, inhibited "endogenous" depressions; irrational inferiority and guilt feelings; hypochondriasis (based on painful physical sensations); alcoholism and drug addiction

Corresponding Activities in Freudian Erotogenic Zones

oral frustration (thirst, hunger, painful stimuli): retention of feces and/or urine; sexual frustration; experiences of cold, pain and other unpleasant sensations

Associated Memories from Postnatal Life

situations endangering survival and bodily integrity (war experiences, accidents, injuries, operations, painful diseases, near-drowning, episodes of suffocation, imprisonment, brainwashing and illegal interrogation, physical abuse, etc.); severe psychological traumatizations (emotional deprivation, rejection, threatening situations, oppressing family atmosphere, ridicule and humiliation, etc.)

Phenomenology in LSD Sessions

immense physical and psychological suffering; unbearable and inescapable situation that will never end; various images of hell; feelings of entrapment and encagement (no exit); agonizing guilt and inferiority feelings; apocalyptic view of the world (horrors of wars and concentration camps, terror of the Inquisition; dangerous epidemics; diseases; decrepitude and death, etc.); meaninglessness and absurdity of human existence; "cardboard world" or the atmosphere of artificiality and gadgets; ominous dark colors and unpleasant physical symptoms (feelings of oppression and compression, cardiac distress, flushes and chills, sweating, difficult breathing)

BPM III

Related Psychopathological Syndromes

schizophrenic psychoses (sadomasochistic and scatological elements, automutilation, abnormal sexual behavior); agitated depression, sexual deviations (sadomasochism, male homosexuality, drinking of urine, eating of feces); obsessive-compulsive neuroses; psychogenic asthma, tics, stammering; conversion and anxiety hysteria; frigidity and impotence; neurasthenia; traumatic neuroses; organ neuroses; migraine headache; enuresis and encopressis; psoriasis; peptic ulcer

Corresponding Activities in Freudian Erotogenic Zones

chewing and swallowing of food; oral aggression and destruction of an object; process of defecation and urination; anal and urethral aggression; sexual orgasm; phallic aggression; delivering of a child, statoacoustic eroticism (jolting, gymnastics, fancy diving, parachuting)

Associated Memories from Postnatal Life

struggles, fights and adventurous activities (active attacks in battles and revolutions, experiences in military service, rough airplane flights, cruises on stormy oceans, hazardous car-driving, boxing); highly sensual memories (carnivals, amusement parks and nightclubs, wild parties, sexual orgies, etc.); childhood observations of adult sexual activities; experiences of seduction and rape; in females, delivery of their own children

Phenomenology in LSD Sessions

intensification of suffering to cosmic dimensions; borderline between pain and pleasure; "volcanic" type of ecstasy; brilliant colors; explosions and fireworks; sadomasochistic orgies; murders and bloody sacrifice, active engagement in fierce battles; atmosphere of wild adventure and dangerous explorations; intense sexual orgiastic feelings and scenes of harems and carnivals; experiences of dying and being reborn; religions involving bloody sacrifice (Aztecs, Christ's suffering and death on the cross, Dionysus, etc.); intense physical manifestations (pressures and pains, suffocation, muscular tension and discharge in tremors and twitches, nausea and vomiting, hot flushes and chills, sweating, cardiac distress, problems of sphincter control, ringing in the ears)

BPM IV

Related Psychopathological Syndromes

schizophrenic psychoses (death-rebirth experiences, messianic delusions, elements of destruction and recreation of the world, salvation and redemption, identification with Christ); manic symptomatology; female homosexuality; exhibitionism

Corresponding Activities in Freudian Erotogenic Zones

satiation of thirst and hunger; pleasure of sucking; libidinal feelings after defecation, urination, sexual orgasm, or delivery of a child

Associated Memories from Postnatal Life

fortuitous escape from dangerous situations (end of war or revolution, survival of an accident or operation); overcoming of severe obstacles by active effort; episodes of strain and hard struggle resulting in a marked success; natural scenes (beginning of spring, end of an ocean storm, sunrise, etc.)

Phenomenology in LSD Sessions

enormous decompression, expansion of space, visions of gigantic halls; radiant light and beautiful colors (heavenly blue, golden, rainbow, peacock feathers); feelings of rebirth and redemption; appreciation of simple way of life; sensory enhancement; brotherly feelings; humanitarian and charitable tendencies; occasional manic activity and grandiose feeling; transition to elements of BPM I; pleasant feelings may be interrupted by *umbilical crisis:* sharp pain in the navel; loss of breath, fear of death and castration, shifts in the body, but no external pressures

Perinatal Matrix I (Primal Union With Mother)
The first perinatal matrix (BPM I) is related to primal union with the mother, to the original state of intrauterine existence during which the maternal organism and the child form a symbiotic unity. When no noxious stimuli intercede, the conditions for the fetus are close to being ideal, involving protection, security and continuous satisfaction of all needs. However, a variety of adverse circumstances can interfere with this condition. These involve diseases and difficult emotional states of the mother as well as disturbing influences from the outside world, such as toxic factors, loud noises, and mechanical concussions or vibrations. The first perinatal matrix has therefore its positive and negative aspects; subjects frequently refer to them as the "good womb" and the "bad womb" experience.

The elements of *undisturbed intrauterine existence* can be experienced in LSD sessions in a concrete biological form or in the form of its spiritual counterpart, *the experience of cosmic unity.* Although the "oceanic feelings" of the embryonal state are not identical with the experience of cosmic unity, there appears to be a deep association and overlap between these two conditions. The experience of cosmic unity is characterized by transcendence of the usual subject-object dichotomy. The individual in this state becomes deeply aware of his or her unity with other people, nature, and the entire universe, and with the ultimate creative principle, or God. This is accompanied by an overwhelming positive affect that can range from peace, serenity and bliss to an ecstatic rapture. In this state the categories of space and time are transcended and subjects can perceive themselves as existing outside of the usual space-time continuum. In the extreme, they may experience eternity and infinity within a period lasting seconds or minutes of actual clocktime. Other typical characteristics of this state are a sense of sacredness and of ultimate insight into the true and real nature of existence. Accounts or descriptions of this revelatory experience are usually full of paradoxes and appear to violate the basic laws of Aristotelian logic. This state of mind is referred to as "contentless yet all-containing," "formless but pregnant with form," one of "cosmic grandeur yet utmost humility," or one characterized by loss of ego while at the same time the ego has expanded and become the whole universe. Different subjects experience and describe this event within different symbolic frameworks. Most frequent references are to Paradise, The Garden of Eden, Heaven, Elysian Fields, *unio mystica,* the Tao, Atman-Brahman union, or Tat tvam asi (Thou art That).

With the eyes closed, the phenomenon of cosmic unity is experienced as an independent complex experiential pattern of oceanic ecstasy. With the eyes open, it results in an experience of merging with the environment and a sense of unity with perceived objects. It is basically this experience that is defined by Walter Pahnke's (76) mystical categories and that Abraham Maslow (63) calls a "peak experience." In LSD sessions, feelings of cosmic unity seem to be closely related to "good womb" experiences, "good breast" experiences, and happy childhood memories. They also appear to represent an important gateway to a variety of transpersonal experiences, such as ancestral memories, elements of the racial and collective unconscious, karmic phenomena, evolutionary memories, and various archetypal constellations. The *disturbances of intrauterine existence* can likewise be experienced in concrete biological form or symbolically as encounters with various demonic appearances, metaphysical evil forces, or malefic astrological influences.

As far as the relation to memory mechanisms is concerned, the positive aspects of BPM I are related to positive COEX sytems. The positive facet of BPM I seems to represent the basis for the recording of all later life situations in which the individual is relaxed, relatively free from needs, and not disturbed by any unpleasant stimuli. Negative aspects of BPM I have similar links to certain negative COEX sytems.

In regard to the Freudian erotogenic zones, the positive aspects of BPM I coincide with the biological and psychological condition in which there are no tensions in any of these zones and all the partial drives are satisfied. Conversely, satisfaction of needs in these zones (satiation of hunger, release of tension by urination, defecation, sexual orgasm, or delivery of a child) results in a superficial and partial approximation to the tension-free ecstatic experience described above.

Perinatal Matrix II (Antagonism With Mother)

LSD subjects confronted with this experiential pattern frequently relate it to the very onset of the biological delivery and to its first clinical stage. In this situation the original equilibrium of the intrauterine existence is disturbed, first by alarming chemical signals and later by muscular spasms. Later, the fetus is periodically constricted by uterine contractions; the cervix is closed and the way out is not yet open.

As in the previous matrix, the corresponding biological situations can be relived in a rather realistic way. The symbolic concomitant of the onset of delivery is the *experience of cosmic engulfment*. It involves overwhelming feelings of increasing anxiety and awareness of an imminent vital threat. The source of this approaching danger cannot be clearly identified and the subject has a tendency to interpret his or her immediate environment or the entire world in paranoid terms. Not infrequently do individuals in this state report experiences of evil influences coming from members of secret organizations, inhabitants of other planets, malevolent hypnotists, black magicians, or diabolic gadgets emanating noxious radiation or toxic gases. Further intensification of anxiety typically results in an experience involving a monstrous, gigantic whirlpool, a Maelstrom sucking the subject and his or her world relentlessly toward its center. A frequent variation of this universal engulfment is an experience of being swallowed by a terrifying monster, such as a giant dragon, octopus, python, crocodile, whale, or spider. A less dramatic form seems to be the theme of descent into the underworld and encounter with various dangerous creatures and entities.

The symbolic counterpart of a fully developed first clinical stage of delivery is the *experience of no exit*. An important characteristic of this experiential pattern is the darkness of the visual field and the ominous and sinister colors of all the images that accompany it. Subjects feel encaged or trapped in a monstrous claustrophobic situation and experience incredible psychological and physical tortures. The situation is typically absolutely unbearable and appears to be endless and hopeless. While under the influence of this matrix the individual cannot see the possibility of any end to his or her torments nor any form of escape from them. Death-wishes and suicidal craving can be combined with feelings of futility and with a conviction that not even physical death would terminate this hellish state and bring relief.

This experiential pattern can be manifested on several levels, which may be experienced separately, simultaneously, or in an alternating fashion. The deepest level is related to various concepts of hell—a situation of unbearable suffering that will never end—as it has been depicted by many religions of the world. In a more superficial version of the same experiential pattern, the subject is confronted with images of our planet and sees the whole world as an apocalyptic place full of bloody terror, senseless suffering, genocidal wars, racial hatred, dangerous epidemics, and natural catastrophes. Existence in this world appears to be completely meaningless, nonsensical and absurd, and the search for any meaning in human life futile. While under the influence of this matrix the individual perceives the world and human existence as if through a negatively biased stencil; he or she appears to be blinded to any positive aspects of life. In the most superficial form of the experience, the subject sees his or her own concrete life situation in terms of circular patterns and as completely desperate, unbearable, and full of insoluble problems. Agonizing feelings of metaphysical loneliness, alienation, helplessness, hopelessness, inferiority and guilt are a standard part of this matrix.

The symbolism that most frequently accompanies this experiential pattern involves various images of hell, Christ's humiliation and suffering, and the theme of eternal damnation as exemplified by Ahasverus, the Flying Dutchman, Sisyphus, Ixion, Tantalus or Prometheus. The most important characteristic that differentiates this pattern from the following one is the unique emphasis on the role of the victim and the fact that the situation is unbearable, inescapable and eternal—there appears to be no way out either in space or in time.

BPM II seems to represent the basis for recording all extremely unpleasant future situations, in which the passive and helpless individual is victimized and endangered by an overwhelming and destructive external force. In regard to Freudian erotogenic zones, this matrix seems to be related to a condition of unpleasant tension in all of them. On the oral level, it is hunger, thirst, nausea, and painful stimuli; on the anal level, retention of feces; and on the urethral level, retention of urine. The corresponding phenomena on the genital level are sexual frustration and excessive tension, as well as pains experienced by the delivering female in the first clinical stage of labor.

Perinatal Matrix III (Synergism With Mother)
Many aspects of this complex experiential matrix can be understood from its association with the second clinical stage of biological delivery. In this stage, the uterine contractions continue, but the cervix stands wide open and makes possible gradual and difficult propulsion through the birth canal. There is an enormous struggle for survival, crushing mechanical pressures, and often a high degree of anoxia and suffocation. In the terminal phases of delivery the fetus may experience immediate contact with a variety of biological materials, such as blood, mucus, fetal liquid, urine and even feces.

From the experiential point of view, this pattern is rather ramified and complicated; beside actual realistic reliving of various aspects of the struggle through the birth canal it almost always involves a variety of phenomena that can be arranged in typical sequences. Its most important facets are an atmosphere of *titanic fight, sadomasochistic orgies, intense sexual sensations, scatological involvement, and the element of purifying fire (pyrocatharsis)* occurring in various combinations. The above elements constitute the *death-rebirth struggle.*

The subject experiences in this state powerful currents of energy streaming through his or her entire body and increasing to a level of concentration and condensation that seems to transcend all imaginable limits. This is followed by episodes of explosive discharge and feelings of ecstatic release. Visions typically accompanying these experiences involve titanic battles of universal proportions, archetypal feats of super-heroes, explosions of atomic bombs, thermonuclear reactions, launchings of missiles and spaceships, power plants, hydroelectric stations, high-voltage power lines, dramatic scenes of destruction in modern wars, gigantic conflagrations, exploding volcanoes, earthquakes, tornadoes and other natural catastrophes. A mitigated form of this experiential pattern is associated with visions of medieval battles, bloody revolutions, dangerous hunts for wild animals, or discoveries and conquests of new continents.

Another important aspect of this experiential matrix is excessive activation of sadomasochistic elements in the personality of the subject. Enormous amounts of aggressive energy are being discharged and consumed in destructive and self-destructive fantasies, images, and vivid experiences. The individual indulges in rapes, various sexual perversions involving pain, bestial murders, tortures and cruelties of all kinds, executions, mutilations, bloody sacrifices, and self-sacrifices. This can be accompanied by suicidal ideation, fantasies, or even tendencies involving brutal and mutilating self-destruction.

Sexual arousal can reach an unusually high degree and be expressed in complex scenes of unbridled orgies, pornographic sequences, visions of Middle-Eastern harems, endless Oriental nuances of the art of loving, lascivious carnivals, and rhythmic sensual dances. In this context, many LSD subjects discover a close experiential link between agony and sexual ecstasy; they realize that intense orgiastic arousal can border on suffering and mitigated agony can be experienced as sexual pleasure.

The scatological facet of the death-rebirth process can be very complete and have not only visual and tactile, but also olfactory and gustatory dimensions. The subject can experience himself or herself as wallowing in excrement, drowning in cesspools, crawling in offal or sewage systems, eating feces, swallowing phlegm, drinking blood or urine, and sucking on putrefying wounds. This is often followed by an experience of passing through a purifying and rejuvenating fire; its overpowering flames seem to destroy whatever is corrupted and rotten in the individual and prepare him or her for the experience of spiritual rebirth.

The religious and mythological symbolism of this matrix is most frequently derived from religions that glorify bloody sacrifice or use it as part of their ceremonies. Quite common are allusions to the Old Testament; images of Christ's suffering and death on the cross; scenes of worshipping Moloch, Astarté or Kali; and visions of rituals from various Pre-Columbian cultures using sacrifice and self-sacrifice, as they were practiced in the Aztec, Mixtec, Olmec, and Mayan religions. Another group of images is related to religious rituals and ceremonies involving sex and wild rhythmic dances: fertility rites, phallic worship, or various tribal religions of the aborigines. A frequent symbol associated with the purifying fire is the image of the legendary bird the Phoenix. A very appropriate symbolization of the scatological aspect of the death-rebirth struggle is Hercules cleaning the stables of King Augeas, or the Aztec goddess Tlacolteutl, Devourer of Filth, a deity of child-birth and carnal lust.

Addendum to the revised edition: Paintings from high-dose LSD sessions governed by BPM I depicting memories of undisturbed intrauterine existence:

The Amniotic Universe. (above) Experiential identification with the blissful experience of the fetus in a good womb accompanied with feelings of cosmic unity. The galaxy shaped as a breast reflects the fact that this experience is also connected with a memory of blissful symbiotic union with the mother during nursing.

The Oceanic Womb. (below) Experiential identification with the fetus associated with a sense of identifying with the ocean and various aquatic forms of life (fish, whales, dolphins, jellyfish, kelp and others).

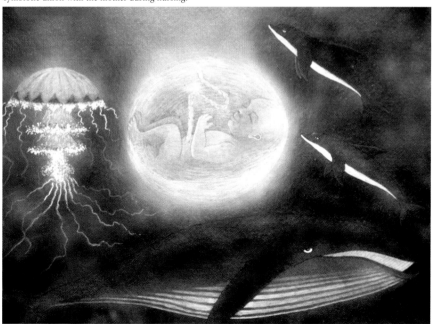

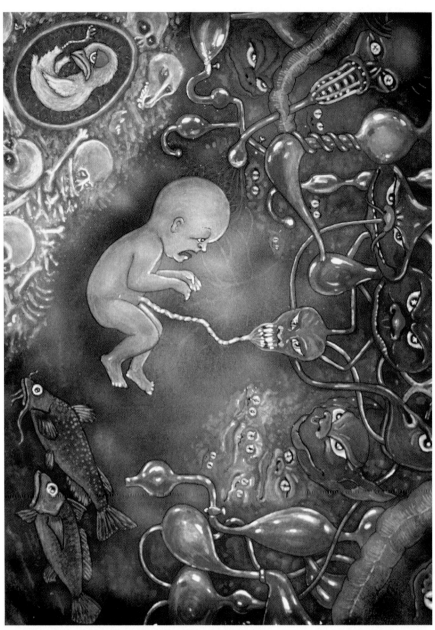

Painting representing a "bad womb" experience in a high-dose psychedelic session.

Toxicity of the womb portrayed as a painful and frightening ordeal in a diabolical laboratory full of insidious demons. This experience is accompanied by identification with fish and polluted waters and with a chicken embryo in advanced stage of development when the inside of the egg is contaminated by metabolic side products.

Painting representing a "bad womb' experience in a high-dose psychedelic session.
Hostility of the womb experienced as attacks by vicious animals. *(By Robin Maynard-Dobbs)*

Visions of giant tarantulas symbolizing the devouring feminine are very common in perinatal sessions governed by BPM II.

Above. A painting representing a vision encountered in a high-dose LSD session. It shows a Mother-Spider exposing helpless fetuses to diabolical tortures.

Below. A similar painting from a holotropic breathwork session, indicating that this motif is not a pathological product of the pharmacological action of the drug, but reflects genuine content of the psyche. The image of the subject as a tightly swaddled mummy emphasizes the element of confinement and constriction during uterine contractions. *(By Jarina Moss)*

From a high-dose LSD session portraying the beginning of the death-rebirth process (transition from BPM I to BPM II), experienced as engulfment by a gigantic Mælstrom. The little boat with a skeleton suggests that this process involves an encounter with death.

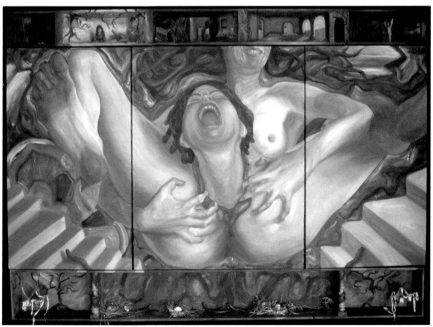

A painting representing the combined experience of giving birth and being born in a session of holotropic breathwork. Experiences of this kind can be very healing and transformative, resulting an a sense of giving birth to a new self. *(By Jean Perkins)*

The horrors of the birth trauma. Bird-like monsters encroach on the helpless and fragile fetus as it hangs from the top of the uterine cupola by its umbilical cord. Their gigantic claws and beaks symbolize the destructive biological forces of the delivery.

Phoenix rising. Color sketch by Stanislav Grof of the mythical Phoenix rising from its own ashes, as experenced in one of his high-dose LSD sessions.

Albert Hofmann said, "If I am the father of LSD then Stan is the godfather. Nobody has contributed as much as Stan for the development of my problem child. It is not unusual that the godfather cares more for a child than the father." Dr.s Hofmann and Grof share a private moment during a visit to the Hofmann's home in 1999.

Stanislav Grof, M.D., began his research into the psychotherapeutic uses of LSD in 1960 at the Psychiatric Research Institute in Prague, Czechoslovakia. He is the founding president of the International Transpersonal Association, and has taught and lectured in academic and workshop settings worldwide. Dr. Grof is the author of numerous other books, the latest of which is *Psychology of the Future: Lessons from Modern Consciousness Research,* published by State University of New York Press, September 2000.

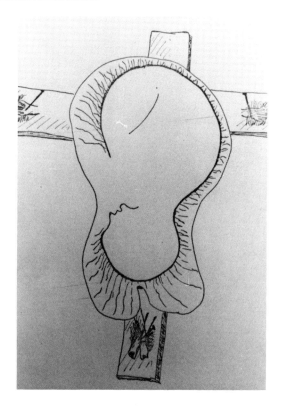

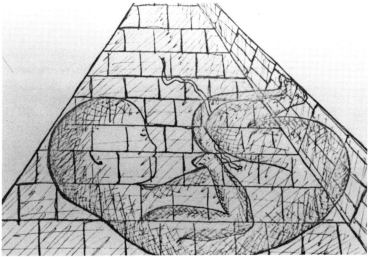

(Above) Insight into the connection between birth and crucifixion—the crucified fetus. (Below) The connection between intrauterine existence and transcendental feelings of peace—a fetus inside a pyramid.

A scatological experience showing the subject drowning in a gigantic cesspool.

Several important characteristics of this experiential pattern distinguish it from the previously described no-exit constellation. The situation here does not seem hopeless and the subject is not helpless. He or she is actively involved and has the feeling that the suffering has a definite direction and goal. In religious terms, this situation would be closer to the concept of purgatory than to that of hell. In addition, the subject does not exclusively play the role of a helpless victim. He is an observer and can at the same time identify with both sides, to the point that it might be difficult to distinguish whether he is the aggressor or the victim. While the no-exit situation involves sheer suffering, the experience of the death-rebirth struggle represents the borderline between agony and ecstasy and the fusion of both. It seems appropriate to refer to this type of experience as "volcanic ecstasy" in contrast to the "oceanic ecstasy" of the cosmic union.

As a memory matrix, BPM III is related to all experiences of the individual involving intense sensual and sexual elements, to wild, hazardous and exciting adventures, as well as scatological exposures. Memories of sexual abuse, orgies, and violent rapes are also recorded in this context. In regard to the Freudian erotogenic zones, this matrix is related to those activities which bring sudden relief and relaxation after a prolonged period of tension. On the oral level it is the act of chewing and swallowing of food (or conversely, of vomiting); on the anal and urethral level, the process of defecation and urination; on the genital level, the mechanism of sexual orgasm, and the feelings of the delivering woman in the second stage of labor.

Perinatal Matrix IV (Separation From Mother)
This perinatal matrix seems to be meaningfully related to the third clinical stage of delivery. In this final phase, the agonizing process of the intense struggle culminates; the propulsion through the birth canal is completed and the extreme intensification of tension and suffering is followed by a sudden relief and relaxation. After the umbilical cord is cut blood ceases to flow through its vessels, and the child has to develop its own system of respiration, digestion and elimination. The physical separation from the mother has been completed and the neonate starts its existence as an anatomically independent individual.

As in the case of the preceding matrices, some of the experiences belonging here seem to represent a realistic reenactment of the actual biological events during this phase, as well as specific obstetric interventions. The symbolic counterpart of this final stage of delivery is the *death-rebirth experience*; it represents the termination and resolution of the death-rebirth struggle. Physical and emotional agony culminates in a feeling of utter and total annihilation on all imaginable levels. It involves an abysmal sense of physical destruction, emotional catastrophe, intellectual defeat, ultimate moral failure, and absolute damnation of transcendental proportions. This experience is usually described as "ego death"; it seems to entail an instantaneous and merciless destruction of all the previous reference points in the life of the individual.

After the subject has experienced the limits of total annihilation and "hit the cosmic bottom," he or she is struck by visions of blinding white or golden light. The claustrophobic and compressed world of the birth struggle suddenly opens up and expands into infinity. The general atmosphere is one of liberation, salvation, redemption, love, and forgiveness. The subject feels unburdened, cleansed and purged, and talks about having disposed of an incredible amount of personal "garbage," guilt, aggression, and anxiety. This is typically associated with brotherly feelings for all fellowmen and appreciation of warm human relationships, friendship and love. Irrational and exaggerated ambitions, as well as cravings for money, status, fame, prestige and power, appear in this state as childish, irrelevant and absurd. There is often a strong tendency to share and engage in service and charitable activities. The universe is perceived as indescribably beautiful and radiant. All sensory pathways seem to be wide open and the sensitivity to and appreciation of external stimuli is greatly enhanced. The individual tuned into this experiential area usually discovers within himself or herself genuinely positive values, such as a sense of justice, appreciation of beauty, feelings of love, and self-respect as well as respect for others. These values, as well as the motivations to pursue them and live in accordance with them, appear on this level to be intrinsic to human nature.[4] They cannot be satisfactorily explained in terms of compensation, reaction-formation, or sublimation of primitive instinctual drives. The individual experiences them as genuine and integral parts of the universal order.

The symbolism associated with the experience of death and rebirth can be drawn from many different cultural frameworks. The element of ego death can be associated with visions of various destructive deities, such as Moloch, Shiva the Destroyer, Huitzilopochtli, and the terrible goddesses Kali and Coatlicue, or experienced in full identification with the death of Christ, Osiris, Adonis, or Dionysus. Typical symbolism of the moment of rebirth involves fantastic visions of radiant sources of light experienced as divine, heavenly blue cosmic spaces, magnificent rainbow spectra, or stylized peacock designs. Rather frequent are non-figurative images of God, as exemplified by the Tao, Atman-Brahman, Allah, or the Cosmic Sun. On occasion subjects may see personified images and traditional representations of God and the various deities of specific religions. Thus God can appear in the Christian form as an archetypal wise, old man sitting on a throne surrounded by cherubim and seraphim in radiant splendor. Also quite common in this context is the experience of union with the Great Mother, such as the Divine Isis of the Egyptians, Cybele, or the Virgin Mary. Joining the Greek gods on Mount Olympus in drinking nectar and eating ambrosia, admission to the Germanic Valhalla, or advent to the Elysian fields are some additional symbolic alternatives for the rebirth experience. Other visions involve gigantic halls with richly decorated columns, marble statues and crystal chandeliers, or beautiful natural scenery —the star-filled sky, majestic mountains, luscious valleys, flourishing meadows, or clear lakes and oceans.

In regard to memory, BPM IV represents a matrix for the recording of all later situations involving major personal success and termination of conditions of prolonged serious danger, such as ends of wars or revolutions, survival of accidents, or recoveries from severe diseases. As far as Freudian erotogenic zones are concerned, BPM IV is associated on all the levels of libidinal development with the condition of satisfaction immediately following an activity that reduced or discharged tension (swallowing of food, relieving vomiting, defecation, urination, sexual orgasm and delivery of a child).

The Basic Perinatal Matrices have a function on the perinatal level which is comparable to the one that COEX systems play in the psychodynamic realm. The phenomena occurring in psychedelic sessions of a predominantly perinatal nature can be understood as the result of successive exteriorization, abreaction, and integration of the content of negative perinatal matrices, (BPM II and III) and connecting with the positive ones (BPM I and IV). When a perinatal matrix dominates the experiential field its content determines not only the subject's emotional reactions, thought-processes and physical manifestations, but also his or her perception of the physical and interpersonal environment. The hegemony of BPM I provides a totally positive stencil which makes the subject see the world as radiant, incredibly beautiful, safe, nourishing, and essentially a manifestation of the divine. Transition from BPM I to BPM II (cosmic engulfment) introduces the element of insidious, but very basic, threat. The world and all its components seem to be closing in on the subject and seem to represent a serious danger to his or her security, sanity, and life. The subject tends to fear entrapment and might make an attempt to escape from the treatment room, not recognizing that the trap is inside. Feelings of panic and paranoia are typical concomitants of this state. In terms of an experiential stencil, BPM II is the exact opposite of BPM I. The world is seen as a hopeless place of diabolic, absurd and meaningless suffering. It can also have an empty cardboard-like quality or the bizarre and grotesque character of a circus sideshow. The influence of BPM III typically gives the world the quality of a dangerous battlefield, where one has to be on guard and struggle hard to defend one's life. The sexual, sadomasochistic and scatological component of this matrix can also find its expression in shaping the perception of the world. BPM IV gives the world a touch of freshness, novelty, cleanliness and joy, associated with a sense of triumph.

The above descriptions reflect only the most general characteristics of the perinatal matrices in their function as governing systems; the individual experiences that occur within this context represent manifestations of their specific content as described earlier (see paradigm on pages 73–76). Like the COEX systems, perinatal matrices show a complicated two-sided interaction with the elements of the environment. After a poorly-resolved LSD session, the dynamic influence of the activated negative matrix can continue in the subject's everyday life for indefinite periods of time. After a well-integrated session of a perinatal nature, the subject can be under the continuing influence of the positive matrix that dominated the experiential field at the time when the effect of the drug was wearing off. Conversely, external influences involving elements characteristic of the individual perinatal matrices can facilitate specific corresponding experiences related to the death-rebirth process.

TRANSPERSONAL EXPERIENCES

The common denominator of this otherwise rich and ramified group of phenomena is the subject's feeling that his or her conscoiusness has expanded beyond the usual ego boundaries and has transcended the limitations of time and space. In the "normal" or usual state of consciousness, we experience ourselves as existing within the boundaries of the physical body (the body image) and our perception of the environment is restricted by the physically determined range of exteroceptors. Both our internal perception (interoception) and the perception of the external world (exteroception) are confined by the usual spatial and temporal boundaries. Under ordinary circumstances we vividly experience only our present situation and our immediate environment; we *recall* past events and *anticipate* the future or fantasize about it.

In transpersonal experiences, as they occur in psychedelic sessions or in various non-drug frameworks, one or several of the above limitations appear to be transcended. Many experiences belonging to this category are interpreted by the subjects as regressions in historical time and explorations of their biological or spiritual past. It is not unusual in psychedelic sessions to experience quite concrete and realistic episodes identified as *fetal* and *embryonic* memories. Many subjects report vivid sequences on the level of cellular consciousness which seem to reflect their existence in the form of a sperm or ovum at the moment of conception. Sometimes the regression appears to go even further and the individual has a convinced feeling of reliving memories from the lives of his or her ancestors, or even drawing on the racial and collective unconscious. On occasion, LSD subjects report experiences in which they identify with various animal ancestors in the evolutionary pedigree or have a distinct feeling of reliving episodes from their existence in a previous incarnation.

Some other transpersonal phenomena involve transcendence of spatial rather than temporal barriers. Here belong the experiences of merging with another person into a state of dual unity or completely identifying with him or her, tuning into the consciousness of an entire group of persons or expanding one's consciousness to the extent that it seems to encompass all of mankind. In a similar way, one can transcend the limits of the specifically human experience and tune in to what appears to be the consciousness of animals, plants, or even inanimate objects. In the extreme, it is possible to experience the consciousness of all creation, of our planet, of the entire material universe. Another phenomenon related to the transcendence of normal spatial limitations is consciousness of certain parts of the body such as various organs, tissues, or individual cells. An important category of transpersonal experiences involving transcendence of time and/or space are the various ESP phenomena, such as out-of-body experiences, telepathy, precognition, clairvoyance and clairaudience, and space and time travel.

In a large group of transpersonal experiences, the extension of consciousness seems to go beyond the phenomenal world and the time-space continuum as we perceive it in our everyday life. Quite common examples are the experiences of an encounter with spirits of deceased human beings or supra-human spiritual entities. LSD subjects also report numerous visions of archetypal forms, individual deities and demons, and complex mythological sequences. An intuitive understanding of universal symbols, or the arousal of the Kundalini and activation of various chakras are additional examples of this category. In the extreme form the individual consciousness seems to encompass the totality of existence and identify with the Universal Mind. The ultimate of all experiences appears to be the *Supracosmic and Metacosmic Void*, the mysterious primordial emptiness and nothingness that is conscious of itself and contains all existence in a germinal form.

Although we have discussed transpersonal experiences in the context of extrapharmacological variables related to the personality of the subject, such an approach presents serious difficulties. On the one hand, transpersonal phenomena occur on the same continuum as psychodynamic and perinatal experiences in the process of the subject's deep self-exploration and probing of his or her unconscious. On the other hand, from the point of view of present conceptual frameworks, their sources frequently appear to be outside the conventionally defined context of the individual—in pre-history, future, remote locations, or other dimensions of existence. The psychodynamic level draws from the individual's history and is clearly biographical in origin and nature. Perinatal experiences seem to represent a frontier between the personal and the transindividual, as is reflected by their deep association with biological birth and death. The transpersonal realm, then, reflects the connections between the individual and cosmos mediated through channels which seem at the present to be beyond our comprehension. All we can say in this respect is that somewhere in the process of perinatal unfolding a qualitative leap seems to occur in which this process of in-depth exploration of the individual unconscious turns into an adventure in the universe-at-large and involves what can best be described as the superconscious mind.

Intimate knowledge of the transpersonal realms is absolutely essential not only for the understanding of the psychedelic process, but for any serious approach to such phenomena as shamanism, religion, mysticism, rites of passage, mythology, parapsychology, and schizophrenia. Transpersonal experiences in LSD sessions as well as in non-drug states tend to occur in thematic clusters. Thus, for example, embryonal experiences are typically associated with evolutionary (phylogenetic) memories and with images of blissful or wrathful archetypal deities, depending on the nature of the intrauterine experience. However, their organization is much looser and does not allow one to speak of dynamic governing systems and matrices as in the case of psychodynamic and perinatal material. In the process of transpersonal unfolding the very principles that would allow for organization and classification, such as the concepts of linear time, three-dimensional space, matter, causality, and ultimately form itself, are progressively questioned, undermined and transcended.

Emerging transpersonal experiences tend to influence the perception of oneself, of the persons present in the room, and of the physical environment. All these elements can appear systematically transformed in a certain direction to fit the content of the emerging theme, whether it is an ancestral or phylogenetic memory, elements of the racial and collective unconscious, archetypal structures, or a karmic pattern. A powerful transpersonal experience that has not been completed in a psychedelic session, such as manifestation of an important archetype or reliving of a past-incarnation memory, can continue to influence the subject for an indefinite period of time after the drug experience has worn off.

PERSONALITY OF THE THERAPIST OR GUIDE

Numerous observations made during clinical research with LSD strongly suggest that the personalities of the therapist, the co-therapist, the sitters, or any persons present are factors of paramount significance in structuring the content, course, and outcome of psychedelic sessions. Probably the single most important element determining the nature of an LSD experience is the feeling of safety and trust on the part of the experient. This is, of course, critically dependent on the presence or absence of the guide, his or her personal characteristics, and the nature of the relationship between the subject and this person. It is absolutely essential for the successful course and outcome of an LSD session that the subject lets go of his or her usual defenses and surrenders to the psychedelic process. This usually requires the possibility of relegating the reality testing and all the decisions on practical matters to a trusted sitter.

A person taking a psychedelic drug alone cannot really fully abandon control at the crucial moments of the experience, because a part of him or her has to continue playing the role of the reality-oriented judge and sitter. However, total surrender is absolutely essential for completing the experience of ego death, one of the crucial steps in the LSD process. Certain important problems that originated in interpersonal situations, such as difficulties with basic trust, can also not be successfully resolved and overcome without the human element providing a corrective emotional experience. I have repeatedly seen in the early stages of our therapeutic work with LSD,[5] when the role of the sitter was not sufficiently understood, that patients were not able to overcome certain recurrent impasses in their LSD sessions until the therapist promised to stay with them through the entire experience and never leave the room.

If psychedelic sessions are conducted for therapeutic purposes, the emotional significance of the therapist for the patient has two distinct components. The first one is based on the reality of the patient's actual life-situation at the time of therapy and reflects the fact that the therapist is a person who is supposed to provide help with crippling emotional symptoms and the difficulties of living. The investment of time and energy, as well as the financial commitment necessary for treatment, further accentuate the intensity of the patient's emotional involvement. The second component of the therapeutic relationship is its transference aspect. In LSD therapy this element is generally much more powerful than in conventional psychotherapy, and tends to increase with the number of LSD sessions until the time it is resolved. It is based on the fact that the patients, in the course of long-term psychotherapeutic interaction in the sessions and outside of them, project on the therapist a variety of strong emotional attitudes derived from important figures of their past and present life, especially close family members. Although there exist techniques which can minimize the transference problems during the free intervals between psychedelic sessions, this element plays an important role at the time of the drug effect. It is not unusual for the actions of the therapist to have a far-reaching influence on the content and course of the sessions. At certain periods of the psychedelic experience, LSD subjects can show unusually strong reactions to the therapists' leaving or entering the room, offering or withdrawing physical contact, or to seemingly indifferent gestures and comments. Occasionally, even such phenomena as the colors of optical illusions and visions, or intense physical symptoms such as severe nausea and vomiting, suffocation, agonizing pain and cardiac distress, can change dramatically as a result of the therapist's behavior, intervention, or interpretations.

The importance of the therapist as a powerful determinant of the session increases considerably if LSD is administered after a long period of systematic intensive psychotherapy or if the drug is given repeatedly within the framework of a psycholytic series. In that case, it is not uncommon for the transference phenomena to play a dominant role in the manifest content of an entire session.[6]

The degree of human and professional interest of the therapist, his or her clinical experience and therapeutic skill, personal security, freedom from anxiety, and current physical and mental condition are very important factors in successful LSD therapy. It is absolutely essential that, prior to the administration of LSD, the therapist examine his or her own motivation and attitudes toward the subject, try to establish a good working relationship, and clarify the transference-countertransference situation. The therapist should never offer LSD as an impressive and "magical" procedure to a patient who is stagnating in psychotherapy, just because he or she can not tolerate the atmosphere of failure, insecurity, or helplessness. Another objectionable approach is to administer the drug to a patient who has been neglected for a long time because of personal or objective reasons, in order to compensate for these circumstances and create a feeling that something important is going on. Perhaps the most dangerous motivation for using LSD is the need to demonstrate power and authority to a troublesome patient who is shattering the therapist's sense of security. All these and similar problems, if not properly analyzed, can easily contaminate the LSD session, especially if they happen to replicate traumatic experiences in the patient's past.

Clarity in the relationship between the therapist and the subject is a necessary prerequisite for a successful course of therapy. As we mentioned earlier, LSD can best be described as an amplifier of mental processes. By activating the intrapsychic elements in the subject, it also amplifies the interpersonal situation between him or herself and other people present in the session. This makes it possible to see the transference aspects of the relationship clearly and thus view also the nature of the maladjustive interpersonal patterns of the patient. If the situation between the therapist and the patient is clear and open, this becomes a great opportunity for therapeutic progress. However, if there are overt or covert misunderstandings, conflicts and distortions in the therapeutic relationship before the session, they can be exaggerated by the drug-effect to such a degree that they become a serious impasse and eventually endanger the treatment process. It is important therefore that the guide be aware during the sessions of his or her own intrapsychic and interpersonal patterns, so that they do not interfere with the psychedelic process.

All the phenomena in LSD sessions that involve the subject, the sitters, and their mutual relationships, are the result of a complicated interaction between the specific personality characteristics of each of them. The proportion of the individual contributions varies from situation to situation and session to session. However, since the mental processes of LSD subjects are powerfully activated by the drug, they usually play a more important role in determining the content and nature of such interactions unless some very serious countertransference problems are involved on the part of the sitters.

The degree of the transference distortion seems to be related to the dosage and to the nature of the unconscious material that is emerging in the session. In periods in which the subject is under the influence of the drug but is not dealing with any difficult emotional material, he or she can show unusual depth and clarity of perception. The ability for intuitive and empathic understanding of others can be sharpened and deepened to a startling degree. In some instances, LSD subjects can make amazingly accurate readings of the sitters even at a time when they are struggling with emotional problems of various kinds. This happens when the nature of the problems they are facing is similar to or identical with problematic areas in the sitters. A deep exploration of certain unconscious structures within oneself can thus mediate an instant intuitive understanding of corresponding elements in others.

In these situations, the personalities of the sitters, their thought-processes, emotional reactions, attitudes and behavior patterns become especially important. We have repeatedly observed that LSD subjects were able to tune into the inner feelings of the sitters with great accuracy. They were able to tell when the therapist was fully concentrated, dedicated to the session, and pleased with its course or, conversely, distracted by other professional or personal problems, bored, tired, dissatisfied with the course of the session, or worried about its unfavorable development. This is quite understandable in those cases where the LSD subject can see the sitters' facial expressions. It is conceivable that the effect of the drug can sensitize an individual to various minor or even subliminal clues to the point where these would provide adequate information and sufficient feedback for accurate reading. This could happen even in those cases where the phenomena involved were so subtle that under the conditions of conventional psychotherapy they would escape the patient's conscious attention. However, in some instances where this happened the subjects had their eyes closed or covered by eyeshades; in others, their eyes were open but they were not facing the therapist.

It is also important to add that the subject's and the therapist's concepts of what constitutes a "good" and productive session do not necessarily coincide, especially at the time it is still underway. Therefore it is not possible for the LSD subject to guess the therapist's feelings about the session automatically from his or her own evaluation. In some instances, the ability of the subjects to "read" the therapist correctly was truly striking and seemed to border on genuine extra-sensory perception. Some patients correctly guessed not only the therapist's emotional tones, but also the specific content of his thought-processes, or they felt connected with his memory system and accurately described certain concrete circumstances and recent or remote events from his life.

Elements of accurate perception are more common in low-dose sessions, in which the amount of LSD is not sufficient to activate important emotional material. In high-dose sessions they occur by and large, at the beginning, before the subject's experiential field is occupied by the emerging unconscious contents, or later, after the difficult aspects of the experience have been worked through and resolved. However, this is not an absolute rule and there exist significant exceptions; episodes of unusual clarity occasionally occur at any dosage level and at any time during the session. They seem to be associated with the nature of the experience or a particular state of mind, rather than a specific time of the drug reaction or its intensity. When LSD subjects are deeply engaged in their problem areas, most of their perceptions, thoughts, feelings and anticipations concerning the sitters have very little substantiation in reality. They are projections, reflecting the subject's inner experiences—his or her emotions, instinctual tendencies, and superego functions.

In high-dose LSD sessions a good therapeutic relationship is an element of critical importance. It is necessary to emphasize that even an ideal interpersonal situation cannot completely prevent the occurrence of significant distortions under the influence of the drug. However, if there is a clear and solid relationship be-tween the experient and the sitters outside of the session context, the drug-induced distortions become an important opportunity for learning and for corrective emo-tional experiences, rather than a danger to the psychedelic process. A good therapeutic relationship helps the patient to let go of psychological defenses, sur-render to the experience, and endure the difficult periods of sessions characterized by intense physical and emotional suffering or confusion. The quality of the therapeutic relationship is essential for working through one of the most crucial situations in psychedelic therapy, the crisis of basic trust.

As long as the guide does not significantly contribute to the interpersonal configuration on a reality basis, in terms of strong countertransference, the sub-ject's LSD experiences concerning the therapeutic situation reflect the nature of the emerging unconscious material. There exist many different forms and degrees of projective distortion in the therapeutic relationship. The most superficial and simple manifestation of this kind is fantasizing or visualizing the therapist as assuming certain specific opinions and attitudes. If this occurs at a time when the subject has eye contact with the therapist, it can take the form of actual illusive transformations of the facial expression. Thus the patient may see the therapist as chuckling, smiling and laughing, or expressing condescension, irony and ridicule. He or she might find clear indications of sexual interest or even arousal in the therapist's face and signs of seductiveness in his gestures. The therapist can appear to be critical, angry, hateful and aggressive, or emanate compassion, under-standing and love. His face may appear to betray uncertainty, concern, fear, or guilt feelings. The nature of fantasies and transformations of this kind reflects the variety of feelings and attitudes that the subject transfers onto the therapist. Quite frequently, the projections take a much more elaborate and intricate form; in the extreme, this can result in complex illusive transformations of the therapist's face, body image, and attire. Sometimes the symbolic meaning of such changes is immediately clear and obvious; at other times their full understanding requires systematic and focused analytical work.

There are several typical categories of problems reflected in these symbolic transformations. The most common are those images that represent *projections of the subject's instinctual tendencies of an aggressive or sexual nature*. Thus the therapist can be illusively transformed into various figures representing violence, cruelty and sadism. Here belong, for example, representatives of professions such as a butcher, boxer, executioner, mercenary, or inquisitor; infamous historical figures like Genghis Khan, Caesar Nero, Voivod Dracula, Hitler, or Stalin; and an entire gallery of murderers, hired guns, robbers, SS and Gestapo members, red commissars, head-hunting savages, and others. Famous characters from horror movies also occur frequently in this context, exemplified by Frankenstein, The Creature from the Black Lagoon, Dracula, King Kong, and Godzilla. Another manifestation of the subject's aggression is the symbolic transformation of the therapist into a bloodthirsty predator—eagle, lion, tiger, black panther, jaguar, shark, or tyrannosaurus. A similar meaning can be associated with the therapist changing into one of the traditional adversaries of such animals—a gladiator, hunter, or tamer of wild beasts. Archetypal images symbolizing aggression are equally common; they range from evil magicians, malicious witches, and vampires to devils, demons, and devouring deities. A subject tuned into aggressive themes in his or her own unconscious may see the treatment room transformed into the cabinet of Dr. Caligari, a dungeon, torture chamber, barrack in a concentration camp, or a death cell. Innocent objects in the therapist's hand, such as a pencil, fountain pen, or a piece of paper, change into daggers, hatchets, saws, guns, and other murderous tools.

In the same way, sexual tendencies can be manifested in the form of symbolic projections. The therapist is perceived as an Oriental harem owner, a lewd lecher, prostitute, suburban pimp, metropolitan swinger, or a frivolous and promiscuous bohemian painter. Don Juan, Rasputin, Poppea, Casanova, and Hugh Hefner were some other sexual symbols observed in this context. Images that express sexual attraction without a pejorative undertone range from famous film stars and legendary romantic lovers to archetypal gods of love. In advanced LSD sessions deified personifications of the male and female principles such as the Apollo-Aphrodite or Shiva-Shakti dyad occur frequently, and images of priests or priestesses in various love cults, fertility rites, phallic worship, or tribal rituals involving sexuality are also quite common. On several occasions, transformation of the therapist's visage into the "leonine face" of a leper or the deformed face of a syphilitic could be deciphered as a projection of sexual wishes combined with the threat of punishment.

Another typical category of illusive transformations involves *projections of the subject's Superego*. The therapist is frequently perceived as various specific personages who evaluate, judge, or criticize the experient. These can be parental figures, teachers and other critical authorities from the subject's life, priests, judges and jury members, various archetypal personifications of Justice, and even

Three representations of illusory transformation of the therapist. He appears as an Arabian merchant dealing with dangerous intoxicating drugs (above left); a wild and primitive African native (left); and as an Indian sage radiating perennial wisdom (above right). Each image reflected the nature and content of the patient's psychedelic experience at that particular time.

Illusory transformation of the therapist. Here he becomes a sadistic monster who enjoys inflicting suffering on the patient. The angelic figure on the left represents the patient's awareness that the tortures will ultimately lead to a spiritual opening. The castle on the right reflects his vague awareness of a medieval scene of torture which he felt as a karmic memory. The experience occurred during a session characterized by the transition from BPM III to BPM IV.

God or the Devil. Some other visions seem to reflect the part of the subject's Superego that represents the ego ideal. The therapist is then perceived as being an absolutely perfect human, a person endowed with all imaginable virtues, possessing and having achieved all that the patient always wanted—physical beauty, moral integrity, superior intelligence, emotional stability, and a balanced life situation.

A typical category of transformations reflects the subject's *strong need for unconditional love and undivided attention*, as well as irritation at not having exclusive possession and control of the therapist. This is most characteristic of psychodynamic sessions that involve deep regression to early infancy and intense anaclitic needs. Many patients find it difficult to accept the fact that they have to share the therapist with other patients, that the therapist has a private life of his or her own, or that the therapeutic framework sets certain clear limits on intimacy. Whether the objective reality justifies it or not, many patients feel they are being treated with professional coolness and scientific objectivity, or as experimental guinea pigs. Even if physical contact is used in the sessions, a client sensitive in this area may experience it as a therapeutic technique or a professional ploy rather than a genuine expression of human affection.

The therapist's curiosity concerning the patient's history or the dynamics of his or her problems can in this context be ridiculed by an illusive change of the therapist into Sherlock Holmes, Hercule Poirot, Leon Clifton, or just a caricature of a detective with a large pipe, spectacles, and a magnifying glass. His professional, objective and "scientific" approach to the patient can be caricatured in an illusive transformation into a funny-looking, learned owl, sitting on a pile of cobweb-covered volumes. The irritating lack of adequate emotional response and professional "coolness" can be reflected in a visual illusion showing him in the thick protective suit of a medieval armored knight, astronaut, fireman, or scubadiver. The recording of the session may irritate the patient, even if he or she not only agreed to it before the session, but specifically requested it. It can be ridiculed by a satirical vision of the therapist as a philistine bureaucrat, ambitious and diligent schoolboy, or provincial clerk. The white coat, a common symbol of the physician, can play an important part in this context; the medical role of the therapist can be attacked by changing him into representatives of other professions who also use white coats, such as grocers, barbers, or butchers. Transformations of the therapist into Doctor Faust, observed in the past, were deciphered as allusions to his sophistication and title, the unconventional nature of his scientific quest, and the magical properties of the drug he uses; in some instances they also reflected the wish that he follow Faust's example and exchange science for mundane pleasure.[7]

> A very interesting, cartoon-like illustration of some of these problems occurred in one of the early sessions of Agnes, who was undergoing psycholytic treatment for a severe chronic neurosis. In the phase of therapy when she desperately wanted the therapist for herself and was jealous of all the other patients, she experienced in her LSD session symbolic sequences from a chicken hatchery, which represented a satire on her LSD treatment. The hatchery symbolized the Psychiatric Research Institute where she was in therapy and her co-patients appeared as eggs with various flaws and defects

Illusory transformation of the therapist into a nosy detective with a large pipe ("Sherlock Holmes"). The patient is depicting his irritation with the therapist's inquisitiveness and objectivity.

that were in different stages of hatching. Since the experience of birth is an important therapeutic step in LSD therapy, hatching symbolized in this context the successful end of treatment and the cure of neurosis. The patient-eggs were competing with each other, trying to expedite the hatching process, but also to win the affection of the therapist. The latter was represented by a system of electric bulbs providing scientifically measured amounts of light and warmth. The patient herself was a dissatisfied little chicken embryo who passionately competed for the artificial heat, since that was all that was available. In reality, she wanted to be the single offspring of a real mother hen and could not put up with the electric surrogate.

As indicated by this example, the transformation of the therapist does not have to occur as an isolated phenomenon, but can be accompanied by simultaneous autosymbolic transformation of the patient and/or illusive change of the entire environment.

Like most LSD phenomena, the illusive transformation of the guide and the environment usually has a multi-level and overdetermined structure. Although one specific meaning or connection may be in the center of awareness, one can usually find a number of additional functions for the same image. As in the case of dreams, there frequently exist several interpretations for the same phenomenon. They involve material from different levels of the unconscious and, quite typically, opposing tendencies and emotions can find joint representation in a single condensed symbolic image. Although we have thus far been discussing visual manifestations, which are the most striking, projective distortions can involve other senses, such as hearing, smell, taste, and touch.

The concrete content of the illusive transformations reflects the type of the LSD experience and the level of the unconscious that is activated. The most superficial changes are of an abstract nature and do not seem to have any deeper symbolic significance. The therapist's face can appear undulating, distorted, or in changing colors. On occasion, his or her skin is covered with mosaics and intricate geometrical designs that look like tattoos or aboriginal decorations. These changes resemble the disturbances on the screen of a television set that is out of tune and seem to reflect chemical stimulation of the sensory apparatus.

On the psychodynamic level, the illusive transformations reflect the basic themes of individual COEX systems colored by the specific content of the layer that is at that time in the center of the experiential field. The therapist can be perceived as a parental figure, sibling, close relative, nanny, neighbor, or any significant person who was instrumental in important childhood experiences. Doctors and nurses who conducted painful medical interventions, acquaintances who played the roles of surrogate parents, adults who physically or sexually abused the subject, and protagonists in various frightful episodes are typical representatives of this category. Occasionally, the therapist may assume the form of favorite animals, such as the family dog, pet rabbit or hen, or even an emotionally important children's toy which was the subject's surrogate companion.

Sometimes the projective transformations do not directly reflect the biographical events recorded in a COEX system, but variations on its central theme. The following example from an LSD session of Renata,[8] a patient who suffered from severe cancerophobia, shows how even a seemingly insignificant partial transformation of the therapist can condense relevant material from different levels.

When Renata looked at the therapist, the light reflection in his eye took the form of a large Sphinx moth. Free associations which Renata volunteered the next day brought out the following material:

The Sphinx is a night moth that visits flowers with intoxicating fragrance and sucks the nectar from them. It has a distinct mark of a human

A Sphinx moth seen in the therapist's eye.

skull on its back and is usually associated in folklore with death. This reflects a theme which was very important for Renata and formed the basis of her cancerophobia. As a result of certain childhood experiences, particularly sexual abuse by her stepfather at the age of eight, sex and death were intimately connected in her unconscious. Summer nights and heavy sweet fragrance suggest the atmosphere of romance and love-making; the Sphinx flying around is a portent of death.

Some additional associations showed the complicated, overdetermined, and ingenious structure underlying this transformation. Renata read somewhere that the Sphinx caterpillars live on *Atropa Belladonna* or the deadly nightshade, which is known for its psychoactive properties and was used in medieval potions and ointments for the Witches' Sabbath. Small doses of Belladonna are hallucinogenic and larger doses extremely toxic. The hallucinogenic properties of Belladonna represent a link to the LSD process. Its relation to the orgies of the Witches' Sabbath alludes to dangerous aspects of sex. Its connection with death, beside reemphasizing the closeness between sex and death, also points back to the LSD process which has the death experience as an important element. Renata also remembered reading somewhere that the Sphinx caterpillars sleep in an erect position. She found a direct link from here to the traumatic situation of seduction by her stepfather during which she was confronted with his penis.

On the deepest level the name of the Sphinx moth pointed to the Egyptian Sphinx. This image of the destructive female—a creature with a human head and animal body, which strangles its victims—occurs frequently in LSD sessions dealing with the agony of birth and transcendence. It was on the perinatal level, in the process of biological birth, that Renata found the deepest unconscious roots of the fusion and confusion in her between sex and death.

The transformations of the therapist in sessions with strong perinatal emphasis have a very different quality. The general direction of the projective change depends on the stage of the death-rebirth process, or the basic perinatal matrix which is activated at that time.

The basic elements and attributes associated with each of the matrices are characteristic and quite distinct. For BPM I it is transcendental beauty, unconditional love, merging of boundaries, an atmosphere of numinosity, and a sense of nourishment and protection. The very beginning of BPM II involves deep metaphysical fear, feelings of threat and paranoia, and a sense of losing autonomy. A fully developed BPM II is characterized by an atmosphere of irreversible entrapment, hopeless victimization, experience of endless, diabolical tortures and loss of one's soul. BPM III imparts the elements of a titanic and bloody fight with sadomasochistic, sexual, and scatological features. The transition from BPM III to BPM IV is experienced as an overwhelming pressure to surrender completely and unconditionally, abysmal fear of annihilation, and expectations of catastrophe. BPM IV then has the unmistakable quality of spiritual liberation, deliverance from darkness, salvation, and illumination.

If the subject is under the influence of one of the negative perinatal matrices, the therapist can appear as a representative of elements and movements that threaten not only individuals but the entire world: the chief of a dangerous underground organization, a representative of an extraterrestrial civilization trying to enslave mankind, an important Nazi or Communist leader, a misguided religious fanatic, a mad-genius scientist, or the Devil himself. Confronted with these images, the subject can lose the critical insight that he or she is involved in a symbolic process and experience a full-blown paranoid reaction. In more superficial and less convincing experiences, a number of specific elements of perinatal symbolism can be projected onto the therapist; he can change into a mythological monster threatening to devour the subject, the Great Inquisitor, the commandant of a concentration camp, or a diabolic sadist. He or she can change into various historical figures known for their cruelty, sexual perverts, coprophiliacs, warriors, severely sick or wounded persons, conquistadors, Pre-Columbian priests, carnival figures, or crucified Christ. The specific form of these transformations depends on the stage of the death-rebirth process, the level on which it is experienced, and the passive or active role of the subject.

When the positive matrices dominate the LSD session, the transformations have a very different quality. If it is BPM IV, the therapist can be perceived as a triumphant military leader celebrating victory over a vicious enemy, the Savior, the embodiment of cosmic wisdom, a teacher of the deepest secrets of life and nature, a manifestation of the divine principle, or essentially God. The activation of BPM I has many of the elements of BPM IV, such as the radiance, sacredness, and humor; however, these have a timeless quality instead of occurring as a stage in the process of transition from death to rebirth. The subject can experience loss of boundaries and a feeling of fundamental oneness with the therapist, associated with a sense of absolute safety and total nourishment.

Quite frequently during the death-rebirth process, the therapist assumes for the subject the role of the delivering mother and may actually be experienced as such; this can occur with both male and female sitters without regard to the actual sex identity. Under these circumstances the transference relationship can assume a symbiotic quality; it is characterized by a deep biologically rooted ambivalence, and its relevance is so basic that it appears to be a matter of life and death. The therapist can become for the patient a magical and powerful figure of cosmic proportions. The patient can have either a sense of participating in this power or of being in a totally passive, dependent and vulnerable position. A critical factor in this situation seems to be the patient's ability to trust the world and human beings, which essentially reflects his or her early history. The nature of the childhood experience determines whether a totally dependent role can be enjoyed or whether it becomes a source of vital threat and paranoid ideation.

Frequently the patient has to go through a profound crisis of basic trust to be able to reconnect with the nourishing aspects of the mother-child relationship. When the early symbiotic situation of the perinatal period is projected on the therapist, LSD patients often lose the ability to differentiate clearly between the therapist and themselves. Their perceptions, emotions and thoughts seem to merge with those of the therapist. This can result in a feeling of being magically influenced or controlled by suggestion, hypnosis, telepathy, or even psychokinesis. The therapist appears to read their minds and know all their thoughts; the opposite is also common, namely, the sense of having access to the therapist's mind and sharing his feelings or thought-processes. Under these circumstances patients frequently find it unnecessary to communicate their experiences verbally. They feel either that the therapist automatically shares and knows the experience in all its details, or that he has prearranged it and controls it, so that everything is happening according to his plan. In critical stages of the death-rebirth process the therapist can become the murderous or life-giving womb, and can also be experienced as the delivering obstetrician or midwife. This is especially frequent if the treatment technique involves actual physical contact and support.

The problems in the transference relationship on the perinatal level culminate when the patient is approaching the moment of ego death, which coincides with reliving the moment of biological birth. This involves totally letting go of all defenses, all effective control, and all reference points, and is typically associated with a profound crisis of basic trust. In this state of ultimate vulnerability the patient questions the character and motives of the therapist in an attempt to assess the degree of danger in total surrender. Important negative aspects of the patient's history emerge in an amplified form and are projected onto the therapist in various symbolic manifestations. In addition, the real flaws in the therapist's personality, attitudes and motives, and the problems and conflicts in the therapeutic relationship, are seen as if through a magnifying glass. The patient's perception of the therapist can be a reflection of his or her experience in the murderous birth canal, and the LSD process can appear at this point as a diabolic scheme to destroy the patients, brainwash them, enslave them for eternity, or steal their souls.

After the crisis of trust has been worked through and the bond of confidence re-established, the transference phenomena tend to swing to the other extreme. A subject influenced by BPM I or IV can see the therapist as the ultimate source of love, security, and nourishment. He or she can experience the therapist as being the good breast and the good womb at the same time. There do not seem to be any more individual boundaries, only a continuous, free flow of thoughts, emotions, and good energy. The patient experiences this as the ultimate process of nursing, in which the milk seems to be coming from a spiritual source and has miraculous healing properties. The same experience also seems to have embryonal qualities; the circulation of different kinds of spiritual emotions and energies seems to have strong elements of the placentary exchange between the mother and child. Once this biological, emotional and spiritual link is established, the therapist can be perceived not only as one's own mother, but as the good mother in general—the archetypal image of the Great Mother, Mother Nature, and ultimately the entire cosmos or God.

In LSD sessions of a transpersonal nature, the transference relationship has a completely different quality. The illusive transformations of the therapist can no longer be interpreted in the same way as those on the psychodynamic level—as complicated symbolic images with a multilevel and overdetermined structure, or as projections reflecting various layers of the COEX systems. These illusive transformations also differ from the perinatal transference phenomena, which can be understood as repetitions of the nourishing and destructive aspects of the symbiotic relationship with the mother. Transpersonal projections are phenomena that *sui generis* defy further psychological analysis.

In general, almost all of the many types of transpersonal experiences can find specific reflections in the therapeutic relationship. Thus the therapist can assume the forms of powerful archetypal images, such as sacralized representatives of various roles, or deities and demons. The transformations into the Cosmic Man, the Wise Man, the Great Hermaphrodite, the Animus or Anima, Shiva, Kali, Ganesha, Zeus, Venus, Apollo, Satan, Isis, Cybele, or Coatlicue, would be examples in this category. Equally frequent are transformations of the therapist into a great religious teacher—Jesus, Moses, Mohammed, Buddha, Sri Ramana Maharishi, and others. When the patient is experiencing elements of the racial and collective unconscious, the therapist may be transformed into a representative of another culture and/or a person existing in a different century. Such an episode can also have a "past-incarnation experiential quality." In that case, the patients feel convinced that they are reliving memories from their past lives and that the present situation is a replica or variation of an event that occurred in the remote past. It is quite common for clients to feel that they have met the therapist in many of their previous incarnations. Occasionally, this can involve very complex situations from different cultures and centuries which may be visualized in considerable detail.

Inclusion of the therapist into ancestral or phylogenetic memories occurs quite frequently. In that case the therapist appears transformed into a specific human or animal ancestor of the same or opposite sex. In general, the projective transformations of the therapist on the transpersonal level are quite different from those of a basically psychodynamic, Freudian nature. The former feel very genuine, authentic and convincing; they frequently contain valid and objectively verifiable information that seems to go far beyond the subject's educational background and level of information. Unlike the projective transformations on the psychodynamic level, they cannot be deciphered and interpreted as symbolic representations of certain aspects of the patient's present existence. Even those patients who enthusiastically help to analyze various projective phenomena on the psychodynamic level refuse the Freudian approach to the transpersonal realm as superficial, inadequate, and inappropriate.

The enormous significance of the therapist or sitter during the LSD sessions has its consequences for psychotherapeutic practice. On the one hand, the role frequently presents serious problems for the therapist, who may come under emotional pressures of various kinds and has to guard against all the intricate pitfalls of the transference and countertransference situation. On the other hand, the intensification of the therapeutic relationship goes far beyond the limits of conventional psychotherapy, frequently reaching the point of caricature. This makes it easier for the patient and therapist to recognize and understand the transference nature of the problems involved. To an experienced therapist, the dimensions of the therapeutic relationship reached in psychedelic sessions offer a unique opportunity to mediate powerful corrective emotional experiences on very deep levels that are not easy to reach by conventional psychotherapy.

To be able to face all the challenges of psychedelic therapy, the therapist has to have special training that involves personal experiences with the drug. Because of the extraordinary nature of the LSD states and the limitations of our language in describing them, it is impossible for the future LSD therapist to acquire deeper understanding of the process without first-hand exposure. Reading about psychedelic experiences, attending seminars and lectures, or even witnessing sessions of other people can only convey a superficial and inadequate knowledge. Personal sessions have another important function: they offer an opportunity to work through one's own areas of conflict and problems on various levels. Some of the crucial issues that a future LSD therapist has to confront remain essentially untouched in most forms of conventional therapy. Fear of death, total loss of control, and the specter of insanity can be mentioned here as salient examples. Unless the therapist deals successfully with these issues, the manifestations of the deep unconscious of the patient will tend to activate his or her own problem areas and trigger difficult emotional and psychosomatic responses. This can be conducive to serious transference-countertransference problems and places increased demands on the defense system and self-control. LSD sessions in which the therapist has to struggle with his or her unresolved problems can become a real burden; they are usually experienced as mutually draining and result in excessive fatigue.

Other important qualities and abilities of a good LSD therapist come from long clinical experience. With the increase in the number of sessions that he or she has witnessed, the therapist becomes more comfortable with and less threatened by various unusual phenomena that are quite common in psychedelic therapy. In everyday practice he or she observes a great number of people suffering through dramatic experiences of dying, going crazy and feeling possessed by evil spirits, or claiming that they went beyond the point of no return. Witnessing positive resolutions of such states and seeing the same subjects only a few hours later radiant and joking, the therapist gradually develops equanimity, confidence and tolerance in regard to the entire spectrum of psychedelic phenomena. This attitude is transferred onto the patients and makes it possible for them to allow themselves to experience whatever is emerging in the LSD sessions in order to find the roots of their emotional problems.

SET AND SETTING OF THE SESSIONS

In addition to the factors associated with the personalities of the subject and the therapist or sitter, there exists a broad complex of non-pharmacological parameters usually referred to as "set and setting." Any understanding of the LSD reaction and its therapeutic use is superficial and incomplete if it does not take into consideration all the determining elements belonging to this category.

The term *set* includes the expectations, motivations and intentions of the subject in regard to the session; the therapist's or guide's concept of the nature of the LSD experience; the agreed-upon goal of the psychedelic procedure; the preparation and programming for the session; and the specific technique of guidance used during the drug experience.

The term *setting* refers to the actual environment, both physical and interpersonal, and to the concrete circumstances under which the drug is administered.

THE IMPORTANCE OF SET

Since LSD is a non-specific amplifier of mental processes, the LSD phenomena cover an extremely broad range, extending potentially to all aspects of human experience and behavior. For this reason there can be many different sets for the LSD sessions. The fierce controversies surrounding LSD could be dispelled easily if those involved in arguing about the dangers and benefits of LSD would clearly recognize the critical relevance of the non-drug factors. In most instances, discussions that pretend to be about LSD are actually about different uses of the drug, and about the influence of set on the outcome of the LSD experience. Humphrey Osmond, an early pioneer of LSD research, analyzed this situation in a conference on LSD psychotherapy. He emphasized the fact that LSD is a tool, and the way it is employed is of crucial importance. To illustrate his point, he asked the audience to imagine a situation in which a group of people with different backgrounds and different sets of observations try to assess whether a knife is a dangerous object or a useful tool. In this context, a surgeon would present statistics of successful surgical operations, a chief of police would talk about murders and mutilations, a housewife would consider the knife in relation to cutting meat and vegetables, and an artist would think about it in connection with carving wood. In such a situation any attempt to choose one view over the other is clearly absurd and inconceivable; it would be obvious to everybody that the critical factor is the use the knife is put to. Nobody would seriously consider that the dangers and positive potentials of this tool represent its intrinsic properties. Yet this is exactly what has been done in the past in various discussions about LSD.

In the following text, we will briefly review the most important sets in which LSD has been administered, and discuss their specific characteristics. The first major conceptual framework for the administration of LSD was the so-called *"model psychosis"* approach. It dominated LSD experimentation in the years immediately following the discovery of the drug. The LSD experiences were viewed in a clearly psychopathological connection and labeled "experimental psychoses" or "chemically induced schizophrenia." In this stage, the drug was administered to volunteers for research purposes, with the aim of exploring the biochemical basis of endogenous psychoses, or to mental health professionals for didactic and training purposes—to send them on a reversible journey into the world of the schizophrenic.

A completely different set for LSD sessions emerged when it became obvious that the drug experiences could enhance creative potential in certain individuals. The drug became popular among artists as a *source of inspiration* and many hundreds of painters, sculptors, musicians, architects, and writers volunteered for LSD experiments. Somewhat later, scientists, philosophers and other highly creative individuals became favorite subjects for LSD sessions. This was based on the observation that the unusual states of consciousness induced by LSD can generate important insights, facilitate problem-solving, and lead to valid intuitions or unexpected resyntheses of accumulated data.

Another important set for LSD sessions was developed after experimenters had repeatedly observed that the drug experience could take the form of a profound *religious or mystical experience.* Some researchers interested in exploring this "instant" or "chemical mysticism" tried to create frameworks and circumstances facilitating the incidence of these spiritual phenomena.

Many different sets have been used in sessions exploring the *therapeutic potential* of LSD for psychiatric patients and the terminally ill. Various methods of LSD therapy have been described in an earlier chapter and will be only briefly reviewed here. In some of these studies LSD was administered routinely, as any other pharmacological agent, without regard to its specific psychedelic properties. This strictly medical model was applied in approaches using LSD as an antidepressive, abreactive, or activating agent. In others, LSD was seen as a catalyst of mental processes and an adjunct to psychotherapy; psycholytic, anaclitic, and hypnodelic therapy are examples of this approach. Certain therapeutic orientations such as psychedelic therapy or Salvador Roquet's psychosynthesis have a clearly religious emphasis and stress the "mysticomimetic" effects of LSD.

The drug can be administered in the context of individual or group psychotherapy and its use may lean in theory and practice on various therapeutic systems —Freudian psychoanalysis, Jung's analytical psychology, Moreno's psychodrama, Perls' Gestalt practice, or existential psychotherapy. The anaclitic approach puts a great emphasis on physical contact and mothering behavior. Psychedelic therapy can use the framework of different religions; its individual variations also stress particular aspects of the set and setting, such as music, elements of nature, the use of universal symbols, or readings of specific passages from sacred books.

Almost infinite variations of set are associated with *non-medical use* and *unsupervised self-experimentation.* Some individuals have a sitter for their sessions while others take LSD on their own or participate in group experiences. The settings for these experiences cover a wide range, from private apartments, beautiful natural locations, or rock concerts to streets with busy traffic and cars on the highways. The quality of the street samples of LSD is questionable, and possible impurities include substances such as amphetamines, phencyclidine, STP, and even strychnine. The quantity of the active substance is equally unpredictable. The unreliability of the drugs, absence of a support system, and illegal framework of such self-experiments are conducive to paranoia and panic reactions. For this reason the incidence of serious psychological complications under these circumstances cannot be considered an indication that the use of LSD is intrinsically dangerous.

LSD and some other psychedelics have been listed as narcotics. This is incorrect and has no scientific justification. No genuine physiological addiction to LSD or related substances has been demonstrated. The reasons for their use and abuse are extremely complex and can have very deep psychological roots. Any legislation that overlooks or ignores this fact is necessarily doomed to fail. The individuals involved in non-medical self-experimentation with psychedelics belong to different categories and have very different motivations. Some of them are immature and irresponsible youngsters who lack or ignore serious information about the nature of the LSD effect and take the drug for kicks, rebellion, or group orgies. Others are pleasure seekers trying to enhance their sensory experience for aesthetic, recreational and hedonistic reasons. Some couples use joint psychedelic experiences to work through emotional problems within the dyad, improve the quality of their relationship, open new channels of communication, and explore various levels and dimensions of their sexual interaction. A not insignificant group of self-experimenters seem to be people with serious emotional problems for whom traditional psychotherapy is inaccessible, or who are disappointed by its inefficacy. They are desperately looking for therapeutic alternatives, and since responsible and professional LSD treatment is not available, they make attempts at self-therapy. There also exists a large group of responsible and sophisticated intellectuals who see repeated psychedelic sessions as a unique opportunity for philosophical and spiritual search, comparable to the way offered by traditions such as Tibetan Vajrayana, Zen Buddhism, Taoism, Sufism, or different systems of yoga.

Thus the motivations for psychedelic experimentation can be extremely serious and reflect the most fundamental needs of human beings—cravings for emotional well-being, spiritual fulfillment and a sense of meaning in life. However, there is no doubt that, whatever the motivations and intentions of the subjects may be, the LSD sessions should be conducted in a safe situation and in the context of a trust relationship with an experienced and responsible sitter. If these requirements are not met, the dangers and risks of such an undertaking far outweigh the potential benefits.

The last area of LSD experimentation that will be mentioned in this context is characterized by what can be referred to as *destructive sets*. Here belong "experiments" which explore the potential of LSD for the psychological liquidation of certain individuals, eliciting of confessions, brain washing, and chemical warfare. We could include here situations in which an individual ingests LSD without knowing it and frequently without any previous knowledge of its effects. The danger of this situation cannot be sufficiently stressed; not only the sanity, but the life of the subject can be at stake under these circumstances. Sometimes this can happen by accident when LSD is mistaken for other pills, or sugar cubes containing LSD for plain sugar. However, secret police, intelligence agencies and military experts have in the past systematically exposed naïve and unprepared subjects to the effects of the drug to test its destructive potential. In several instances this even has been done by psychiatric researchers; the objective of these experiments was to test whether in unprepared and surprised subjects the LSD reaction would resemble schizophrenia more closely than when the drug is administered with informed consent.

It has also happened quite frequently in the past that irresponsible individuals added LSD secretly into the food or drink of relatives, friends or strangers, as an "initiation," "psychedelic defloration," entertainment, or just a mischievous and vengeful act. Sometimes this has been combined with other activities that further accentuate the hazards of this situation. I can refer here to an encounter with a group of youngsters several years ago in Washington Square in New York City. When they heard that I had been doing research with LSD, they proudly shared with me their own "experiments," in which strangers were given LSD without knowing it. After ingestion of the drug, these involuntary guinea pigs were taken into a private apartment. Here the "experimenters" performed a wild dance around their victims clad in bizarre aboriginal masks and costumes, swinging daggers and spears. The objective of this "research" was to study the reactions of various subjects to this unusual situation. It is obvious that under these circumstances, LSD can have a profoundly disorganizing effect and precipitate acute, uncontrollable panic and even psychotic decompensation. If LSD is given to another person covertly, without his or her informed consent, I would not hesitate to use the term *criminal set* for such a situation.

During the last twenty years I have had the opportunity to conduct, observe and personally experience psychedelic sessions in several different sets. I started working with LSD at the time of the "model psychosis" approach, and I also ran didactic sessions with my professional colleagues during this period. Occasionally, artists, philosophers and scientists came to our facility and had LSD sessions for inspiration and insight. Later, I started using LSD as an adjunct to systematic dynamic psychotherapy and conducted an exploratory study of its diagnostic and therapeutic potential within the framework of a specially structured patient community. During this work, I developed a therapeutic technique using repeated administrations of LSD. Although it was originally conceived as drug-assisted psychoanalysis leaning in theory and practice on Freudian concepts, it gradually became a treatment modality *sui generis*. In addition to working through traumatic material from childhood, as practiced in psychoanalysis and psycholytic therapy, this approach puts great emphasis on the importance of the death-rebirth process and transpersonal experiences.

After many years of clinical experimentation with LSD in Prague, I was able to spend some time in London and to acquire first-hand experience of anaclitic therapy as it was practiced by Joyce Martin and Pauline McCririck. In 1967, I moved to the United States and joined the research team at Spring Grove in Baltimore, where I learnt and practiced the psychedelic treatment technique. During this time I was occasionally called in as a consultant on cases of non-medical experimentation with LSD which involved various complications and I became quite familiar with the counterculture's use of psychedelics. All these experiences have been a rich source of important observations, and they clearly indicate the paramount significance of set as a determinant of the LSD reaction.

Certain aspects of set are quite obvious and explicit. It is not difficult to see that specific programming during the preparation period, certain techniques of conducting the sessions, or props and paraphernalia to which the subject is exposed can influence the LSD experience. However, some other important factors have been overlooked in the past, or were not appreciated sufficiently because they are much more subtle and not easily identifiable. One of them is the presence or absence of verbal communication between the subject and the sitter. Talk that goes beyond a certain necessary minimum during psychedelic sessions tends to make the experience more superficial and is generally counterproductive in terms of effective self-exploration. However, in those situations where there is a continuing dialogue between the subject and the sitter, the nature of their verbal exchange becomes a factor of considerable importance. This is particularly true in regard to the choice and formulation of the questions that are asked. In addressing the subject, the sitter continuously reinforces and redefines the set that has been established in the preparatory period of the session. A specific wording of the questions can attract the subject's attention to certain aspects of the multidimensional and multifaceted content of the LSD experience. In the extreme, it can significantly determine the direction in which the experience moves, modify its content and influence its course.

In the *descriptive approach* to an LSD session, which tries to capture the phenomenology of the drug reaction, the subject is encouraged to focus on some formal and relatively superficial aspects of his or her experience. The elements that are of interest in this context are the presence or absence of physical symptoms, direction of emotional changes, quality of perceptual distortions, and the degree of psychomotor excitement or inhibition. The experimenter wants to know if the subject's vision is sharp or blurred, if objects are perceived as steady or undulating, if the visions are of a geometrical or figurative nature, if hearing is more or less acute than usual, and if synaesthesias are present. Under these circumstances, the subject usually experiences all the LSD phenomena in a rather impersonal way, as a spectator watching an interesting movie. Whatever is happening in the session is seen as a result of the interaction between the drug and the subject's brain; the experient is used as an observer and reporter of these changes. Even if relatively strong emotions are involved, they are attributed to the chemical effect of the drug rather than seen as a manifestation of the subject's personality; they are simply noticed and recorded. In the sessions focusing on psychopathological description, relevant dynamic material is seldom recognized and never pursued any further. Typical questions redefining this experimental framework are sentences such as: "Are you sweating?", "Are your hands trembling?", Do you feel dizzy?", "Are the colors different from the usual?", "Do you have any strange feelings in your body?" The records of early LSD experiments and the questionnaires used in this period abound in questions of this kind.

When LSD was administered in the context of the *model psychosis* research, the sessions were connected with strongly negative programming. They were explicitly referred to as "experimental psychoses" and psychedelic drugs as "hallucinogens," "psychotomimetics" or "psychodysleptics." The subjects would both expect and selectively focus their attention on phenomena that are usually associated with schizophrenia, such as paranoid feelings, panic anxiety, dissociation between affect and thought, various perceptual distortions and disturbances, delusional interpretation of the environment, or disorganization and fragmentation of the ego. In LSD sessions conducted with mental health professionals for training purposes, the psychopathological focus was particularly strong. These individuals would try to properly identify and diagnose various perceptual disturbances, abnormal thought-processes, and unusual emotional qualities, assigning the appropriate clinical labels to them, and comparing them with those occurring in schizophrenic patients.

The questions characteristic of this approach would be: "Do you have any visual or acoustic hallucinations?", "Are your emotions inappropriate to the content of your thoughts and visions?", "Do you have any strange sensations or bizarre changes of your body image?", "How does your experience compare with schizophrenia?", "Are you getting any insights into the psychotic process?"

In sessions where the emphasis is on *aesthetic experiences and artistic inspiration*, LSD subjects are primarily interested in changed perception of forms, colors and sounds. They focus their attention on such phenomena as the intricacy of geometrical patterns, dynamics of optical illusions, and richness of synaesthesias. They frequently try to relate their experiences to various modern movements in art or the work of individual artists. Abstractionism, impressionism, cubism, surrealism, superrealism, and concrete music seem to be particularly relevant from this point of view. Another typical feature of these sessions is preoccupation with technical problems and difficulties in expressing these unusual phenomena in artistic forms. The following questions would be characteristic of this type of session: "Do your visions resemble the work of some famous artist?", "What are the predominant colors you see?", "Are your visions geometrical or figurative?", "What material and what technique would be best to express what you see?", "Is this a picture of a vision you had or an automatic drawing?", "How is your coordination?", "Is it difficult to concentrate on painting?", "Does the music you are hallucinating remind you of any piece you know?", "Which instruments would you use in composing this music?", "Do you now have a better understanding of modern art?"

In *psychotherapeutic sessions of psycholytic orientation*, the patients are encouraged to use the sessions for self-exploration and dynamic understanding of their emotional problems. The LSD phenomena are seen as complex symbolic formations that reflect important unconscious processes in the patient. There is a systematic effort to decipher all the manifestations of the experience and use them as clues in the process of tracing psychopathological symptoms back to their original sources. The psychodynamic set is continuously redefined by such statements as: "Try to understand why you have this particular experience," "What do you think it means?", "Does this remind you of something in your past?", "Try to attach these feelings of aggression to the original target!", "Where does your fear come from? Trace it back to its source!", "Why do you think you see me transformed in this particular way; could it have some symbolic meaning?", "Do you have any associations or memories connected with this vision?"

In sessions where the main objective is to have a *religious or mystical experience*, there is a definite tendency to deemphasize or ignore descriptive aspects, psychopathological phenomena, and traumatic personal material. The aesthetic elements are considered important, but the major focus is on the supraindividual, transpersonal, and transcendental. To a great extent, this is also characteristic of *psychedelic therapy*. In sessions aimed at achieving a psychedelic peak experience, there is usually very little verbal interaction between the therapist and the patient. If it occurs, it tends to take the form of simple directive statements rather than a question. Some typical examples would be the following: "Don't be afraid to die; this is not really dying. The moment you can accept death, you will experience rebirth" . . . "It is not really annihilation and disintegration—it is dissolving, dissolving in the universe" . . . "Try to use the music—let the music carry you; be in it and stay with it, try to become the music" . . . "Do not fight it; let it happen, let go, try to surrender completely to the experience" . . . "We can think and talk later; for now just try to experience whatever is happening, be yourself, simply be!"

THE IMPORTANCE OF SETTING

During my clinical work with LSD, I have made numerous observations indicating clearly that the physical and interpersonal elements of the setting can also profoundly influence the nature of the LSD reaction. Most situations in which external stimuli have a strong influence on the subject and modify his or her LSD experience can eventually be understood in terms of the content of underlying dynamic governing systems and their complicated reciprocal interaction with the environmental stimuli. If the setting involves elements that characteristically occur as components of positive COEX systems or positive perinatal matrices, they tend to facilitate the emergence of pleasant or even ecstatic experiences. Since such experiences have a great healing potential and therapeutic value, this association should be systematically utilized in psychedelic sessions and as many elements as possible that are related to positive systems should be incorporated into the treatment setting. The importance of this principle was empirically discovered and is utilized by psychedelic therapists.

The treatment room should be quiet, comfortable, tastefully decorated, and furnished in a homelike fashion. Much attention should be paid to the choice of fabrics, pictures, and flower arrangements. Beautiful natural scenery or certain objects that reflect nature's creativity usually have a very positive influence on the LSD experience. This can be understood from the fact that visions of beautiful landscapes occur in the context of BPM I as part of the intrinsic symbolism of this matrix. Similarly, memories of excursions to or stays in beautiful and nourishing natural settings constitute important layers of some positive COEX systems. There exists sufficient empirical evidence that the ideal location for psychedelic facilities of the future would be in a natural environment such as by mountain lakes, on ocean beaches, on little islands, in deserts, in wooded areas, or in old parks. Clean water in any form seems to have a particularly powerful impact on LSD subjects; a swim, shower, or bath can frequently dispel negative experiences and facilitate an ecstatic reentry. One of the most significant factors of the setting is good stereophonic music of high aesthetic quality.

In contrast, elements that are usually associated with negative COEX systems tend to precipitate unpleasant LSD experiences when they are part of the setting or occur as accidental stimuli. An extreme example of this would be a small, ugly, claustrophobic and tastelessly furnished treatment room, with a window overlooking unpleasant scenery such as industrial areas with factories, junkyards, high smokestacks, and an atmosphere of chemical pollution. Loud human voices, unpleasant music, the noises of machinery, and sounds of sirens, ambulances, fire-engines and jets, exemplify the interferences that can have a very disturbing influence on a psychedelic experience. For the same reason, the setting of the sessions should not remind the subject of a hospital, doctor's office, or laboratory. As a result of COEX and BPM dynamics, medical elements such as white tiles, medicine cabinets, white coats, syringes, vials with pills, and generally sterile surroundings tend to facilitate experiences related to diseases, operations, accidents, pain, agony, and death. For obvious reasons, the traditional atmosphere of psychiatric facilities can, in addition, facilitate experiences related to prisons, concentration camps, or military barracks.

Similar relations exist in regard to the elements of the interpersonal setting of the sessions. In this sense, the optimal arrangement seems to be the presence of a few well-known persons whom the subject trusts; this generally has a very favorable influence on the course of the session. As will be discussed later, a therapeutic dyad that combines the male and the female element in an atmosphere of trust seems to be the ideal solution. Negative consequences can be expected from frequent changes in the interpersonal situation, where many persons unknown to the subject appear and disappear in an unpredictable way. This is the case with LSD experiences in party settings or even for some sessions in university hospitals where medical students occasionally drop by, observe the subject for a short time, make jokes or inappropriate comments, and leave. The same is true for experimental settings in which the subject is sent from one testing situation to another, is wired up and attached to various gadgets, has to undergo strange laboratory examinations, and is asked to urinate into containers and give samples of blood every hour on the hour.

It has already been mentioned that certain physical stimuli from the environment can change the session in a very dramatic way if they happen to be similar to or identical with the elements of a COEX system or a perinatal matrix which is activated at that time. This may be observed in connection with certain accidental sounds; thus barking of a dog, sound of a jet, explosions of fireworks, factory or ambulance sirens, or a particular tune may have a specific biographical meaning that can elicit quite unexpected responses from the subject. Sometimes the general character of the treatment room, specific pieces of furniture and trivial objects, or certain aspects of the view from the window can function as powerful selective triggers of experiences.

The same mechanism can be observed in regard to the people the subject sees during the session. Various persons tend to evoke quite specific and differentiated responses. We have observed numerous situations in which dramatic reactions occurred every time certain nurses entered the treatment room. The manifestations triggered in this seemingly innocent way covered a rather wide range and involved such diverse reactions as violent shaking, nausea with vomiting, intense headache, disappearance of colors from the vision, and hallucinations of a particular color. Conversely, we have also noticed sudden experiences of light, ecstatic feelings, a sense of tranquility, or feelings of emotional nourishment. Occasionally the entire character of the session changed in a specific way with the change from the day shift to the night shift, when a new team of nurses entered the patient's experiential field. With some of the nurses the patients felt safe and protected and had predominantly positive experiences; with others, the same subjects on the same session day became anxious, hostile, or suspicious. These differences were to a great extent individual and were mostly biographically determined. We did not find that some nurses always had with absolute constancy and just because of their personalities, a positive or negative influence on all the subjects.

Subsequent analysis usually provided an explanation of these idiosyncrasies in terms of the personal history of the subject and his or her interaction with a particular nurse. In some instances the clue seemed to be physical resemblance of the nurse to a relevant figure in the subject's past; in others, similarity of behavior patterns, habits, or approach to the subject. Sometimes the patients' reactions could be explained by the fact that they put the nurse into an interpersonal category toward which they had either a particularly good or a conflict-laden attitude, for example, a possible sexual partner, dangerous seductress, erotic rival, competitor, maternal woman, understanding person, domineering type, authority figure, or personified superego.

Successful therapy with LSD requires intimate understanding of the significance of set and setting, so that these factors become powerful tools in the therapeutic process instead of operating in an elemental fashion and presenting unpredictable problems and complications.

NOTES

1. The interested reader will find more information on the multilevel over-determination of LSD experiences in the first volume of this series, Stanislav Grof: *Realms of the Human Unconscious.* (32)
2. It is interesting to compare this psychedelic cartography with the four levels and stages described by R.E.L. Masters and Jean Houston in their pioneering book *The Varieties of Psychedelic Experience.* (65) The authors distinguish (1) The sensory level (eidetic images and other perceptual changes, altered body image, temporal and spatial distortions), (2) The recollective-analytic level (reliving of important emotional experiences from the past, confronting personal problems, conflicts in relationships, life goals), (3) The symbolic level (historical, legendary, mythological, ritualistic, and archetypal images), and (4) The integral level (religious enlightenment, mystical union, illumination, psychological integration). The first two levels of both cartographies show essential correspondence with each other. The Masters-Houston map does not specifically mention the level of the death-rebirth process which plays an important part in my conceptual model. Their symbolic and integral levels are combined in the cartography presented here and appear in the category of transpersonal experiences.
3. In this context, the significance of COEX systems for the dynamics of LSD sessions can only be briefly outlined. The interested reader will find a detailed discussion of this theme with several clinical examples in my first book, *Realms of the Human Unconscious.* (32) Another source of information about this topic is Hanscarl Leuner's book, *Die experimentelle Psychose* (Experimental Psychosis) (57). His concept of *"transphenomenal dynamic systems"* is closely related to, but not identical with, that of COEX systems. C. G. Jung's (43) definition of a *"complex"* represents yet another approach to the same problem area.
4. It is interesting to point in this context to the striking parallels between this observation from psychedelic therapy and Abraham Maslow's (64) concept of metavalues and metamotivations derived from the study of spontaneous peak experiences occurring outside the drug context.
5. The therapeutic philosophy of those early days can be exemplified by the

approach of Dr. van Rhijn (2) from Holland, who described at an LSD conference his vision of the psychiatric facility of the future. It involved a system of small treatment cells in which patients would spend their days alone working through their emotional problems with the help of LSD.

6. The interested reader will find a good example of an LSD session entirely dominated by the transference aspects in my first book, *Realms of the Human Unconscious.* (32) (The case of Charlotte, p. 224).

7. The description of the LSD session of Charlotte, published in my first book, *Realms of the Human Unconscious*, p. 224, has many good examples of the illusive transformations described above. (32)

8. The interested reader will find a condensed case history of Renata in my book *Realms of the Human Unconscious.* p. 52. (32)

PSYCHOLYTIC AND PSYCHEDELIC THERAPIES WITH LSD: TOWARDS AN INTEGRATION OF APPROACHES

3

The Search for an Effective Technique of LSD
    Psychotherapy
Advantages and Drawbacks of the Psycholytic
    Approach
Pros and Cons of Psychedelic Therapy

THE SEARCH FOR AN EFFECTIVE TECHNIQUE OF LSD PSYCHOTHERAPY

It would be very difficult to describe in a systematic and comprehensive way the therapeutic procedure used in my clinical research with LSD psychotherapy in Prague. When this study began, very little was known about LSD and its therapeutic potential. The purpose of the research was to investigate whether LSD might be a useful tool for personality diagnosis and the therapy of emotional disorders. Since the project was a pilot study designed to collect new observations, in its initial phases it combined therapeutic efforts based on conventional understanding of the psychotherapeutic process with first orientations in an entirely new world of clinical phenomena. As a result, the treatment technique was being developed and constantly modified as the research proceeded. The changes of therapeutic approach reflected my increasing clinical experience, deeper understanding of the effects of LSD, and immediate inspirations from various accidental observations. In the following text I will briefly outline the major trends and stages of development of the new therapeutic technique.

When I started conducting therapeutic LSD sessions with psychiatric patients, as an enthusiastic and convinced psychoanalyst I automatically chose the classical Freudian arrangement. I had no doubts about the conceptual framework of psychoanalysis and the validity of its therapeutic technique. My intention was to explore the possibility of intensifying and accelerating the psychoanalytic process, which I found intellectually fascinating in theory but painfully ineffective in practice. I hoped that the use of LSD as an adjunct to the therapy would yield more impressive results than classical analysis, which requires years of intensive work and offers relatively meager returns on an enormous investment of time and energy. However, in the course of my LSD research I was led by everyday clinical observations to drastic departures not only from the Freudian therapeutic technique, but also from its conceptual framework and basic philosophy.

In the first therapeutic LSD sessions I conducted I asked the patients to lie on a couch, and I sat in an armchair situated near the head of the couch so that they could not easily see me. I expected to get almost continuous accounts of their LSD experiences and occasionally offer interpretations. It soon became obvious that this arrangement was not appropriate for LSD psychotherapy and I was not able to maintain it for more than a few sessions. The nature of the experience and of the process seemed to be incompatible with the Freudian technique and required a more human approach, genuine support, and personal involvement. I first moved my chair to the side of the couch, and later kept leaving it more and more frequently to sit on the side of the couch, entering into direct physical contact with the patient. This ranged from simple support such as hand-holding, reassuring touches or cradling to deep massage, bioenergetic-type maneuvers, or psychodramatic enactment of struggle. Because of my training as an analyst, the shift from a detached attitude to direct participation in the process occurred gradually and not without hesitation and conflict. It appeared quite appropriate to offer this degree of support to subjects who were suffering through extraordinary emotional ordeals and frequently showed signs of quite authentic regression to early periods of infancy. However, the description of this process has to be considered in its historical context; it might appear almost comical in the age of growth centers, encounter groups, sensitivity training, neo-Reichian therapies, and nude marathons. Yet I made the first moves to violate the Freudian taboo of touch while attending seminars in which my teachers seriously discussed whether shaking hands with patients presented dangers to the transference-countertransference process. Another major modification of the treatment technique was a shift from extensive verbal interaction and occasional eye contact to internalized sessions with minimal exchange of words, and use of eyeshades, headphones, and stereophonic music.

Even more drastic than the modifications of the therapeutic technique were the changes in the conceptual framework and basic paradigms underlying psychotherapy. Everyday observations from psychedelic sessions put many commonly held scientific assumptions to serious test, and showed an urgent need for revision on such fundamental issues as the cartography and dynamics of the unconscious, the nature of memory, the origin of consciousness, the definition of mental health and illness, the therapeutic goals and hierarchy of values, the philosophy and strategy of psychotherapy, and even the nature of reality and of human beings. We will discuss here only those observations that are of direct relevance for psychotherapy. The ontological and cosmological insights from psychedelic research and their relationship to the revolutionary concepts of modern physics will be described in a future volume.

At present, many professionals recognize the need to acknowledge the wisdom of ancient and Oriental spiritual disciplines, and assimilate it into psychology and psychiatry. Transpersonal psychology is becoming increasingly popular, and obtaining wide recognition. It is hard to expect a professional living in the late seventies to appreciate the difficulties that we faced in the late fifties and early sixties, exploring LSD psychotherapy equipped with the conceptual framework and world-view of Freudian psychoanalysis. Almost every day, we were confronted in psychedelic sessions with new and puzzling phenomena such as sequences of death and rebirth; intrauterine, ancestral, racial, and phylogenetic memories; animal and plant consciousness; or past-incarnation experiences. The therapeutic changes associated with some of these unusual experiences were often much more dramatic than those achieved in the context of biographically oriented work. A typical early LSD researcher, encountering some of these extraordinary episodes, risked having his or her own rationality severely tested, and quickly learned to censor reports of them to avoid having sanity questioned by others. At present, twenty years later, we are much more open to the existence of these phenomena, but still lack a comprehensive conceptual framework to account for them.

Descriptions of the exciting adventures in early clinical research that led to the development of the present therapeutic technique might be of historical interest, but are of little practical value. Instead of guiding the reader through a complicated sequence of trials and errors I will focus on the final product of this process—a therapeutic technique that has emerged from years of clinical experimentation and crystallized into a more or less standard procedure. In my experience, this approach minimizes the risks and maximizes the benefits of the psychedelic process. It makes LSD-assisted psychotherapy a powerful, effective and relatively safe method of treatment and personality change.

At this point, it seems appropriate to briefly discuss the major existing techniques for the therapeutic use of LSD, and indicate their advantages and drawbacks. This discussion should provide a basis for understanding the rationale of the treatment procedure which will be described later in detail. In an earlier section of this book, I described the techniques and underlying concepts of what I consider to be the four viable approaches to LSD psychotherapy, the psycholytic, psychedelic, anaclitic, and hypnodelic methods. The use of LSD in a hypnodelic context seems to be the least useful of these. It is a specialized procedure, discussion of which would require a considerable detour into the theory and practice of hypnosis. It has been used by only a few researchers in the past and will probably not be widely used in the future. Similarly, anaclitic therapy in its extreme form—the fusion technique—is practiced only exceptionally, although a mitigated version has been assimilated by many LSD therapists. For practical purposes we can focus our discussion on the two most important approaches, psycholytic therapy and psychedelic therapy, with occasional reference to specificities introduced by anaclitic treatment.

At first sight, psycholytic and psychedelic therapies seemed to differ both in theory and in practice to such an extent that most LSD therapists found them irreconcilable. They felt the gap between them and between their underlying philosophies to be so fundamental that they could not conceive of bridging it; as a result, they committed themselves clearly to one or the other modality. Only a few researchers were able to feel comfortable with both approaches and use them alternately. This dichotomy is quite surprising in view of the fact that both approaches use the same chemical compound, deal with emotionally disturbed human beings, and have the same goal—therapeutic help for the patients. Although extrapharmacological factors, such as the personality of the therapist or the set and setting, play a very important role in the LSD experience, it seems reasonable to assume that psycholytic and psychedelic therapists deal with phenomena that occur on the same continuum and are closely related, if not identical. The differences seem to lie, not in the nature of the experiences themselves, but in the quantitative incidence of certain elements in the sessions, and the therapists' emphasis on certain phenomena and tendency to discourage others.

It is well known that psycholytic therapists frequently see transpersonal phenomena in their clinical practice. However, they tend to discard them, either as an escape from important traumatic childhood material, or as undesirable "psychotic" enclaves in the LSD procedure.[1] Within the psycholytic framework, transpersonal phenomena are not acknowledged and their therapeutic value is not recognized. Patients are thus implicitly or explicitly discouraged from entering transcendental states; moreover, the low and medium dosages used in psycholytic therapy are generally less conducive to perinatal and transpersonal experiences than the high dosages employed by psychedelic therapists.

The frequent occurrence of transpersonal states in psycholytic treatment has its counterpart in the fact that many patients in psychedelic therapy relive traumatic childhood memories and are confronted with other material of a clearly biographical nature. Many psychedelic therapists, with their one-sided emphasis on transcendence and on mystical and religious experiences, have very little appreciation of or even tolerance for psychodynamic issues. The implicit or explicit message in psychedelic therapy usually is that a session spent in this way is inferior to one that involves transpersonal experiences. Under these circumstances patients who have predominantly biographical sessions in the course of psychedelic therapy tend to develop a feeling of personal failure. Not infrequently, the sense of "a lost opportunity" is shared by the average psychedelic therapist, no matter how important the biographical material uncovered and worked through in such a session.

As mentioned earlier, my own development was such that I had first-hand experiences of psycholytic, psychedelic, and anaclitic therapies. Being an orthodox psychoanalyst, I started my LSD work in Prague following the principles of psycholytic therapy. When numerous observations in my everyday clinical practice made this orientation untenable, I moved far beyond the narrow psychoanalytic framework to full recognition of the practical and theoretical significance of the death-rebirth process and transpersonal phenomena. During my stay in London in 1964, I participated in the work of Joyce Martin and Pauline McCririck, and acquired intimate insights into the nature of anaclitic therapy as both experient and observer. Since my arrival in the United States in March 1967, I have practiced psychedelic therapy for a number of years in the Maryland Psychiatric Research Center in Baltimore, working with alcoholics, heroin addicts, neurotics, mental health professionals, and individuals dying of cancer.

In addition, I have met most of the therapists practicing in the psycholytic and psychedelic orientations during various LSD conferences and during my visits to therapeutic facilities in Europe, the United States and Canada. The discussions during these encounters, study of LSD literature, and my own clinical experiences have gradually convinced me that the differences between these two treatment techniques are not as irreconcileable as is usually assumed. I came to the conclusion that it is possible to reduce the phenomena involved in both approaches to certain common denominators and to formulate a comprehensive general theory of LSD psychotherapy. The practical implication of this new understanding of the mechanisms operating in LSD sessions is the development of an integrated treatment procedure combining the advantages of psycholytic and psychedelic therapies, and minimizing their shortcomings.

ADVANTAGES AND DRAWBACKS OF THE PSYCHOLYTIC APPROACH

An unquestionable advantage of psycholytic therapy is its heuristic value. The slowly progressing unfolding of various levels of the unconscious has been compared by some patients to chemoexcavation, the careful archaeological work that sequentially explores layer after layer and studies their mutual interrelation. Other subjects refer to this process as "peeling the onion" of the unconscious mind. THe richness of the material obtained in repeated sessions using medium dosages of LSD provides unrivalled insights not only into the nature of the LSD reaction, but also into the dynamics of emotional disorders and the functioning of the human mind in general.

This aspect can be important not only for the therapist, but also for many scientifically, artistically, or philosophically oriented subjects. In addition to therapeutic benefit, these individuals receive unique lessons about human nature, art, philosophy, history, and the natural sciences. Psycholytic therapy usually takes much longer than psychedelic therapy to achieve comparable results; however, it gives an individual a much better knowledge of the territories of the mind and the mechanisms through which the change was achieved, and it may be the preferred treatment for subjects with less serious and urgent problems who have deep intellectual interest in the nature of the process. As an open-ended situation, psycholytic therapy gives a better opportunity for the patient to work through and resolve important problems of his or her life than the hit-or-miss approach of psychedelic therapy, which is limited to just one or a few high-dose LSD sessions.

At the present stage of development, psycholytic therapy is more understandable and acceptable in conventional professional circles and to the "scientifically-minded," since it leans in theory and practice on widely accepted psychotherapeutic concepts. This seems to be true despite the fact that many observations from psychedelic research clearly and unequivocally demonstrate the limitations of the existing paradigms and the need for their revision and reformulation.[2] However, the psycholytic emphasis makes it possible to ignore or disqualify most of these challenging discoveries.

An obvious disadvantage of psycholytic therapy is that it is much more time-consuming. Although according to one of its foremost representatives, Hanscarl Leuner, psycholytic therapy can shorten the psychotherapeutic process to take approximately one-third of the time required by psychoanalysis, it still requires an enormous amount of the therapist's time. The first statement is based on clinical impressions; no comparative study of psycholytic and psychedelic therapies has ever been conducted. Any attempt to compare the efficacy of these two approaches on the basis of the existing literature runs into considerable difficulty. In addition to the general problems related to the evaluation of psychotherapeutic results, which have been discussed in the literature over the last two decades, one encounters certain complications specific to LSD therapy.

Whereas psychedelic therapy has been used in the past primarily with alcoholics, drug addicts and terminal cancer patients, psycholytic treatment has focused on other categories of emotional disorders, such as psychoneuroses, character disorders, and psychosomatic diseases. It has been pointed out that the result of psycholytic therapy is more solid and permanent, because the underlying material gets thoroughly worked through, than the dynamic shift or transmodulation that occurs in psychedelic treatment. If the results of the two methods could somehow be compared, the time aspect would be very much in favor of psychedelic therapy. My impression is that the use of higher dosages and internalization of the process, as practiced by psychedelic therapists, deepens the effect of LSD and is much more productive therapeutically. However, I would still like to see an open-ended situation, which would allow for a series of such experiences if necessary, instead of the all-or-nothing philosophy of the psychedelic approach. As mentioned above, a systematic and well-controlled comparative study, though highly desirable, does not exist at present.

For those who want to take a conservative stance, the number of exposures to LSD and the overall amount of the drug used in psycholytic therapy can represent an important issue. Although none of the suspicions about the biological dangers of LSD have been substantiated, it should still be considered an experimental substance whose long-term physiological effects have yet to be fully determined.

Another aspect of psycholytic therapy that should be discussed is the use of low and medium dosages of LSD as compared to the high or very high dosages used in psychedelic treatment. Although this might be contrary to popular belief, high-dose sessions are generally much safer. There is no doubt that high-dose sessions present more real or potential problems at the time of the actual pharmacological effect of the drug. Under the circumstances of unsupervised use, the collapse of psychological defenses, the massive emergence of deep unconscious material, the loss of effective control and the resultant lack of reality testing occurring in high-dose experiences present grave potential dangers. An experienced therapeutic team, however, can usually handle these quite easily. In the long run, the very aspects of high-dose exposures that make them a greater risk at the time of the drug action turn out to be their advantages. Lessened ability to fight the effect of the drug and more complete surrender are conducive to better resolution and integration of the experience. Low and medium dosages activate latent unconscious material very effectively and bring it closer to the surface, yet they also allow an unwilling subject to avoid having to face it fully and deal with it effectively. Sessions of this kind can result in feelings of excessive fatigue after the experience, a sense of incompletion, various unpleasant emotional and psychosomatic aftereffects, and prolonged reaction or a precarious emotional balance conducive to later recurrences ("flashbacks"). In the next chapter we will discuss various principles and techniques of conducting psychedelic sessions that lead to better resolution and reduce the incidence of prolonged reactions and flashbacks.

Psycholytic therapy involves series of medium-dose LSD sessions, (sixteen to eighty or more, depending on the nature of the clinical problem) and thus presents numerous opportunities for temporary activation and insufficient completion of unconscious gestalts. In the course of psycholytic therapy, the patient's clinical condition undergoes dramatic changes in both directions, and sometimes the therapist has to face a serious transitional worsening of the symptoms or even decompensation, when the patient is approaching an area of deep and important conflicts. This intensification of symptoms sometimes occurs after earlier therapy had brought about a considerable improvement, and the therapist continues the sessions with an intent to "insure the result and prevent a relapse." Although psychedelic therapy does not eliminate the possibility of activation followed by an incomplete integration of unconscious material, it certainly considerably decreases the probability of such an occurrence.

A potentially negative aspect of psycholytic therapy is the enormous intensification of transference that almost inevitably develops in its course. This presents unique therapeutic opportunities, and also considerable dangers and difficulties. The issue of transference and its analysis is an important theoretical and practical problem in LSD psychotherapy and in psychotherapy in general. There is no doubt that the quality of the therapeutic relationship is one of the most important factors determining the course and outcome of LSD sessions. However, it is much less certain that the development of transference and its analysis is essential for therapeutic progress. This is something which is taken for granted in classical psychoanalysis and in psychoanalytically oriented psychotherapy, but that does not exclude the possibility that there exist other effective mechanisms of therapeutic change. Observations from LSD psychotherapy suggest very strongly that the intensity of transference is directly proportional to the resistance to facing the original traumatic material. In a certain sense, therefore, an LSD therapist who puts great emphasis on identification and analysis of transference phenomena, instead of acknowledging them and directing the patient's attention beyond them, is cooperating with the defense mechanisms. It happens quite regularly in the course of LSD psychotherapy that various transference problems clear up automatically after the subject has been able to face and work through underlying unconscious material of a psychodynamic, perinatal or transpersonal nature.

A definite disadvantage of psycholytic therapy is its theoretical dependence on conventional dynamic psychotherapy. For this reason, it does not offer an adequate framework for many experiences that occur in the LSD sessions. Some of them have extraordinary therapeutic potential, such as the death–rebirth process, past-incarnation memories, various archetypal phenomena and, especially, the experiences of cosmic unity. The latter are closely related to, although not identical with, the oceanic feelings experienced by the infant at the breast and in the womb. They seem to have as fundamental a significance for the success of LSD therapy as the natural experiences of symbiotic unity with the mother have for the development of an emotionally healthy and stable personality. A tendency to discard and discourage perinatal and transpersonal phenomena, or to interpret them in terms of more superficial levels, limits the therapeutic potential of LSD psychotherapy and frequently confuses the patient.

PROS AND CONS OF PSYCHEDELIC THERAPY

Some of the advantages of psychedelic therapy are practical, others are of a theoretical nature. In general, the therapeutic changes achieved in a single psychedelic session are much more dramatic and profound than those observed as a result of a single psycholytic session. Certain aspects of the psychedelic treatment technique represent a great acceleration and deepening of the therapeutic process, as well as a definite increase in its efficacy and safety. This approach seems to have fully appreciated the importance of positive experiences, which are usually underestimated in psycholytic therapy; the latter shares with psychoanalysis a one-sided emphasis on psychopathology and traumatic material. Explicit focus on the positive potential in human beings is an important therapeutic factor; so is the emphasis on positive structuring of the set and setting for psychedelic sessions. External circumstances have a profound effect on the termination period of the session and thus on the final outcome of the psychedelic experience. The discovery of the critical importance of this phase represents a major contribution of psychedelic therapists to the LSD procedure.

There seem to be several reasons for the greater efficacy and safety of psychedelic therapy. High dosages and internalization of the process lead to greater depth, intensity, and spontaneous flow of the experience; this results in more emotional turmoil, but also in a better chance for a positive breakthrough. A single psychedelic session can achieve dramatic therapeutic results by penetrating or bypassing the psychodynamic levels and utilizing powerful mechanisms of transformation on the perinatal and transpersonal levels. This is facilitated by full theoretical acknowledgement and validation of transpersonal realities. Careful positive structuring of the reentry is another important factor of therapeutic change.

As a result of a favorable combination of the above factors, a good therapeutic outcome can be obtained even if the patient does not explicitly confront certain areas of major difficulty and conflict on the psychodynamic level; in systematic psycholytic treatment these would inevitably have to be faced. Under these circumstances, there is certainly less risk of a worsened clinical condition, even with severely emotionally disturbed patients, than after individual psycholytic sessions.

If we consider the other important advantages of psychedelic therapy, such as reduced time investment, less intense exposure to the drug, and fewer transference problems, it would seem that the psychedelic procedure is clearly superior to the psycholytic approach. It is therefore important to discuss some of the theoretical and practical disadvantages of psychedelic therapy, which should be taken into consideration in the formulation of an integrated therapeutic approach. An important question that would have to be clarified is the nature of the changes observed in psychedelic therapy. The major objection raised against these sudden clinical improvements and personality transformations is that they represent only temporary shifts rather than deep changes of dynamic structures. From this point of view psycholytic therapy, dealing slowly and patiently with various levels of unconscious conflicts, would provide more lasting results. There are no comparative studies that would answer the fundamental question whether deep and lasting therapeutic changes are possible without working through early childhood material, reenacting the original traumatic relationships in the transference situation, and subjecting these anachronistic replicas to transference analysis. Although observations from LSD research strongly suggest that there exist important alternatives, these will have to remain on the level of clinical impressions until they are systematically studied and validated.

A much more serious problem that psychedelic therapy—as presently practiced—has to face is the fact that in spite of the efforts at positive structuring of the LSD sessions, it is not possible to guarantee that all the subjects will have deep transformative experiences. In the Spring Grove program, where the therapeutic potential of psychedelic therapy utilizing just one session was systematically explored in various categories of subjects, the incidence of "psychedelic peak experiences" ranged between 25 and 78 per cent, depending on the population studied. It was the lowest in neurotic patients and highest for narcotic drug addicts, with mental health professionals, individuals dying of cancer, and alcoholics falling in between.

The psychedelic peak experience is certainly an important factor mediating deep personality transformation; however, its occurrence is not a *conditio sine qua non* of successful therapy. Different degrees of improvement can be observed in many patients who have not reached the transcendental level of consciousness in their psychedelic sessions. Unfortunately, the candidates for a productive and successful psychedelic session cannot be selected in advance with a reasonable degree of certainty by any known criteria. Since the important variables determining the outcome of the session are insufficiently understood, the psychedelic approach, with its extreme "all-or-none" philosophy, still remains very much a "hit-or-miss" procedure.

The theoretical drawbacks of psychedelic therapy are probably more important than its practical shortcomings. This approach may produce very dramatic therapeutic changes with minimal understanding of the underlying mechanisms. The material from psychedelic sessions can offer new insights into some phenomena of a very general nature, such as the dynamics of positive and negative memory systems, the existence of new mechanisms of personality transformation, dimensions of human experience and the human mind, states of consciousness associated with dying, or the mystical nature of the universe. It contributes relatively little to our knowledge of the effects of LSD, cartography of the human mind, psychodynamics of mental illness, or mechanisms of therapeutic change.

This aspect of psychedelic therapy will be seen as a great disadvantage by those who judge the scientific returns of this procedure by Western standards. It will be highly rewarding for those who seek an alternative to linear, rational and logical approaches to knowledge. The insights emerging from high-dose psychedelic sessions are of a global, intuitive and holographic nature. The transcendental "aha!" experience of this kind cannot be dissected easily by the Western analytical mind, nor can it be exploited in a pragmatic sense. It is an illuminating insight into the very essence of existence. The experient does not gain rational understanding of the cosmic process, but reaches instant comprehension by losing his or her separate identity and literally *becoming* the process.

This intuitive insight into the universal scheme of things is quite similar to the process described in the Upanishads as "Knowing That, the knowledge of which gives the knowledge of everything." This does not involve a total and all-encompassing intellectual comprehension of the universe, in the sense of causal connections and pragmatic know-how concerning objects and events in the phenomenal world, but a transcendence of phenomena, space, time, and causality.

It is necessary to add that this is frequently accompanied by the conviction that some of the questions that were previously considered important or even urgent are irrelevant in the context of the new system of reference. Instead of finding answers to specific questions, one reaches a state in which those questions do not exist or are not relevant, or where there is no need to ask them; both finding the answers and transcending them represent solutions to the problem, although on different levels and of differing kinds.

The fact that certain questions appear irrelevant to LSD subjects in the context of mystical consciousness will not relieve the frustration of a scientifically-minded researcher trying to draw some general conclusions from the observations of psychedelic therapy. The enormous interindividual variability precludes any valid generalizations based on the material from single sessions with many different subjects. The definite spiritual emphasis of psychedelic therapy, its recognition of mystical states of consciousness, and the inclusion of what might appear to a superficial observer as elements of religious indoctrination, will certainly make this approach less appealing to skeptical and critical professional audiences. This will continue to be true until an adequate paradigm is developed that will make it possible to assimilate all the extraordinary new phenomena into the body of existing psychiatric knowledge and general scientific theory.

NOTES

1. Arthur Janov has a similar approach to the spiritual experiences occurring in some patients during primal therapy. His original emphasis was exclusively on early childhood material. Later, he was forced by clinical observations to incorporate the birth trauma, whose significance he originally denied, into the theory of primal therapy. At present, he still lacks genuine recognition of the value of transpersonal experiences, and considers them a "cop-out from primal pain." The most serious dilemma of primal therapy is the fact that it uses a tool that has the power to elicit experiences for which the limited primal theory does not have an adequate conceptual framework.
2. Transpersonal psychology and the mystical world-view are frequently, and erroneously, referred to as unscientific. This reflects the fact that psychology and psychiatry (as well as the general public) still adhere to the old model of the world, based on the Newtonian image of the universe and the Cartesian dichotomy between mind and matter. In actuality, the mystical world-view is surprisingly compatible with revolutionary discoveries in modern science, such as relativity theory and quantum physics. Both modern physics and the mystical world-view violate common sense and are inconsistent with what can be called "the pedestrian consciousness and world-view," which has not caught up with either. The interested reader will find an excellent discussion of the convergence of modern physics and mysticism in Fritjof Capra's book *The Tao of Physics*. (18)

PRINCIPLES OF
LSD PSYCHOTHERAPY   *4*

The Preparation Period
Psychedelic Sessions
Integration of the Drug Experiences

Having discussed the most general problems related to LSD psychotherapy, I will describe the basic principles of an LSD procedure which, according to my past clinical experience, can bring the best therapeutic results in the shortest possible time and with the least risk of complications. The procedure is also in full agreement with clinical common sense and with present theoretical understanding of the mechanisms of the LSD reaction.

An ideal course of LSD psychotherapy involves an open-ended situation in which the number of sessions is not limited *a priori*. In general, the treatment process consists of three separate but mutually interrelated phases. The first of these is the *preparation period*: it involves a series of drug-free interactions during which the subject is prepared for the drug experience. For obvious reasons, the nature of the preparatory phase will be quite different for the first psychedelic session; when the sessions are repeated, certain generalities will be omitted and in-depth attention will be focused on certain specific problems suggested by earlier sessions. The second phase is the *drug session* itself; during the session day the patient spends many hours in a special treatment suite assisted, ideally, by a male-female therapeutic dyad. The third phase involves several *non-drug interviews in the post-session period*; the purpose of these is to help the subject integrate the content of the psychedelic experiences into his or her everyday life.

THE PREPARATION PERIOD

A sufficiently long period of drug-free interaction between the subject and the sitters should precede the first LSD session. The amount of time that is necessary to prepare a person adequately for a psychedelic session depends on the nature of the problems involved and on the circumstances; normally the range is somewhere between five and twenty hours. It is understandable that it takes much less time to work with an emotionally relatively stable subject who volunteers for the LSD session for the purpose of professional training, personal growth, or enhancement of creativity, than to prepare a severely disturbed patient with serious neurotic, psychosomatic or borderline psychotic symptoms.

Since every situation is different and every client presents quite specific problems, no concrete and detailed guidelines can be offered for the nature, content and duration of the preparation period. However, it is possible to give some general recommendations and outline certain basic principles and strategies for preparatory work.

If the session is run for therapeutic purposes the therapist should discuss in considerable detail the subject's present life situation, emotional, interpersonal and professional adjustment, and the dynamics of various psychopathological symptoms. It is also important to get sufficiently acquainted with the candidate's biographical data from early childhood to recent past. This will be very useful for a deeper understanding of various episodes of a psychodynamic nature that might occur in the LSD sessions. A therapist who is familiar with the client's developmental history will be able to offer much effective support and guidance. Knowledge of the subject's family dynamics, characteristic interpersonal patterns, and idiosyncratic emotional reactions in different periods of his or her life makes it much easier to recognize specific biographically determined distortions in the therapeutic relationship and deal with them effectively. A particularly important part of the preparatory work is to recognize certain recurrent themes, repetitive patterns, vicious circles, and self-perpetuating elements in the client's interpersonal interaction, since these are likely to be reenacted in the transference relationship.

During the exploration of the subject's life history, the therapist should share any meaningful insights and observations that he has concerning the emerging material. One important task is to develop an effective framework for organizing the subject's understanding of the relationship between his or her traumatic past and the existing problems and difficulties. Another area that deserves special attention is the connection between psychopathological symptoms and interpersonal maladjustment. It is very important to depart at this point from the classical psychoanalytic approach, and conduct the interviews in the spirit of the basic philosophy underlying psychedelic therapy. The psychoanalytic approach is primarily concerned with psychopathology, and thus focuses selectively on the negative aspects of the patient's personality. The Freudian image of man is instinctivistic and essentially pessimistic. Psychoanalysis sees human behavior as motivated by primitive impulses of a sexual and aggressive nature, and interprets any higher values as reaction formation or compromise with the repressive forces of society. Unhappiness is the normal human condition; the purpose of psychotherapy is to change the excessive suffering of the neurotic into normal human suffering. The psychoanalyst is basically non-directive; he or she avoids value judgments and any active guidance of the patient. It is very rare that a psychoanalyst trained in the classical tradition gives a clear answer to a specific question.

In the preparation for an LSD session, we also discuss symptoms and life problems. However, the therapist tries to relate to whatever is available of the healthy core of the patient's personality. The basic message is that there is a deep positive potential in every human being that is hidden behind the symptoms, however overwhelming and crippling they might seem. The traumatic past is seen as a complex of factors and situations that has alienated the patient from his real self.

The image of human nature on which this approach is based is closer to Hindu philosophy than to Freudian psychoanalysis. Behind the barrier of negative instinctual forces associated with early biographical traumas and the hellish realms of the perinatal matrices there exist vast transpersonal realms of the superconscious mind, and a system of positive universal values not dissimilar to Abraham Maslow's metavalues. In the psychedelic model the human mind is not limited to biographically determined elements of the Freudian unconscious; it has no boundaries or limits and its dimensions are commensurate with those of the entire universe. From this point of view, it is more correct to see human nature as divine than as bestial. Although the specificities of this philosophy are not communicated to the patient as part of the preparation for the sessions, this worldview characterizes the approach of a psychedelic therapist.

In working with LSD patients, whether during the preparation or later on, it is not necessary to avoid all value judgments and direct advice. The therapist should not try to give the patient specific guidance on concrete life situations, such as whether or not to get married, file for a divorce, have children, get an abortion, and leave or change a job. Here the psychoanalytic principles are certainly justified. The situations involved are usually too complex and contain many unpredictable factors; the therapist cannot evaluate them objectively enough to suggest the optimal course from the point of view of the client's needs. Under these circumstances, it is very likely that the advice would reflect the therapist's unconscious fears, wishes and needs, instead of representing an "objective professional judgment." However, a directive approach seems to be indicated and useful in regard to a general philosophy of existence and life strategy. Here the LSD therapist can base his or her guidance on a set of values that seems to be intrinsic and universal. These values tend to emerge independently and quite consistently during successful psychedelic therapy with various subjects and appear to be associated with healthy functioning.

One of the basic messages of this existential strategy is the emphasis on life in the here-and-now—the present moment, this hour, today—as compared to rumination of memories from several past decades and indulgence in fantasies or plans for many years to come. At the same time, the awareness of the client is directed from grandiose schemes toward simple and ordinary situations in everyday life, not only as a new and untapped source of potential gratification but as the *only* real basis of satisfaction in life. The client is not necessarily discouraged from pursuing complicated and involved long-term projects, but is led to an insight that external achievements alone will not bring the expected satisfaction and peace of mind. A deep confrontation with death, which is an important part of the psychedelic process, will inevitably make people realize that a good self-image and positive feelings about oneself, the ability to enjoy the life process, and a deep sense of meaning with regard to one's existence are not contingent on complicated external conditions. They represent a primary organismic state and a way of being in the world that is basically independent of the material conditions of life, with the exception of some drastic extremes.

If this fundamental affirmation of existence is present, then even the commonest life conditions can be experienced as worthwhile. In a sense even the simple fact of participating in consciousness and in the cosmic process, in whatever way, appears to be very precious. Ordinary activities such as everyday work, physical exercise, eating, going for a walk, watching a sunset, or making love can become a joyful expression and celebration of life. When this basic appreciation of the fact of existence is missing then external success and achievement of any kind and any scope will not provide it. Under these circumstances, frantic pursuit of what appear to be self- and life-validating goals will trap the individual into a net of vicious circles without bringing the expected satisfaction. The positive life feelings, if absent, have to be sought inside, through a process of deep self-exploration and inner transformation, not by manipulation of external circumstances alone. The philosophy underlying psychedelic therapy thus definitely emphasizes orientation on the process, rather than on the outcome or goal. How and with what attitude one performs certain activities becomes very important in this context, not only what the specific choices are and what the final result of one's effort will be.

During the preparation for the session, the above system of values can be explicitly and implicitly communicated to the client whenever there is a good opportunity. It seems appropriate to actively discourage excessive dwelling on the past for sentimental reasons or nostalgia, questioning of old decisions and choices, examination of actions associated with guilt, or retrospective rumination on failures. In a similar way, clients can be warned that they might not achieve the expected happiness by pursuing elaborate plans for the future involving money, power, status, or fame. This is particularly important if the schemes for the future are irrational, unrealistic, and exaggerated, or if the client is obviously wasting time in futile daydreaming and building "castles in the air."

It seems fully justified to emphasize the deep wisdom of the emotional and philosophical (though not necessarily pragmatic) orientation towards the present moment, and of a reliance on ordinary situations for basic life-satisfaction. We can also point to the futility and self-defeating nature of various attitudes and behaviors reflecting desperate needs to prove oneself, to please or convince one's parents, peers or unidentified "others," or to fight irrational authority. Since the above value system and life strategy was derived from the psychedelic process, there is a good possibility that the drug sessions will provide a powerful experiential validation of various issues conveyed during the preparation in a more or less intellectual way.

An important part of the initial work focuses on philosophical and religious issues. Although it has occasionally been done by psychedelic therapists, I would not recommend the use of a specific religious system as part of the framework for the sessions, whether it is Christianity, Judaism, Hinduism, or Tibetan Buddhism. This can frequently interfere with a symbolic framework that is emerging spontaneously from the subject's collective unconscious and is the most appropriate form for that person's spiritual experience. In addition, explicit introduction of the elements of a specific religion or church affiliation can be experienced as inappropriate and irritating not only by atheists and skeptics or followers of other creeds, but also by those who have been brought up in that same tradition and have developed serious conflicts about it. However, it seems useful to increase the client's awareness of the aesthetic aspects of the world, his or her interest in basic philosophical questions of life, and recognition of the spiritual dimension of existence in a non-specific way.

Clarification is frequently required in regard to the subject's understanding of the term "religion," the role of spirituality in human life, the relationship between religion and science, and conflicts between various creeds. For those clients who *a priori* have strong negative feelings about the religious aspects of psychedelic therapy, it is helpful to emphasize that spiritual experiences in LSD sessions usually do not take the form outlined by orthodox religions. More frequently, they are close to what Albert Einstein described as cosmic religion. This form of spirituality does not involve a personified godhead, a pantheon of intermediary saints, regular church attendance, and formalized divine service. The focus is on the failure of the rational approach to grasp the many mysteries of nature and on the awe and wonder experienced in confrontation with the creative forces of the universe.

In this context, spiritual feelings are associated with such issues as the enigma of time and space; the origin of matter, life, and consciousness; the dimensions of the universe and of existence; the meaning of human life; and the ultimate purpose underlying the process of creation of the phenomenal world. Spiritual experiences of this kind can occur in individuals of high intellectual caliber and rigorous scientific training, in fact, they are fully compatible with observations accumulated by various branches of modern research. An important illustration of this point, for those who emphasize the scientific world-view, is the recent convergence of quantum-relativistic physics and various mystical traditions.

In some instances, perinatal and transpersonal experiences in psychedelic sessions can occur in specific symbolic forms typical of certain cultures and historical periods. Without special training and sophistication in archaeology or mythology, knowledge of the cultural heritage involved, or even adequate general intellectual background, an individual may experience mythological and symbolic sequences from ancient Egypt or Greece, Africa, India, Tibet, China, Japan, Australia, or Pre-Columbian countries. However, images of specific personified deities from these cultures are not usually felt to be the supreme and ultimate force in the universe. Like the endless variety of beings and objects constituting the phenomenal world, such deities appear to be manifestations of a creative principle that is transcendent and beyond form. If the psychedelic experience occurs in the context of one of the traditional sacred frameworks, it is usually congruent with the teachings of the mystical branches of that particular religion rather than with its orthodox mainstream form. It is thus closer to Christian mysticism than traditional Christianity, to the Kabbalah or Hassidism rather than Old Testament Judaism, or to Sufism rather than the Moslem faith.

The psychedelic experience frequently involves elements totally alien to an individual's own religious tradition. Thus a Buddhist can experience identification with the crucified Christ and emerge from the session with a new understanding of Christianity; a Christian can have experiential sequences in which he or she discovers and appreciates Sufism; a Moslem may get insight into the law of karma and cycles of reincarnation; and a Rabbi may experience a conversion toward Zen Buddhism. In whichever way the subject experiences and conceptualizes the transcendental realities, he or she will usually accept that form as appropriate and fully compatible with his or her personality.

A very important element of the preparation is the development of a trust relationship between the guide and the client. The ability of the subject to let go of psychological defenses and surrender to the experience, which is crucial for successful outcome of the session, is directly proportional to the degree of trust in the sitters. Trust is thus the single most important prerequisite of safe and effective

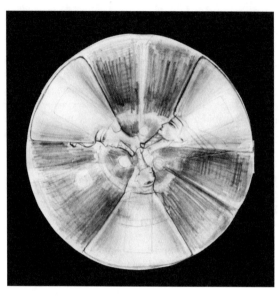

Through illusory transformation, the rotating plastic wheel of a tape recorder becomes an ancient Egyptian ornamental motif showing the heads of three hierophants.

psychedelic therapy. In the most general sense it is of great relevance to the course of any LSD session; however, there are certain specific situations in which the element of basic trust plays a particularly crucial role. Any work on the roots of one's distrust of other people and the world at large is critically dependent on the quality of the relationship between the experient and the guides. Similarly, the ability to face the experience of ego death in all its complexity and depth usually requires good external grounding in a dependable therapeutic situation. In view of the importance of the relationship between the guides and the client, the preparation for a session should not be just a one-sided flow of information but should give the subject a chance to get to know the future sitters. Ideally, instead of being a conventional exchange of clichés, the preparation period and the therapeutic process should represent a genuine human encounter.

When the therapists feel that the preparation has accomplished the objectives described above and the client is psychologically ready for the first drug experience, they schedule one last meeting before the session. This focuses exclusively on various technical aspects of the procedure and usually takes place on the day immediately preceding the drug session. The discussion concerns the nature of the psychedelic experience, the range of unusual states of consciousness that can be induced by LSD, and the most useful ways of dealing with the experience. At this point, unless it happened earlier in the process, the therapists should encourage the client to voice all the fears and doubts that he or she might have about the drug and the procedure. This is the last opportunity to answer general or specific questions and to clarify all the misconceptions and half-truths that the subject might have picked up from sensational publicity and even from professional literature. Of these, the most important are concepts of the LSD state as "model schizophrenia" and of LSD as a substance that can cause or precipitate psychosis; the issue of prolonged reactions and "flashbacks"; the danger of organic brain damage; and the possible adverse influence of LSD on chromosomal structure and heredity.

The "model psychosis" concept was discussed earlier; it is outdated and was replaced by a new understanding of LSD as a catalyst or amplifier of mental processes. The occurrence of transitional psychotic states after some sessions represents one of the risks of LSD therapy even under supervised conditions. However, in supervised LSD work these occur very rarely, and only in people with severe emotional problems and borderline symptomatology. They are not created by the drug but represent exteriorization of important, deep unconscious material. The activation and conscious manifestation of large quantities of such material can present a clinical problem; however, it is also an opportunity for therapeutic change, if approached and handled properly. In a later section we will discuss in detail the mechanisms of prolonged reactions, "flashbacks," and psychotic decompensations associated with the administration of LSD, as well as certain principles of conducting sessions that can minimize the occurrence of these phenomena.

The only serious and unquestionable somatic danger associated with psychedelic sessions is the stress on the cardiovascular system caused by the intensity of emotions and physical tensions typically triggered by the drug. Careful selection of the candidates and screening out of persons with a history of myocardial infarction, decompensated heart failure, malignant hypertension, severe arteriosclerosis, tendency to brain hemorrhage and similar conditions, eliminates this risk. A disposition to seizures may be a contraindication for a psychedelic session unless a well-equipped pharmacy is readily available. In individuals with a history of epilepsy LSD can occasionally trigger a sequence of seizures, or *status epilepticus*, which can be extremely difficult to control outside of a medical setting.

There are no indications that pharmaceutically pure LSD in the dosages that have been used in psychotherapy (50–1500 micrograms) causes organic brain damage. The allusions to this possibility that have occurred in professional literature were based on two observations. The first of these was the frequent occurrence of tremors, jerks and complex twisting movements in the subjects during LSD sessions. These motor manifestations can be observed even in individuals without an epileptic disposition and they bear a certain similarity to symptoms seen in a variety of organic diseases of the central nervous system. According to clinical observations from LSD therapy, they represent release and discharge of deep, pent-up energies associated with emotional abreaction and actually have a great therapeutic potential. The most dramatic motor abreactions of this kind occur in connection with the death-rebirth process. They tend to diminish or disappear when the individual moves beyond the perinatal level, despite the fact that by then the total amount of the drug ingested is much higher than at the time when they first occurred. Also, the great individual variability and lack of a direct dose-effect relationship weigh strongly against there being an organic basis for the motor phenomena in LSD sessions. In general, testing of LSD subjects during various stages of the psycholytic series failed to detect any indications of brain damage, even in those cases where the total number of sessions was close to one hundred. The techniques used in this context were basic neurological examination, electroencephalography, and psychological tests that are routinely used for establishing organic brain damage in clinical practice.

The second observation that some authors interpreted as indicative of brain damage was the incidence of certain personality changes observed in some LSD users. Among these were loss of ambition, dropping-out from school, growing long hair and a beard, wearing unusual clothes, a lessened concern about personal hygiene, departure from a rational orientation, and preoccupation with philosophical and religious issues. Careful analysis of the "hippie personality" clearly indicates that it cannot be attributed exclusively to the use of psychedelic substances. It is a complex phenomenon which involves important sociopolitical factors and elements of juvenile revolt reflecting the deepening generation gap. It was clearly demonstrated in our patient population that profound personality changes, including philosophical and spiritual transformation, can occur without the external changes characterizing the hippie personality. To equate the personality changes of American LSD users with the deterioration observed in patients with organic brain diseases such as prefrontal tumors shows grave misunderstanding of the problems involved. In addition, the poor quality of many of the street samples of LSD and the overlapping of the psychedelic scene with the use of amphetamines, barbiturates, phencyclidine, STP and other drugs, raises serious doubts whether one can draw any conclusions about LSD from observations made in connection with the non-medical use of so-called "street acid."

Unfortunately, the negative publicity concerning LSD and other psychedelics not only influenced the attitudes of the general public, educators and legislators, but also the opinion of many professionals. The national hysteria of the sixties and sensational newspaper headlines had a greater influence on psychiatrists and psychologists than the results of clinical studies indicating the relative safety of LSD when used under responsible circumstances. As a result of this, many of the statements made about the drug by professionals reflected a strongly irrational emotional bias rather than solid scientific evidence. This is best illustrated by the fact that among the psychiatrists who raised fierce objections to the use of LSD as a therapeutic tool, because they were concerned it may cause some subtle brain damage not yet detectable by our current methods, there were some individuals who did not hesitate to recommend patients for pre-frontal lobotomy.[1]

The last area that should be mentioned in this context is the effect of LSD on the chromosomes, fetal development and heredity. Sensationalizing has succeeded in programming the general public so thoroughly that this issue is almost bound to come up during the preparatory talks. The problem is of critical importance for psychedelic psychotherapy and its future, and one of the appendices to this book presents a critical review of over one hundred scientific papers on the subject. I will only briefly summarize my own opinion on this matter, based on twenty years of clinical experience and a thorough study of the existing literature. There does not seem to be any indication that the administration of pharmaceutically pure LSD has any specifically deleterious effect on chromosomes or heredity. It should not be administered to a pregnant woman, however, because of an increased danger of abortion and possible interference with fetal development.

LSD thus appears to be a very safe substance biologically, if we screen out persons with serious cardiovascular problems and pregnant women, and proceed with caution when there is a predisposition to epileptic seizure. All other dangers seem to be of a psychological nature. To a great extent these are not inherent in the drug itself, but are determined by a complex of extrapharmacological factors, such as the personality of the subject, the set and setting, and the specific techniques used in the process. The most important aspects of this problem are discussed in detail in other parts of this book.

After all the fears, doubts and apprehensions have been discussed with the client, the therapist should convey his or her understanding of the effect of the drug and of the therapeutic potential of the experience. It is important to emphasize that LSD is a catalyst or amplifier of mental processes, a tool facilitating deep self-exploration. Ingesting it does not send one into an alien world of "toxic psychosis" or "chemical phantasmagoria," but mediates an adventurous journey into the hidden recesses of one's own unconscious mind and through it into realms that can best be described as superconscious.

In the early years of LSD research, influenced by the "model schizophrenia" hypothesis, psychedelic sessions were routinely referred to as "experimental psychoses" even when they were conducted for therapeutic purposes. It is important to avoid terminology and metaphors of this kind, since they are not only scientifically incorrect, but involve a danger of heavy negative programming for the session. In such a context, episodes of anxiety, aggression, mistrust and other difficult emotions will be interpreted by the subject as indications of the "psychotomimetic" effect of the drug, instead of being seen as unique opportunities for confronting and working through certain problematic areas in one's own mind. In addition, the allusion to schizophrenia or psychosis has a frightening connotation of irreversible and permanent loss of sanity. More appropriate and useful metaphors are those using the images of an "intrapsychic movie," a "vivid fantasy," or a "waking dream." It is particularly helpful to remind the future candidate for psychedelic therapy that in our sleep we all have episodes of unusual states of consciousness during which we can vividly see, hear, smell, taste, and feel things that do not exist in the phenomenal world. This reference to dreams is a useful emphasis of the fact that all phenomena which deviate from the common experience of reality and the usual logic of things do not necessarily imply insanity.

Another important part of the preparation is to inform the client briefly of the range of experiences that can occur during the session, such as perceptual changes in various sensory areas, reliving of emotionally relevant experiences from childhood, sensations related to diseases and operations, elements of the death-rebirth process, and various transpersonal phenomena. Since many of these are beyond the conventional frameworks, it is useful to encourage the client to give up intellectual analysis during the session and focus on the experience itself. Otherwise, reason can become a powerful obstacle to exploring new areas of experience. The intensity of psychedelic states also deserves notice; it is important to prepare the client for the fact that the dimensions of the experience will probably be beyond anything that he or she has ever faced before or could even imagine in the usual state of consciousness. Although no words can adequately communicate the intensity of a high-dose LSD experience, such a warning can save the candidate from shock and panic during the session.

It is essential to discuss in advance several situations that are the most frequent sources of difficulty in LSD sessions. The first of these is the *experience of dying*, which can be so dramatic, realistic and convincing that the subject can easily mistake it for a real physiological emergency. This is particularly true for the confrontation with death that occurs on the perinatal level; it may be associated with many acute biological signs that can alarm not only the subject but also an inexperienced sitter. The drastic changes of color, seizure-like motor activity, projectile vomiting, profuse sweating, and fast thread-like pulse that accompany the experience of dying can be very convincing as indicators of physical crisis, and may contribute to the failure to recognize its symbolic nature. There exists another type of confrontation with death that occurs on the transpersonal level. It does not usually have the same heavy biological emphasis or the form of a violent life-threatening assault. The major focus of the transpersonal form of confrontation with death is on the relative ratio between attachment to the world and the desire to leave it. As a process it is much more subtle, and tends to have the quality of relatively free decision-making. It is primarily the perinatal encounter with death that presents problems in the sessions, and it should be discussed with the subject in advance. It is important to convey that the perinatal experience of dying occurs in the context of the death-rebirth process, and that total surrender to it is always followed by feelings of liberation, whereas struggle against it prolongs the suffering.

The second frequent problem in LSD sessions is the *feeling that the experience will never end or that permanent insanity is imminent*. A special instance of this state is the no-exit experience described earlier. It is of critical importance for the subject to know that the fastest way out of this condition is to accept the content of the experience. No judgments about the outcome of the session made while it is still in progress should be considered valid assessments or predictions; they should be treated as part of the experience. Thus, paradoxically, accepting that one will stay in the hellish experience forever leads to its termination, and total surrender to permanent insanity results in a move to higher sanity. As in the case of the death experience which frequently accompanies the fear of psychosis, fighting the specter of impending doom and insanity prolongs the unpleasant state and keeps the subject in the sphere of its influence.

The third most common source of panic is the *fear of becoming homosexual*. It is usually initiated by feelings of very authentic identification with representatives of the opposite sex. A male subject can experience not only an authentic female body image, but also a very genuine sense of what it feels like to be pregnant, to deliver a child, or to have a vaginal and clitoral orgasm. The less frequent equivalent experience in the female usually does not involve a sense of having a masculine body, but male psychological characteristics. It is necessary to reassure the subject that this is a very unique opportunity to gain access to the experiential world of the opposite sex. It will ultimately strengthen the sense of one's own sexual identity rather than cause a homosexual transformation. Another source of homosexual fears can be sudden feelings of physical attraction to the sitter of the same sex. These can usually be deciphered as transference of early sensual feelings toward the parent of the same sex. The deepest source of homosexual panic in a male subject seems to be the emergence of frightening birth memories; in this context the vagina appears to be a murderous organ and the individual cannot imagine ever approaching it again as a source of pleasure.

Various physical feelings that can occur in LSD sessions should be mentioned here. On occasion, they reach sufficient intensity to present real problems. It is important to make it clear to the client that LSD in the dosages commonly used in psychotherapy does not produce any somatic symptoms just by virtue of its pharmacological effect. Nausea, vomiting, headaches, various muscular pains, suffocation, painful cramps of the uterus or the gastrointestinal tract, increased motor activity, and other physical manifestations in LSD sessions are always of a psychosomatic nature. They are associated with important psychological material and experiencing them fully is of great therapeutic value.

Every preparation for a psychedelic session should involve discussion about the possibility that the client might experience at some point a profound *crisis of basic trust*, no matter how good the therapeutic relationship seems to be before the drug experience. The essential characteristics of this important crisis were described earlier. It is vital to prepare the client for this possibility and strongly suggest that he or she try to look inside themselves for possible sources of such mistrust before focusing their attention on the external circumstances. It is obviously more reasonable to assume that one's perception was changed by the influence of a powerful psychoactive drug, than to suspect that within half an hour a drastic and unexpected change occurred in the external situation or in the personalities of the sitters. The very fact that the possibility of the crisis involving trust was discussed in advance usually helps to mitigate it when it occurs.

A basic rule that is of critical importance in LSD psychotherapy is to keep the sessions internalized. Since the psychedelic experience represents a process of deep self-exploration, a journey into one's own mind, consistent introspective orientation is by far the most productive approach. LSD subjects are therefore encouraged to stay for most of the experience in a comfortable reclining position with their eyes closed; the best technical solution here is the use of soft eyeshades. Exposure to complex stimuli from the external world, especially if combined with moving around, excessive talking and social interaction is, in general, counterproductive. It tends to keep the experience on a superficial level and interferes with the process of self-exploration. On occasion, expressive dancing can be very useful in psychedelic sessions if the subject keeps his or her eyes closed and does not lose the introspective connection with the inner process.

I would not like to deny that there can be positive value in psychedelic experiences in which the subject is oriented toward the external environment. The drug can open and sensitize all the sensory channels to an extraordinary degree and make it possible for the subject to perceive the world in a totally new way. The ensuing aesthetic, emotional and spiritual participation in the environment can be a very profound and valuable experience, especially if the session takes place in a beautiful natural setting. An externalized psychedelic experience in the mountains, on the seashore, in the woods, or even in one's own garden can become a unique and unforgettable event. However, if one is taking LSD for this purpose, it is important to stay in the lower dosage range, below 100 micrograms. Higher dosages tend to activate important unconscious material that can surface and distort the perception of the environment. For a person who takes LSD in a complex physical and social setting, relevant psychological elements and external sensory stimuli fuse into an inextricable amalgam that obscures the emerging personal material. Under these circumstances, the LSD state tends to become an incomprehensible mixture of external perception and experiences of one's inner world; as a result of this, such situations are generally not very conducive to productive introspection. Sessions using higher dosages for the purpose of personal growth, working through the emotional problems, and philosophical or mystical quest should, therefore, be internalized.

An even more important reason for keeping the focus on the inner process is the element of safety. The ratio between the potential benefits and possible risks is much more favorable for internalized sessions conducted in a simplified and protective setting, than it is for the outward-oriented experiences practiced by many people in the subculture. It is essential for a good outcome of the session that a balance be kept between the lowering of psychological defenses and effective working through of the emerging unconscious material. Whatever deep contents have been released, the energy associated with them should be channeled to the periphery. Maximum awareness of the inner process and its full emotional, perceptual and physical expression is of paramount importance for a good integration of the LSD experience. Sessions in which the drug activates areas of difficult emotional material and the individual tries to avoid facing them can lead to prolonged reactions, unsatisfactory integration, subsequent residual emotional or psychosomatic problems, or a precarious mental balance that becomes the basis for later "flashbacks."

In view of the above observations, much emphasis is placed during the preparation period on explaining to the client how important it is to maintain a reclining position during the LSD session, to keep on the eyeshades and headphones, and to face, experience and express fully whatever is surfacing. Most of the technical problems in the sessions occur when the client, instead of treating the experience as an internal process, projects the emerging unconscious material onto the sitters and the treatment situation. This attitude functions as a powerful defense and represents a serious obstacle to therapeutic progress. Instead of facing the problem in the inner world where it can be identified and resolved, the client creates a pseudoreal situation by projecting and focusing attention on manipulation of the external world. Preventing such counterproductive situations is one of the important tasks of the sitters and it begins in the preparation period with a detailed description and explanation of the basic rules.

One more important aspect of psychedelic therapy should be discussed with the patient in considerable detail. In medicine and conventional psychiatry, there is an implicit rule that in successful therapy the degree of improvement should be directly proportional to the number of therapeutic interventions or to the duration of treatment. In the psychedelic procedure, as in other forms of uncovering therapy that focus on solving the problems instead of relieving symptoms, this is not necessarily true. Here it can happen that the symptoms are temporarily intensified after some of the sessions; this frequently occurs just before a major therapeutic breakthrough. It should be explicitly stated in the instructions that it is not a failure of LSD therapy if after certain sessions the client feels worse. It simply reflects the fact that important unconscious material was activated in the preceding session and remained unresolved. The concept of temporary worsening as an unfinished gestalt helps the patients to tolerate difficult post-session intervals, approach them constructively, and maintain optimism in regard to the final outcome of the treatment.

Before I start describing the actual technique of conducting the LSD sessions, I would like to mention briefly several observations from my European study of psycholytic therapy. They can be used as empirical and theoretical justification of some of the principles outlined later. During psycholytic therapy, the clinical condition of the patients in the free intervals between LSD sessions showed considerable oscillations in both directions. After some sessions, clinical symptoms were alleviated or even disappeared and patients felt "cured," free from conflicts and problems, and ready to start a totally new chapter in their lives. After other sessions the clinical condition obviously deteriorated, as compared to the pre-session period. Sometimes the original symptoms were intensified, at other times entirely new and unexpected forms of psychopathology emerged, after a poorly resolved session. Occasionally, we witnessed prolonged reactions or even temporary psychotic decompensations in some borderline patients. In several instances a striking clinical improvement was reached in patients who had a very dim prognosis, but continuation of LSD therapy with the intention of stabilizing the results in fact opened new areas of problems.

Although there is a general trend toward more positive LSD experiences and better functioning in life with the increasing number of sessions, it seems impossible to eliminate all areas of conflicts and problems. However, the nature of these problems changes successively from psychodynamic, autobiographically determined issues through derivatives of the death-rebirth process to various transpersonal elements. In the most general sense, and with some reservations, it is possible to talk about the Freudian, Rankian, and Jungian phases of psychedelic therapy. It is important to emphasize that the sequence of these stages is not necessarily linear and that there exist many individual patterns of unfolding. However, if we look statistically at a large number of records from serial LSD sessions, the biographical material tends to occur in early sessions, the middle part of therapy is dominated by the death-rebirth process, and advanced sessions tend to be all metaphysical and philosophical in nature. In all these stages, there seems to exist the possibility of the negative outcome of a particular session with an adverse effect on the clinical condition.

Retrospective analysis of the records from psycholytic therapy shows that good, free intervals usually followed sessions in which important partial resolutions were achieved. The termination periods of such sessions were characterized by tension-free, pleasant or even ecstatic experiences of the here-and-now. In this state, there were no unpleasant physical or emotional symptoms and no preoccupation with the past or future; only a sense of pure being with enhanced sensory awareness of the present moment. The achievement of such a condition should be the ideal goal of every psychedelic experience. Since the positive outcome of an LSD session seems to correlate with a good resolution of the activated unconscious material and with a pleasant termination period of the session, the sitters should exert active effort at the time when the pharmacological action of the drug is wearing off to facilitate a successful completion of the experiences.

Observations from psycholytic therapy provide important clues to how this can be done most effectively. Spontaneous experiences of tension-free, oceanic ecstasy in psychedelic sessions are typically associated with visions of beautiful natural scenes such as clear lakes, calm oceans, tropical islands, luscious forests, flourishing meadows, and blue or star-filled skies. Equally common in this context is experiential confrontation with artistic creations of high aesthetic value— visions of beautiful temples, sculptures or paintings, and spontaneous hallucinations of inspiring music. The experience quite regularly has a definite spiritual and mystical emphasis, and this typically takes the form of enchantment with the mysteries of nature and the creative forces of the Universe, although concrete archetypal symbolism related to specific religions and mythologies of different cultures is as frequent. Some patients also report quite authentic experiences of the good womb and good breast, as well as episodes involving ideal maternal care, love, and friendship.

Many of the above elements that occur spontaneously in the context of ecstatic episodes in LSD sessions have been routinely used by psychedelic and anaclitic therapists as tools facilitating positive experiences. Walks in nature and the use of various objects reflecting nature's creativity, beautiful pieces of art, symbolic paintings of the sacred traditions, sculptures related to various spiritual disciplines, readings from religious texts, and the use of physical contact can be mentioned here as salient examples. Although the positive influence of these factors was discovered empirically, their use can be theoretically justified and their unusual efficacy explained on the basis of a deep unconscious association between oceanic ecstasy and the experiences of natural beauty, inspired artistic creations, spiritual feelings, and highly satisfactory human relationships. Some of these elements and principles should be integrated in a comprehensive program of LSD therapy; they facilitate the occurrence of positive experiences during psychedelic sessions, as well as in the termination periods. This makes psychedelic treatment more meaningful and effective and increases its therapeutic potential.

PSYCHEDELIC SESSIONS

In the following text, I will outline the most important characteristics of an ideal treatment setting as I see it on the basis of past clinical experience with psychedelic therapy. Obviously, in practice these absolute demands will seldom be met and LSD therapists have to be prepared for various degrees of compromise. Ideally, LSD sessions should be conducted in a specifically designed treatment unit or suite. This should be situated on the ground floor and isolated from the rest of the facility, with a separate entrance. A small kitchenette and easily available lavatory would make it possible for the therapists to stay with the patient the entire day without undue interruption, and to choose the optimal moments for a physiological break or a snack. It is important that the patient be able to reach the bathroom in a short time without having to interact with the external world and to face a complex social situation. At times, the abreactive episodes in sessions make it necessary to encourage loud noises such as screaming, growling, or banging, which can be quite upsetting for other patients or visitors. Adequate provision should be made for such situations so that the therapist and the patients do not feel constrained or restricted by external concerns and can follow fully the dynamics of the process. If the unit is not in a small separate building but part of a larger complex, adequate acoustic insulation might be necessary.

The treatment room should be homelike, comfortably furnished and tastefully decorated. Soft padding and cushions are preferable to sharp edges and hard metallic surfaces. This not only gives the patient a sense of comfort and protection, but can become an important safety factor in more animated episodes in sessions that involve physical movement or psychodramatically enacted struggle. Freshly cut or potted flowers, a bowl of assorted fresh and dried fruits and nuts, a collection of inspiring pictures and art books, and various natural objects of great beauty such as shells and stones, have become over the years a standard and integral part of our treatment setting. Music is an essential part of psychedelic therapy, and a high fidelity stereo record player and tape deck, several sets of headphones, and an extensive collection of tapes and records of good quality should always be available.

If possible, the treatment facility should be situated in a beautiful natural setting. Although this is of little relevance in the first four to five hours which the patient spends with the eyeshades and headphones on, it becomes important during the termination period of the session. The psychedelic experience tends to bring the subject into intimate contact with nature and dramatically enhances his or her sensory perception of the world, and an encounter with nature at its best can become an aesthetic and spiritual experience of lasting value. It not only contributes considerably to a good integration of the session, but connects the positive energies and emotions to elements of the everyday world. Water deserves special notice; during the session it assumes an almost magical significance for many LSD subjects and has extraordinary capacity to facilitate a positive outcome of the session. A swim in the ocean, a clear lake, or a stream can work wonders in the termination period of LSD sessions. Under more modest circumstances, the use of a swimming pool or bathtub, or a good shower will serve a similar purpose.

It is preferable to start LSD sessions in the morning; if the drug is taken in the afternoon, the experience can continue until late in the evening and the subject might find it difficult to sleep that night. The optimal dosage of LSD seems to be somewhere between 200 and 400 micrograms for most patients. It is determined primarily by the nature of the psychological problems involved, the personality structure of the subject, and certain physical concerns such as age and general health. Body weight seems to play a relatively minor role; the sensitivity or resistance toward the drug appears to be primarily a function of the system of psychological defenses. We mentioned earlier that patients with severe obsessive-compulsive neuroses seem to represent an extreme of resistance, while persons with a hysterical personality structure or symptomatology are at the other end of the spectrum. There seems to be a saturation point for LSD somewhere around four or five hundred micrograms; increase of the dose beyond this point does not seem to produce much additional effect. It is generally more useful to identify the specific mechanisms of resistance and try to influence them psychologically than to use heroic dosages in an effort to "break down the defenses."

LSD is fully effective orally in most individuals and administration by injection is of little practical value. The slight shortening of the latency period that this gives is usually not worth the inconvenience of the injection technique and the introduction of a powerful element of the traditional medical model into the setting. Intramuscular administration is occasionally useful for patients whose clinical problems involve a predisposition to nausea and vomiting. In the case of vomiting early in the session, an uncertainty might arise as to the actual amount of LSD that was resorbed. For similar reasons, LSD was administered by injection to some cancer patients where there was concern about the degree of resorption because the gastrointestinal system was afflicted by the disease.

In general, fasting for a day or two before the LSD session seems to have some advantages. It tends to potentiate the effect of LSD, make the subject more open to unusual states of consciousness, and reduce the incidence of unpleasant gastro-intestinal symptoms in the session, particularly nausea and vomiting. A compromise solution should be used almost routinely if the subject has not fasted; we usually recommend a light dinner on the night immediately preceding the session and only liquids (milk, fruit juice, or tea) for breakfast. This tends to shorten the resorption time and reduce the incidence of nausea.

The subject should have light, casual and comfortable clothes; any restricting garments or potentially dangerous personal belongings should be removed from the body. If this is not done before the session the patient might ask for it later in the experience, or it may become necessary in view of certain special situations. It is thus easier to eliminate beforehand bras, belts, tight pants, watches, pieces of jewelry, artificial dentures, glasses, contact lenses, keys, pocket knives, and similar objects.

LSD should be administered without much delay, after a brief focusing on the "here-and-now." Many patients show a high level of excitement, apprehension, or anxiety, and as a result lose a few hours of sleep before the session. This is quite common before the first psychedelic experience, but is not exceptional even for experienced LSD subjects. It is useful to discuss briefly the physical and emotional conditions and give time for last-minute questions that might be the product of a sleepless night. However, much delay tends to increase the anxiety instead of reducing it. Facing the drug state once it sets in is usually easier than dealing with all the fantasies as to what the experience will be like.

After the administration of LSD there is a latency period of about twenty to forty minutes before the drug takes effect. Its duration depends on the route of administration, the amount of food in the stomach if the drug is ingested, and the level of psychological defenses. The time before the onset of the drug effect can be spent in meditation, listening to quiet music, looking at pictures, or in relaxing discussions. Sometimes it is interesting to leaf through the family album or look at pictures of close family members if one wants to use the experience for a deeper insight into and work on relationships with close relatives.

As the patient begins to feel the effect of the drug, he or she is encouraged to lie down on the couch and put on eyeshades. This helps the individual to focus on the inner world that is beginning to unfold and prevents distraction and interference from the outside. From then on the reclining position is generally encouraged for the next four or five hours, and the experience is almost fully internalized. The subject receives stereophonic headphones and listens to specially selected music; the objective is to let go and surrender to the experience. The task of the sitters is to give support and protection to the subjects, take care of their various psychological and physiological needs, facilitate the full unfolding of the experience, and deal with various forms of resistance as they occur during the session.

In general, excessive talking should be discouraged during the period of intense drug effect; this is particularly true for the compulsive, incessant talking and intellectual analyzing that is usually a manifestation of resistance and interferes seriously with the experience. Long explanations and interpretations offered by the therapist, or involved discussions, are also usually counterproductive. The psychedelic experiences in high-dose sessions usually have many levels and facets; their rapid unfolding and change make comprehensive reporting impossible. In addition, the ability to articulate and communicate verbally is frequently impaired by the influence of the drug.

Verbal exchange between the therapists and the client, although very useful during the preparation, in the termination period of the sessions, and on the following days, should be kept at an absolute minimum during the culminating hours of the drug session. The subject is occasionally asked to give a brief report limited to a few sentences to provide clues for the sitters. An experienced sitter can usually get a sufficient understanding of the nature of the subject's psychedelic state on the basis of external behavior and sporadic verbal communications. This is particularly true if the sitter can draw on his or her own experiences of a similar kind. Thus, general tension, an aggressive facial expression, clawing or clenching of the hands, and occasional primitive sounds, together with statements like: "All this incredible butchery" or "I have been in all the wars since the beginning of the world" give sufficient information to the sitter. Similarly, a statement such as "I cannot differentiate boundaries anymore; all seems to be coming together, flowing into One" from a relaxed, ecstatic subject does not require any further explanation. Sensual movements of the body with an intense involvement of the pelvic area and occasional utterances about love-making, sex, or orgies convey enough content. Any further narratives and descriptions serve the needs of the sitters rather than the experient. Memories of the session are usually quite adequate and discussions and analyses can be postponed to a later time. The only exception is a situation of strong resistance where the sitter needs to have exact information to help the experient through the impasse.

If the client is not giving any feedback, the therapist should interrupt briefly every half-hour or so; the purpose of this "checking-in" is to re-establish contact, obtain some clues about the process, and give reassurance if necessary. One of the reasons the sitters should know the nature of the subject's experience is that music for the session should be chosen with sensitivity to match the psychological state of the experient. Apart from this, mostly non-specific support should be given through non-verbal channels. This can involve hand-holding, reassuring touches, cradling, or various forms of psychodramatic involvement in the experience. It might prove helpful at times to provide resistance for a client who needs to struggle or push, to emphasize certain physical feelings by pressure or massage, or to use some other maneuvers of a similar kind. This becomes more common as the session is approaching the termination period. Early in the experience physical interventions require great sensitivity and good rapport. It is important to maintain a trusting relationship, a sense of cooperation, and a general framework of a play. However, the "as if" atmosphere of synergistic play can be easily lost in the intensity of the experience and the therapist might risk being perceived as an attacker rather than as a helper. Unless the sitters have intuitive certainty about the quality of the relationship, these maneuvers should not be used in the early stages of the session. Another important aspect of the therapeutic interaction is sensitive response to the client's needs—offering a blanket when he or she appears to be cold, wiping the sweat off the brow, cleaning mucus or saliva from the face, wetting the lips when they are dry, or bringing a glass of water.

All that has been said above applies to psychedelic sessions which have an uncomplicated and relatively smooth course. In such sessions, the client is able to maintain the reclining position, stays with the eyeshades and headphones on, keeps the experience internalized, and is capable of handling the emerging unconscious material adequately. In the best sessions of this kind, there is very little for the sitters to do; they listen to music, meditate, and try to tune empathically into the client's experience. A very different situation occurs when the subject is not able to tolerate the experiences and refuses to "go with it."

Minor examples of this are various evasive maneuvers, such as a tendency to take off the eyeshades and sit up, have a cup of coffee or a cigarette, chat about trivial things, pace around, or go for a walk. A more dramatic manifestation of resistance is projection of the emerging material onto the sitters and the treatment situation. The client wants to look at the sitters, get involved in intellectual arguments, discuss their life situation or their problems, or criticize the rules and circumstances of the session. Extreme complications involve a total loss of awareness of the symbolic nature of the experience and confusing it with reality. These usually occur in connection with the experience of dying, fear of insanity, or homosexual panic. The patient may experience acute mistrust and want to escape the situation and the room, confusing the internal danger with the external situation.

When the client cannot maintain the recommended position, starts perceiving and interpreting the situation in a grossly distorted way, or shows a tendency for acting-out behavior, the sitters must move from their passive stance to active intervention. A less urgent indication for therapeutic action is a situation in which the patient stays in the eyeshades and headphones but tends to project his or her feelings on the sitters, rather than tracing them back to their origins. The basic strategy and techniques for dealing with various difficult situations in psychedelic sessions will be discussed later in a special section. (pp. 154-201)

An atmosphere of security, privacy, and full committment is absolutely necessary for a successful psychedelic session. Sitters who answer telephone calls during the sessions, permit people to knock on the door, or leave the treatment room to carry out various parallel activities can hardly expect smooth, fully productive and successful sessions. A single major distraction or unpredictable withdrawal of support at a critical time in the session can become a long-term obstacle in treatment. The patient can lose trust in the unconditional and constant support of the therapist and never again dare to abandon control and face certain difficult aspects of his or her unconscious.

Ideally, the patient should be attended during the entire time of the drug action by two sitters, a male-female therapeutic dyad, who never leave the treatment unit. The sitters should know each other well, get along with each other, and be used to working together. There are several reasons for having therapists of both sexes in the sessions. There are certain activities which are much more natural for men than for women, and vice versa. By and large, women seem to be more appropriate for comforting, cradling, and physical support, unless the nature of the experience calls specifically for a male figure. This is true for situations in which the subject is dealing with the psychological impact of the absence of his or her father in childhood, or feels a need to express affection in relation to a father-figure.

Conversely, psychodramatic enactment of struggle might require physical strength and be better suited to a male therapist, unless the content of the experience calls specifically for a female. It is also quite common that various problems related to the Oedipal triangle in the client's childhood first become manifest as projective distortions of the relationship with the therapeutic dyad. There are also certain transpersonal experiences, such as archetypal constellations and past-incarnation memories, for which the presence of both sexes is important or facilitating. Thus representation of both the male and the female element is useful not only in terms of division of tasks, but also as specific facilitation of certain experiences and for evocative projection screens. Although deep involvement in projections is generally counterproductive and should be discouraged, the projective distortions can become an extremely powerful source of insight if approached by the subject in a constructive way.

Since music is such an important and integral part of LSD psychotherapy, we will briefly discuss its role, the basic principles of selecting appropriate pieces, and the specific way in which these are used in the sessions. Music seems to serve several important functions in the context of psychedelic therapy. It tends to evoke a variety of powerful emotions and facilitates deeper involvement in the psychedelic process. It provides a meaningful structure for the experience and creates a continuous carrier wave that helps patients to overcome difficult parts of the sessions and move through impasses. LSD subjects frequently report that the flow of music helps them to let go of their psychological defenses and surrender fully to the experience. Another function of music is to provide a sense of continuity and connection in the course of various unusual states of consciousness. It is quite common that clients have difficulties with the periods when the music stops and the records or tapes are being changed; they complain that they feel suspended in midair, and sense a painful gap in the experience. An additional function of the music deals more specifically with its content; it is often possible to facilitate the emergence of a certain emotional quality such as aggression, sexual feelings, "psychedelic breakthrough," or a transcendental experience, by a specific choice of music. The significance of music for the positive structuring of the reentry period has already been described.

As far as the choice of music is concerned, I will outline only the general principles and give a few suggestions based on my own experiences.[2] Each therapeutic team develops after a certain time, a list of its favorite pieces for various phases of LSD sessions and for certain specific situations. The basic rule is to respond sensitively to the phase, intensity and content of the experience, rather than to try to impose a specific pattern on it. Preference should be given to music of high artistic quality, but little concrete content. One should avoid playing songs and other vocal pieces in which the verbal content suggests a specific theme. Where used, vocal compositions should involve a language unknown to the experient so that the human voice becomes an unspecific stimulus. For the same reason, it is preferable to avoid pieces with which clients have specific intellectual associations. Thus, the beginning of Beethoven's Fifth Symphony in C minor is usually associated with the imminence of a fateful event (Symphony of Destiny); the use of the wedding marches from Wagner's *Lohengrin* or Mendelssohn's *A Midsummer Night's Dream* suggest a nuptial atmosphere; and Bizet's *Carmen* would evoke through a similar mechanism the theme of a bull-fight. In Czech subjects, Liszt's *Les Préludes* tends to bring memories of the war, because it was used by Nazi propagandists as an introduction to the daily news broadcasted on street loudspeakers.

The major objection to the use of music in psychedelic sessions is that even if we avoid the gross programming illustrated by the above examples, we will exert a strong structuring effect on the experience by our choice of music. This seems to be in sharp contrast with the tendency to internalize the sessions and eliminate specific optical stimuli by the use of eyeshades, and there is a certain element of truth in this objection. The ideal solution seems to be to play a tape of "white noise"—a sequence of random acoustic patterns produced by a sound generator. Listening to intense white noise through headphones, LSD subjects usually create their own inner music which seems to fit the nature and content of the experience perfectly, since it is coming from the same source. Thus, only non-specific acoustic stimulation is provided, which is then illusively transformed by the subject into music. Monotonous sounds, noises coming from various electric appliances, or recordings of the ocean tide can play a similar role.

However, the danger of programming associated with specific music is not as serious as it might seem. The potential for manipulating and controlling the experience is rather limited. If the subject is in an extremely difficult emotional place, any music, no matter how inspired and ethereal, will be distorted and may sound like a dirge. Conversely, during a deep positive experience just about any music will be enthusiastically accepted by the subject, who will find it fitting and interesting from some point of view. Only in the medium range somewhere between these two extremes can music effectively shape the experience. Even then, although a certain general atmosphere or emotional tone will be suggested from the outside, the subject will elaborate it very specifically. The resultant sequences will still be manifestations of the individual's own unconscious, reflect the content of his or her memory banks, and represent a meaningful self-revealing gestalt. Moreover, the external input does not seem to reduce the therapeutic significance of the psychedelic experience that it triggers or modifies.

It is useful to discuss the subject's taste in music before the session and get an idea of his or her preferences, idiosyncrasies, and general level of musical sophistication. However, the actual selection usually reflects more the sitters' understanding of the process than the experient's choice. Only the late hours of the session, when no more therapeutic work has to be done, are an exception; this is a period of relaxation and the subject is given the opportunity to determine the nature of the entertainment. In general, the music chosen reflects the usual experiential trajectory of the psychedelic sessions. In the latency period, before the onset of the drug effect, quiet, flowing and calming music seems appropriate. This changes after the experience begins into music which has an opening-up and building-up quality. Within about an hour and a half, the patient is fully under the influence of the drug; this is the time for powerful and emotionally highly-evocative music. If we are choosing from the Occidental repertoire, good classical music, such as less well-known symphonies, concertos, or overtures of famous masters would be appropriate. Johannes Brahms, Robert Schumann, Sergei Rachmaninoff, Edvard Grieg, Ludwig van Beethoven, Hector Berlioz, Richard Strauss, Richard Wagner, Antoin Dvořák and especially Alexander Nikolaevich Scriabin are examples of composers whose music was frequently used by the Spring Grove therapists in this phase. In the fourth hour the LSD session tends to culminate, and in most instances seems to build up to a resolution. This is an opportunity for a major emotional or spiritual breakthrough, depending on the level on which the session is experienced. It seems appropriate at this point to introduce powerful, overwhelming music with a transcendental quality; oratoria, requiems, and masses, combining a full orchestra with a multitude of human voices, can be extremely evocative and effective. Sacred music of Wolfgang Amadeus Mozart, Johann Sebastian Bach, George Frederick Handel, Hector Berlioz, Giuseppe Verdi, Charles Gounod, or Francis Poulenc would be typical examples of this category. The music of the American composer of Armenian-Scottish extraction, Alan Hovhanness, can be unusually powerful and effective in this context. It is extremely evocative and transcendental, yet not sufficiently well-known to produce standard associations. For the termination period of the session quiet, relaxing, and flowing music with a timeless quality is chosen, such as the classical guitar, compositions for harp, and certain pieces by Johann Sebastian Bach or Antonio Vivaldi. Many records of contemporary composers such as Georg Deuter, Steve Halpern, Paul Horn and Paul Winter are also useful in this context. Oriental selections would include records of Ravi Shankar, music for Zen meditation, Japanese music for the bamboo flute, or Polynesian songs.

The above directives represent a very general outline; in practice the choice of music will depend on the LSD subject and on the circumstances. The sitters should respond very sensitively to the specific content of the sessions, providing Russian, Middle Eastern, Indian, African, Chinese, or other music if the subject reports experiences in those cultural contexts. Specific pieces of music might also be selected to deepen an experience of aggression, sexuality, physical and emotional pain, or transcendental feelings.

Over the years I became particularly impressed by the profound impact of ethnic music, especially those sound performances from certain religious traditions which were specifically designed as techniques for altering consciousness. Some of these are so unusual for an average Westerner that they should be used only with sophisticated individuals familiar with these traditions. Among the most powerful recordings in this category are the multivocal chanting of the Tantric Buddhist tradition in Tibet; the Hindu kirtans; the monkey chant, or ketjak, and other trance-inducing music from Bali; shamanic music from various parts of Asia, North America and South America; the hocketing of the Congolese Pygmies; trance music of the ¡Kung! Bushmen of the Kalahari desert; and chants from the Sufi ceremonies. Similarly, Greek sirtak dances, flute music from the Andes, recordings of the African oud, songs of the Bauls of Bengal, Armenian liturgical chants, Spanish flamenco guitar music, and other interesting ethnic pieces are useful for psychedelic sessions.

If the subject can stay with the experience, the therapist's task is to change records with sensitivity to the process, give support, protection, and encouragement, and take care of the patient's basic needs. The time when the pharmacological effect of the drug is wearing off—usually the sixth hour after ingestion—is the most critical period of the session. This is the time for the sitters to move into an active mode and try to facilitate a good resolution and integration of the experience. The emotional and psychosomatic condition of the subjects at the time the session terminates is of crucial importance to the final outcome of the session and the longer lasting effects. Even if the LSD subjects had deep transcendental experiences earlier in the session, they can have negative aftereffects if, during the reentry, they get "stuck" in some unresolved psychodynamic material. Conversely, a very difficult session with paranoid states and hellish experiences can be extremely therapeutic if it is well resolved. Two ways in which the sitters can facilitate the resolution and increase the probability of a good outcome of the session are by helping the subject to work through the unresolved material, and by introducing into the situation certain elements that are conducive to positive emotional states.

At the time when the effect of the drug is decreasing it is important to engage in verbal exchange with the subject, to get detailed feedback on his or her emotional and psychosomatic condition. If at this time he or she is experiencing discomfort, such as depression, anxiety, blocked aggression, feelings of guilt, circular thinking, headaches, nausea, muscular pains, intestinal cramps, or difficulties in breathing, this is the time to suggest active intervention. The possibility of this happening should have been discussed during the preparation period. The first step is to find out exactly what type of experience is involved; whether it is an unfinished reliving of a childhood memory, a perinatal sequence, a past-incarnation theme, or some other type of transpersonal phenomenon. It is also important to encourage the subject to scan his or her body for signs of physical pain, tension, or other forms of distress indicating energy blockage. There is, in general, no emotional distress or disturbing and incomplete psychological gestalt that does not show specific somatic manifestations. These concomitant psychosomatic symptoms then become the entry points for the sitters' intervention.

The sitters ask the experient to remain in the reclining position with eyes closed or covered by eyeshades. The instruction is to stop intellectual analysis ("turn off the head") and start intense hyperventilation. The breathing should be faster than usual and very deep; the experient should follow the air in his or her mind's eye all the way down into the pelvis. This hyperventilation tends to activate any available emotional material. The sitters ask the subject to pay attention to his or her body and surrender fully to the experience that starts unfolding—to allow any postures, movements, grimaces, sounds, shaking, crying, coughing, or gagging. At a certain point, the sitters enter the picture and, after having reached agreement on their roles, they start artificially increasing the physical feelings described earlier by the subject. For example, if there is pressure on the head or a headache, one of the sitters produces more of the same kind of pressure by laying hands on the subject's head. If the complaint is constriction of the chest or difficulties with breathing, more pressure is applied on the rib cage or under the clavicles. Nausea can be activated by rhythmic stimulation of the upper abdomen, combined with massage of the stomach; muscular pains enhanced by deep pressures approaching rolfing, and tension in the pelvic area intensified by holding the loins in an elevated position. All this has to be done in synchrony with the breathing rhythm and in tune with the general theme of the experience. The sitters have to use their imagination and intuition to enact the content of the unfin-ished gestalt in the most realistic way. Although this technique was developed in the context of LSD work, I have since used it with great success in experiential workshops where the drug was not administered.

The basic concept underlying this approach is that the subject's conscious emotional and physical distress is a mitigated version of the actual content of the unconscious matrix that is trying to emerge. The resolution of that matrix occurs when the unconscious content is experienced consciously in its original form and full intensity. By intensifying the existing sensations one thus facilitates the con-vergence of the conscious experience and the emerging unconscious gestalt, to the point that they become identical and merge. In this way the unconscious theme is energetically reduced and ceases to exist as a symptom-producing dynamic struc-ture; this is followed by sudden relief and a feeling of completion. Although it is not always possible to reach optimal resolution and a tension-free, "oceanic" state, the sitters should work toward this goal.

The above technique seems to be a most powerful way of reaching positive closure and good integration of an LSD session. As will be described later, it is fully compatible with other approaches of experiential psychotherapy and can be combined with them. An eclectic therapist can use techniques of gestalt practice, bioenergetic exercises, rolfing, guided affective imagery, asanas from Hatha yoga, elements of primal scream, and many other methods to great advantage. If the sessions are conducted in the context of a therapeutic community, other group members can be introduced into the process during the termination period to assist the experient in working through the residual problems. They can facilitate the experience by enacting a simulated struggle in the birth canal, offering comforting physical support, working with the subject in a warm pool, or creating a transper-sonal field by group chanting.

When it becomes obvious that the available pent-up energy has been re-leased and further uncovering work would require maneuvers that were too forceful, the sitters offer positive inputs to facilitate integration. Physical contact, individually or in a group, can induce nourishing feelings of comfort and security. A walk in nature, with its variety of sensory experiences, seems to be conducive to positive or even ecstatic emotional states. Looking at flowers or trees, sitting in the grass, smelling hay, or watching the sunset can be powerful experiences long to be remembered. It was already mentioned that exposure to water in the form of a swim, bath or shower seems to be of special significance. LSD subjects frequently experience contact with water at this stage as being not only physically cleansing, but also emotionally and spiritually purifying. It can bring them into touch with memories of infant bathing, prenatal existence, or early phylogenetic stages, and can induce a state of blissful merging and undifferentiated unity.

When all major residual problems have been worked through, it is time for socializing. At this point the sitters invite into the treatment room, with the previous agreement of the patient, friends or relatives who have been waiting out-side. Depending on the circumstances this may be just one person, such as the spouse, a sexual partner or good friend, or a group of family members and friends. All participants in this "reunion" are asked to respond to the needs of the experient and respect his or her special state of mind. It is up to the subject whether this meeting will take the form of a quiet meditation and wordless get-together, or a jovial social event. New channels of straight and honest communication can often be opened in this situation.

In our arrangement, a special "psychedelic dinner" was usually prepared by relatives or friends. It consisted of a variety of meals, snacks and fruits of interesting colors, tastes, and textures. Mandarin, Indonesian, Indian and Japanese dishes became particularly popular in this context. After well-resolved psychedelic experiences most subjects love to experiment with food, and discover that eating can be an adventure involving qualities and dimensions they had never imagined. However, it may happen that the individual feels nauseated or does not show interest in food. This is accepted with understanding and no pressure is put on him or her to participate in the prepared meal. The instruction given to the participants in the "reunion" is to respect the psychological space of the experient. This approach is in essential congruence with the basic orientation of the entire session day. The subject should feel free to do what he or she wants to do or has to do, and see the sitters and later the friends and relatives as helpers or assistants. "This is your day" is the implicit and explicit message given to the subject before the session and reinforced or repeated in various ways during the day. The issue of a reunion is an important one and should be approached with great sensitivity. It should not be done routinely, but always with respect to the specific circumstances. In some instances, it might be wiser and more appropriate not to invite the relatives, or even to cancel previous arrangements if the general condition or special emotional state of the subject seems to indicate it.

On the night following the session the subject should stay in the special treatment suite. Unless the circumstances or the condition of the client do not allow it or make it inadvisable, the spouse, close relative or good friend should spend the night with the subject. A nurse and at least one of the sitters should be on call in case any difficulties arise. On occasion, especially after poorly resolved sessions, a belated upsurge of intense emotions might occur in the hypnagogic period, later at night, or in the morning during the hypnopompic state.

If the session started in the morning there are generally no problems with sleep: this is particularly true if the experience was well resolved and integrated and the termination period was positive. After sessions that had a late start, or where the subject did not complete the emerging emotional and psychosomatic gestalt, sleep may not be easy. Generally, it is better not to use hypnotics and tranquillizers at this time, since they also inhibit the process of natural integration of the unconscious material. Even if the subject loses a few hours of sleep, the completion is usually cleaner and the long-term results better without these. If too much excitement interferes with a good night's sleep and this becomes a strong emotional issue for the subject, Librium, Valium, or a barbiturate might be appropriate.

The basic rule is that the subject should not be left alone for twenty-four hours after the ingestion of LSD. During the evening and the night it is recommended that he or she maintains a quiet meditative mood and does not embark on solving heavy interpersonal problems. If the companion for the night is a sexual partner, the suggestion is to spend the time in quiet non-verbal communication. Talking and sexual interaction should not be enforced by the partner and should reflect the inclinations of the subject.

INTEGRATION OF THE DRUG EXPERIENCES

The morning after the session the client should be able to sleep as long as is necessary. The general suggestion for the day is to rest, relax and stay in a meditative state of mind. Quiet walks in nature, basking in the sun, or swimming are highly recommended. Listening to music, especially to the pieces that were played during the LSD experience can be particularly useful. Later that day the sitters should schedule a long interview with the client. This is an opportunity to share in detail the experiences of the preceding day and also to discuss any puzzling aspects of the psychedelic session; it also serves to facilitate the integration of the material and its application to everyday life. Special attention should be paid to transference phenomena that occurred during the session, and to their analysis. At the Maryland Psychiatric Research Center both treatment units were equipped with closed-circuit television. Those subjects who requested or agreed to have their LSD sessions videotaped usually watched the tape the following day. We found this procedure extremely useful; it provided a unique opportunity to complement the subjective dimension of the experience with a more objective point of view.

The subject should be encouraged to write a detailed account of his or her psychedelic experience. This process involves concentrated attention and seems to facilitate recall of otherwise forgotten episodes. Intense emotions can emerge during this work, and the client might have an opportunity to complete an unfinished gestalt. In general, it seems that the work on the account greatly facilitates the integration of the session and later this write-up becomes a basis for a deeper and more detailed discussion of the psychedelic experience with the sitters. If the sessions are continued detailed records become essential, since old material can frequently assume new dimensions of meaning in view of later psychedelic experiences.

The clients should also be given ample opportunity to express their experiences in various artistic forms, such as paintings, mandala drawings, poems, written stories or plays, sculptures, dancing, or musical compositions. In addition to their aesthetic, cathartic, and documentary value, these creations often provide valuable material for a deeper understanding of the session. In several of our patients, impulsive drawing and painting became an important channel for coping with difficult unconscious material.

Sometimes the integration of the session takes days or weeks. It is important to encourage the client to keep the emotional channels open and continue the uncovering process, rather than try to shut them off prematurely by psychological means or with tranquillizers. Belated completion of an unconscious gestalt is most likely to occur in the intermediate states between waking consciousness and sleep that characterize the hypnagogic and hypnopompic periods. Another important opportunity of this kind is the dream life. After a well-integrated session, the nights tend to be dreamless and sleep very deep and refreshing. Conversely, a session in which the subject did not reach emotional and psychosomatic closure is usually followed by extraordinarily rich and intense dream life. A powerful dream can often mediate completion and final integration of material that had been activated by the drug but remained unresolved.

When the spontaneous process does not have enough dynamic strength to complete itself, the sitters should do intense activating work with the client, following the principles outlined earlier for the reentry period. An interesting alternative to the approach that encourages exteriorization and abreaction is the use of prolonged hyperventilation. This technique, based on the Indian science of breath, *pranayama*, was recently rediscovered by Leonard Orr (72) and adopted in his *rebirthing* programs. Intense breathing, continued for a period of about thirty to forty-five minutes, tends to collect the tensions in the body into a stereotyped pattern of armoring and eventually release them. This is associated with activation of important material from various levels of the unconscious. The muscular tensions concentrate in the arms and legs (the so-called *carpopedal spasms* of medical terminology)[3] and in several circular constrictions of the head and body corresponding to the levels of the different chakras in the Indian system of Kundalini yoga. In this technique, vocalization and conventional abreaction is generally discouraged, and the subject is asked to continue breathing until all the tensions are released. This is a very effective way of clearing residual problems after a psychedelic experience. Even without previous administration of the drug this method can mediate access to deep and dramatic experiences of a biographical, perinatal and transpersonal nature in a very short time. The use of this technique requires certain background information and special instructions, and it will be discussed in greater detail in the following volume.

If neither of the above techniques brings a satisfactory psychological resolution, another psychedelic session should be scheduled as soon as possible. The general principle applied here might seem paradoxical to a conventional psychiatrist: Psychedelic therapy can be discontinued at any time after a successful session that was well integrated. If it resulted in an intensification of clinical symptoms or a prolonged reaction, continuation of therapy is indicated. The basic idea is that this is not due to some unpredictable effect of LSD, but represents an unfinished unconscious gestalt that should be completed.

The use of group psychotherapy as part of a comprehensive LSD treatment program deserves special discussion. After several unsuccessful attempts at using LSD as an adjunct in group psychotherapy, we moved away from this model. However, it proved extremely useful to combine individual LSD treatment with drug-free group work in the context of a therapeutic community. The atmosphere of collective responsibility and support, opportunities for mutual help, and the specific power of the group process represent extraordinary therapeutic potential. In the context of a therapeutic community, LSD patients spend the late hours of the sessions in the company of their co-patients. At this time they can have various interesting perceptions of other people and of their interaction; conversely, others make valuable observations of the persons coming down from LSD sessions and of their own reactions toward them. In the next meeting where the patient shares his or her psychedelic experiences, this material becomes an important addition to the group dynamics. The subject's interaction with other members in the group can contribute considerably to a deeper understanding of the material from the LSD session, and also provides new insights into the problems of other patients in the group. These group meetings typically have such evocative power that some patients, instead of communicating verbally, are moved into deep emotional states that can lead to experiential therapeutic sessions.

The use of the material from psychedelic experiences in meetings of the therapeutic community results in an unusual deepening and intensification of the group process. LSD sessions regularly bring forth powerful unconscious material which would otherwise rarely appear in group work. The spectrum of experiences discussed in these meetings ranges from episodes involving various sexual perversions, murderous aggression, sadomasochistic drives, incestuous tendencies, and primitive indulging in biological material, to states of ecstatic rapture, feelings of cosmic unity, and past-incarnation memories. This provides fairly unique opportunities for indirect corrective emotional experiences for group members, in terms of the therapist's reactions toward potentially objectionable unconscious material emerging in the LSD sessions of their co-patients. The therapist's matter-of-fact approach to issues such as sadistic tendencies, grandiose fantasies and day-dreams, forbidden sexual wishes, or loss of control over bladder or bowels which may have occurred in the sessions of various members of the group, helps others to accept such elements and to allow themselves to experience such situations if they start emerging in their own psychedelic sessions. In this context, unconscious material that is usually anxiety-, guilt-, and conflict-laden can be treated with lightness and even humor. In addition to the advantages described above, the use of group work also saves time for the LSD therapist; many of the general principles of therapy, experiential strategies, and interpretive possibilities can be communicated to the entire group instead of having to be repeated for each participant individually.

In the above discussion I have outlined only the most general principles of a comprehensive program of LSD psychotherapy. The detailed therapeutic strategy and tactics in each individual case depend on many factors and have to be creatively developed by therapists on the basis of their clinical experience and their own first-hand explorations in LSD training sessions. The actual practice of psychedelic therapy is ultimately based as much on intuition as it is on knowledge of therapeutic principles, and it will probably always combine elements of art and science.

NOTES

1. Prefrontal lobotomy is a psychosurgical procedure developed by the Portuguese neurologist, Edgar Moniz, and awarded a Nobel Prize for medicine in 1949. It was used for chronic psychoses, impulsive behavior and some severe obsessive-compulsive states. Its original form involved blind severing of connections between the frontal lobes and the rest of the brain. The damage was occasionally so excessive that most of the brain hemisphere turned into a large blood cyst.
2. The interested reader will find more information on the use of music in psychedelic sessions and non-drug experiential work in a special article by Helen Bonny and Walter Pahnke, *The Use of Music in Psychedelic (LSD) Therapy* (14) and in Helen Bonny and Louis Savary's book *Music and Your Mind*. (15)
3. In medical handbooks this is referred to as the *"hyperventilation syndrome,"* and presented as a mandatory physiological reaction to intense breathing. Repeated observations from psychotherapeutic work utilizing breathing techniques clearly indicate that this is not true. If the subject is encouraged to continue hyperventilating after these spasms have developed, this will paradoxically release the tensions. Moreover, after several initial sessions employing this method the organism stops responding to intense breathing with the "hyperventilation syndrome."

COMPLICATIONS OF LSD PSYCHOTHERAPY: OCCURRENCE, PREVENTION, AND THERAPEUTIC MEASURES 5

Physical and Emotional Contraindications
Critical Situations in LSD Sessions
Adverse Aftereffects of LSD Psychotherapy
Prevention and Management of Complications
in LSD Psychotherapy

While discussing the risks and dangers of LSD psychotherapy, we must distinguish between those that are intrinsic to the drug and to the psychedelic process and those that are critically dependent on extrapharmacological factors. The former are involved every time the drug is taken without regard to the specific circumstances; the latter are to a great extent conditional and their incidence, degree and relevance can be influenced by set, setting and the technique of conducting the sessions. The dangers of LSD psychotherapy can be reduced considerably if we screen out individuals who represent high risk, and if we conduct the sessions with an awareness of and respect for the specific dynamics of the LSD reaction.

PHYSICAL AND EMOTIONAL CONTRAINDICATIONS

All clinical and laboratory evidence accumulated during the last three decades indicates that from the biological point of view pharmaceutically pure LSD is a surprisingly safe substance. This statement should not be automatically applied to so-called "street acid." The quality of samples sold in the black market varies considerably and some of the impurities and admixtures are physiologically much more dangerous than LSD. Chemical analysis detected amphetamines, strychnine, STP, phencyclidine (PCP or "angel dust"), and other substances in several street samples of what was sold as LSD.

In clinical work with pure LSD, the major physiological danger is not the drug *per se*, but the intensity of emotions that it triggers. Only rarely is there a high-dose LSD session in which the client does not experience at some point extreme degrees of emotional and physical stress, the dimensions of which are beyond anything encountered in everyday life. It is therefore essential to screen out in advance individuals for whom intense emotions can be dangerous or even fatal. It was mentioned earlier that this involves in the first place persons with serious cardiovascular problems, such as a high degree of arteriosclerosis, thrombosis with a danger of embolism, malignant hypertension, vascular aneurysms, a history of myocardial infarction, myocarditis, decompensated cardiac failure, and brain hemorrhage. Where there is the slightest doubt, the candidate for an LSD session should have a physical examination, including an electrocardiogram. In case of mild cardiovascular problems, one should be conservative with the dosage and proceed with caution. We have to bear in mind that we are not talking about direct noxious effects of LSD on the heart or vessels, but the risks associated with intense emotions. Although higher dosages usually evoke more powerful affective responses, this relationship is not linear. In individuals who are very emotional or who have enormous amounts of unconscious material close to the surface, a relatively small dose of LSD can trigger a very strong reaction.

Pregnancy should be an absolute contraindication. Although the existence of a direct teratogenic effect of the usual doses of LSD is questionable, there is a danger of disturbing the biochemical balance between the fetus and the maternal organism. An even greater risk is the intense uterine contractions that are part of many high-dose sessions, especially those involving perinatal material. As a result of a powerful LSD session female subjects may often start menstruating in the middle of their cycle. The issue of chromosomal damage and adverse effects on heredity has caused much controversy in the past; at present very few scientists believe that such dangers really exist. Because of their practical significance these problems are discussed in a special appendix to this book. (pp 320-47)

All other biological dangers are relative. Many clinical observations suggest that special caution is indicated in persons who have an epileptic disposition, especially those with a history of *grand mal* seizures. In these individuals LSD can occasionally trigger not only individual attacks but entire chains of seizures following each other in a rapid sequence. This so-called *status epilepticus* can be very difficult to control. However, certain forms of epilepsy and other types of seizure-like motor activity have responded favorably to LSD treatment in the past, and so this issue has to be considered individually for each case. This observation seems to be particularly true for temporal lobe epilepsy, though there is as yet no clear organic finding.

Sometimes the excessive muscular activity that frequently occurs in high-dose LSD sessions can be a specific danger for some of the patients. Extreme tension, tremors, cramps, jerks and complex twisting movements might lead to complications in individuals with pathological fragility of the bones, insufficiently healed fractures, or a disposition to recurrent dislocation of the joints.

There are some indications that individuals with severe liver damage have a tendency to prolonged LSD reactions, because the liver plays an important role in detoxifying LSD and excreting it from the body. Some researchers therefore tended in the past to screen out persons with insufficient liver function associated with cirrhosis, a history of hepatitis, or other pathological conditions. Our experience with chronic alcoholics and cancer patients, many of whom had considerable liver damage, indicated that this factor is negligible unless the dysfunction is of a critical degree.

If we follow the rules outlined above, LSD appears to be a drug with a wide range of biological safety. Dosages between 25 and 2000 micrograms have been used in clinical settings without any detectable adverse physiological effects. In our own research, we have administered LSD to persons up to the age of eighty-three and to a number of cancer patients in the terminal stages of their illness, without a single casualty. Our experience shows that the laboratory examinations routinely used in medical practice to detect diseases and dysfunctions, such as electroencephalography, electrocardiography, blood count, sedimentation, urine analysis and liver tests do not show any pathological changes even after a series of eighty to one hundred LSD sessions.

The situation is much more complicated in regard to emotional risks. Here the degree of safety is critically dependent on the pre-session emotional balance of the subject, and on the external circumstances. I have never seen adverse after-effects of an LSD session in an individual who did not have considerable emotional problems prior to the session. In a person who is reasonably balanced and adjusted, the negative sequelae the day after a supervised psychedelic session seldom go beyond such complaints as feelings of fatigue, headache, or hangover. These negative consequences can be much more serious after experiences in complex and erratic social situations, in those instances where the drug was given to an unprepared or even unsuspecting individual, or where traumatic circumstances and pathological interaction complicated the course of the psychedelic reaction.

The risk of adverse aftereffects increases considerably when the drug is administered to persons who have serious emotional problems, show severe interpersonal maladjustment, or had psychiatric hospitalization in the past. Work with psychiatric patients, even when conducted by an experienced LSD therapist under the best circumstances, involves certain risks. Careful preparation of the patients, internalization of the experience, and active psychotherapeutic work reduces the hazards, but does not eliminate them completely. There will always be a risk that in spite of all the precautions and palliative measures some important unconscious material may remain unresolved. This can mean an intensification of pre-existing complaints, the occurrence of a new set of symptoms, incidence of prolonged reactions, or later recurrence of unusual states of consciousness (flashbacks). When we work with persons who have borderline schizophrenic symptoms or have had psychotic episodes in the past, triggering serious emotional reactions of a temporary nature represents a calculated risk.

Unlike the case of somatic contraindications, where certain caveats are absolute, screening of LSD candidates on the basis of their emotional condition depends on many external factors. Under optimal circumstances, which involve a specially structured treatment facility and an experienced therapeutic team, LSD psychotherapy can be experimentally conducted with any psychiatric patient whose condition is clearly not of an organic nature. However, this requires an open-ended situation where no limits are placed on the number of sessions. In treating emotionally severely disturbed individuals, we have to be prepared to deal occasionally with transient psychotic states, aggressive behavior, or suicidal tendencies inside and outside of the sessions themselves. Experienced therapists, trained nurses, and the supportive atmosphere of a therapeutic community are necessary prerequisites for such an endeavor. Under circumstances where these criteria are not met, we have to carefully screen out individuals with borderline psychotic problems and a psychotic disposition. An example of this was the situation at the Maryland Psychiatric Research Center. There the number of LSD sessions for all categories of subjects except cancer patients was limited by the research design to three. The center had laboratories and treatment suites, but no bed facilities. In the case of a prolonged reaction or other complications, LSD patients had to be hospitalized at the Spring Grove State Hospital and, according to the routine local policies, this meant a stay in a locked ward and administration of phenothiazines. Despite these unfavorable conditions we worked with very severely disturbed patient populations, such as chronic alcoholics and heroin addicts who were prison inmates, and we were not overly anxious during the screening process. We had only two instances of prolonged reactions in our LSD subjects, both occurring in patients who had psychotic episodes in the past. They lasted only a few days, and could be handled easily by conventional means.

CRITICAL SITUATIONS IN LSD SESSIONS

While seriously adverse aftereffects of supervised LSD sessions tend to occur only in individuals who had considerable emotional problems prior to the drug experience, in the actual course of high-dose psychedelic sessions various emergencies can occur in anybody, without regard to his or her emotional stability. It is essential to inform a client during the preparation period that he or she may have difficult experiences during the sessions, and that these represent a meaningful and integral part of the procedure. One of the major problems in the non-supervised use of psychedelics was a false notion that the subject would experience only states of transcendental bliss and have a uniformly wonderful time. The occurrence of difficult emotional states was therefore perceived as an unexpected complication, and easily caused panic in the subject and his or her friends.

The most common problem in psychedelic sessions is resistance to the emerging unconscious material and an unwillingness to "go with the experience." The form this resistance takes is usually indicative of the client's habitual mechanisms of defense. The evasive maneuvers that the sitters have to deal with cover a very wide range. Sometimes, the subject accepts the eyeshades and headphones, but argues against the use of evocative music. Here the therapists must be careful to distinguish constructive and appropriate objections from anxious efforts to fence-off the emerging emotions. Constant talking and intellectualizing which does not leave space for deeper experiences is another common escape. Some individuals try to focus in their mind's eye on the external environment and recall the surrounding reality in the most minute details. They try to remember the names of the co-patients, reconstruct the ground plan of the facility, and visualize the form and color of furniture in the room. Sudden sobering-up in the middle of a high-dose session is another common form of psychological resistance against the psychedelic experience.

The next step involves unwillingness to keep the session internalized. Sometimes the subject asks for permission and offers a reason—taking a break, smoking a cigarette, drinking a cup of coffee, having a chat, or going for a walk. Frequent visits to the bathroom are a particularly common technique; sometimes they are physiologically justified, but often they have purely psychological motives. A more serious form of resistance involves removing the eyeshades and headphones and simply refusing to continue, without excuse or explanation. When this happens the sitters should use all their psychological skills to return the client into the original introspective mode. The only exceptions to this rule are situations where the subject wants to explore the external world and there is no doubt that the request is genuine and does not serve the purpose of avoiding the inner experience. While negotiating with the client in these situations, the sitters can refer to the original contract made during the preparation period, when various forms of resistance were explicitly discussed with the subject and he or she accepted the importance of keeping the session internalized.

In an extreme case, the relationship between the sitters and the LSD subject can be disrupted to the point where the latter perceives it as being not cooperative but antagonistic, and tries to act on his or her own. This can culminate in the client attempting to leave the treatment situation altogether. These episodes are not very frequent, but they are extremely critical for LSD therapists. The basic rule here is to keep the subjects on the premises and guard against their hurting themselves or someone else. Various degrees of compromise have to be made between the needs to restrain the subject, and to avoid an open confrontation and fight that would further impair the therapeutic relationship. In the most dramatic situations of this kind, the best one can do is to play for time and keep the subject safe until the receding pharmacological effect makes him or her more amenable to active cooperation. Fortunately, such extreme situations are rather exceptional in therapeutic LSD sessions conducted by experienced sitters.

Before discussing the specific difficulties and complications that can occur during LSD sessions, we will mention some of the general principles. The most important factor in crisis-handling is the therapist's emotional reaction to the emergency situation. A calm, centered, and supportive attitude toward the various manifestations that occur in psychedelic sessions is much more important than anything the therapist says and does. The ability to remain unperturbed while facing dramatic instinctual outbursts, sexual acting-out, hostility and aggression, self-destructive tendencies, paranoid reactions, or extreme emotional and physical pain increases with clinical experience and the number of sessions one has conducted. Participating in a number of critical situations and witnessing their positive resolution is the best training for future emergencies. Working through one's own emotional difficulties in psychedelic sessions conducted for training purposes is equally, if not more important. Any serious unresolved problems in the sitters may easily be activated by participation in other people's sessions.

If the emergency situation evokes anxiety, aggression, guilt or some other inappropriate "countertransference" reaction in the therapists, this can result in a highly dangerous type of interaction with the patient. Since the sitters are the patient's only hold on reality, their reaction is his or her ultimate criterion of the seriousness of the situation. Thus, anxiety manifested by the therapist represents final proof to the patient that the situation is really dangerous. Not only are the sitters sober and supposedly in a state of adequate reality-testing, but in the eyes of the client they are experts in dealing with unusual states of consciousness. Their evaluation of the situation and their emotional reaction thus reflects professional judgment. Whenever the therapists show strong negative reactions to emergency situations in LSD sessions, destructive vicious circles are likely to develop between the clients and themselves. The therapist may be upset by certain behavior or experiences that the patient manifests, and his or her emotional reaction has a reinforcing effect on the patient. This intensification of the patient's difficulties causes in turn more emotional distress in the therapist. Because of this snowballing effect, such situations can reach critical proportions in a very short time. Similar patterns have been described in psychodynamic literature as "diabolic circles" (*circuli diaboli*); although this term might seem slightly exaggerated when used for situations in everyday life, it is certainly appropriate and justified for the dramatic circumstances that might develop in LSD sessions.

Adequate handling of critical situations is one of the crucial problems in LSD psychotherapy. A session in which the process gets out of control is not only fruitless, but harmful; it creates frustration and disappointment in both the therapist and patient, undermines their mutual trust, and can shatter their feelings of personal security. For the therapist adequate experience and training, including his or her own LSD sessions, is therefore of paramount importance. At the time of my LSD research in Czechoslovakia, the training for future LSD therapists more-or-less followed the psychoanalytic model. It required a minimum of five personal LSD sessions under the guidance of an experienced therapist, and thirty therapeutic sessions with psychiatric patients conducted under supervision. LSD training sessions were also found very useful for those psychiatric nurses who functioned as female co-therapists or came into contact with patients under the influence of LSD.

The use of tranquillizers is an issue of considerable practical significance and deserves a special notice. In general, an experienced therapeutic dyad can handle all, or almost all, situations that occur in LSD sessions by psychological means alone. I have personally conducted more than three thousand sessions over the years, and only three were terminated by tranquillizers. All three occurred in the early years of my LSD research when my experience with drugs was very limited. Thorazine and other major tranquillizers are not specific neutralizers of the LSD effect. Used in high dosages, they have a general inhibiting effect that overrides and masks the psychedelic action of LSD. Detailed retrospective analysis of this situation usually shows that the patient experiences the action of both drugs simultaneously, and that the combined effect is rather unpleasant.

The use of tranquillizers in the course of psychedelic sessions is potentially very noxious. The most dramatically negative LSD experiences have a strong tendency toward positive resolution; if they are well resolved they are extremely beneficial for the subject in the long run. If tranquillizers are administered in the middle of a difficult psychedelic state they tend to prevent its natural resolution and positive integration. They "freeze" the subject in a negative psychological frame and thus contribute to the incidence of prolonged reactions, negative aftereffects, and "flashbacks." The routine administration of tranquillizers in the middle of negative psychedelic experiences is therefore a harmful practice that should be discontinued. This is even more true of their use in the context of LSD psychotherapy, which follows in general the strategy of an uncovering technique. Unpleasant experiences are caused by the emergence of highly-charged emotionally traumatic unconscious material. Since this material is the source of the patient's difficulties in everyday life, negative episodes in LSD sessions, if properly approached and handled, represent great opportunities for therapeutic change.

In LSD psychotherapy, there is a continuity in the content of consecutive sessions. If we terminate an unpleasant experience by administering tranquillizers, the unresolved material will continue to surface in future sessions till the patient reaches the point where he or she is capable of confronting and resolving it. Therefore, the therapist should first exhaust all possibilities of a psychological intervention before considering tranquillizers. If a specific vicious interaction has developed between the sitter and the client, and the situation appears to be irresolvable, another therapist should be called to take over the session; provisions for such situations should always be made in advance.

If all psychological approaches fail and tranquillizers have to be used, it is much better to start with Librium (30–60 milligrams) or Valium (10–30 milligrams), which seem to alleviate painful emotions without interfering with the course of the session. As soon as possible, the patient should resume a reclining position with eyeshades and headphones, to continue the introspective approach to the experience.

The situation that creates the most problems in psychedelic sessions is the *experience of dying* that occurs in the context of the death-rebirth process. This encounter with death is so authentic and convincing that it can easily be mistaken for a real, vital emergency, not only by the experient but also by external observers and inexperienced sitters who are in a normal state of consciousness. Because of this confusion between symbolic and biological dying, the resistance against the psychedelic process can be particularly powerful. Deep seated anxiety and activation of survival programs can make the subject fight the effect of the drug with the intensity and determination characteristic of an actual life-and-death struggle.

From the technical point of view this is a most critical and important situation. It is absolutely essential to the smooth course of the session and its positive outcome that subjects stay with the eyeshades and headphones at this point, and keep the process internalized. If the psychological aspects of this experience are projected onto the therapeutic situation, this can result in dangerous acting-out behavior. Subjects may feel drawn to windows and doors, seeing them as escape routes out of the unbearable psychological situation; they may physically fight with the sitters, seeing them as the oppressive element; or be driven to violent self-destructive actions mistaking them for the liberating ego death. The dangers of the externalization of this process extend beyond the framework of the drug session itself. Unresolved psychedelic experiences of this kind can result in very difficult emotional states in the post-session period, which may last for days or months unless properly treated.

If the client tries to tear off the eyeshades, and create a projective pseudoreal situation of the above kind, this is the time for active intervention. Since the issue has been discussed during the preparation period, the sitters can make references to that conversation to connect the client's intellectual knowledge of the process with the actual experience. This in itself can be helpful, although there is usually a fundamental gap between the death experience and its verbal description. This process can be so elemental and of such unimaginable experiential dimensions that no words in the world are adequate to convey it. In any case, the critical factors in dealing with this situation are the non-verbal aspects of the sitters' approach; under these circumstances, metacommunication is more effective than anything that is said or done.

The sitters should emphasize, repeatedly if necessary, that the client is not facing real biological death, however convincingly he or she might feel this. They should offer reassurance that the feeling of a lack of oxygen is only subjective, and that the breathing itself is adequate. It is also important to encourage the subject consistently to surrender to the process and accept the psychological death. Insistence that the quickest way out of this experience lies in going through its most difficult parts, and references to the positive "other side" can be of great help. However, the sitters' centeredness, familiarity with the process, and trust in its intrinsic trajectory are ultimately the most critical factors, since they supply the non-verbal or metacommunicative components which make their statements experientially real and convincing.

In the course of repeated LSD sessions that focus on the perinatal level, the experiences of dying usually become deeper and more complete. When the process reaches the stages of the final *ego death*, special technical problems can occur. The ego death involves an experience of the destruction of everything that the subject is, possesses, or is attached to. Its essential characteristics are a sense of total annihilation on all imaginable levels, loss of all systems of relation and reference, and destruction of the objective world. As it is approached in different directions and on different levels, the process requires more and more psychological sacrifice. In the final stages, subjects have to face and confront experiences, situations and circumstances that are unacceptable or even unimaginable to them.

The nature of the experiences that represent the final obstacle for the completion of the death-rebirth process varies from subject to subject. For some, it can be certain critical physical conditions, such as a high degree of suffocation, agonizing physical pain, blacking out, or violent seizure-like activity. Others have to face a situation which is psychologically utterly unacceptable to them, and surrender to it. The most frequent of these are vomiting, losing control of the bladder or bowels; sexually unacceptable behavior; confusion and disorientation; making various inhuman sounds, and humiliation or loss of prestige. A very difficult and important experience that occurs in the context of the ego death is the expectation of a catastrophe of enormous dimensions. Subjects face agonizing tension increasing to fantastic proportions and develop a conviction that they will explode and the entire world will be destroyed. This fear of disintegration represents a difficult experiential barrier; in their special state subjects may generate a strong conviction that not only their own fate, but the fate of the entire world depends on their ability to hold on. In this situation it is extremely important that the sitters repeatedly emphasize the safety of this experience. No matter how catastrophic it might appear from the subjective point of view, this explosion is ultimately emotionally and spiritually liberating. What is destroyed in this process is the old, limiting concept of oneself and the corresponding restricting view of existence and of the universe. Once the process reaches this point, it is absolutely essential to complete the experiential gestalt. Unfinished and poorly integrated sessions in this area can result in serious destructive behavior and suicidal ideation.

Another situation that can become a source of considerable problems in LSD sessions is the *experience of no exit*. Although it occurs most frequently in the context of BPM II, there exist close parallels that can be observed in advanced sessions on the transpersonal level. The transpersonal versions lack the concrete element of mechanical imprisonment and the gross biological dimension, and have a purely metaphysical quality. A person who is in a no-exit state experiences extreme distress of various kinds and is unable to see any end to this situation or any way out of it. Thinking seems to have a circular quality and subjects frequently compare their thought-processes with closed loops running on a tape-recorder. A more appropriate and accurate description of this state is to liken the peculiar circularity of ideas and emotions to a moving Moebius strip that turns into itself while also involving a paradox in regard to the usual spatial and temporal configurations.

The basic strategy in dealing with the no-exit situation should be to emphasize and clarify the distinction between psychological time and clock-time. The feeling of eternal doom with no hope of escape is an *essential experiential characteristic* of the no-exit situation. In order to work through and integrate this experience one has to accept its full content, including the feeling that it will last forever and that there is no way out.[1] Paradoxically, a person who desperately resists and fights what he or she feels would be an experience of endless suffering, prolongs his or her tortures; conversely, if he or she capitulates and accepts staying in hell forever, the very depth of the infernal matrix has been experienced, that particular gestalt is completed, and the process will move further.

A difficult situation that seems to be closely related to the no-exit matrix involves *repetitive verbal or motor behavior*; in classical psychiatric terminology this is known as verbigeration and perseveration. For a period of time that can last anywhere from minutes to hours the individual behaves like a robot whose mechanism has been broken. Subjects in this state keep repeating the same movements, sentences, or words. There is usually no meaningful contact with them, and no external intervention of any kind can break the automaton-like behavior. In most cases, the only solution is to wait until the reaction spontaneously terminates and contact with the client can be re-established. This problem seems to occur when the drug activates unconscious material with excessive emotional charge. Less dramatic forms of this pattern can accompany the emergence of a particularly strong COEX system; extreme cases are almost always associated with the perinatal process. Subjects frequently have total amnesia, or very incomplete memory, regarding episodes of this kind.

One of the common problems in psychedelic sessions is *fear of insanity*, usually associated with a feeling of losing control. It occurs most frequently in individuals who have a strong need to maintain control and are afraid of losing it even under circumstances of everyday life. The general strategy, discussed during the preparation period and reinforced verbally during the session when loss of control becomes an issue, is to encourage giving up control. The usual misconception underlying this problem is the fear that even a momentary abandoning of control will result in its permanent loss, and insanity of some type would ensue. The new concept offered to the patient is that giving up control creates a situation in which the suppressed material that has been kept in check can emerge and be worked through. After an episode of dramatic and often chaotic release of pent-up energies through various available channels, the problem loses its charge and the individual achieves effortless control. This new type of mastery does not involve stronger self-control, but no need for it, since there is nothing to control. The frequent association of problems related to loss of control with concerns about sphincter function will be discussed later in the chapter.

In general, any kind of "psychotic" experience should be encouraged during the sessions, and in specially structured situations also in the free intervals between sessions, as long as they do not endanger the client or anyone else. We are not dealing here with experiences produced by the drug but with areas of potential psychotic activity within the client that have been chemically exteriorized. It is more appropriate to see such episodes as unique therapeutic opportunities rather than as clinical problems. Psychotic reactions that deserve special attention are those associated with *paranoid perception*. They present particular technical difficulties since they affect the very core of the therapeutic cooperation, the relationship with the sitters. Problems in this area cover a wide range, from minor mistrust to full-blown paranoid delusions. They also occur in many varieties and can be anchored in different levels of the unconscious. During the work on the psychodynamic level they can usually be traced back to situations in childhood in which the client was actively abused and mistreated, or to episodes in early infancy involving emotional deprivation and abandonment. Important sources of paranoid feelings are BPM II and BPM III, particularly the onset of the no-exit situation. Biologically, this would correspond with the beginning of the delivery, when the intrauterine world of the fetus is invaded by insidious and intangible chemical forces and starts to collapse. Some of the paranoid feelings can be traced back to early embryonal crises, traumatic past-incarnation experiences, negative archetypal structures, and other types of transpersonal phenomena.

Less serious forms of mistrust can be approached by reminding the clients of earlier discussions concerning basic trust, and by encouraging them to turn within and search for the sources of this mistrust in the emerging unconscious material. This is usually possible only where there is enough trust left for the subject to be able to communicate about the loss of trust. In more serious forms the client will deal with the paranoid thoughts and feelings internally, and the sitters might not discover this until the experience is over and the trust bond reestablished. Extreme degrees of paranoia can involve acting-out behavior; situations where an acutely paranoid LSD subject tries to leave the room or attempts to attack the sitters are among to the most difficult challenges of psychedelic therapy. Here the only resort might be to guard against irreversible damage to persons and objects, and play for time. When the reaction subsides the sitters should return the patient to the reclining position, eyeshades, and headphones, and try to facilitate complete resolution and integration of the problem by the methods described earlier.

On occasion, *sexual acting out* can present technical problems. When it does not involve the sitters directly, as in the case of genital or anal masturbation, the sitters should be sufficiently open-minded to allow it. Occasionally, one episode of this kind properly handled by the therapists can provide a powerful corrective experience that will heal a long-lasting psychological trauma caused by insensitive parents, who may have drastically punished infantile instinctual activities. If the sitters have difficulty accepting such behavior, this should be an incentive towards and a unique opportunity for exploration of the roots of their own attitudes and reactions.

The situation is more difficult if the acting-out behavior involves sexual activities directed toward the sitters. The general rule here should be to exclude any explicit adult interaction that involves genitals, breasts, or the mouth. The reasons for this are serious and go beyond considerations of a moralistic nature. Sexual activity of this kind on the part of the patient is frequently a manifestation of

A patient's representation of the dynamic and colorful displays of ornamental patterns which char- acterize the early stage in a psy- chedelic session.

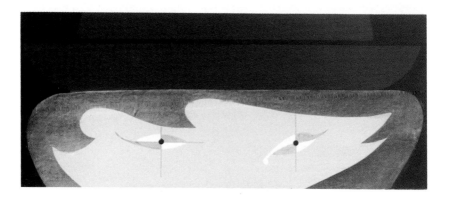

Illusory transformation under the influence of LSD. Two represen-tations of a psychiatric nurse seen in her street clothes.

Above. The 'psychedelic break-through' during a perinatal experience. The lower part of the painting shows a scatological area which the patient described as the 'quagmire' of her unconscious: numerous dangerous animals represent the negative emotions. In the upper part a heavenly blue tunnel symbolizes rebirth and transcendence. The patient is sitting on a porpoise-like animal made friendly by the presence of the divine element. She is represented as a little naked princess with a golden crown, a divine child. This experience was related to the moment of biological birth ('crowning').

Below. Influences from the external world destroy the newly achieved positive state; on a deeper level, uterine contractions encroach on the oceanic peace of the womb.

The transition from BPM III to BPM IV.

Left. A gigantic and threatening Golem-like figure blocks the access to the source of light.

Above. The subject at a later stage faces and embraces the unobstructed rising sun. (From the collection of Dr. Milan Hausner, Prague, Czechoslovakia.)

Above. In an experience from the final phase of the death-rebirth process, a subject is attacked by vicious predatory birds as he climbs a steep mountain towards the sun.

Below. The transition from BPM III to BPM IV in the context of the death-rebirth process. The lower section represents dark, restricting forces and the upper the cosmic source of light. The middle section symbolizes the physical and emotional agony accompanying the opening of the heart chakra. The flaming heart with the peacock design is stretched beyong any imaginable limits.

Above. A perinatal experience of abysmal nausea. It shows the naked, sick, dejected subject vomiting into a gigantic vaginal corridor.

Below. A depiction of torture, mutilation and being cut off from one's senses; experienced in the context of the perinatal process.

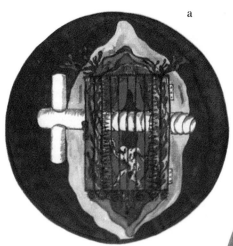

a

b

c

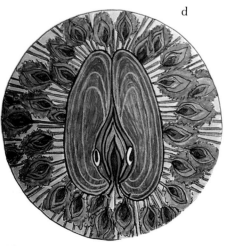

d

A unique sequence of paintings illustrating the transformation of the maternal genitals from a murderous instrument into a symbol of security, beauty and transcendence.

Left a. The delivering vagina as a combination of prison, torture chamber and gigantic press.

Left b. The genitals seen as ugly and disgusting (the 'vagina of Kali').

Left c. In a more advanced stage of the birth process the emphasis shifts from the frightening and biological aspects to the decorative, and to a smooth flow of cosmic energy through the organ.

Left d. The vaginal features are all but lost in a glorious peacock aureole.

Above. The last painting of the series represents the final experience of biological and spiritual birth. The subject appears in a peacock mandala framed by a halo of purifying fire; she is supported, protected and nourished by divine hands. The vagina of her mother, her own genitals and the sustaining hands of the goddess bear identical peacock ornaments.

An experience of death and re-birth from a perinatal session. The subject's body rises into the light from the realm of darkness, cemeteries, coffins and candles; her arms reaching to embrace the sun, her head melting into the transcendental source.

Left. An experience of over-whelming threat combined with disgust. The element of danger was associated with the bird-like monster in the upper half of the picture, the feelings of revulsion with the 'mangy rat-tail' at the bottom.

Right. A terrifying vision of an encounter with the devil, the 'Master of Hell'.

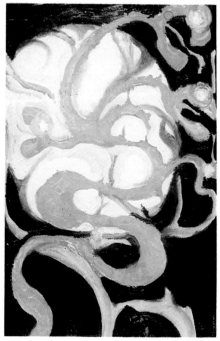

172

Three illustrations of the role of snake symbolism in the death-rebirth process.

Upper left. Deep anxiety is associated with visions of dangerous, poisonous snakes with exposed fangs and forked tongues.

Lower left. The serpentine elements are still present but the patient can envision the possibility of escaping from this situation; the enclosed 'snake pit' has changed into a tunnel and she can see the light at its end.

Above. A representation of what LSD therapists call 'psychedelic breakthrough'. The newly discovered core of the patient's personality is represented by a human embryo and a germinating seed, both symbolizing the perspective of new life, new beginning. The snake now represents the forces in her unconscious that might endanger and destroy this oceanic state of consciousness.

An ecstatic experience of divine epiphany following the ego death. The patient felt flooded with transcendental love and a light of indescribable radiance; her deep feelings of alienation dissolved and for the first time in her life she had the feeling that she 'belonged'.

'The Flagellant' is the title of this attempt to portray the experience of volcanic ecstacy characterizing the final stages of the death-rebirth process (BPM III), where agony and pleasure fuse in an inextricable amalgam. Various parts of the painting can be perceived as related either to physical suffering or to sensual pleasure: wounds with torn flesh, drops and traces of blood after flagellation or beautiful patterns of exotic fabrics and Persian rugs.

The experience of volcanic ecstacy in perinatal sessions is frequently associated with visions of purifying fire (pyrocatharsis). While releasing enormous amounts of destructive energy, LSD subjects identify with erupting volcanoes, atomic explosions, thermonuclear reactions, and even cosmic catastrophes.

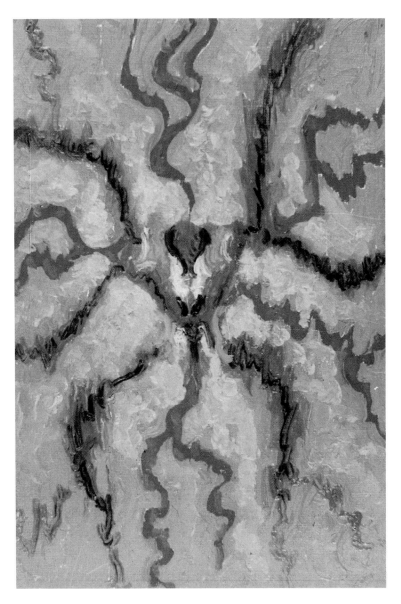

The last seconds before biological and spiritual birth in an LSD session. The triangular area in the center of the picture is where the top of the head or vortex breaks through; the highly charged currents of energy reflect the extreme tension that is typically associated with this moment. Individuals facing the final release experience expectations of apocalyptic catastrophe, such as the fear of an impending explosion in which the entire world will be annihilated.

A representation of identification with the universe. This experience, from an advanced stage of LSD psychotherapy, is associated with ecstatic rapture and visions of cosmic processes on a galactic scale.

Identification with the crucified Christ in the context of BPM III.
Top. Jesus surrounded by the hatred of the hostile mob.
Middle. The brutal biological aspects of crucifixion.

Above. The anger that would be an appropriate human reaction to the tortures that were inflicted upon Jesus.

Three manifestations of the same theme on the psychodynamic, perinatal and transpersonal levels.

Above. 'Pega', an important fantasized childhood companion of the subject.

Upper right. Soldiers in ancient costumes are crushed between two gigantic cylinders. In this basically perinatal symbol the soldiers represent elements of an underlying transpersonal experience which is depicted in the last drawing.

Lower right. A military expedition of an ancient (African?) army. The image of 'Pega' now re-appears as a motif on the standard.

Above. The explosive energies and overwhelming emotions involved in the final stages of the perinatal unfolding (BPM III). **Right.** The connection between this process and the opening of the heart chakra.

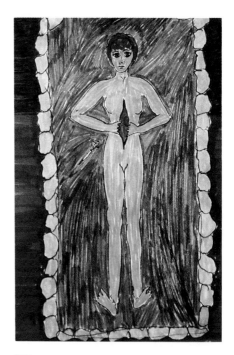

The experience, during a transpersonal session, of elements of the collective unconscious. The patient became a member of an ancient culture that she could not identify by name, historical period or geographical location. However, she was able to draw and paint in its artistic style.

184

Three paintings depicting embryonal, tissue and cellular consciousness.

Upper left. An early intrauterine experience with an awarenesss of the placentary circulation and a sense of the complex communication with the maternal organism.

Left. Consciousness of rapidly growing tissues within the same embryo; the chemical energy of the metabolic processes is seen as explosions of golden light.

Above. The conscious experience of the individual cells constituting the embryonal tissues. This is associated with the insight that consciousness is not limited to the human brain, but pervades all manifestations of life.

Archetypal demonic entities en-
visioned during transpersonal sessions.
Above. A stylized dragon of cosmic proportions representing the
principle of metaphysical evil.
Right. An image of a winged
demonic creature that screens the
source of divine light and prevents
the subject from reaching and
uniting with it.

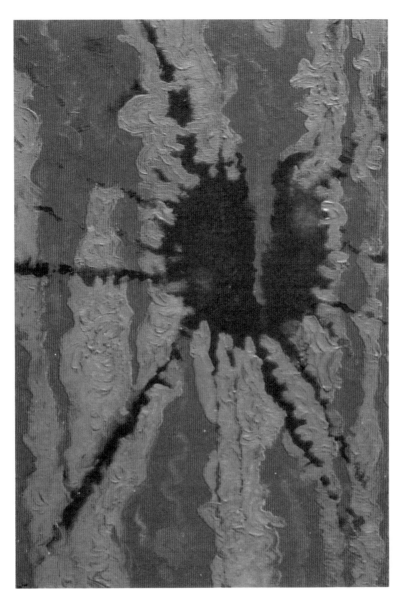

A unique series of paintings from transpersonal sessions representing insights into the nature of reality and the relationships between the ego, the Self and the universe.

Above. 'Through Suffering to the Black Sun', the manifestation of the innermost core of the human being, the divine Self. It is symbolized by the Black Sun which, unlike the *sol niger* of alchemy, is associated with transcendental bliss. The red stripes represent the suffering which must be endured in order to realize one's real nature.

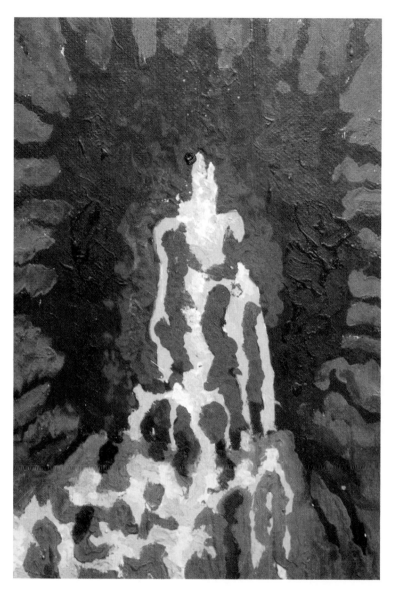

The Black Sun is here depicted as the ultimate source of creative energy in the cosmos. In combination with the preceding painting this gives rise to the idea of the 'Beyond Within', the essential identity between the individual Self and the universal Self. The insight shows a similarity to the Hindu concept of the relationship connecting Jiva with Atma-Brahma and is especially striking as the subject was not familiar with Indian philosophy.

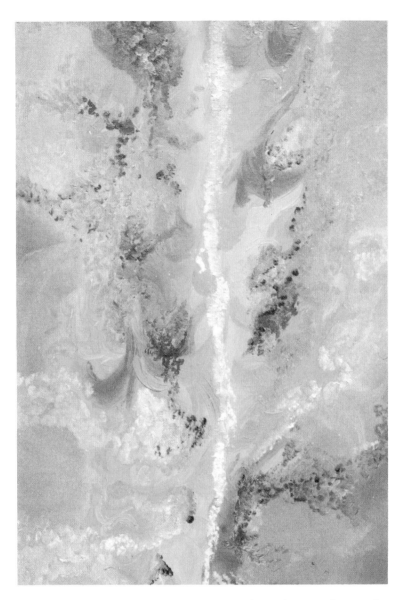

The process of creation and its relationship to the individual as well as the universal Self. The stream of creative cosmic 'energy-consciousness' emanates from its source, the Black Sun, and gen-erates the infinite richness of form. In this case the created elements are related to the vegetable kingdom: blossoming trees, flour-ishing meadows and aquatic plant forms.

The process of cosmic creation through volcanic activity. The patient, who in the perinatal process had experienced the destructive power of volcanoes, was now appreciating the creative, mountain-forming potential of the glowing magma. She related it to a primordial, intermediate state between consciousness and matter out of which all forms emerge and into which they eventually return.

Motifs related to the North American Indian tradition; from transpersonal sessions.

Egyptian motifs from an advanced LSD session of a subject who had spontaneous Kundalini experiences in her everyday life. **Upper right.** An insight into the similarities between the Indian concept of the Serpent Power and Egyptian symbolism involving snakes. Special emphasis was placed on the parallels between the chakra system and the *djed* or spinal column of Osiris and the relationship between the opening of the third eye and the symbol of the uraeus.

Upper left. The blocking of the Kundalini energy in the left eye is connected to the symbolism of the Eye of Horus (*udjat* eye).

Above right. The subject's eye, while watching the sunset, is transformed into a combination of the *udjat* eye and the winged solar disk of Egyptian mythology.

The artist Harriette Francis documented an LSD experience during a psychedelic program at Menlo Park, California. Much of it had typical perinatal features and she has expressed many of the symbolic sequences of the death-rebirth process. After the initial visions of geometric ornaments (1), the process gradually deepens (2,3) and the artist faces an engulfing whirlpool drawing her into the world of death (4). In the underworld she is subjected to piercing pains (5) and crushing pressures (6,7), experiences a strange combination of birth and death (8), meditates on mysterious symbols on a cruciform altar (9) and is offered assistance (10). In a sequence strongly resembling shamanic initiation she faces reduction to a

skeleton and annihilation (11), followed by renewal, ascent and return to life (12). After what appears to be symbolic crucifixion (13) and reminiscence of some surgical intervention (14), she experiences rebirth, which is associated with the vision of a peacock (15). The next drawing, of the oceanic womb, suggests that the experience of birth opened the way to the unitive state of prenatal consciousness (16). She returns from her journey with a sense of rejuvenation and revitalization (17).

(From LSD Journals of an Artist's Trip. Drawings by Harriette Frances. Courtesy of the International Foundation for Advanced Study, Menlo Park, California.)

resistance to deeper issues. A typical example would be a male patient who feels the need for comforting contact on the infantile level and, fearing the dependency and helplessness that this entails, attempts to approach a female therapist in an adult sexual way. In situations like this the sitters should always direct the client to a deeper experiential level and discourage acting-out. This can be done in a constructive way and does not have to involve rejection. Reference to the explicit rules agreed upon before the session can make this situation easier for the sitters.

Adult sexual activities in LSD sessions can be very tricky; no matter what the external circumstances are, they are experienced by the client on many different levels since the ability for narrow and accurate reality-testing is impaired by the drug. Frequent involvement of the infantile levels can result in a specific vulnerability, particularly fear associated with the incest taboo. There is danger that such experiences will be traumatic and have lasting negative consequences for the client and the relationship with the sitter. I have seen several deterring examples of this kind outside of the medical context, especially in communes where young people were sharing psychedelic experiences involving free sexual exchange. The result, in some instances, was contamination of everyday interpersonal relationships by deep unresolved transference problems and sexual confusion. In general, there should be no limits to what the client can experience on the fantasy level. However, the sitters should be very clear about their own attitudes and motives, and approach the subject with integrity and sensitivity. In my experience, there is no need or justification for adult sexual activities in psychedelic therapy, and whenever a sitter considers it seriously, he or she should examine his or her own motives. The only place for adult sexual activities during a psychedelic experience should be between partners who have an emotional and sexual commitment to each other in everyday life. Such an approach can add interesting dimensions to sexual interaction, but is not without dangers and pitfalls even under these circumstances; it should occur only between mature partners with deep knowledge of the nature of the psychedelic process.

It is clear that the question of sexual boundaries is much more problematic in sessions that involve physical intimacy than in those where the sitters maintain a detached attitude toward the clients. Since the use of close physical contact is extremely useful in psychedelic therapy this issue will be briefly discussed here. Deep age-regression in LSD sessions is frequently accompanied by intense anaclitic feelings and tendencies, especially in patients who experienced serious emotional deprivation in early childhood. They might want to hold, fondle, or suck the sitters' hand, put their head in someone's lap, or cuddle up and be cradled and caressed. Sometimes the regressive quality of these phenomena is beyond doubt and the patients show convincing signs of deep regression. At other times these activities can present technical problems because it may not be easy to distinguish whether a certain behavior is an authentic regressive pehnomenon, an inadvertent occurrence, or a sexual overture on a more-or-less adult level. This is particularly true in later stages of the sessions when the drug effect has subsided. Sometimes both levels seem to be involved simultaneously, and the client can oscillate from one to the other.

In the early years of my therapeutic work with LSD I used to discourage or refuse such manifestations, in accord with my strict Freudian background. Later, it became clear to me that periods of deep regression with strong anaclitic needs are of crucial importance from the therapeutic point of view. I realized that the therapist's approach to such situations can represent a deep corrective emotional experience or, conversely, perpetuate and reinforce old, pathological patterns of deprivation and rejection. Even at a time when I was already using physical contact almost routinely, I tended to withdraw it when the client crossed the sexual boundaries. At the present time, I do not see this as an either/or situation. The boundaries can be defined and negotiated in very subtle verbal and non-verbal ways. If the situation moves into problematic areas, it is possible to restore acceptable limits without withdrawing close contact altogether. The key here seems to be the therapist's clarity about his or her own motives and the ability to communicate clearly with the client, verbally and non-verbally. It is the therapist's ambiguities and conflicting messages that allow or breed problems. This is a complex and sensitive area and it is difficult to establish any fixed rules. The therapist has to rely on intuition and clinical experience in every individual case. The nature and specific characteristics of the therapeutic relationship and the degree of trust in it will remain the most important factors in charting the course.

One of the most important areas for psychedelic therapists to deal with is the various forms of *hostility and aggression*. If the sessions are conducted in the framework of a good working relationship, real technical problems with aggressive manifestations are extremely infrequent, even in sessions in which destructive tendencies are predominant. In most instances it is possible to maintain a synergistic relationship even in the context of intense psychodramatic struggle. Most of the technical problems occur when the sitters get physically involved with LSD subjects in a playful fight which involves pressing, pushing, restricting, and sometimes inflicting pain. Under these circumstances, it is absolutely essential to redefine the "as if" framework and prevent the situation becoming absolutely real and serious for the subject. A skillful combination of verbal communication and metacommunication can keep the play in that territory of experiential ambiguity which seems to be optimal for therapeutic work. On the one hand, the situation has to be sufficiently real for the subject to allow his or her full involvement and release of emotions; on the other hand, it must not be so real as to be mistaken for a dangerous or traumatic situation. Maintaining a trusting relationship has to be the primary consideration.

In contrast to the frequency, intensity and scope of experiences involving aggression, elemental and uncontrolled acting-out of destructive tendencies is extremely rare in supervised LSD sessions. When a situation of this kind seems to be impending, the best approach is to encourage external expression in a cooperative framework, as described above. Another effective technique is to relate to the deeper level of anxiety, hurt, and helplessness usually underlying aggressive phenomena. Thus, comfort and reassurance can sometimes have an almost magical influence on a patient who is aggressive and tries to threaten the sitters with an ostentatious display of power. Most effective approaches to aggression entail identification of the specific problem involved in the case, and finding the appropriate solution. As in other kinds of emergencies, the factor of critical importance is the sitter's own reaction and attitude to the situation. If the patient's behavior evokes anxiety or aggression in the sitter, they can get locked into a

A symbolic self-portrait from a session which was characterized by intense aggression oriented both inward and outward. A stylized bird of prey crushes a helpless mouse with its
right claw; the left claw is transformed into a cannon turned against its own head. The an-
tique car on top represents a play on words (self-portrait = auto-portrait), but also suggests
the relationship between the mixture of aggressive and self-destructive impulses frequently
encountered in perinatal sessions and also in reckless, perilous driving.

vicious circle of interaction that tends to reinforce the pathological reactions. The following example from our early work in Prague can be used to illustrate some of the above points.

One day when I was conducting an LSD session with a neurotic patient, I was interrupted by loud knocking. Surprised by this interference, which was against the rules, I went to answer the door. An alarmed nurse told me that my presence was urgently needed in the other treatment room where Henry, another LSD patient, had gone "berserk." I left the nurse in attendance and hurried to the place of the emergency. I found the treatment room in a catastrophic condition; the patient had broken a mirror against the wash-basin, overturned all the furniture, and torn several books and journals to shreds. He was standing in the middle of the room screaming and growling; his appearance was reminiscent of an angry ape. In the corner stood Julia, a young colleague who had recently joined our team. She had sat in on LSD sessions before, although this was the first one she had run independently. She was pale, obviously frightened, and her hands were shaking.

I came up to Henry and took him by the hand; this established contact and also reduced the chances for his attacking me. "It's alright, don't be afraid, nobody is going to hurt you," I told him in a reassuring tone of voice, and pointed to the couch. "Can we sit down? I would like to find out what you have been experiencing." We sat down and I started asking him questions, trying to find out what triggered his aggression. It soon became apparent that earlier in the session he had regressed into early childhood and experienced a need for closeness and affection. He was seeking physical contact with Julia and put his head into her lap. She panicked, pushed him away, and admonished him for introducing sexual elements into therapy. This triggered a very painful memory of a childhood situation in which Henry was caught masturbating by his mother. She made a big scene and reported it to his father who punished him in a very cruel way. This sequence of events effectively blocked Henry's access to both the channel of childhood dependency and that of sexual feelings. In addition, the combination of sexuality with punitive feedback and anxiety made the perinatal level of his unconscious experientially available. At this point, Henry "chose" the path of aggressive behavior.

During this discussion, Julia recovered from the shock of her psychedelic baptism. With my psychological support, she allowed Henry to put his head on her lap and held his hand. However, another difficult test was yet to come. About half an hour later, Henry, by that time back in the experience with his eyes closed, started playing with his penis. While doing this he occasionally opened his eyes, obviously checking our reaction. When the expected feedback was not forthcoming, he gradually unzipped his pants and started to masturbate by pulling his foreskin back and forth. His ejaculation brought a dramatic relief of Henry's physical and emotional tension; its psychological impact went far beyond that of the physiological release. Henry felt that being able to masturbate in the presence of surrogate parental figures without being rejected had helped him to overcome a sexual trauma from his childhood and brought about a lasting liberation of his sexual life.

This session was also quite important for Julia's development. In retrospect, she appreciated this difficult experience as a great learning opportunity. It helped increase her tolerance of various unconventional manifestations in LSD sessions and, subsequently, she became a better and more effective therapist.

To complete the list of difficult situations that can occur in LSD sessions, we should discuss various *physical manifestations* that are common concomitants of psychedelic experiences. In their milder form, they usually do not present a particularly serious technical challenge, but their extreme forms can be quite alarming. As I mentioned earlier, none of them are simple pharmacological effects of LSD; they represent complex psychosomatic manifestations. The general strategy toward somatic aspects in LSD sessions should be to experience them as fully as possible; clinical experiences have repeatedly confirmed the therapeutic value of this approach.

Probably the most common physical manifestations in LSD sessions are various motor phenomena, such as generalized muscular tension, complex postures and twisting movements, and a wide variety of tremors, jerks, twitches, and seizure-like episodes. The subject should be encouraged to let these happen; they represent extremely valuable channels for effective discharge of deep, pent-up energies. It is important that the sitters watch for any attempts on the part of the subject to control such phenomena, for aesthetic or other reasons. They should consistently encourage uninhibited discharge of energy, even if full manifestation takes the form of a violent temper tantrum or an epileptiform seizure. If the drug effect is not strong enough to bring about a spontaneous release of tension, this can be induced by the subject forcefully tensing-up the areas involved, and holding sculpture-like postures for long periods. Intense external pressures and deep massage are also quite useful for this purpose.

Breathing difficulties are very common in psychedelic sessions. On occasion, they can take the form of genuine asthmatic attacks; these usually occur in persons who have had problems of this kind in the past. In the context of LSD sessions it is important to encourage full experience of the unpleasant feelings of suffocation, at the same time reassuring the subject that there is no real danger, since the breathing difficulties are only subjective and respiration is adequate. It is essential that the sitters give the experient honest and objective feedback on this issue. Frequently gagging, coughing, or screaming, if it forms an integral part of the experience, can bring dramatic release. It should be encouraged if the process moves in that direction, but not mechanically suggested as a specific remedy.

Physical pain is an important and integral part of the psychedelic process and should also be experienced fully if it starts emerging in the session. It usually occurs in the context of reliving actual physical traumatizations such as diseases, accidents and operations, or the birth trauma, although it can also have various symbolic connotations. Intense physical pain may sometimes be associated with various transpersonal phenomena such as past-incarnation memories and ancestral or phylogenetic experiences. In later stages of the sessions, when the pharmacological effect of the drug is not strong enough, it is useful to increase the sensations by pressure or deep massage in the places indicated by the patient. In working with pain the sitters should always emphasize full experience of the pain, and the physical or emotional expression of the emotion that is inevitably behind it. Quite commonly patients themselves ask for more intense pressure, sometimes considerably beyond the point which the therapists feel comfortable with. Under unsupervised conditions individuals may actually try to hurt themselves to exteriorize the pain. This seems to be the mechanism behind some of the self-mutilations and self-inflicted injuries in LSD sessions which have received so much publicity in the media.

Nausea and vomiting usually occur in individuals who have suffered from this problem in childhood or in whom this is a habitual reaction to stress in everyday life. Nausea should not be alleviated by any means and the sitters should encourage vomiting whenever the patient seems to be fighting it. Breakthrough vomiting has a powerful purging effect, and in many instances means a positive turning point in a difficult LSD session. It can be of particular significance in persons who have a very strong negative charge about it in everyday life. Unwillingness to vomit can represent a very important block and may be associated with powerful emotional material on various levels. After having thrown up in the middle of an LSD session, some patients talk about having dumped generations of garbage. Others feel that they rid themselves of the introjected image of a bad parent or step-parent. In some instances, projectile vomiting can be associated with a sense of expelling alien transpersonal energy forms, almost in the sense of exorcism.

Problems related to urination and defecation are unusually frequent in psychedelic sessions. They either take the form of urethral and anal spasms and an inability to evacuate or, conversely, an intense physiological urge in these areas and fear of losing control over bladder and bowels. Difficulties with urination typically occur in persons who in their everyday life respond to various stresses by frequent micturition (pollakisuria), or show the classical Freudian characteristics of a urethral personality, such as intense ambition, concerns about prestige, a disposition to shame, and fear of blunder. If the LSD subject had problems with enuresis (wetting the pants or bed) at some point in his or her past, one should expect the problems in this area to be reenacted sooner or later in the sessions. This is also true for women who suffer from an orgastic insufficiency or frigidity that is associated with fear of losing bladder control at the same time as sexual orgasm is supposed to occur. On the psychodynamic level, urethral problems are associated with specific traumatic biographical material in agreement with psychoanalytic descriptions. However, they always have deeper roots on the level of the birth process; there exist quite specific associations between urethral dysfunction and certain aspects of perinatal matrices. Thus, a block of urination comes in the context of BPM II, a painful urge to void and conflicts about it is an almost standard component of BPM III, and loss of bladder control characterizes the transition from BPM III to BPM IV.

In the early years of my LSD work, patients with the above problems often delayed confrontation with the urethral material for weeks or months by interrupting the experience and leaving for the bathroom. Some of them made fifteen to twenty visits to the toilet in a single session, most of them unnecessary. When I recognized that this was a very powerful form of resistance, I made the necessary provisions for involuntary urination in the form of a rubber sheet and discouraged the adult approach to urethral urges. Patients who had strong objections to this arrangement and an insurmountable resistance to it were advised to use surgical rubber pants. With this approach, severe urethral conflicts and blockages could be resolved in a few sessions, whether or not involuntary urination actually occured. When a patient loses control of the bladder during an LSD experience, it is usually associated with reliving traumatic incidents from childhood which involved ridicule by peers or parents for urethral accidents. This release opens the way to the libidinal pleasure originally related to unrestricted urination, removes the psychological block, and facilitates letting go. On a deeper level, it frequently connects the patient with the moment of birth, where a fundamental relief after hours of agony can sometimes be associated with reflex urination.

Problems related to defecation follow a similar pattern. They typically occur in obsessive-compulsive patients of both sexes, in males with latent or manifest homosexual tendencies, and in anal personalities. On the psychodynamic level they are usually associated with conflicts around toilet training, gastrointestinal disorders in childhood, and a history of enemas. Deeper perinatal roots of anal retention are in BPM II; an urge to defecate and conflicts about it characterize BPM III, and explosive bowel release or loss of anal control is psychologically associated with the ego death and the moment of birth. Although anal problems of various kinds are very common in LSD sessions, actual uncontrolled defecation and manipulation of feces has been extremely rare; I have encountered it only about ten times in over five thousand LSD sessions I have studied. This may be an artifact of cultural programming and therapeutic technique rather than clinical reality. Our taboo against feces is much stronger than that against urine, and the common unwillingness of the experient and the sitters to deal with the aftermath of anal letting-go is also a factor that should not be underestimated. I realize retrospectively that for many years we discussed with LSD candidates the possibility of loss of bladder control and tried to alleviate their concerns about it; at the same time, however, similar reassurance was never offered in regard to defecation. In 1972, I saw a dramatic improvement in a patient with severe obsessive-compulsive neurosis which had resisted classical psychoanalysis for eighteen years; it occurred in an LSD session in which he lost control of his bowels and in a deeply regressed state played for several hours with his feces. That made clear to me some of the factors that might have been responsible for our chronic therapeutic failure with patients with severe obsessive-compulsive neuroses. If problems of an anal nature keep occurring in LSD therapy, the patient should be encouraged to give up adult concerns and be willing to abandon control if it becomes necessary during the experience. As in the case of urination, surgical pants can be a great psychological help, for the patient as well as the sitters.

ADVERSE AFTEREFFECTS OF LSD PSYCHOTHERAPY

LSD psychotherapy involves activation of deep unconscious material, its exteriorization, and conscious integration. Although the LSD sessions represent the most dramatic aspect of this treatment modality and ideally form a relatively completed psychological gestalt, psychedelic therapy is a continuous uncovering process which includes the dynamics of the free intervals between sessions. Within the framework of an LSD series, no clearcut boundaries can generally be drawn between the sessions and the events preceding and following them. The dynamic unfolding of various governing systems in the unconscious continues in a more or less subtle way for a long time after the actual pharmacological effect has subsided. A very convincing illustration of this process is found in dreams. The content of the dreams seems to form a continuum with the content of the psychedelic sessions. It is quite common that pre-session dreams anticipate the content of the LSD experience and post-session dreams are attempts to complete the gestalts that remained unfinished and to elaborate on the material involved.

Although internalization of the LSD sessions and active psychological work in the termination periods can considerably facilitate the integration of the material, there is never any guarantee that all the psychological gestalts will be completed by the time the pharmacological effect of LSD terminates. The risk that the integration of a session will be incomplete and will result in real clinical complications seems to be directly proportional to the degree of preexisting emotional problems in the subject and the negative circumstances in the session that prevent consistent introspective work. The extreme examples of this are intensification of the original symptoms, emergence of new forms of psychopathology, prolonged reactions, psychotic breaks, and reoccurrence of LSD symptoms at a later date ("flashbacks"). All these should be seen as comprehensible phenomena which are part of the dynamic unfolding of the uncovering process and represent calculated risks of LSD psychotherapy.

Some of the papers discussing the probable mechanisms of these complications entertained the possibility of actual pharmacological presence of a certain amount of LSD in the brain for indefinite periods of time. This explanation is inconsistent with the basic principles of pharmacology and also with concrete laboratory findings on the metabolism and distribution of LSD in the body. According to these, the drug has left the brain by the time the psychedelic experience culminates. There seems to be sufficient clinical evidence that the adverse aftereffects of LSD sessions reflect deep, basic dynamics of the unconscious processes and should be understood and approached in this context.

The psychopathological symptoms that can manifest as a result of incompletely resolved LSD sessions cover a very wide range. Essentially, any aspect of an activated dynamic matrix or specific unconscious material that remains unresolved can persist after the session for an indefinite period of time, or recur at a later date. Most frequently, these are various emotional qualities, such as depression, a sense of inferiority, suicidal feelings, affective lability or incontinence, a sense of loneliness, anxiety, guilt, paranoid feelings, aggressive tension, or manic elation. Psychosomatic symptoms that can occur in this context involve nausea and vomiting, difficulties with breathing, psychogenic coughing and gagging, cardiovascular distress, constipation or diarrhea, headaches and pains in various parts of the body, chills and hot flashes, increased sweating, "hangover" feelings, flu-like symptoms, hypersalivation, skin rashes, and different psychomotor manifestations such as general inhibition or excitement, muscular tremors, twitches, and jerks. An activated and unresolved unconscious gestalt can also specifically influence the subject's thought-processes. Certain ways of thinking about various issues such as sex, men, women, marriage, and authority, or philosophical speculations about the meaning of existence, the role of religion in life, suffering, injustice, and many other problems can be direct reflections of the underlying unconscious material. Strong opinions, judgments, and systems of values in various areas can change drastically when a previously unfinished unconscious gestalt is completed.

The occurrence of various perceptual changes after unresolved sessions is relatively less frequent. Long after the pharmacological effect of the drug has subsided, the patient may still report anomalies in color-perception, blurred vision, after-images, spontaneous imagery, alterations in body image, intensification of hearing, ringing in the ears, or various strange physical feelings. Sometimes, various combinations of the above emotional, psychosomatic, ideational and perceptual changes constitute completely new clinical syndromes which the subject has never experienced before. The occurrence of new forms of psychopathology can be understood as a result of activation and exteriorization of the content of previously latent unconscious matrices. These symptoms usually disappear instantly when the underlying material is fully experienced and integrated.

The general nature and specific characteristics of the adverse aftereffects of LSD sessions depend on the level of the unconscious that was activated and the specific content of the matrix involved. An active and unresolved matrix, whether of a psychodynamic, perinatal, or transpersonal nature, will influence the subject's perception of himself or herself and of the world, emotional reactions, thought-processes, and behavior patterns in a specific way. The clinical symptoms that are psychogenetically connected with the activated functional system may persist for days or weeks and even for unlimited periods of time. Sometimes the adverse aftereffects of the session are limited to accentuation and intensification of the original emotional, psychosomatic or interpersonal problems of the patient. At other times the post-session difficulties represent a recurrence of symptoms which he or she suffered from in childhood, adolescence, or some later period of life. In still other instances, the adverse aftereffects constitute a repetition of the situation that typified the onset of the subject's manifest neurotic or psychotic symptoms; this is true not only in terms of clinical symptoms, but also for specific interpersonal patterns.

One mechanism of crucial relevance has to be mentioned at least briefly in this context. We described earlier how an activated dynamic matrix determines the nature of the patient's experience and the specific ways in which he or she perceives the environment. This is quite regularly associated with a strong tendency to exteriorize the content of the unconscious constellation and enact its replica in the treatment situation, as well as in everyday life. If we carefully analyze the psychodynamics of this phenomenon, we find a very interesting underlying mechanism that can be described as intolerance of emotional-cognitive dissonance. Apparently, it is very difficult and disturbing to experience a deep incongruence between one's inner feelings and/or sensations and the nature of events in the external world, as cognitively interpreted. It seems to be much more acceptable to experience various unpleasant emotions as being reactions appropriate to or at least congruent with actual circumstances existing in objective reality, than to perceive them as incomprehensible and absurd elements coming from within.

Thus irrational feelings of anxiety and a sense of threat originating in the unconscious can result in maneuvers aimed at provoking hostility in the therapist, spouse, or employer. When these maneuvers succeed, previously incomprehensible feelings of anxiety assume the form of concrete and familiar fears of losing the therapist's support and endangering the continuation of treatment, worries about the disintegration of the marriage, or unsubstantiated concerns about losing one's position or job. In more intense forms of such fear that border on vital threat, the patient might actually seek out dangerous situations in activities such as hazardous car driving, parachuting, walks in bad neighborhoods, or visits to bars and night clubs of questionable reputation. Similarly, an LSD patient tuned into deep irrational guilt feelings may behave in an utterly inappropriate way, break the basic rules of therapy, and try to offend, irritate, or verbally attack the therapist. He or she can also do things in everyday life that are highly objectionable and guilt-provoking. As a result of this, the pre-existing guilt feelings can be rationalized, since they become attached to actual external events and appear to be congruent with the objective situation. The above are just a few concrete examples of very common mechanisms that can present considerable difficulties in the therapeutic situation, as well as in the patient's everyday life. It is absolutely essential for a successful course of psychedelic therapy that the therapist is familiar with this phenomenon and capable of handling it appropriately.

The changes caused by activation of different levels of COEX systems are usually not very dramatic and stay within the range of various neurotic and psychosomatic manifestations, unless the activated layer is from very early childhood and/or its emotional charge is excessive. When an important COEX system is activated and remains unresolved, the subject experiences in the post-session period an intensification of the clinical symptoms related to this system and perceives the environment with specific distortions reflecting its content. In addition, he or she may manifest a tendency to exteriorize the general theme of the system, or certain specific characteristics of one of its layers, in the treatment situation and in various aspects of everyday life. He or she may show peculiar idiosyncrasies and overreact to certain circumstances. The behavior of subjects under these conditions can involve complicated psychological maneuvers that tend to provoke specific reciprocal attitudes in the partners of their various interpersonal relationships. The external situations that result from such interaction represent approximate replicas of the original traumatic events that remained unresolved in previous sessions. Since this section focuses on complications of LSD therapy, we are naturally discussing activation of negative COEX systems. However, it is important to emphasize in this context that activation of a positive COEX system can have powerful positive consequences of a very similar kind.

When the adverse aftereffects of an LSD session result from an incomplete resolution of a COEX system, their general nature and specific content can be understood once the unconscious material becomes fully availiable. The basic characteristics of the emotional and interpersonal problems involved will reflect the general theme of the system; specific details will then make sense in terms of the individual layer of the COEX constellation that was activated. The therapist will frequently not be able to understand the dynamics of the problem when it occurs and he or she might have to wait until the time when the underlying unconscious material surfaces and the gestalt is completed. However, an experienced LSD therapist is not always dependent on retrospective understanding. In many instances the nature of the material to be experienced can be anticipated, at least in a general form, from the specific characteristics of the adverse reaction. Many of the elements discussed above are illustrated by the following clinical example:

Tom, a 26-year-old dropped-out student, was accepted into the program of LSD therapy for a severe impulsive neurosis with periodic running away from home, vagabondism, and excessive abuse of alcohol and various drugs (poriomania, dipsomania and toxicomania). His behavior during these episodes involved many distinctly antisocial elements. He usually did not pay in restaurants and inns: he either escaped without settling the bill or left some personal belongings as guarantee for later payment. Occasionally, he stole money or various objects from relatives, friends or strangers to cover his expenses. He slept in forests, public parks, and railway stations, and grossly neglected his personal hygiene. Tom was referred to the LSD program after two years of unsuccessful therapy by various conventional methods. Some of his previous psychiatrists had diagnosed his case as schizophrenia, and the history of his treatment included a series of insuline comas.

His first twenty-six LSD sessions followed an unusually monotonous course. He experienced anxiety, occasionally mounting to panic, and showed great agitation associated with massive muscular jerks and tremors. This was accompanied by recurrent visions of a pale, grimacing female face. In later sessions, another element was added to the content of his experiences. Every time he heard the sound of water running in a nearby bathroom, he was overcome by anger and had great difficulty in controlling his aggression. He also could not tolerate the presence of a female therapist or nurse, even briefly, and responded to them with irritation and rude verbal attacks. The visions of the pale female face were now supplemented by images related to water. In this context, various dangerous situations associated with seas, lakes and rivers alternated with courageous sailors and aquatic animals of prowess, symbolizing mastery over the water element.

At this time, Tom's problems in the free intervals between LSD sessions bordered on psychosis. He experienced bouts of unmotivated panic anxiety and felt intense hatred towards women. His idiosyncrasy in regard to running water continued and he almost physically attacked everyone who turned on the water tap. Tom's behavior resulted in numerous conflicts with the co-patients and nurses since he tended to provoke hostility by his intolerance, recklessness, and aggression. He appeared agitated and manifested a variety of involuntary motor phenomena, particularly massive jerks.

Several sessions later, new elements appeared in the visions accompanying Tom's LSD experiences. At first, their content was quite puzzling and incomprehensible. He saw rapid sequences of various trivial objects related to bathing, such as shower nozzles, water taps, soap bars, tile patterns, sponges, bath brushes, and bath toys. The innocent nature of these visions seemed quite incongruent with the intensity of anxiety and the powerful motor discharges that accompanied them. Tom was very dissatisfied with these sessions and found them confusing; he referred to his experiences as "a crazy pell-mell," "mish-mash," or "chaos." All these disconnected experiences suddenly made sense when Tom relived in a complex way certain traumatic memories from his early childhood. When he was two and three years old, he had an emotionally disturbed nurse who finally turned out to be psychotic. She used to maltreat him and frighten him in a very sadistic way, particularly during bathing. The authenticity of Tom's recollections was later verified by his step-mother; she fired the nanny after having discovered how much she had abused the child. After full and complex reliving of these traumatic memories, most of the elements described above disappeared from Tom's sessions. However, the anxiety and muscular jerks persisted, despite the fact that they originally seemed to belong to the traumatic memory involving the nanny. At this point, the anxiety in Tom's LSD sessions became much more primitive and elemental; the twitches now appeared to be associated with very unpleasant tastes and oral sensations. This gradually developed into reliving of early childhood experiences that involved the application of various disinfectant solutions to the mucous membranes of his mouth when he suffered from a fungus disease. The musuclar jerks were particularly emphasized around Tom's head and neck and he identified them as escape reactions associated with these medical interventions. In the intervals between these sessions, Tom showed a strong negative attitude toward hospitals and medicine; he criticized and ridiculed the medical aspects of our treatment procedures and revolted against them.

Following this phase, intense hunger and thirst, feelings of cold and emotional starvation were added to his anxiety. In his LSD sessions, he was now reliving traumatic experiences from a nursery where he was kept for the first seven months of his life. At this time, he craved the presence of and physical contact with women, and asked for the female therapist and nurses —persons whom he previously could not stand—to be present. In this context they seemed to compensate for the frustration and emotional deprivation which he had experienced in the nursery, where the superficial professional attitudes of the personnel had failed to satisfy his infantile needs. In the free intervals between these sessions, Tom was haunted by the desire to find the ideal woman; his depression was accentuated and he felt an irresistible urge to consume great quantities of alcohol and various drugs.

When Tom started to relive his difficult birth, during which his mother had died and he himself had barely survived, he recognized that many of his symptoms were actually rooted on the perinatal level. His panic anxiety, aggression, guilt, and driving tension suddenly made sense as derivatives of the birth trauma. He now saw his massive muscular jerks and twitches as belated discharges of pent-up energies related to the "hydraulic" aspects of the delivery. Tom's behavior around the birth sessions was impulsive, ruthless and erratic; it was characterized by acting out of strange ambivalent tendencies and conflicts between dependence and independence. Much of this was expressed in the context of the transference relationship; by conventional standards Tom's behavior during this period would be labelled psychotic.

In his sixty-fifth psycholytic session, Tom seemed to have completed the birth process and had his first deep trancendental experience, followed by a dramatic but not lasting improvement. It took six more sessions and several months of unstable clinical condition before he reached a new equilibrium.

In the years following his LSD therapy Tom has not needed hospitalization and did not have to rely on psychiatric help. He married and was able to maintain a job and take care of his two children.

Sometimes seemingly bizarre sensations, emotions, and thoughts occurring in the context of an adverse LSD reaction can be explained naturally and logically when one uncovers and identifies the underlying unconscious material. The fear of a male patient that his penis is shrinking can thus be traced to an emotional fixation on a body image corresponding to the age of an unfinished childhood memory. In a similar way, a female patient who is psychologically tuned into an activated memory from the preadolescent period can lose the awareness of her breasts from the body image, or can develop a conviction that she is losing her hair when she connects emotionally to ·early infantile memories. Naive and childlike perception of the environment, inappropriate fears, increased dependency needs, or doubts about bladder or bowel control are some other examples in this category. Of particular interest for psychosomatic and internal medicine are those instances in which, following an LSD session, an apparently somatic problem turns out to be an integral part of a traumatic memory from childhood. Because of the special clinical importance of this phenomenon, I will illustrate it with several examples.

Renata, a patient suffering from severe cancerophobia, relived in one of her sessions a sexual episode that supposedly happened when she was four years old. In this scene, her stepfather was lying in bed and she crawled under the blanket with him expecting to be fondled and caressed. During their play, however, he gradually directed her to his genital area and abused the situation for his sexual gratification. The discovery of his erect penis was a particularly exciting and frightening aspect of this situation. While reliving a part of this episode, in which her forearm was the most important area of contact with her step-father's body, she suddenly developed a massive circumscribed infiltration and reddening of the skin. In front of my eyes and within a matter of minutes this area reached the consistency of shoe-leather; it became thick, hard and covered with protruding skin eruptions. This condition, which was diagnosed as eczema by a consultant dermatologist, persisted for ten days until the next LSD session. After the traumatic memory had been fully relived and integrated, it disappeared over several hours.

In another of her sessions, Renata relived a childhood scene in which she had fallen on ice while figure-skating and badly hurt her head and knee. During the following week she experienced intense pain in the "injured" parts of her body. She could not turn her head, was limping considerably, and maintained a typical protective posture of her right leg. All these phenomena disappeared after the incident was fully relived.

Another interesting example of a similar kind was observed during the LSD therapy of Dana, a patient with complicated neurotic problems. In one of her sessions, she started reliving a traumatic episode which had occurred at a time when she suffered from severe bronchitis. In this context, she suddenly began manifesting all the typical symptoms of a bronchial infection. These symptoms persisted even after the actual pharmacological effects of LSD had worn off; during the following week, she continued to cough excessively and complained about severe chest pain. The internist who saw her as a consultant diagnosed bronchitis on the basis of elevated temperature, characteristic rales during stethoscopic examination, coughing, and production of thick phlegm. The only signs that distinguished this condition from genuine bronchitis were its sudden onset at the time when the traumatic memory started to emerge and its equally abrupt termination when the psychological gestalt was completed.

The governing influence of activated basic perinatal matrices on the post-session intervals is usually much more dramatic, and is of great practical and theoretical importance. If the subject is under a strong influence from one of these matrices at the time that the pharmacological action of the drug is wearing off, he or she can experience its influence in a mitigated form for days, weeks or even months. If a deep level of a negative matrix is activated, the individual difficulties following the session can reach psychotic proportions. The consequences are quite distinct and characteristic for each of the perinatal matrices.

When the termination period of an LSD session is governed by BPM II and the subject stabilizes under its influence, the post-session interval is characterized by deep depression. Under these circumstances, individuals are vexed by various highly unpleasant feelings, thoughts, and physical sensations. They have access only to unpleasant memories and cannot see any positive elements in their entire life history. Guilt, inferiority, and shame seem to dominate their thinking about the past. Their present life appears to be unbearable and fraught with problems that have no solution; they do not have any perspective on anything, and the future looks equally hopeless. Life is devoid of any meaning, and there is an absolute inability to enjoy anything. The world is perceived as threatening, ominous, oppressive and without colors. Suicidal ideation is not uncommon in this situation; it typically has the form of a wish to fall asleep or be unconscious, forget everything, and never wake up again. Persons in this state of mind have fantasies about taking an overdose of sleeping pills or narcotics, drinking themselves to death, inhaling domestic gas, drowning in deep water, or walking into snow and freezing. (suicide I) Typical physical symptoms accompanying this condition are headaches, oppression of the chest, breathing difficulties, various cardiac complaints, ringing in the ears, severe constipation, loss of appetite, and a total lack of interest in sex. Feelings of exhaustion and fatigue, drowsiness and somnolence, and a tendency to spend the entire day in bed or in a darkened room are also common.

Stabilization of an LSD session under the dominance of BPM III results in feelings of intense aggressive tension, frequently associated with strong but vague apprehension and anticipation of a catastrophe. Subjects in this state liken themselves to "time bombs" ready to explode at any minute. They oscillate between destructive and self-destructive impulses and are afraid of hurting other people or themselves. A high degree of irritability and a strong tendency to provoke violent conflicts is typical. The world is perceived as a dangerous and unpredictable place, where one has to be constantly on guard and prepared to fight and struggle for survival. Painful awareness of one's real or imagined handicaps and limitations is combined with exaggerated ambitions and efforts to prove oneself. In contrast to the inhibited and tearless depression related to BPM II, the clinical picture here can take the form of an agitated depression accompanied by emotional incontinence and psychomotor excitement. Suicidal thoughts, fantasies and tendencies are quite frequent, and follow a pattern distinctly different from that described for BPM II. Individuals in this state contemplate bloody and violent suicides, such as throwing themselves under trains, jumping from a window or cliff, hara-kiri, or shooting themselves. (suicide II) The only suicidal fantasies observed in this context that do not involve blood are related to strangulation and hanging. This seems to reflect the fact that high degrees of suffocation are frequently experienced in the final stages of birth. Typical physical symptoms associated with this syndrome involve intense muscular tension, frequently resulting in tremors, twitches, and jerks, pressure headaches, pains in various other parts of the body, nausea with occasional vomiting, intensification of intestinal activity and diarrhea, frequent urination or urethral spasms, and profuse sweating. A characteristic manifestation in the sexual area is excessive augmentation of the libidinal drive, for which even repeated orgasms do not bring satisfactory relief. In male subjects, this intensification of sexual tension is sometimes associated with impotence[2] and premature ejaculation; in females, with an inability to achieve sexual orgasm, premenstrual emotional turbulence, dysmenorrhea, and painful genital cramps during intercourse (vaginism).

Subjects whose LSD session terminates under the influence of BPM IV present a very different picture. The most remarkable aspect of this state is a dramatic alleviation or even disappearance of previous psychopathological symptoms, and a decrease of emotional problems of all kinds. Individuals feel that they have left the past behind and are now capable of starting an entirely new chapter in their lives. Exhilarating feelings of freedom from anxiety, depression and guilt are associated with deep physical relaxation and a sense of perfect functioning of all physiological processes. Life appears simple and exciting, and the individual has the feeling of unusual sensory richness and intense joy.

As far as BPM I is concerned, the individual can stabilize under the influence of its positive or negative aspects. In the former case, the postsession interval resembles the one described for BPM IV. However, all the feelings involved are much deeper and are experienced in a religious or mystical framework. Subjects see new dimensions in the world and in the universe, have strong feelings of being an integral part of creation, and tend to regard ordinary things and activities in everyday life—such as eating, walks in nature, playing with children, or sexual intercourse—as manifestations of the divine. The experience of cosmic unity has an unusual therapeutic potential and can have lasting beneficial consequences for the individual.

If the subject remains after an LSD session under the influence of the negative aspects of BPM I or negative transpersonal matrices, he or she experiences various forms and degrees of emotional and physical distress associated with conceptual confusion. These difficulties are typically interpreted in a metaphysical framework—in spiritual, occult, mystical, or religious terms. These unpleasant conditions are attributed to the adverse forces of destiny, "bad karma," malefic astrological or cosmobiological influences, or various evil spiritual entities. In extreme cases this condition can reach psychotic proportions. After the individual works through and integrates the experience, he or she assumes a more tentative and metaphorical approach to such extreme interpretations.

The four major complications of LSD sessions that are of great practical relevance and should be specifically discussed are *activation of preexisting symptoms, prolonged reactions, psychotic decompensations,* and *"flashbacks."* They can all be reduced to a common denominator, namely, the weakening of the defense system and incomplete resolution of the unconscious material that was thus made experientially available. The weakening of resistance is most apparent in those situations where the symptoms that the subject originally had are activated and intensified after a particular LSD session. In this case, no major change has occurred; the underlying matrix remains the same but its dynamic influence is experienced more strongly than before. In the case of a prolonged reaction, the specific defense system collapses but the material behind it is not worked through. The experience then continues not because of the persisting pharmacological action of the LSD, but as a result of the emotional charge of the unleashed unconscious material. The emerging unconscious theme is now too energetically charged and too close to consciousness to be repressed and covered up again, but a subject unfamiliar with the psychodynamics of this process usually tries to prevent it from emerging fully and completing itself.

A temporary psychotic decompensation after an LSD session can be seen as a special example of a prolonged reaction. It occurs when the unconscious material that became activated and remained unresolved is a theme of fundamental relevance and carries excessive emotional charge. It may occasionally be a major trauma from very early infancy; however, in most instances such an episode involves perinatal material or some powerful negative transpersonal matrix. I have never seen an incident of this kind after supervised LSD sessions with persons who showed a reasonable degree of emotional, interpersonal and social adjustment prior to the experience. In individuals who have serious psychiatric problems that border on psychosis, or have had schizophrenic episodes in the past, occurrence of transient adverse reactions of this depth is not uncommon.

The recurrences of LSD-like states days, weeks, or even months after the actual administration of the drug has stirred much publicity and deserves special attention in this context. Careful study of the psychodynamics of the LSD reaction over many years has convinced me that these episodes, popularly known as "flashbacks," have a very similar basis to the prolonged reactions and psychotic breaks immediately following the sessions. The difference is that in this case the defense mechanisms are strong enough to cover up the activated and unresolved material in the termination period. The experience appears to be completed, but this is true only on the surface; the result is a very precarious dynamic balance between the unconscious forces and the psychological resistance against them. As time passes, any number of circumstances can disturb this problematic equilibrium, and the individual starts consciously experiencing the unfinished gestalt. Since it is a continuation of a process that started during the LSD experience, the uninformed subject will usually see it as an insidious, belated attack of the drug, rather than as a manifestation of his or her unconscious. Less urgent episodes of this kind occur under circumstances which physiologically involve weakening of defenses, such as the periods between waking and sleep (the hypnagogic and hypnopompic state), physical fatigue, or sleep deprivation. More dramatic instances are usually associated with the use of drugs such as alcohol, marijuana, and psychostimulants, or virus diseases and other somatic processes. On occasion, later psychotherapeutic sessions, especially those that involve techniques using hyperventilation, can facilitate what the subject considers to be an LSD "flashback." Meditation and various other spiritual practices or the individual and group exercises used in growth centers can have similar effects.

In addition to the above factors which have a general catalyzing influence, the mechanism of "flashbacks" frequently involves an element of very specific psychological stress. This mechanism is of such importance that it deserves special emphasis. Powerful triggers for the recurrence of the LSD state are situations of everyday life that involve elements similar or identical to the unconscious matrix or theme that remained unresolved. An example of this would be a subject whose last LSD session, spent mainly under the influence of BPM II, did not end with a satisfactory resolution. Under these circumstances a crowded, overheated, poorly ventilated, and noisy subway can provide an experience which is extremely close to the basic characteristics of the "no exit" situation. Driving a car in the rush-hour on a busy highway or use of a crowded elevator can have a similar impact. All these situations can thus function as powerful facilitators of the content of the second perinatal matrix.

In a similar way, a subject psychologically tuned into BPM III could have a "flashback" as a result of watching a movie or TV-show involving rape, sadism and violence, or while driving a car and reaching a speed that appears dangerous. Sometimes the triggering stimuli come from the external world, more or less accidentally and without active participation of the subject. In some other instances, the subject is instrumental in creating a situation in everyday life that is an approximate replica of the unresolved traumatic gestalt. The mechanism underlying such situations was described earlier in detail. Since this process typically involves interpersonal partners and external circumstances it takes some time for it to reach critical dimensions. The period necessary for such development would then explain the frequently long period that elapses between the drug experience and the "recurrence." Examples of this mechanism would be: recreating for oneself a "no-exit" situation in everyday life, contaminating a sexual relationship by elements of the third perinatal matrix, reenacting an unresolved father problem in the daily interaction with one's employer.

Understanding that the adverse aftereffects of LSD sessions are comprehensible and lawful phenomena reflecting the basic psychodynamics of the unconscious, and not capricious spin-offs of the pharmacological effects of a bizarre and unpredictable substance, suggests a general strategy and certain specific techniques for their prevention and therapy.

PREVENTION AND MANAGEMENT OF COMPLICATIONS IN LSD PSYCHOTHERAPY

Occasional activation of the unconscious material associated with various kinds and degrees of emotional and psychosomatic discomfort is part of every uncovering process. Instances of this have been observed occasionally even in the course of conservative and traditional psychoanalytic treatment, and it is a common occurrence in various experiential psychotherapies—neo-Reichian work, primal therapy, Gestalt practice, encounter groups—where no psychoactive drugs are used. Dramatic intensification of emotional or psychosomatic symptoms and interpersonal maladjustment indicates that a patient has approached areas of important unconscious problems. In LSD therapy, which considerably deepens and intensifies all psychological processes, this mechanism is more apparent than in more conservative forms of therapy, but is in no way specific to it.

Understanding the basic dynamics of the complications that arise in LSD psychotherapy is absolutely essential for their prevention and treatment. An important part of this work has to be done during the preparation for the first LSD session. The therapist has to explain clearly to the patient that intensification of symptoms, deep emotional turmoil, and even psychosomatic manifestations in the course of LSD therapy do not mean failure of treatment but are logical and meaningful parts of the process. As a matter of fact, such phenomena frequently occur just before a major therapeutic breakthrough. Another important message that has to be communicated before the drug is administered is that the incidence of these complications can be considerably reduced by consistent internalization of the LSD sessions. Full, unselective experiencing of whatever surfaces during the drug sessions, and finding appropriate channels for discharging deep pent-up energies are of crucial importance for safe and effective psychedelic therapy. It is also essential that patients understand the function and importance of active work during the termination period on unresolved issues. Explaining the rationale, basic principles, and rules for cooperation increases the chances for good integration of the sessions and reduces the incidence of prolonged reactions or "flashbacks."

The basic principles of conducting the LSD sessions have already been described and will be only briefly summarized here. A patient who removes the eyeshades to avoid confrontation with difficult emotional material that is surfacing is not likely to have a smooth and clean reentry and should be prepared for difficulties in the post-session interval. Similarly, unwillingness to work hard on unfinished material in the termination period of the session might mean a prolonged process of integration with investment of the therapist's and patient's time and energy for days to come.

Even if the above criteria are met, it is not possible to eliminate with any certainty the belated occurrence of various emotional and psychosomatic aftereffects. Psychedelic experiences represent powerful interventions in the dynamics of the unconscious and it takes time to integrate them. Even a well-resolved session may be followed by later upsurges of additional unconscious material, because the experience might have removed an important block and made available new contents that were previously successfully repressed.

I remember in this context a very beautiful and fitting simile which one of my Czech patients used to describe the process. Lumberjacks floating trees down a river occasionally encounter a situation in which the trunks form a barrier that obstructs the stream. Their approach to this situation is not to remove every log systematically, but to look for what is called a key-log, one piece that holds a strategic position. Experienced lumberjacks will approach the obstruction paddling against the stream, find the key-log, and remove it with a hook. After this intervention, the logs start moving in a way that ultimately reestablishes the free flow of the river. This process can take days or weeks, but it is made possible by removing the crucial block. Similarly, LSD sessions can eliminate dynamic blocks in the unconscious; this opens the way to emotional liberation, although the actual mechanics of it may extend over a long period of time.

For patients who are properly instructed and guided, these reactions usually do not represent serious problems. They are trained in dealing with unusual states of consciousness and see them as windows into their unconscious and opportunities for self-exploration, rather than as threats to their sanity. Since the emotional material usually tends to surface in the hypnagogic and hypnopompic periods, it is not difficult to take some time and approach such episodes as "micro-sessions." A short period of hyperventilation can help to activate the underlying problem and facilitate its resolution through fuller experience and energy discharge. This approach is far preferable to the usual effort to suppress and control the emerging material, which prevents lasting solution and binds much of the patient's energy. Frequently, difficult emotions and physical symptoms can disappear after half an hour of introspective work.

This situation is more complicated if the material is so close to the surface and its affective charge so strong that it tends to emerge unpredictably under the circumstances of everyday life. In that case, the patient should be instructed to arrange for situations where it is possible to face and express whatever is emerging. If this is not available, regular therapeutic sessions should be scheduled and systematic uncovering work done on the unresolved issues with the assistance of the sitters. The techniques used in this work are essentially the same as those that we described for the termination period of the LSD sessions. After a short episode of hyperventilation that tends to unspecifically activate the underlying emotional structure, the sitters assist the patient by accentuating the physical sensations and states that he or she is already experiencing. Depending on the nature of the problem, they can use a combination of bioenergetic exercises or other neo-Reichian approaches, Gestalt technique, psychodrama, guided affective imagery, and deep massage to mobilize and work through the unfinished matrices. Stereophonic music, especially the pieces that were played in the session, can be of great help during this work.

If LSD therapy is being conducted in the atmosphere of a therapeutic community, it can be very useful to engage a group of co-patients in this uncovering work. For example, the group can enact in a very convincing way the experience of the encroaching birth canal, the atmosphere of a life-and-death struggle, or the comforting and nourishing womb. On occasion, stimulating or comforting sounds produced by the group members during this work can be very effective. Individuals in this team may also volunteer or be chosen by the patient or therapist for specific psychodramatic roles—surrogate mother, father, sibling, spouse, child, or employer. This approach is not only very effective for dealing with unresolved gestalts, but can also have a very powerful catalyzing effect on the assisting persons. It is not infrequent that under these circumstances the intense experiences of the protagonist can trigger valuable emotional reactions in some of the helpers. The material and observations from such therapeutic events can become an important addition to later group sessions. The experience of the role of helper also has an important function for the self-esteem of the group members and contributes to their sense of mastery. Collective efforts of this kind tend to create a sense of closeness, intimacy and togetherness which contribute to the social cohesion of the therapeutic community and its healing potential.

In the rare instances where the adverse aftereffects are very intense and the patients are potentially dangerous to others or to themselves, it may be necessary to keep them in the therapeutic facility twenty-four hours a day until these reactions subside. Nurses and co-patients should be trained to assume collective responsibility in these situations, and provide continuous assistance and surveillance. If the non-drug work fails to bring desirable results it is advisable to shorten the free interval and run another LSD session as soon as possible, to complete the unfinished gestalt. An interval of less than five to seven days tends to decrease the intensity and the therapeutic efficacy of the next session, because of the biological tolerance incurred by the previous administration of LSD.

In particularly resistant cases the therapist may decide to resort to the use of other pharmacological substances. Major or minor tranquillizers should be avoided, since their effect is contrary to the basic strategy of any uncovering approach and psychedelic therapy in particular. By inhibiting the process, blurring the experience, and obscuring the nature of the underlying problem, they prevent its resolution. In those instances where the unconscious material is close to the surface but is blocked by a barrier of intense psychological resistance, inhalation of Meduna's mixture (thirty percent of carbon dioxide and seventy percent of oxygen) can be very useful. A few inhalations of this mixture can cause a brief but powerful activation of the underlying unconscious matrix and facilitate a breakthrough. A session with Ritaline (40–100 milligrams) can occasionally help in the integration of material from the previous LSD session. Psychedelic drugs with a certain affinity for positive dynamic systems, such as tetrahydrocannabinol (THC) or methylenedioxyamphetamine (MDA) can be used with advantage. A drug that holds great promise in this indication but has not been sufficiently explored, is ketamine (Ketalar). It is a drug approved for medical purposes, which has been used by surgeons for general anesthesia.[3] This anesthesia is of a dissociative type, which is very different from the one induced by conventional anesthetics. Under the influence of ketamine consciousness is not obliterated but deeply changed and drastically refocused. An out-of-body state is induced in which the patient loses contact with and interest in objective reality and gets involved in various cosmic adventures, to a degree that makes surgical operations possible. Optimal dosages for psychedelic purposes are relatively small, 50–150 milligrams, which is about one-twentieth to one-sixth of the standard anesthetic dose. The psychoactive effect even in this low-dose range is so powerful that it catapults the patient beyond the point of impasse from the previous LSD session, and can make it possible for him or her to reach a better level of integration. This approach should be explored with individuals who have developed long-term psychotic states as a result of unsupervised self-experimentation with LSD.

NOTES

1. Since the deepest level of BPM II involves experiences described by many religions as *being in hell*, a few references to spiritual systems seem appropriate at this point. Hell is crossculturally defined as involving unbearable tortures without end; it is an experience of eternal suffering. The element of hope-

lessness is a necessary experiential attribute of hell; the experience of enormous physical and emotional pain where there is hope for release is not hell but *purgatory*. It seems that mainstream Christian theology has made the same mistake as some LSD subjects and confused psychological time with clock-time. In spiritual systems that have a deeper understanding of consciousness, such as Hinduism and Buddhism, one does not stay forever in hells or heavens; when one is experiencing infernal or paradisiacal states, it subjectively feels like they will last forever. Eternity should not be confused with an infinitely long period of historical time. It is a state where linear time is experientially transcended and ceases to exist.

2. This apparent paradox requires a few words of explanation. According to observations from LSD psychotherapy, most cases of impotence and frigidity are not based on lack of libidinal drive, but on excess of volcanic instinctual energies related to BPM III. It is unconscious fear of unleashing these forces and a need to control them that interferes with the sexual act. When these excess energies are discharged in a non-sexual context, they reach a level of intensity which the individual can comfortably handle in a sexual situation. This understanding of sexual disturbances is supported by the clinical observation that impotence and frigidity change into temporary hypersexuality in the course of successful treatment along these lines.

3. In recent years there has been a trend among surgeons to use ketamine only in children and old persons despite its biological safety and special advantages as an anesthetic. The reason for this has been the occurrence of certain psychological states during awakening that have been referred to as *emergence phenomena*. This reflects basic ignorance of the nature of the ketamine effects. Since extraordinary psychedelic-type experiences are the very essence of the ketamine action, every administration of this drug should be preceded by specific instructions which make it clear that a very unusual type of anesthetic is being used.

THE COURSE OF
LSD PSYCHOTHERAPY   6

*Changes in the Content of Psychedelic Sessions
Emotional and Psychosomatic Changes in the
    Post-Session Intervals
Long-Term Changes in the Personality Structure
    World-View, and Hierarchy
    of Basic Values*

The discussion of the course of LSD psychotherapy presented in this section is based to a great extent on the observations made during a study which was conducted at the Psychiatric Research Institute in Prague between the years 1960 and 1967. This was a clinical project exploring the potential of LSD for personality diagnosis and as an adjunct to psychotherapy. The orientation in the early phases of this study was psycholytic; however, in the course of clinical work with LSD, many of the principles characteristic of the psychedelic approach were discovered and assimilated into the treatment procedure. The most important of these were increased dosage, internalization of the process, use of music, and appreciation of the healing potential of perinatal and transpersonal experiences. The final outcome of this development was the therapeutic method of using LSD described in this book.

Most of the subjects in this study were psychiatric patients, although psychiatrists, psychologists, psychiatric nurses, scientists from various disciplines, and artists were occasionally given serial LSD sessions outside of the therapeutic context for training, insight, and inspiration. In selecting the patients for this project we followed three basic criteria. We wanted to have all the major psychiatric diagnoses represented in the study, to assess indications and contraindications of this form of therapy and to explore whether the LSD process had specific characteristics related to clinical diagnosis and personality structure. There was a definite bias toward selecting patients who had severe chronic and fixated emotional disorders that had lasted many years and had not responded to conventional therapies. This emphasis seemed to provide ethical justification for subjecting patients to experimental treatment with a new, powerful and insufficiently known psychoactive drug. Since high-quality feedback about the psychedelic experiences and therapeutic results was essential for the study, we tended to select people with an above-average level of intellectual functioning, a good educational background, and a talent for introspection.

We kept detailed records of each drug experience, as well as of the intervals between the sessions. These records came mainly from two sources—the patients themselves, and the therapists who were conducting LSD sessions. Additional information was occasionally provided by the nurses and co-patients who spent some time with the LSD subjects during the late hours of the psychedelic experience. With the help of two colleagues who joined me later in the project, I collected records from the serial sessions of fifty-four patients. The dosages ranged between 150 and 450 micrograms and the overall number of LSD sessions per patient was between fifteen and one hundred-and-three.

The study thus involved intelligent patients with a variety of severe emotional and psychosomatic disorders of a chronic and fixated nature. Among the conditions we treated with serial LSD sessions were inhibited and agitated depressions, all major forms of psychoneuroses, psychosomatic diseases such as asthma, psoriasis and migraine headaches, various sexual dysfunctions and deviations, alcoholism and narcotic drug addition, character disorders, borderline psychotic states, and several patients with manifest schizophrenic symptoms. Later, when I was heading the psychedelic research project at the Maryland Psychiatric Research Center in Baltimore, I also had the opportunity to conduct serial LSD sessions with cancer patients. The variety of subjects and circumstances made it possible to draw general conclusions about the natural course of LSD psychotherapy, as well as the therapeutic strategies that can influence it in a favorable way.

Keeping detailed records of the psychedelic experiences and of the intervals between consecutive sessions is a very important part of LSD psychotherapy. It is absolutely essential for research purposes, if one intends to draw generalized conclusions and use the observations as a basis for theoretical speculation. Good and detailed records are also extremely useful in everyday clinical practice. A therapist treating a large number of patients in serial LSD sessions usually forgets many details, and even patients themselves do not remember all the sequences from their previous psychedelic experiences. Occasionally, material from a much earlier session unexpectedly acquires new meaning in view of later episodes; reliable records can be of great value under such circumstances. This can become even more evident if the patient has documented the course of his or her therapy with drawings and paintings.

During my own research, careful retrospective study of the LSD records revealed many connections that I had missed during the actual treatment process, which extended over periods of months or years. While reviewing and reconstructing the unfolding of the psychedelic process of each single individual as reflected in the notes, I could recognize certain repetitive themes, recurrent experiential clusters, important underlying trends, typical stages, and characteristic turning points. This gave valuable insights into the nature and course of the LSD procedure in specific individuals and allowed comparison with the significant findings from similar data about other patients. This in turn provided a rough dynamic cartography of the inner spaces made available through LSD and thus expanded the model of the human unconscious. It also threw light on the basic characteristics of the transformative process facilitated by repeated administrations of the drug.

In the following text we will discuss in detail the processes unfolding during the course of LSD therapy, focusing on its three important aspects:

a) changes in the content of psychedelic sessions;

b) emotional and psychosomatic changes in the post-session intervals;

c) long-term changes in the personality structure, world-view, and hierarchy of basic values.

CHANGES IN THE CONTENT OF PSYCHEDELIC SESSIONS

In an earlier section of this book, we discussed abstract, psychodynamic, perinatal and transpersonal phenomena as being the four major categories of experiences occurring in LSD sessions. The arrangements of the generative matrices of these experiential modalities and their interconnections are intricate and complex. They cannot be reduced to any linear model, and are best understood in holonomic terms.[1] It is, therefore, not quite accurate to talk about the unconscious as stratified, and to refer to some of its manifestations as more superficial than others. Yet in everyday clinical work with LSD some of these phenomena seem to be generally more available than others, and in serial psychedelic sessions they tend to emerge in a certain characteristic sequence.

In the first few LSD sessions, especially if the dosage is kept within the range of 100–150 micrograms, there is usually a preponderance of abstract experiences of various kinds. With the eyes closed, most LSD subjects have incredibly colorful and dynamic visions of geometric designs, architectural forms, kaleidoscopic displays, magic fountains, or fantastic fireworks. Sometimes, this can take the more complex form of interiors of gigantic temples, naves of Gothic cathedrals, cupolas of monumental mosques, or decorations in Moorish palaces ("arabesques"). When the eyes are open, the environment appears to be in flux or in rhythmic undulating movement. Colors are unusually bright and explosive, color contrasts much stronger than usual, and the world can be perceived in a way characterized by various movements in modern art, such as impressionism, cubism, surrealism, or superrealism. Sometimes inanimate objects are described as coming to life; at other times the entire world can appear geometrized and ornamentalized. Probably the most interesting perceptual phenomena in this group are optical illusions. Various ordinary elements of the environment may be seen transformed into fantastic animals, grotesque faces, or exotic sceneries. Although the changes of perception are most striking in the optical field, they can also involve hearing, touch, smell, or taste. Characteristic occurrences at this stage are synaesthesias, where external stimuli produce responses in inappropriate sensory organs; thus LSD subjects can report such extraordinary phenomena as seeing music, hearing pain, or tasting colors.

The above experiences, although fascinating from the aesthetic and artistic point of view, seem to have very little relevance from the point of view of therapy, self-exploration, and personal growth. The most important aspects of these experiences can be explained in physiological terms as resulting from chemical stimulation of the sensory organs and reflecting their anatomical structure and functional characteristics. Many of them can be produced by anoxia, hyperventilation, inhalation of carbon dioxide, or various physical means, such as mechanical pressure on the eyeball, electric stimulation of the optical system and exposure to stroboscopic light or sounds of various frequencies. LSD subjects occasionally refer in this context to certain phenomena in everyday life that approximate some of these experiences. Thus the television screen of a set that is out of tune can produce a close replica of the visual distortion or geometrization of an image. Similarly, the illusive acoustical changes produced by LSD can be simulated by a radio receiver that is registering the noises from intermediate bands between stations.

Visions of geometrical patterns are so common in the low-dose LSD sessions of beginners that they were originally considered a regular and typical reaction to the drug. However, they tend to disappear from the sessions when the dose is increased or the administration of LSD repeated. This is an observation that is not easy to explain. There is a possibility that they actually represent a replay of the sensory phenomena induced by the lack of oxygen during delivery, and thus form the most superficial level of the memory of birth. Their affinity to the third perinatal matrix seems to point in this direction. To prevent misunderstanding it is important to emphasize that not all abstract and geometrical experiences in LSD sessions belong in this category. LSD subjects can have various visions of a geometrical nature in advanced transpersonal sessions. These two kinds of geometrical visions are quite different and can be easily distinguished from each other. The advanced geometrical images are related to specific forms of the micro- and macrocosm or represent elements of spiritual geometry. Typical visions from this category represent atomic and molecular structures, cellular and tissue elements, shells, honeycombs, flowers and blossoms, or various universal symbols and complex mandalas. The rich philosophical and spiritual content of these phenomena clearly distinguish them from the abstract and aesthetic experiences described earlier.

Sometimes, the abstract sensory changes can assume a distinct emotional quality, and even a specific content. They can become sharp, dangerous, and aggressive, with a dark red color that suggests accident, operation, murder, or incest. Their colors might be very fecal with accompanying feelings of revulsion, disgust, or shame. Some other forms and colors of abstract visions can be perceived as lascivious and obscene, or very sensuous, sexually stimulating and seductive. Similarly, warm, soft, and soothing forms and colors can be suggestive of the world of the satisfied infant. Such specific qualities in the imagery always reflect underlying emotionally-relevant biographical material. The same is true for perceptual changes in other areas, whether they occur spontaneously or as specific illusive transformations of some concrete sensory input. Experiences of this kind represent a transition from the abstract to the psychodynamic level.

In the study of psycholytic therapy in Prague most patients had, in the initial stages of their LSD treatment sessions, psychodynamic and abstract elements in various combinations and proportions. With the increasing number of sessions, the abstract phenomena progressively disappeared from the content of psychedelic experiences and the process focused on complex biographical self-exploration. Certain aspects of the psychodynamic sessions represented reliving of emotionally important events in the individuals' lives, from early childhood, later life or even the recent past. Most other experiences on this level could be identified, either immediately or at a later date, as various derivatives of such biographical material. The deciphering of these more complex formations often occurred spontaneously in the course of LSD therapy when they could eventually be traced back to their original sources. However, since these psychodynamic phenomena have a structure similar to dreams, they can also be subjected to further analysis by various techniques used in dream interpretation.

The understanding of the content and dynamics of LSD sessions on this level is facilitated if we think in terms of the specific memory constellations, or *COEX systems*, which were described earlier. These help to explain the otherwise puzzling observation that in sequential LSD sessions the specific content tends to undergo constant change, yet the overall structure of the experience, the quality of the emotions, and the accompanying psychosomatic symptoms can remain relatively stable for long periods of time. This reflects the fact that every COEX system has a general theme that characterizes it, but each of the historical layers represents a concrete and specific version of this theme linked with many biographical details. Once the entire COEX system is revealed, the sequential changes in the specific content of the sessions (and the corresponding illusive transformations of the therapist and the setting) can be retrospectively understood as reflecting its various historical levels. With some clinical experience, it is also possible to use the knowledge of COEX systems for anticipating the approximate nature of the experiences in their deeper layers before these are actually manifested in the LSD process. As we discussed earlier, the concept of COEX constellations, and of governing dynamic systems in general, is particularly useful in understanding the complications of LSD administration, such as prolonged reactions or recurrences.

In our research in Prague, the content of psychodynamic sessions tended to proceed, by and large, from reliving traumatic memories of a psychological nature to memories of serious diseases, operations, and accidents. This should be understood in statistical terms, as a trend in a large number of patients; it does not mean that this development is absolutely linear or that it is mandatory for every single individual or every treatment situation. At a certain stage of their LSD treatment, many patients moved from conflicts, problems, and memories of emotionally relevant events to reliving situations that had endangered their survival or bodily integrity. Biologically threatening events and severe psychological traumas in early infancy seem to represent a thematic link between the biographical level and the perinatal level of the unconscious. Since there is usually considerable experiential overlap between these two realms, the transition may be gradual and almost imperceptible. Thus, many LSD patients who were reliving episodes of near-drowning, diphtheria, whooping cough, childhood pneumonia, or tonsillectomy, suddenly recognized that some of the pain, fear, and suffocation that seemed to be related to these biographical events was actually part of the birth trauma. Similarly, other patients who were working through murderous rage seemingly related to early oral disturbances frequently recognized that some of the enormous aggression which they had attributed to their infantile dissatisfaction with the conditions of nursing was on a deeper level associated with the struggle to

be born. In the perinatal context, the tension and locking of the jaws characterizing oral aggression appeared to be a natural situation in the final stage of birth,
where the head is being pressed against the resisting walls of the birth canal. An
experienced LSD therapist can thus frequently recognize emerging perinatal
elements behind certain excessive emotional reactions and psychosomatic
manifestations that the patient associates with various childhood memories.

When serial psychedelic sessions were continued, sooner or later every single
LSD subject transcended the biographical stage and moved fully into the perinatal
area. The number of sessions necessary for this development varied considerably
from one individual to another. By and large, in the context of the psycholytic
study conducted in Prague, subjects without serious emotional problems spent
very little time dealing with biographical material and moved relatively quickly
to problems of dying and being born, philosophical questioning of the meaning of
human life, and discovery of the spiritual dimensions of existence. In contrast,
psychiatric patients with severe neurotic and psychosomatic problems sometimes
needed twenty to thirty sessions before they fully entered the realms of the death-
rebirth process. Retrospectively, many of them realized that their dwelling on the
psychodynamic level had been defensive in nature; they had been avoiding the
much more frightening perinatal material. This attitude was, of course, supported
and encouraged by the exclusive emphasis on biographical data implicit in the initial Freudian orientation of the therapists. The time needed for psychodynamic
work can be considerably shortened if the sitters are familiar with the perinatal
and transpersonal dimensions of the psychedelic experience and are comfortable
with them.

Once patients are fully involved in the death-rebirth process, the main focus
in many consecutive LSD sessions is on the perinatal unfolding,with all its
ramifications and nuances. In the most general terms, this process consists of a
large number of experiential sequences involving the symbolism of individual perinatal matrices. We have not been able to detect any universal patterns or regulari-
ties as to the order in which these matrices are confronted. Some exceptional subjects have direct experiential access to elements of BPM I and transpersonal
phenomena before they confront the elements of negative perinatal matrices.
More typically, the access to BPM IV and I increases as LSD subjects
deal with the difficult aspects of BPM II and III. In general, the perinatal sequential patterns are very individual; the factors determining them are complex and at
the present time only insufficiently understood. The nature and circumstances of
the actual biological birth process, and specific features of the individual's history
that reinforced and accentuated certain facets of the birth trauma seem to be of
considerable importance in this sense.

In addition to elements built into the personality structure of the subject, a
variety of external factors seem to be of potential or actual significance. These include the personality of the therapist, his or her general orientation and
therapeutic approach, and the elements of set and setting in the broadest sense.
Various unsystematic observations seem to suggest the potential relevance of
seasonal influences and calendrical events, such as birthdays, important anniver-
saries, Christmas, or Easter. Some interesting clues can occasionally be derived
from the subject's astrological chart and from the data on planetary transits,[2] and
the most interesting area for future research may be that of possible cosmobiological determinants of psychedelic sessions in general and the perinatal process in

A complex experience combining feelings of constriction with painful genital and umbilical sensations. It illustrates the origin of the castration complex and its roots in the birth trauma.

The horrors of the birth trauma. Bird-like monsters encroach on the helpless and fragile
fetus as it hangs from the top of the uterine cupola by its umbilical cord. Their gigantic
claws and beaks symbolize the destructive biological forces of the delivery.

particular. While the major experiential focus in the LSD procedure is on the perinatal level, several important episodes related to the individual matrices can be experienced in a single session. However, in each of these sequences the emphasis is on a different aspect, facet, or level of the main experiential pattern. In some sequences involving the negative matrices, the central focus is on the emotional quality, such as depression, anxiety, guilt, anger, aggression, or revulsion. In others the emphasis can be on one or several psychosomatic manifestations—a feeling of suffocation, pressures on the head and body, various physical pains, discharge of tension in tremors, nausea and vomiting, or cardiac difficulties. In addition, each of the stages of the perinatal process can be experienced on different levels, from various superficial symbolic allusions to sequences of a primordial and elemental nature that have mind- and world-shattering dimensions.

The richness of the experiential content is augmented by the fact that the process involves an endless variety of illustrative material from biology, zoology, anthropology, history, mythology, and religion. These elements also contribute to the content of positive perinatal matrices, whose emotional and physiological manifestations are much more uniform and simple than those of the negative ones. For these reasons, psychedelic sessions focusing on the death-rebirth process not only have great therapeutic potential, but are a source of invaluable scientific, sociopolitical, philosophical, and spiritual insights.

Although LSD subjects can have several sequences of death and rebirth in a single psychedelic experience, it usually takes many sessions before this process is finished and the perinatal material completely disappears from their content. This is in agreement with anthropological observations in various non-Western cultures where powerful sequences of death and rebirth are induced by drugs or various non-drug methods in the context of so-called rites of passage. There are indications that in the second half of life the episodes of unusual states of consciousness during such rituals become less dramatic and lack the perinatal elements. Kilton Stewart's (96) description of the Senoi culture can be cited as an important confirmation of this. As the perinatal process unfolds, the intensity of negative experiences tends to increase and the feelings of release and liberation thereafter become deeper and more complete.

Certain aspects of the perinatal process can be used as rough indicators of its progression. If the LSD subject spends large periods of several consecutive sessions in the role of the suffering victim—helpless, hopeless, and with "no-exit" feelings—it usually means that he or she is in the initial stages of the process. Increasing access to aggressive feelings and an active role in the experiential sequences are characteristic of more advanced stages of the death-rebirth process. It was mentioned earlier that, in the context of the third perinatal matrix, physical and emotional agony are intimately interwoven with intense sexual arousal. As a result of this connection, during LSD therapy using lower dosages some of the birth agony can be discharged and worked through in the form of orgastic sequences of painful intensity. If high dosages are used in the LSD process, the increase of sexual content in the sessions is an important indicator that the perinatal process is moving into the final stage. The same is true for intimate encounters with biological material such as blood, phlegm, feces, urine, or various other foul-smelling substances. Another typical sign that the death-rebirth process is coming to an end is experiential predominance of the element of fire, in the form of concrete images of volcanoes, thermonuclear reactions, explosions and conflagrations, and especially in the more abstract and transcendental form of the purifying and rejuvenating fire (pyrocatharsis).

It is of critical importance for the practice of LSD psychotherapy to know the concomitants of the experiential transition from death to rebirth intimately. Some of the states the subject has to face in this context are so unbearable that he or she may not be able to do it without sufficient acquaintance with this territory on the part of, and constant encouragement and support from the sitter. If this is not available, desperate avoidance of the frightening aspects of the critical turning-point can become a long-term impediment or even a permanent block to the completion of the perinatal process. The expectation of a catastrophic global explosion, excessive degrees of suffocation, feeling an impending loss of consciousness ("black-out"), a sense of bodily disintegration, and the collapse of all reference points are the most frequent final obstacles that subjects have to face in the death-rebirth process.

Perinatal experiences have an interesting intermediate position between the biographically determined individual unconscious and the transpersonal realms of the collective unconscious. The relative degree of involvement of psychodynamic or transpersonal material in perinatal sessions is another indicator of progress. In early phases there is considerable biographical emphasis; while LSD subjects are dealing with traumatic childhood memories the experience occasionally deepens into a perinatal sequence. Later, the main focus shifts almost entirely to the content of perinatal matrices and the psychodynamic elements are usually reduced to an occasional reliving of diseases, operations, or accidents. At the same time, various transpersonal realms are increasingly represented in the sessions, either as illustrations and concomitants of the perinatal sequences or as independent episodes. Quite frequently, LSD subjects experiencing various aspects of the birth trauma report a simultaneous reliving of past-incarnation memories which involve similar elements. Feelings of suffocation in the birth canal can thus be associated with what feels like a memory of being drowned or hanged in another life-time. Sharp perinatal pains can take the form of being gored by a sword or a wild animal in a previous incarnation, and the no-exit feelings of BPM II can be paralleled by a scene of imprisonment in a medieval dungeon. In a similar way, experiences of the ego death can coincide with executions, murders, or ritual sacrifices.

Many other forms of transpersonal phenomena can make their first appearance in connection with perinatal sequences. Various archetypal images of deities and demons can accompany the birth experiences, as individual visions or in the context of entire mythological sequences. Versions of the Terrible or Great Mother, Satan, Moloch, Shiva the Destroyer, Osiris, Dionysus and Jesus Christ seem to have specific association with individual perinatal matrices and various aspects of the birth process. In some instances, memories from the lives of the individual's human ancestors, or experiences of various phylogenetic crises can occur in the same function as described above for karmic elements. An identification with persons of different races, professions, social groups, and predicaments, such as soldiers in wars, ambitious military leaders, revolutionaries, dictators, prisoners in concentration camps, inmates of insane asylums, adventurers, explorers, martyrs, saints, and sages is quite characteristic. Similar identification may be experienced in regard to entire groups of people, and be accompanied by various relevant insights into the dynamics of important religious, historical, and sociopolitical movements. In the extreme, the death-rebirth experience can seem to have transcended all boundaries and become a drama involving all of mankind.

The number of psychedelic sessions necessary for the completion of the perinatal process varies considerably from person to person and also depends critically on external factors such as dosage, therapist, set and setting. For this reason, any absolutely valid numerical estimate is impossible. In my experience, some individuals were able to work through and integrate the perinatal material in less than ten fully-internalized high-dose LSD sessions. Others needed several scores of psychedelic experiences in the same framework before they were able to move fully into the transpersonal phase. I have also met a number of people who had taken LSD on their own, in an unsupervised externalized way and in a social context, and had not really even begun this process in spite of hundreds of exposures to the drug.

If high dosages of pure LSD are used and the sessions are approached as indepth self-exploration, most individuals sooner or later complete the process of ego death and rebirth. Beyond this point, all their sessions are transpersonal in nature and represent a continuing philosophical and spiritual search. Whether the process was originally approached as therapy or for another reason, it becomes at this stage a cosmic adventure in consciousness aimed at solving the riddles of personal identity, human existence, and the universal scheme.

In the program of psycholytic therapy in Prague a typical psychiatric patient with neurotic or psychosomatic problems moved successively from work on psychodynamic issues through the process of death and rebirth to the philosophical and spiritual exploration of the transpersonal phase. If we want to relate this development to existing schools of psychotherapy, we can refer to the first phase as *Freudian*, because much of the LSD process on the psychodynamic level can be understood in psychoanalytic terms. Since an important aspect of the perinatal process is the reliving of the birth trauma, we can refer to it as *Rankian*. One of the essential characteristics of this phase is enormous release of pent-up energies through orgasm-like discharges and the dissolving of the character armor; it thus also has an important *Reichian* dimension. The only psychiatrist who systematically explored and described many of the transpersonal phenomena was Carl Gustav Jung. Although his conceptual framework does not cover the entire range of transpersonal experiences, it is appropriate to call the third stage *Jungian*. Much of the experiential cartography of the perinatal and transpersonal areas has also been covered by various religious and mystical systems and traditions.[3]

The progression through the above stages and the corresponding changes of content can be illustrated in the series of LSD sessions of Erwin, a twenty-two-year-old patient with an extremely severe obsessive-compulsive neurosis. Although from the point of view of therapeutic outcome he was one of the few absolute treatment failures, his sessions were an interesting example of the change of symbolic content. They showed how the snake, a classical Freudian phallic symbol, took on different meanings depending on the level of the psychedelic process. During his LSD therapy, Erwin successively experienced various psychodynamic, perinatal, and transpersonal phenomena, but all of a negative nature. He was never able to experience the ecstatic unitive states that, according to our observations, have the greatest therapeutic potential.

Erwin was accepted into the LSD treatment program after four years of unsuccessful psychiatric therapy with various conventional methods. His most tormenting clinical problem was a strong compulsion to conceive in his mind a geometrical system with two coordinate axes, and find within this system the proper location for different persons, situations and problems in his life. When he resisted this urge, he became overwhelmed by intolerable fear and other highly unpleasant emotions. This activity absorbed so much of his time and energy that it interfered with his everyday functioning and frequently totally paralyzed him. Sometimes he spent hours attempting to find the appropriate coordinates for a certain aspect of his life, but was never able to complete the task to his satisfaction. Shortly before his admission, he developed an alarming feeling that the center of his imaginary system was shifting to the left. This was accompanied by a sense of urgency, tension, depression, and general insecurity. At that time he had also developed various psychosomatic symptoms and tended to interpret them in a hypochondriacal way. He was referred to LSD therapy after several psychiatric hospitalizations and unsuccessful treatment with tranquillizers, antidepressants, and drug-free psychotherapy.

In the beginning, Erwin showed extreme resistance toward LSD; at one point, he was able to fight with full success the impact of 1500 micrograms of Sandoz LSD administered intramuscularly.[4] A long series of high-dose sessions was entirely uneventful; the content of most of them consisted in massive somatization and struggle for control. After this, he gradually started to gain access to some recent biographical material, such as certain memories from his military service. Finally, in his thirty-eighth LSD session, he suddenly regressed into childhood in a very convincing and realistic manner. He felt small and helpless and had various strange sensations around his genital area. It seemed to him that his penis had shrunk and was as tiny as that of a child. This was associated with anxious concerns about losing control of his bowels, and embarrassing feelings of having his pants wet and soiled. His usual obsessive urge was intensified to an enormous degree and seemed to be intimately linked to visions of moving reptilian bodies and patterns of snake skin. The shifts of various elements within his imaginary geometrical system seemed to be perfectly synchronized and at times even identical with the movements of the snakes. In these sessions, he was working through problems related to toilet training and to rebellion against parental authority. The excretory functions had a strongly ambivalent meaning for him, being simultaneously or alternately pleasurable and repulsive.

In this context, he relived in a complex way and in full age-regression an event which occurred when he was two and a half years old. His mother had taken him to a circus, and he was watching the show while sitting on her lap in the front row. After a performance that involved a female belly dancer with a large boa constrictor, her male partner carried the snake around the arena, exhibiting it to the audience. When he approached Erwin and his mother, the snake made an unexpected movement. In a sudden state of panic, Erwin wet and soiled his pants while sitting on his mother's lap. She was greatly embarrassed by the incident and left the circus immediately. The authenticity of this memory was later independently verified by Erwin's mother.

It took a long time to work through all the complicated emotions associated with this event. They ranged from disgust, embarrassment, shame, and inferiority feelings to strong libidinal pleasure and a sense of triumph related to breaking through exaggerated parental restrictions regarding cleanliness. On this level, the image of the snake and the neurotic symptoms had clear anal connotations: the serpentine forms represented feces and the obsessive preoccupation with the shift of the coordinate system reflected the movements of the bowels.

Later on, entirely new elements appeared in Erwin's LSD sessions. The visions of the snake skin and of the serpentine loops now became associated with strong erotic excitement and sexual tension. On occasion, Erwin now saw scenes involving naked male and female bodies in sexual intercourse. These sequences finally opened into a complex reliving of a classical Freudian primal scene—observation of sexual activities of his parents to which he gave a sadistic interpretation. He felt that this event took place at approximately the same time as the circus scene. The two memories seemed to have a deep similarity; both of them involved a male and female figure with himself as an observer. The boa constrictor from the circus scene and the penis from the primal scene appeared to be symbolically equivalent. On this level, the snake was clearly a phallic symbol in full accordance with the Freudian tradition.

When Erwin progressed to the perinatal level, many of the previously described phenomena were meaningfully related to the birth agony. In this context, the snake became the symbol of the destructive female element, crushing and smothering the baby during delivery. Erwin recalled books and films showing constrictor snakes strangulating the prey and swallowing it. The similarity between these acts and birth or pregnancy seemed to represent the associative bridge between the phallic connotation of the snake symbol and its relation to the process of death and rebirth. The obsessive symptoms continued to be closely related to the movements of the snake's body, but now they symbolically reflected the conflicting forces during the propulsion through the birth canal. The feelings of uncleanliness extended from the genital and anal areas to the entire body and could be identified as the condition of the newborn during and immediately after the delivery. The problems of losing control of the bowels and bladder were now related to reflex urination and defecation, which occurs as a reaction to the agony of birth.

The serpentine visions persisted even in some later sessions that had elements of a transpersonal nature. Here the snake was perceived in a variety of archetypal and mythological contexts. Erwin described numerous visions of high priestesses attending and worshipping sacred pythons, snakes embodying the primordial forces of nature, gigantic Ouroboroses swallowing their tails, plumed serpents, and other mysterious serpent deities.

The LSD experiences on all the levels described seemed to make perfect sense in regard to Erwin's symptoms. Unfortunately, none of these seemingly relevant connections proved to be therapeutically useful. Although Erwin frequently felt that he was coming close to the solution of his problems, the long series of psychedelic sessions failed to bring the desired results.

EMOTIONAL AND PSYCHOSOMATIC CHANGES
IN THE POST-SESSION INTERVALS

The changes that occur in the content of LSD sessions during the course of psyche-delic therapy have their counterparts in parallel changes in the subjects' clinical condition following the drug experiences. The specific dynamics of the post-session intervals and the therapeutic approach to complications have been discussed in an earlier section. Here we will describe certain general patterns of change associated with serial LSD sessions. We will focus our attention on the course of therapy in the psycholytic study in Prague, before we introduced the principle of strict inter-nalization of the sessions and active efforts at positive resolution and structuring of the termination period. The use of these two principles decreases the incidence of negative after-effects considerably, and thus reduces the oscillations of the clinical condition.

The discussion of the course of the LSD process under less-structured cir-cumstances is important for two reasons: it provides a better understanding of the dynamics involved, and gives a rationale to future LSD therapists for active in-tervention in the reentry period. Although the LSD sessions were supervised, the lack of therapeutic intervention in the reentry period made the procedure more like non-medical self-experimentation. The observations made in this context are therefore also of great potential value for those professionals who practice crisis in-tervention and treat complications of unsupervised LSD self-experimentation.

Even when no active therapeutic help is offered during the termination period, negative aftereffects of LSD sessions are minimal in individuals who show reasonable emotional stability. As mentioned earlier, I have never seen in this category aftereffects that had the form and intensity of clinical psychopathology. Occasionally, we observed feelings of sadness, irritability, fatigue, existential questioning, headaches, or "hangover" on the day following the session; such manifestations, however, always remained within the normal range. Even at a time when these individuals were dealing with difficult perinatal material, the negative sequelae of their LSD sessions did not interfere with their everyday func-tioning. In fact, to focus one sidedly on the negative consequences of LSD sessions in "normal" persons would be misleading. In most instances, one observed a dis-tinct enhancement of vitality, an increase of zest, a sense of elation, unusual per-ceptual richness, and other distinctly positive changes for days or weeks following the psychedelic session.

The situation was quite different in psychiatric patients with severe neurotic and psychosomatic disorders. At the time when these patients were working in their LSD sessions on psychodynamic material, their clinical condition showed a considerable degree of variation and oscillation. After some LSD sessions, they would manifest signs of very dramatic improvement; because our knowledge of the nature and dimensions of the LSD procedure was rather limited at that time, this occasionally created a false impression that the therapy was approaching a successful termination. However, other LSD sessions were quite unexpectedly followed by a dramatic accentuation of pre-existing symptoms. In the remaining cases, the positive or negative changes were small and sometimes negligible. In addition to these oscillations in terms of alleviation or worsening of clinical symp-toms, we occasionally observed dramatic transformations of the symptoms.

Within a few hours of the LSD session, old psychopathological manifestations, which in some instances had persevered for many years, disappeared as if by magic and were replaced by different clinical symptoms that the patient had never had before. For a detailed discussion of the dynamics underlying these changes, see p. 283 ff. of this book. In some instances, these changes were so fundamental that the patient moved into a completely different clinical category. This phenomenon is so striking and of such theoretical and practical significance that it deserves to be illustrated by a short clinical example:

Richard was a twenty-six-year-old student who had suffered for more than four years from severe unrelenting depression, and had made six serious suicidal attempts, one of them with rat poison. In addition, he had frequent attacks of free-floating anxiety, excruciating headaches, agonizing cardiac pains and palpitations, and severe insomnia. Richard himself related most of these emotional problems to disturbances in his sexual life. Although he had many friendly relationships with women, he was not able to approach them sexually and had never had sexual intercourse with a female. He tried to reduce his sexual tension by occasional masturbation; however, this resulted in self-hatred and tormenting guilt feelings. At irregular intervals, he got involved in homosexual activities, always in the role of the passive partner. Although he could reach momentary satisfaction in these situations, the feelings of guilt associated with them reached self-destructive proportions. In the state of despair that followed his homosexual affairs, he made several attempts at suicide and once tried to castrate himself by taking a large dose of estrogen hormones.

In his eighteenth LSD session, Richard completed the reliving and integration of a powerful negative COEX system that was functionally related to BPM II.[5] This was followed by an ecstatic experience of several hours' duration. He felt self-assured, cured, whole and optimistic. However, during the reentry period he tuned experientially into a different memory constellation, one associated with the third perinatal matrix. It was an unpleasant surprise for him after what he believed to be the final resolution of his illness. Disappointed, and unwilling to face the new problems, he mobilized his defenses prematurely. He returned from his LSD session radiant, happy, and with a sense of physical well-being; however, to our surprise, the complex of his old symptoms was replaced by a classical hysterical paralysis of his right arm. It had all the typical features of a hysterical conversion reaction, including the "belle indifférence"—a surprisingly indifferent emotional attitude toward a seemingly serious and crippling symptom.

The continuation of psychedelic treatment brought about interesting results. In several subsequent sessions, Richard's paralysis was lifted every time the LSD started taking effect. Two important areas of problems underlying his hysterical paralysis kept emerging and had to be worked through. The first was Richard's relationship with his father, fraught with aggression and conflicts about patricide. His father was a brutal and despotic alcoholic who physically abused both Richard and his mother. On several occasions, his father had hurt him so seriously that Richard had to be taken to a hospital. In puberty, Richard used to have violent fantasies and dreams about killing his father.

In the LSD sessions of this period, Richard repeatedly saw me as transformed into his father. As soon as his arm and hand could move under the influence of the drug, he would inevitably aim his fist toward my face. However, he never completed the movement; his hand would stop several inches from my nose, withdraw, and strike again with new force. At times, his fist would oscillate in this way for several hours in front of my face, as if tossed around by contrary impulses of the Freudian id and superego. As this was happening Richard kept reliving various traumatic memories involving his father, and had a number of symbolic visions related to patricide.

The second theme underlying Richard's paralysis involved problems around masturbation. As he experienced strong conflict between his overwhelming desire to masturbate and his guilt and fears associated with it, his hand kept reaching toward the genital area and then pulling back into a position near his hip joint. While his hand was involuntarily oscillating back and forth, Richard had numerous experiences involving sex and punishment. Finally, he relived with intense emotions a traumatic memory of being caught and severely punished by his father for masturbating.

Both areas of conflict described above had their deeper roots in the perinatal area and thus also reflected Richard's relationship with his mother. In these sessions, sequences of the death-rebirth struggle were closely interwoven with biographical material related to his relationship with his father. It took seven sessions to work through these two areas of conflict. When this was completed, Richard regained full control of his hand and arm; this time no new symptoms emerged and his old complaints did not return. Several weeks later, he had the first heterosexual intercourse of his life.

In spite of the oscillations in their clinical condition, a general trend toward improvement was observed in most neurotic patients in our study. After a certain number of sessions, which varied greatly from person to person, many of them temporarily reached a point where their symptoms were considerably alleviated or even non-existent and there was a good level of overall adjustment. With a few exceptions, they could be discharged and continue LSD therapy on an out-patient basis.

This degree of improvement was probably comparable to the result of very successful psychoanalysis or some other type of systematic long-term psychotherapy. In retrospect, from a conventional point of view this would have been a good time to terminate therapy. However, with most of our patients this did not happen. For several reasons, it seemed appropriate at the time to continue LSD psychotherapy beyond this point. My orthodox psychoanalytic training and background were very important factors in the decision to continue, which eventually opened up for me an entirely new avenue of research into the human mind.

Although at this stage these patients showed a satisfactory level of symptomatic improvement in the periods between LSD sessions, their psychedelic experiences still involved episodes of aggression, anxiety, guilt, and various psychosomatic symptoms. In a way these were actually becoming more primitive and elemental. Much of the material that these patients were dealing with had a definite oral emphasis. This was for me an indication that their therapy was coming to an end, and I continued the LSD sessions in the belief that we just had to work through a few "residual problems," to prevent a relapse. According to psychoanalysis, we are born a "tabula rasa"—a blank tablet—and the psychological problems of our development start in the oral period; there is nothing from before birth and thus there was not much further to go. My expectation at that time was that the amount of biographical material would be limited and that we would eventually reach a point where no new areas of problems would be detected and activated by LSD. Since the reliving of traumatic memories was frequently followed by ecstatic and contentless episodes, I expected serial administration of LSD to ultimately result in undifferentiated and unitive experiences with a great potential for healing and integration. This basic premise proved to be correct, but the way to such experiences was much longer and more complicated than I had expected.

The continuation of therapy was thus a result of ignorance of the nature and basic laws of the LSD process; it also reflected the use of an inadequate and limited theoretical model which underestimated the dimensions of the human personality. The toll paid for this was much unexpected emotional and psychosomatic suffering on the part of my patients, and much conceptual confusion and a real testing of therapeutic optimism and endurance on my part. Despite all these difficulties, this period became the most fascinating intellectual and spiritual adventure of my life. It revealed for me new and uncharted areas of the human unconscious, led to countless unsuspected situations and events, and confronted me with hundreds of incomprehensible and puzzling observations. The final outcome of this process was a radical break with the old conceptual frameworks, a much broader understanding of the human mind, and even a drastic change in my concepts concerning the nature of reality.

As the LSD sessions proceeded into the perinatal realms, the emotional qualities and psychosomatic sensations that had to be confronted, broadened and deepened beyond all imaginable limits. Sooner or later, every single patient started to experience agonies and ecstasies of cosmic proportions. As the patients dealt with various aspects of the death-rebirth process, a similar dichotomy also occurred in the intervals following psychedelic experiences. After some LSD sessions, the clinical condition of the patients would deteriorate drastically. On occasion, persons who came into treatment with severe neurotic symptoms and then at a certain point appeared almost cured, suddenly showed transitory psychotic symptoms. Not infrequently, temporary rehospitalization was necessary in patients who had already returned to their ordinary life situation and were continuing therapy on an out-patient basis. Less frequently, the LSD sessions of this stage terminated in deep ecstatic states and were followed by clinical improvement of an order qualitatively different from anything observed earlier on the psychodynamic level. These changes were characterized by not only a considerable reduction of symptoms, but also an actively joyful approach to existence with a distinctly spiritual undertone ("psychedelic afterglow").

As LSD patients come closer to the moment of the final ego death, some of the free intervals become rather precarious. Deep depressions, aggressive tension, self-destructive tendencies, and manic states are not uncommon at this stage. Although complications of this kind can be considerably decreased by active work in the reentry period, a special treatment facility with trained personnel should be available when individuals with severe emotional problems reach this critical phase of LSD psychotherapy.

At this time, some of the original clinical symptoms that had been alleviated or even eliminated by previous therapy might temporarily be accentuated or reappear. As the patient moves during the psychedelic process from the psychodynamic realm into the perinatal area, various psychopathological syndromes may gradually lose their specific characteristics and be reduced to their perinatal roots. Psychiatric patients who started LSD therapy with the most variegated clinical problems typically show a striking convergence, and ultimately manifest in the LSD sessions and in their free intervals a quite similar symptomatology. In this stage, there may be little difference between patients who started with symptoms of claustrophobia, alcoholism, or inhibited depression; they all manifest symptoms characteristic of an activated second perinatal matrix. Similarly, sadomasochism, asthma, hysterical seizures, and agitated depression can be stripped of their biographically determined specific differences and reduced to typical BPM III phenomenology. Observations of this kind throw an entirely new light on the dynamic structure of various psychopathological syndromes and make it possible to construct a revolutionary model of mental illness and of psychotherapy. Theoretical implications of this kind will be discussed in the next volume.

After many sequences of agony, death, and rebirth, LSD patients in the psycholytic study in Prague typically reached the final experience of ego death. This is an important turning point in LSD psychotherapy; beyond this point, elements characteristic of BPM II, III, and IV no longer appear in the sessions or as determinants of the free intervals. The first perinatal matrix and various combinations of transpersonal matrices take over and govern the psychedelic experiences from then on. From the clinical point of view, this is usually associated with dramatic improvements over a broad spectrum of neurotic and psychosomatic disorders. However, full experiential shift from the perinatal into the transpersonal area does not mean that all negative experiences are permanently eliminated from the content of LSD sessions or from the post-session intervals. The content of purely transpersonal sessions shows the same dichotomy as that of biographical and perinatal experiences. The same is true for the dynamics of the post-session periods; here too, the emotional and psychosomatic condition of the individual can be strongly influenced by positive or negative transpersonal matrices. Thus the everyday feelings, thoughts, behavior, entire world-view and life style can reflect elements of the oceanic bliss of the intrauterine state or the all-encompassing horror of fetal crises; positive karmic patterns or past-incarnation tragedies; and the energy of nourishing or destructive archetypal constellations.

The fact that the subject has transcended the biographical and perinatal levels does not mean that from then on the content of his or her LSD sessions has no personal significance or relevance. The biographical history is now freely available on the adult level without repression and emotional distortion. There is no more painful reliving of individual traumatic events nor narrow emphasis on deciphering the dramas in the nuclear family and their impact on one's life. Similarly, the life-and-death struggles, the claustrophobic nightmares, scatological scenes, and sadomasochistic orgies of birth do not reappear in the sessions. However, no matter how grandiose and cosmic the scale of transpersonal experiences, they are always intimately connected with the everyday life of the individual. Working through negative transpersonal matrices and connecting with positive ones has a therapeutic influence on the subject's emotional, psychosomatic and interpersonal processes. It also provides new levels of understanding of one's own identity, the dimensions of being, human life, and existence in general. Although there is no more specific "archaeological" work to be done on one's present life history, the interpretation of its meaning changes constantly as the conceptual frameworks are expanded to accomodate new experiential data.

One aspect of everyday existence that shows particularly intimate connections with the psychedelic process is the individual's dream life. In a course of psychotherapy involving serial LSD sessions, there is a clear continuity between the nature and content of the drug-induced experiences and mental activity during sleep and the hypnagogic period. Dreams before the LSD session often anticipate the content of the psychedelic experience, and dream life in the post-session periods typically elaborates on various themes from the preceding drug session. This is particularly striking when important gestalts remain unresolved in the preceding session and much unconscious material with strong emotional charge becomes experientially available.

When the emphasis in the psychedelic process is on biographical issues, the dreams have the typical dynamic structure known from Freudian psychoanalysis. Much of their content seems to make sense in terms of the individual's emotional history, and can be easily deciphered by an interpreter who is familiar with the basic principles of dream work. When LSD patients experientially enter the perinatal area, the quality of their dreams changes and the Freudian approach to interpretation is no longer adequate. Although formal analysis usually produces some material from the individual's history that appears to be relevant and thematically associated with the content of such dreams, any purely biographical interpretation remains superficial and unconvincing. The dreams of this phase are very primordial, elemental, and fraught with intense emotion. Their content is usually a more or less direct derivative of the typical themes associated with the individual perinatal matrices. Thus perinatal dreams related to BPM II involve passive experiences of tortures in prisons, concentration camps, and gas chambers; frightening claustrophobic experiences in caves, underwater passages, or progressively narrowing corridors, tunnels and pipelines; and a world of meaningless cardboard figures, circus sideshows, and automatons or robots. More mitigated forms of these dreams involve a variety of hopeless no-exit situations on different levels. Various aspects of BPM III generate dreams of titanic warfare or natural catastrophes of enormous proportions; murders, accidents, bloody massacres, rapes, and sadomasochistic orgies; pornographic scenes full of outrageous sexual deviations and perversions; and an atmosphere of decay and unimaginable dirt. Final phases of this matrix are associated with dreams of exciting adventures in military expeditions, hunts, amusement parks, and particularly in colorful carnivals. The transition from BPM III to BPM IV is reflected in dreams about individual and mass death, enormous fires, volcanic eruptions, atomic wars, and the destruction of the world. Dreams derived from BPM IV involve elements of divine revelations, triumphant victories, escape from dangerous situations, loving reconciliation or reunion, and joyful celebration. Heavenly realms, paradisiacal atmosphere, beautiful natural sceneries, and oceanic states in dreams reveal the involvement of the first perinatal matrix.

The following description is an excellent example of a dream whose content reflects perinatal dynamics. In this case the subject himself recognized its relation to the birth process.

> It was a Sunday afternoon and all my family was in the large livingroom of a house situated on a cliff overlooking the Pacific. Everyone was enjoying themselves in our usual family holiday manner when I noticed that a storm appeared to be gathering force outside. Suddenly, the wind and rain acquired such power that it began to penetrate the windows; at this point my father said in a very significant tone, "It is the Fifth Wind." Then, in a moment that seems magnificent even in retrospect, the entire house began to rotate on its foundations and to fall off the cliff into the Pacific far below. During the few seconds between the time it began its descent and the moment of impact, I realized that all my family and myself were going to die in the cataclysm. At the very moment that I had accepted totally my own death and that of my loved ones, I awoke, just before the house hit the ocean.

> Upon awakening, I was left with an extraordinary exalted feeling, and then I recognized the dream as bearing a deep resemblance to certain sensations I had had in recent LSD sessions. In these sessions I appeared to be reliving my birth, and the elements of accepting my death, the end of the world, tremendous elemental forces involved in a cataclysmic explosion, and finally the peculiar sensation that my head (perceived as much greater than usual), the room and building I was in, and indeed the entire universe seemed to be about to spin on its axis in the most inexplicable and awesome manner—all these elements had appeared in various parts of the sessions and were repeated in a beautiful fashion in the dream. Finally, I recalled how, in the birth of my son, the head seemed to rotate at the culmination of the birth process, and the entire picture seemed to fit together—this dream seemed to represent in a symbolic manner many of the essential aspects of the ego death.

Once the individual moves into the transpersonal stage of the LSD process, this has important consequences for the nature and content of his or her dreams. Many of the elements and sequences, or even the entire content of certain dreams can represent transpersonal phenomena in a more or less pure form. Such dreams cannot be adequately interpreted in Freudian terms and the results of such analysis are bound to be superficial and inaccurate. These dreams do not show the distortion and condensation characteristic of those that are biographically determined, and have the quality of past-incarnation memories, ancestral or phylogenetic experiences, encounters with archetypal entities, various types of extrasensory perception, or out-of-body travels. Recognition and acknowledgement of the specific nature of such dreams is essential for their correct understanding and interpretation. Because of the deep organic link between the dream life and psychedelic experiences, the work with dreams should be an integral part of every comprehensive program of psychedelic therapy.

A synoptic representation of a dream which the author had during his analytical training. He was in a horrible dungeon, chained to a slab and exposed to various inhuman tortures. These were associated with the motif of the little cup that provides unlimited amounts of cream of wheat to anyone knowing the magic word—a theme from a popular Czech fairy tale.

In the dream this magic cup was outside the prison, pouring out enormous quantities of nourishing liquid. It was clear that the torments would end at the moment the cream of wheat reached the window and started flowing in. Free associations arising from this dream included the Spanish Inquisition and the ingenious torture instruments used; the instinctual life of apes; many oral themes, including the buccal repositories of hamsters; and details concerning a Czech king who spent his entire life in prison. Various concrete childhood incidents, involving discomfort in erogenous zones, were also recalled: the mouth being burned by hot milk, an operation for fimosis, painful enemas, and others. The analyst consequently interpreted the dream as a composite formation condensing all the interferences with libidinal satisfaction which the analysand suffered in his early life.

This explanation appeared superficial and unsatisfactory. Later the elements of the dream reappeared in a high dose LSD session and made perfect sense in the context of the birth trauma. The dungeon is the delivering uterus and the tortures will end when the nursing stage is reached. Identification with the king illustrates the connection between birth and the child-king archetype ("crowning"). Identification with monkeys and their uninhibited biological indulgence points to the unleashing of a variety of instinctual impulses (polymorphous perversion) in the perinatal process.

The above discussion focused on the course of LSD psychotherapy for subjects with neurotic and psychosomatic symptoms that were serious enough for them to require psychiatric hospitalization. A few words should also be said about the individuals who were at the two extreme ends of the psychopathological spectrum—"normal" persons and schizophrenic patients. Those subjects who did not have serious emotional problems and participated in the LSD program for training purposes or because of intellectual curiosity, basically followed the same general course as neurotic patients. However, this group was characterized by a rapid progression from abstract to perinatal experiences. These individuals did not spend much time on biographical issues and entered very quickly the realm of the death-rebirth process. In the perinatal sessions, the difficult experiences were usually limited to the time at which the drug-effect culminated, and most of the reentries were pleasant or even ecstatic without any active assistance from the sitters. Negative carry-overs from the contents of the LSD sessions to the free intervals were rare and only minimal, and no prolonged reactions or psychotic breakdowns were observed in persons who had not had serious emotional problems prior to the administration of the drug.

The number of psychotic patients we treated was too small to allow any safe generalization. However, the LSD process in these patients had certain interesting characteristics which deserve to be mentioned. Those persons whom we began treating with LSD at a time when they had manifest schizophrenic symptomatology showed considerable oscillation in their clinical conditions after the initial sessions. Although these fluctuations were deeper and more dramatic, the over-all process resembled that described for the neurotic group. Just before these patients entered the perinatal realm, their clinical condition appeared to be greatly improved. Their psychotic symptoms were alleviated or had altogether disappeared, and they showed surprising critical insight into and psychological distance from their previous difficulties. They typically displayed a variety of neurotic and psychosomatic complaints. Their LSD sessions and clinical symptoms in the intervals between them seemed to be similar to those of the neurotic group, and their perinatal process was equally stormy.

The major difference occurred after the completion of the death-rebirth process. At this point these patients suddenly developed various degrees of what can best be described as "transference psychosis." This condition is characterized by recurrence of the original psychotic symptoms, but with the therapist as the main focus and target of all the patient's thoughts, emotions, and behavior. I will return to this process in more detail in a later section and illustrate it with a typical clinical example, (see p. 254) When the LSD sessions were continued despite the deteriorating clinical condition and the persisting transference psychosis, the patients were eventually able to reach an entirely new level of integration and mental functioning. A specially structured treatment unit is absolutely necessary for therapeutic experimentation of this kind and the therapist has to be prepared to work for several weeks under the difficult and demanding conditions of transference psychosis.

The course of LSD therapy is considerably different from the one described above if the therapist uses the approach outlined in this book. The use of high dosages, eyeshades, and stereophonic music deepens the experience considerably.

Under these circumstances, one does not see the gradual unfolding of various levels of the unconscious from one session to another as described for the psycholytic approach. Instead, all the categories of psychedelic phenomena can be sequentially encountered in a single LSD experience. At the beginning of a session the subject usually experiences a short period of an abstract nature when he or she sees colors and dynamic geometrical patterns. Then the focus shifts to the psychodynamic realm, and the individual might briefly come in touch with some biographical elements related to a particular COEX system. As the LSD session culminates, he or she usually confronts deep levels of memory constellations dealing with survival and bodily integrity, or the material of the basic perinatal matrices. Memories of near-drowning, injuries, operations, and dangerous diseases, as well as profound encounters with death that go beyond concrete biographical events are quite common. After several sequences of death and rebirth, the session can stabilize on the level of BPM I, or the subject can enter the transpersonal realm and experience various mythological sequences, ancestral and phylogenetic memories, elements of the collective unconscious, or past-incarnation phenomena.

During reentry, when the effect of the drug is diminishing, episodes of a psychodynamic nature might be repeated. At this time, the insights acquired earlier in the session are frequently applied to the concrete conditions and circumstances of one's life. However, the fact that the subject has had experiential access to the transpersonal level does not mean that he or she has completed the death-rebirth process. It will still take a series of internalized high-dose LSD sessions of a kind similar to the one described above to work through and integrate all the perinatal material and the associated psychodynamic elements. However, if the principles of psychedelic therapy are applied, the overall time required to complete this process is much shorter than in psycholytic therapy. In addition, there are fewer difficulties and complications in the intervals between the sessions, especially when the therapeutic approach involves intense experiential work in the termination period and the sitters make an active effort at positive structuring of the reentries.

LONG-TERM CHANGES IN THE PERSONALITY STRUCTURE, WORLD-VIEW, AND HIERARCHY OF BASIC VALUES

Since we have been discussing the LSD procedure primarily in a therapeutic context, the question of its lasting influence on various personality characteristics is of particular interest. Under certain circumstances even a single psychedelic experience can have profound and lasting consequences. If the subject's personality structure has intrinsic potential for a fundamental positive or negative shift, the administration of LSD can catalyze and precipitate a sudden dramatic transformation. On occasion, one LSD experience has drastically changed an individual's world-view, life philosophy, and entire way of being. It has mediated a profound spiritual opening in atheists, skeptics, and materialistically oriented scientists, facilitated far-reaching emotional liberation, and caused radical changes in value systems and the basic life style.

At the other end of the spectrum, less-fortunate individuals have been deeply shattered by a single exposure to the drug and the psychedelic experience became for them the "last straw" that led to a psychotic episode. Serious emotional disturbances triggered by ingestion of the drug and lasting months or even years are not uncommon among persons who approach self-experimentation with LSD casually and take it under poor circumstances. This should not happen in the context of supervised LSD work. Individuals with serious emotional problems that border on psychosis should be screened out in advance, unless the therapeutic team is willing and equipped to work through all the problems that might be activated by the administration of the drug, and bring the therapy to satisfactory completion. In this section, we will discuss changes that occur in the course of systematic and judicious long-term LSD psychotherapy following the principles described in this book.

Although the process of psychedelic transformation shows many individual variations, it is possible to outline certain basic trends that are reasonably constant and predictable. In the Freudian stage of LSD psychotherapy, which involves biographical self-exploration, subjects tend to discover that various aspects of their life are "inauthentic." Certain perceptions of the world, emotional reactions to persons and situations, and specific behavior patterns suddenly appear to be blind and mechanical automaton-like processes that reflect psychological fixations from childhood. As the traumatic material from the past is confronted and worked through, LSD subjects free themselves from certain idiosyncratic perceptions, inappropriate emotional responses, rigid value systems, irrational attitudes, and maladjustive behavior patterns that are products of their early programming. This process can also lead to elimination or alleviation of some psychopathological symptoms and various life problems of less serious proportions. Since the life history varies greatly from one person to another, the changes on this level can take many different forms.

Perinatal experiences have a much more fundamental and uniform impact on the LSD subjects. The insights that occur in this profound confrontation with the extremes of human experience can drastically change one's perception of oneself and of the world, and result in an entirely new strategy of existence. In this process, many individuals realize that the inauthenticity of their life is not limited to certain biographically determined partial distortions, such as lack of confidence and poor self-image, chronic problems with authority figures, or difficulties with sexual partners. They suddenly see that their entire concept of existence and approach to it had been contaminated by a deep, unconscious fear of death. A strong need to prove oneself, a chronic sense of dissatisfaction and inadequacy, exaggerated ambitions, tendencies to compare and compete, feelings of pressure and lack of time, and the "rat-race" or "treadmill" type of existence that were previously considered intrinsic and inevitable aspects of life, suddenly appear in an entirely different light. They seem to reflect subliminal awareness of the perinatal energies and their insidious influence on the ego. An individual who is under their spell is, in a sense, still psychologically involved in the life-and-death struggle in the birth canal. This entails a peculiar paradoxical mixture of unconscious feelings; from one point of view, one has not yet been born, from another, one is afraid of death. Under these circumstances, many trivial situations become symbolic equivalents of the birth process and are seen as having survival relevance. In a more concrete sense, certain fundamental approaches to problems, projects, and situations are, at this point, seen to be repetitions of the basic aspects of one's biological birth.

As the individual moves through the perinatal process, he or she discharges and integrates enormous amounts of physical tension and negative emotions, and gains experiential access to unitive states associated with BPM I and BPM IV. This tends to change the way of being in the world and the basic approach to life. The ability to relax physically and emotionally and enjoy ordinary things in life is greatly enhanced. The emphasis shifts from pursuit of complicated external schemes to appreciation of simple aspects of existence. The individual discovers new ways of enjoying his or her own physiological processes and develops more respect for life in all its infinite manifestations. Deep satisfaction can now be derived from a number of things that have been available all along but were previously ignored or barely noticed. Full participation in the process of life becomes more important than pursuit of any specific goal. It appears quite obvious that one should be concerned about the quality of the experience of life rather than the quantity of external possessions and achievements. Feelings of separation and alienation are replaced by a sense of belonging or being part of the life process. This is typically accompanied by a definite shift from a competitive orientation toward synergistic behavior patterns. A selfish and competitive approach to existence is seen as ignorant, inferior, and ultimately self-destructive. Complementary and synergistic arrangements become the new ideal, to be applied on all levels—in intimate relationships, working situations, large social groups and in regard to the entire population of the planet.

The old belief that "more and bigger" automatically means better, on both the individual and social scale, is rejected as a delusion and a dangerous fallacy. The Western life philosophy, which confuses conspicuous consumption with richness of life is replaced by a new emphasis on "maximum well-being with minimum consumption" and a definite shift toward "voluntary simplicity." The new holistic world-view quite automatically includes increased ecological awareness and a need to live in basic harmony with the environment. It seems that the need to control and manipulate people and nature is related to the influence of negative perinatal matrices and reflects the memory of life-and-death struggle with the maternal organism. Conversely, the holistic and synergistic approach to the human and natural environment seems to be related to positive perinatal matrices and based on the memory of a mutually satisfying and nourishing exchange with the maternal organism.

Another striking aspect of the psychedelic transformation is the development of intense interest in consciousness, self-exploration, and the spiritual quest. A spontaneous inclination toward mysticism, ancient and oriental spiritual disciplines, the practice of yoga and meditation, and a fascination with mythology and religious art is particularly common. It is associated with the spontaneous emergence of a new transcendental ethic, quite similar to Maslow's concept of metavalues and metamotivations. The individual seems to gain access to a value system that is not understandable in terms of his or her early history or cultural norms. It entails a sense of compassion, tolerance, basic justice, and aesthetic appreciation that has a transpersonal or even cosmic quality. Successful completion of the death-rebirth process thus results in a more joyful, interesting, and satisfactory way of being in the world, with a sense of belonging, meaning, natural spirituality, and synergistic participation.

This development involves a great conceptual expansion in many ways, but does not seem to influence certain basic philosophical cornerstones of the Newtonian–Cartesian world-view. The world is still seen as objectively real and material in its essence. Space is three-dimensional, time is linear and causality is accepted as a mandatory principle governing the course of events, although its roots have been extended far into the transpersonal realms. Intrauterine experiences, racial and phylogenetic memory, metaphysics of the DNA, archetypal dynamics, and the law of karma might have to be incorporated into the subject's thinking to account for the enormous expansion of the experiential world. A scientifically trained individual still typically accepts at this point the Cartesian division between mind and matter and tries to find material substrates for all his or her LSD experiences in the structures of the central nervous system.

As the psychedelic process continues and the subjects explore the world of transpersonal phenomena, many of the above attributes of the Newtonian–Cartesian world-view become philosophically untenable. The possibility of transcending the limitations of matter, time, space, and linear causality is experienced so many times and in so many different ways that it has to be integrated into the new world-view. Although for the practical purposes of everyday life the individual still thinks in terms of matter, linear time and causality, the philosophical understanding of existence approaches that of Kashmir Shaivism, Taoism, Tantric Buddhism, or modern physics. The universe ceases to be a gigantic assembly of material objects; it becomes an infinite system of adventures in consciousness. The new understanding has distinct holonomic features, and the dichotomy between the part and the whole, experiencer and the experienced, determinism and free will, form and emptiness, or even existence and non-existence has been transcended.

Since much of the information in this book has been obtained in a clinical context, a few words should be said about the implications of the above transformation for the understanding of emotional disorders and psychotherapy. The LSD process can be viewed as therapy in the traditional sense as long as the self-exploration remains limited to the biographical areas. Once it reaches the perinatal level, it can be better described in terms of a rite of passage or spiritual transformation. Although the client is still working on emotional, psychosomatic and interpersonal problems, the emphasis tends to shift toward a philosophical and spiritual quest. Many symptoms and difficulties in living disappear in the process, some of them in a psychodynamic context, others during the death-rebirth process, or as a result of certain transpersonal experiences. However, as the process deepens, each client without exception also has to deal with a number of problems that were previously latent and only emerged during the LSD procedure. In general, the emphasis should be on a good integration of each LSD session in the series, rather than on long-term maximalistic goals such as eliminating all negativity from the sessions, which is unrealistic.

There are aspects of the psychedelic approach however, that are much more important than concerns about simple symptomatic relief. The intensity and magnitude of the LSD experiences are so great that they change the basic tolerance for difficulties in life and alter the very concept of what constitutes a hardship. The simplistic approach to life, which tries to eliminate any difficult experiences and create a utopian world free of problems, is replaced by a "transcendental realism" which sees the dark and light side of the universe as two intrinsic and inseparable components, in the sense of the Taoist yin and yang. From this point of view, the objective is not to eliminate the negative elements from life, but to develop an attitude that would affirmatively embrace the universe as it is in its complex cosmic dialectics. In this context, various aspects of the life process that previously would have been considered negative appear to have multiple new dimensions and can be seen from so many different points of view that they become intriguing and interesting. The ultimate reconciliation with the universe—not necessarily with its *status quo* but with the unfolding cosmic process—comes from the insight that the totality of existence forms a unified field or network which is experientially available to each of us. From the point of view of an advanced LSD subject, we are all ramifications of the principle that has created this universe in its infinite complexity and are thus responsible for all the processes involved.

NOTES

1. The *holonomic theory* of the universe and the human brain was developed by physicist David Bohm (13) and the neuroscientist Karl Pribram (81, 82). It is a revolutionary paradigm that offers the possibility of a new synthesis of such seemingly disparate fields as mysticism, modern consciousness-research, parapsychology, neurophysiology and quantum-relativistic physics. This model makes it possible to bridge the differences between the part and the whole, or between separate objects and undifferentiated unity. It also offers a new approach to the understanding of spatial and temporal characteristics of the phenomenal world. Because of its importance to a comprehensive theory of the human mind, it will be discussed in detail in the next volume.
2. Dr. Rick Tarnas (99), who has been systematically studying the correlations between various aspects of the process of spiritual development and major planetary transits, drew my attention to the fact that the archetypal features of the planets Neptune, Saturn, Pluto and Uranus, as described by astrology, show striking parallels with my descriptions of the experiential characteristics of BPM I, BPM II, BPM III and BPM IV respectively.
3. A similar understanding of the connection between various schools of psychotherapy and specific levels of consciousness was recently expressed by Ken Wilber (103) in his concept of spectrum psychology.
4. This episode is described in detail in my book, *Realms of the Human Unconscious*, p. 30. (32)
5. See the description of this memory constellation in *Realms of the Human Unconscious*, pp. 57–60. (32)

INDICATIONS FOR LSD PSYCHOTHERAPY, THERAPEUTIC POTENTIAL, AND CLINICAL RESULTS

7

Problems in the Evaluation of Clinical Results
Depressions, Neuroses and Psychosomatic
  Symptoms
Alcoholism, Drug Addiction, Character
  Disorders and Sexual Deviations
Borderline Psychotic States and Endogenous
  Psychoses
Emotional Distress and Physical Pain of Dying
  Individuals

PROBLEMS IN THE EVALUATION OF CLINICAL RESULTS

Disagreement about the potential and efficacy of LSD therapy has been one of the most striking aspects of the LSD controversy. Professional literature discussing the clinical significance of the drug falls into three distinct categories. The first group of publications consists of enthusiastic reports by LSD therapists according to whom remarkable and relatively quick results have been achieved in the therapy of emotional disorders, not only those that usually respond to conventional treatment but also many that otherwise have a very poor clinical prognosis. In some LSD studies, the success reported with chronic alcoholics, heroin addicts, subjects with severe character disorders, criminal recidivists, and individuals dying of cancer was quite dramatic. The second group of articles on LSD therapy involves those studies that produced essentially negative clinical results, and tend to deny the enthusiastic reports of the first group. Finally, the third group of clinical reports on LSD focuses on descriptions of various deleterious aftereffects of LSD self-experimentation. The images of LSD in professional literature thus cover a wide range, from therapeutic panacea for psychogenic disorders to dangerous psychosis-producing substance. Without a deeper dynamic understanding of the nature of the LSD effect, therefore, it is difficult to draw any clear conclusions from the published material about its clinical use.

The evaluation of the therapeutic potential of LSD psychotherapy presents many serious problems. Some of them are not specific to LSD-assisted therapy, but relate to any kind of psychotherapy or to psychiatric therapy in general. These include not only the difficulties with the accuracy and reliability of the measuring instruments, but a lack of agreement as to what the basic indicators of therapeutic change should be. Those authors who limit their efforts to symptomatic approaches tend to emphasize the reduction of emotional and psychosomatic distress as the major criterion of therapeutic progress. Those who are more dynamically oriented prefer to focus on the patient's ability to solve conflicts or problems of living and on the quality of interpersonal relationships. Some authors value more objective but less specific indices, such as changes in certain psychophysiological or biochemical parameters. This is further complicated by various criteria which reflect contemporary societal values, such as income, professional achievement, or residential adjustment. The difficulties in assessing psychotherapeutic results can be best illustrated by the fact that researchers of the stature of Eysenck seriously argue that there exists absolutely no scientific evidence for the therapeutic efficacy of any psychoanalytically oriented psychotherapy. (25)

The evaluation of LSD psychotherapy presents several additional problems of a more specific nature. This treatment modality involves much more than just administration of a powerful psychoactive substance; it is a complex process which is critically dependent on many non-drug variables. The personality and approach of the therapist and a variety of factors related to set and setting have to be considered integral parts of the treatment process. In the past, many authors approached LSD therapy simply as a chemotherapy, expecting therapeutic results from the administration of the drug alone without regard to all the extrapharmacological factors involved. Others had various degrees of understanding of the complexity of the process and appreciation for the importance of the psychotherapy that precedes, accompanies, and follows the drug sessions. Unfortunately, most clinical reports about LSD therapy do not give sufficient information about the degree and quality of psychotherapeutic care involved. In discussing the therapeutic results achieved with the use of LSD it is essential to realize that all the drug can do is to bring previously unconscious material into consciousness; the outcome of this process depends critically on the way this material is dealt with and integrated. There is nothing inherently beneficial or detrimental about the effect of the drug *per se*.

The state of mind and level of consciousness of the therapist is also an important variable in the treatment process. His or her ability to remain calm and supportive in the face of various extraordinary experiences and unusually intense emotions, and the degree of open-mindedness, tolerance, and permissiveness maintained towards the entire spectrum of psychedelic phenomena are factors critical to therapeutic success. The role of the therapist in the process is so vital that it is impossible for him or her to make an objective evaluation of the efficacy of LSD psychotherapy without critically assessing his or her role in it. For this reason, specialized training of the therapist, which includes first-hand experiences of psychedelic states of consciousness, is an important element in LSD psychotherapy. It is easier for LSD therapists to tolerate, encourage, and appreciate certain unusual experiences of a perinatal or transpersonal nature that have therapeutic value if they have successfully confronted them in their own psychedelic sessions.

Evaluation of the therapeutic results of psychedelic therapy is further complicated by the fact that the clinical improvement is frequently associated with profound changes in life strategy, philosophical and scientific world-view, and the basic hierarchy of values. Alleviation of severe psychopathological symptoms can be accompanied by a distinct loss of interest in the pursuit of power, status, and position. An orientation toward competition and achievement can be replaced by one toward maximum well-being at minimum expenditure of energy and effort. Previously pragmatic and materialistic individuals can develop deep interest in and genuine appreciation of the spiritual aspect of existence. A tendency to control and dominate other people and nature might be replaced by synergistic and ecological concerns. A psychiatrist who sees the present Occidental value system, based on ambition and competition, as natural, healthy, and ultimately mandatory, may consider the above changes in a psychopathological framework and describe them as showing lack of initiative, loss of interest in socially desirable goals, or even development of psychotic delusional systems. This can be illustrated by an episode which occurred during my lecture at the Harvard University School of Medicine in 1968, after I described dramatic clinical improvements that I had observed in several of my patients during LSD psychotherapy. These changes followed death-rebirth experiences, feelings of unity with the whole universe, and various transpersonal phenomena. In the discussion, one of the participants offered the interpretation that the previously neurotic condition of these patients had actually changed into psychosis, because they had now become interested in spiritual pursuits, were seriously considering the possibility of reincarnation, and had become deeply interested in yoga and meditation.

At present, the situation in the world is quite different from what it was ten years ago. The limitations and dangers of the Occidental value system are more than obvious. Criticisms of the one-sided orientation toward unlimited industrial growth come from many different directions, the failures of competitive politics and technocracy are beginning to overshadow the successes, and ecological consciousness is gaining ground in view of the impending environmental disaster. The criteria of sanity are changing rapidly; according to Abraham Maslow and other humanistic and transpersonal psychologists, feelings of oneness with the universe or other mystical experiences need not be considered psychopathological phenomena. They can occur in healthy individuals and are conducive to self-actualization and self-realization. Oriental systems of thought and spiritual practices are attracting increasing numbers of mature and well-educated individuals who cannot be easily dismissed as ambulatory schizophrenics. Transpersonal psychology and psychiatry, a recently developed discipline that represents an attempt to integrate spirituality and mysticism into modern psychology and psychiatry, is gaining wider and wider acceptance among professionals.

Many theoretical physicists are coming to the conclusion that the mystical world-view is perfectly compatible with the philosophical implications of modern science, particularly relativity theory and quantum physics.[1] It is quite possible, if the present trend continues, that individuals resisting mysticism will in the near future be considered evolutionary throwbacks. At present, however, the theory and practice of mainstream psychology and psychiatry is based on the Newtonian mechanistic model of the universe and on the Cartesian dichotomy between mind and matter. Perceptual and cognitive congruence with the Newtonian–Cartesian world-view and agreement with the present Occidental value system are used as important criteria of sanity. This fact cannot be ignored in evaluating the results of psychedelic therapy.

Because of the above factors, I will present my personal view of the potential of LSD psychotherapy, rather than a balanced synopsis of the clinical literature on the subject. Although I will occasionally refer to the work of others, the statements in the following sections should be seen in the context of the therapeutic philosophy and practice described in this volume.

In general, LSD psychotherapy is indicated in those conditions that have a psychological rather than organic basis, and are a result of learning in its most general sense. That does not necessarily exclude disorders with clear physical manifestations, as long as psychogenic factors have played an important role in their development. This definition of the indications for psychedelic therapy is rather loose and leaves much space for individual therapeutic experimentation. Whether a certain disorder is considered psychogenic or somatogenic depends on the level of development of medical science in general and on the degree of understanding of a specific disease in particular. Since medical opinion concerning the nature and genesis of various disorders is seldom unanimous, the diagnosis of a problem as functional or organic will frequently also reflect the personal philosophy of the clinician.

There are conditions for which the degree of agreement among different researchers will be very high. Psychological factors are clearly of great importance in the genesis of various psychoneuroses, such as anxiety or conversion hysteria and obsessive-compulsive neurosis. Similarly, in character disorders, alcoholism, drug addiction, and various sexual dysfunctions and deviations, the psychogenic component seems to be unquestionable. Bronchial asthma, peptic ulcers, psoriasis, and ulcerous colitis are traditionally considered to be of psychosomatic origin. The opinions of clinicians about the ratio of psychogenic and somatogenic factors in various depressions, borderline psychotic states and so called endogenous psychoses such as schizophrenia and manic-depressive disease, vary considerably. In some other conditions only a minority of researchers consider psychological factors to be of any relevance; cancer and collagenous diseases are important illustrations of these.

Fortunately, the nature of the LSD reaction seems to offer help in those cases where the therapist experiences uncertainty. One or two exploratory psychedelic sessions will usually make it clear for the client and the therapist whether the disorder has an important psychological component or not. Emotional and physical symptoms of psychogenic origin tend to be accentuated by the effect of LSD, and the content of the psychedelic experience will bring relevant insights into the psychodynamic, perinatal, and transpersonal roots of the problem. During the initial experiences, the patient also usually gets a clear feeling about the possibility of influencing the disorder by psychotherapeutic work in the LSD sessions. As I mentioned earlier, one of the most remarkable aspects of the effect of LSD is its ability to detect dynamic structures with intense emotional charge and bring their content to consciousness, making it available for introspective analysis and working through.

Despite the fact that LSD psychotherapy can be beneficial over a very broad spectrum of emotional and psychosomatic disorders, it should not be considered an easily available psychiatric panacea. It is a highly demanding and specialized procedure, and requires a rigorous training of the therapist. The course of LSD treatment is not always equally smooth and safe, nor is its outcome always predictable and successful. There are certain patients who require a large number of LSD sessions, and for whom the therapeutic progress is slow and painful. For reasons that are still insufficiently understood, there appears to be a small percentage of severely disturbed individuals who show very limited therapeutic gain despite large numbers of psychedelic sessions and a great investment of time and energy. In some others, the process is not limited to the time of the pharmacological action of the drug and the intervals between the sessions are difficult or even potentially dangerous.

Clinical conditions in which LSD psychotherapy has been successful fall into four major categories: 1) depressions, neuroses, and psychosomatic symptoms; 2) alcoholism, drug addiction, character disorders, and sexual deviations; 3) borderline states and endogenous psychoses; 4) emotional distress and physical pain of the dying, particularly cancer patients.

DEPRESSIONS, NEUROSES, AND PSYCHOSOMATIC SYMPTOMS

In general, the less serious the clinical problem, the quicker and more dramatic are the results and the safer the treatment procedure. The best candidates for LSD psychotherapy seem to be subjects who have a good intellect and adequate interpersonal and professional adjustment, but lack zest for life and a sense of meaning. Although they might appear to be highly successful by the standards of the society that surrounds them, they cannot connect emotionally with their achievements and enjoy them. These symptoms would fall into the category of what Victor Frankl calls noogenic depression. A single high-dose psychedelic session with LSD is frequently enough to change this situation dramatically. The selective accentuation of negative aspects of the world and the basically pessimistic philosophy of existence associated with this condition can be dissipated within a few hours. These previously almost-depressed individuals typically emerge from a successfully integrated LSD session with elevated mood, joyful appreciation of existence, enhanced self-esteem and self-acceptance, and greater capacity for meaningful human relationships. Their inner life is enriched, they are more open, and they show an increased appreciation of beauty in nature and art. In addition, many of them are able to apply various insights from their psychedelic sessions in a creative way in their professional lives.

Various forms of depression seem to respond unusually well to LSD psychotherapy. In general, depression is the most changeable psychiatric symptom, one which shows great fluctuations even without any specific treatment. Two different kinds of changes of depression can occur as a result of psychedelic sessions, and it is important to distinguish between them. A single LSD session, well resolved and integrated, can totally dispel clinical depression, occasionally even a deep one that has lasted for months. However, that does not mean that the depression has been permanently cured and cannot recur; the patient may have a relapse as a result of various psychological or physiological factors.

This can best be illustrated by the influence of LSD on so-called periodic depressions. A patient suffering from this disorder has regular attacks of depression following a rather rigid pattern, in terms of occurrence of symptoms at certain times of the year and the specific duration of the episodes. A single LSD administration can frequently terminate a deep periodic depression that according to the usual recurrent pattern would have lasted several more weeks or months. However, this does not necessarily change the general course of the disorder, and the next episode of depression might appear on the usual date and last the expected period of time. Systematic work in sequential LSD sessions is necessary to change the complex underlying dynamic structure and influence the overall pattern of the disease.

Most neurotic disorders tend to respond well to LSD psychotherapy; however, even with the powerful catalyzing effect of the drug one should not expect therapeutic magic and overnight cures. Various psychoneuroses require long-term psychedelic sessions. In general, most authors seem to agree that the prognosis is best in those cases where anxiety and depression are important components. Psychiatric patients who suffer from free-floating anxiety or anxiety neuroses, as well as those whose anxiety is bound in the form of various phobias, respond well to psychedelic treatment. Conversion hysteria usually presents greater difficulties, but LSD therapy is frequently successful with this disorder. As in conventional psychoanalysis, anxiety and conversion hysteria might present special problems in terms of transference and countertransference. Monosymptomatic neuroses are not necessarily easier to treat than those that have rich, ramified, and complicated clinical pictures. Frequently, a single torpid symptom condenses problems from many different areas and levels in the patient, and a great number of LSD sessions might be necessary to resolve this.

Although success in treating obsessive compulsive neurotics has occasionally been reported,[2] in my experience they seem to have the dimmest prognosis of all the patient categories. Less debilitating obsessive-compulsive states have been successfully influenced by long-term systematic LSD therapy, but severe cases of this category belonged to our most painful failures. Usually much higher dosages have to be used to overcome the excessive resistances of these patients and a large number of sessions is necessary for any therapeutic progress. However, it is conceivable that these therapeutic failures reflect our limited understanding and inadequate technique, rather than an intrinsic aspect of this emotional disorder. The fact that the psychological resistances of these patients are intimately linked to the problem of control of the anal sphincter might be one of the important variables.

Traumatic emotional neuroses resulting from singular major traumas, such as war situations, natural catastrophes, or mass accidents, have in the past been the best indications for drug-assisted abreactive therapy (narcoanalysis) or hypnotic interventions (hypnoanalysis). LSD can be used with great success for these disorders because of its unique properties as an abreactive agent. A single high-dose LSD session can frequently alleviate or remove very debilitating symptoms in these cases. On occasion, it is possible to use the same approach in cases where the traumatization was prolonged and chronic. We should mention in this context a unique LSD program for victims of the Nazi regime conducted by A. Bastians and his team at the University of Leiden in Holland. These researchers have reported success in working through delayed traumatic consequences of incarceration in former inmates of a concentration camp (the so-called "concentration camp syndrome"). (7)

Sexual experiences and behavior can be deeply influenced by the LSD process. The intensity, depth and completeness of the sexual orgasm and the ease with which it occurs seems to be closely related to the process of letting go of psychological defenses. Many problems in this area can be traced back to unconscious confusion between the pattern of genital orgasm and that of the total physical release that characterizes the orgasm of birth. As LSD subjects learn to let go in the death-rebirth process, their orgasmic ability increases considerably; this improvement of sexual experiences can be observed in both males and females. In those individuals who did not have any major psychopathological symptoms prior to the LSD session, the same effect can usually be observed after one or several high-dose psychedelic experiences. Sexual neuroses, such as frigidity, vaginal spasms (vaginism), genital pain during intercourse, impotence and premature ejaculation frequently respond well to LSD psychotherapy; however, effective treatment of these disorders usually requires serial administrations of the drug and experiential confrontation of the roots of these disorders on the perinatal level.

A wide variety of psychogenic physical problems have in the past been favorably influenced by LSD psychotherapy; this applies equally to organ-neurotic manifestations, symptoms that have the dynamic structure of hysterical or pregenital conversions, and psychosomatic diseases. Painful conditions of various kinds, such as ordinary or migraine headaches, severe menstrual cramps, gastric or intestinal spasms, pains in the neck muscles or in the lumbar area, and even arthritic pains without a detectable organic basis can be traced back to their origins and worked through in the course of LSD therapy. Neurotic disorders of various organs, such as cardiac dysfunction, gastric distress, breathing difficulties, excessive sweating, muscular tremors, constipation or diarrhea, and menstrual irregularities often disappear in the course of LSD treatment. Far-reaching improvements of myopia, which occurred as an unexpected side-effect during LSD psychotherapy with two neurotic patients in Prague, suggest that in some cases of this disorder there is a substantial component of psychogenic muscular tension that can be resolved by psychedelic treatment. Pregenital conversions, such as psychogenic asthma, various muscular tics, and stammering are usually relatively resistant to LSD therapy, which may be related to an underlying obsessive-compulsive personality structure. However, the situation is far from hopeless, and patients with these disorders have on occasion been successfully treated with serial LSD sessions. An especially interesting indication for LSD psychotherapy seems to be psoriasis; dramatic improvements even in severe cases have been independently reported by several therapeutic teams. Clearing of various skin disorders, particularly various eczemas, are rather common observations in psychedelic treatment.

In some patients, LSD psychotherapy can lead to dramatic improvement of certain recalcitrant physical problems that are traditionally considered organic in origin; certain chronic infections such as cystitis, bronchitis, and sinusitis are examples of this. A possible therapeutic mechanism is suggested by the fact that such physical changes immediately follow the resolution and integration of a psychological gestalt in which the corresponding area is meaningfully involved. The experience of Tanya described in a later section can be mentioned here as an illustration of this. (p. 290) This suggests that the infectious agent is just one element in the development and perpetuation of the condition, and possibly even a secondary one. A much more important factor seems to be decreased vitality of the organ or tissue, which accounts for the ineffective defense against the bacterial invasion. It is not difficult to see how psychological factors could play an important role in this situation. One of the possible mechanisms could be, for example, psychogenic constriction of the afferent vessels resulting in limited blood supply to and reduced immunobiological resources in the afflicted area. It is interesting that during the session immediately preceding the clinical improvement of a physical problem of this kind, LSD subjects usually report that a block has been removed and free flow of blood and energy established in the afflicted area. This is typically associated with an invigorating feeling of pleasant warmth, and tingling sensations.

ALCOHOLISM, DRUG ADDICTION, CHARACTER DISORDERS, AND SEXUAL DEVIATIONS

Many of the emotional and psychosomatic disorders described above are, by and large, within the range of indications for traditional analytically oriented psychotherapy. The use of LSD as an adjunct in these cases will intensify, deepen, and accelerate the therapeutic process. However, LSD psychotherapy can be successfully applied in some diagnostic categories which are outside the realm of the traditional indications for dynamic psychotherapy. Many clinical studies of psychedelic therapy have reported dramatic results in chronic alcoholics. Unfortunately, in a great majority of them the evaluation was based on clinical impressions. Like most results reported in psychoanalytic literature, these are open to questioning and criticism from the point of view of rigorous research methodology.

In a large, controlled study conducted by our team at the Maryland Psychiatric Research Center, 135 hospitalized alcoholics were randomly assigned to either high-dose (450 micrograms) or low-dose (50 micrograms) LSD treatment. After six months, an independent evaluation team rated fifty-three percent of the high-dose group as "essentially rehabilitated," as compared to thirty-three percent of the low-dose group. In statistical terms this difference had only five chances out of one hundred of being coincidental. Differences between high- and low-dose groups were no longer as great after eighteen months, with 54 percent of the high-dose patients considered greatly improved versus 47 percent of the low-dose patients.

The overall results of this study were quite impressive, considering that the patients were volunteers selected from the population of the Alcoholic Rehabilitation Unit of a state mental hospital, and that most of them had only one high-dose LSD session and several hours of drug-free psychotherapy preceding and following it. An interesting and unexpected research finding was the dramatic improvement in some patients in the control group who received only 50 micrograms of LSD on a double-bind basis, as compared to 450 micrograms for the experimental group. In our original thinking the dosage of 50 micrograms was considered to be an active placebo, the therapeutic effect of which should be negligible. In reality, several patients in the low-dose group had quite significant experiences, while a few of the individuals in the high-dose category had uneventful psychedelic sessions. The interested reader will find a more detailed description of this study in a paper by the Spring Grove team entitled *The Experimental Use of Psychedelic (LSD) Psychotherapy.* (77)

The above results of the Spring Grove team are in sharp contrast with the outcome of an extensive controlled study conducted by Ludwig, Levine and Stark (59) at the Mendola State Hospital in Madison, Wisconsin. The authors randomly assigned the 176 alcoholic patients who had volunteered for this project to one of the following four groups: 1. "psychedelic therapy" with LSD, 2. hypnodelic treatment with LSD, 3. administration of LSD alone, and 4. no specific therapy at all (milieu therapy). In addition, half of each group was offered Antabuse medication after the completion of the experiment. The results of this study were devastatingly negative; the authors did not find significant differences between any of the groups, and the overall remission rate was extremely low. After six months between 70 and 80 percent of the patients in all the categories were drinking, and after a year this number ranged between 80 and 90 percent. Even the introduction of Antabuse did not make any difference in this context.

This study met the formal criteria of contemporary medical research so well that it received the Hoffheimer Award from the American Psychiatric Association. For this reason the negative results of this project deserve special attention; they can be used to demonstrate some of the basic principles emphasized in this book. In the following text I will refer to an incisive critique that Charles Savage presented in March 1971 at a staff-meeting of the Maryland Psychiatric Research Center, of which he was Associate Director. He pointed out that very serious deficiencies could be detected in this study, which on the surface appeared to be methodologically sound and meticulously designed. In the past, substantial claims for fast and dramatic therapeutic success in alcoholism have only been made for the psychedelic model; no LSD therapist has ever indicated that one psycholytic session with LSD can have a profound effect on alcoholic patients. Ludwig and his associates were familiar with the essential characteristics of psychedelic therapy, as evident from the accurate definition given in their book. However, in the actual study they rejected the psychedelic model, while pretending to test it, and neglected many of the elements that psychedelic therapists consider mandatory for therapeutic success. The therapists engaged in this project were thirteen residents and state hospital psychiatrists who were not committed to the work and performed it as a peripheral activity. None of them had personally explored the psychedelic or hypnotic state; they were not experienced in either LSD therapy or hypnotherapy and had only a superficial "crash-course" in both. The preparation for the LSD session was limited to one two-hour session, half of which was spent on measurements of suggestibility. The *ex-post* justification that the authors gave for this drastic condensation of the preparatory work was that none of the patients became psychotic. This fact might be used as an illustration of the safety of LSD,

but certainly does not prove that the procedure was adequate for therapeutic purposes. Although the dosages they used were in the lower range of those used in
psychedelic therapy, (3 micrograms per kg.) the approach was essentially psycholytic. There was continuous verbal exchange, which is known to increase the patient's resistance and interferes with deep regression. The therapists attended the
patients for only three hours of the session and left them alone for the remaining
hours of the drug action. The mystical experiences that are considered of utmost
importance in the psychedelic model were reported by only 8.4 percent of the patients, as compared to the 78 percent of the Spring Grove study. Charles Savage
concluded that the project reflected a strong bias in the authors. At a time when
LSD was popular, Levine and Ludwig (58) had reported positive results using the
hypnodelic technique with addicts, a group generally much more difficult to treat
than alcoholics. When LSD fell out of favor and the positive results became
politically unwise, they obtained negative results. Unconsciously or consciously
they built into their study a number of antitherapeutic elements that guaranteed a
therapeutic failure. The use of inexperienced and unmotivated therapists, defective preparation, antimystical orientation, violation of the basic rules of
psychedelic therapy, and a critical lack of human support and care can be mentioned here as important elements. LSD can best be described as a facilitator, and
in the above study it seems to have facilitated mediocrity, however brilliantly
reported and adumbrated with elegant statistical techniques.

On the basis of encouraging results with alcoholics, the team at the Maryland Psychiatric Research Center carried out a study of LSD psychotherapy with
heroin addicts. All volunteers for this program were male addicts serving a sentence in Maryland correctional institutions, mostly for theft, robbery, and involvement in illegal drug traffic. Those who were interested in participating in the
study were recommended by the research staff for an early parole hearing by the
Board of Parole and Probation. Only individuals who had been granted parole
were accepted into the research program. One half of the volunteers had one high-
dose psychedelic session after an average of twenty-three hours of intensive
psychological preparation, while the other half participated in a regular program
of non drug therapy at the out-patient clinic, which lasted a comparable amount
of time. The assignment of patients to the experimental and control group was
done on a random basis. Both groups were required to remain in regular contact
with the outpatient clinic after treatment and give samples of urine for chemical
analysis. The results of this experimental treatment program were reported by two
members of the Spring Grove team, Charles Savage and Lee McCabe (93). Eleven
of the thirty-four patients in the LSD group did not return to narcotics during the
six-month follow-up period, while only one control subject showed a comparable
improvement. At the one-year follow-up, eight LSD patients were still abstaining
as compared to none in the control group. Although not dramatic in absolute
terms, this has to be considered a very promising result for this extremely difficult
category of patients. Short-term follow-up studies of narcotic addicts indicated
that typically 94–97 percent of the patients return to drug use within a few weeks
following conventional treatments.

One aspect of psychedelic therapy with alcoholics and heroin addicts
deserves special notice. While successful treatment of psychoneuroses and psychosomatic disorders usually requires a whole series of therapeutic psychedelic ses-

sions, in these two categories quite striking improvements may frequently be observed after a single LSD experience. It was mentioned earlier that this might be related to the ease with which many alcoholics and drug addicts achieve transcendental states of mind. In the Spring Grove program, the number of sessions per patient was limited by the research design. All heroin addicts and most alcoholics received only one LSD session; some alcoholic patients had two or, quite exceptionally, three sessions. There is good reason to believe that much better clinical results could have been achieved if the research design had been less rigid. In a more open-ended situation in Prague, where it was possible to administer serial LSD sessions without any limitations, we observed in several instances not only lasting abstinence but deep positive restructuring of the alcoholic's or addict's personality.

Another category of difficult patients with poor prognosis that can occasionally be reached by LSD-assisted psychotherapy should be mentioned in this context. There are indications that certain individuals with asocial, antisocial, and criminal tendencies can benefit from LSD treatment. Several aspects of the psychedelic process seem to make it possible to achieve positive results with these subjects. The most serious obstacle to effective psychotherapy of sociopathic individuals under normal circumstances is their inability to form, develop and maintain relationships. This interferes significantly with the treatment process, since a strong emotional connection with the therapist is considered an important element of therapeutic change. It is well-known that during psychoanalysis just the sharing of intimate personal material tends to result in development of a transference relationship in most subjects. This factor is much more powerful in psychedelic therapy; merely sitting in an understanding and supportive way in a person's LSD sessions will automatically result in formation of a strong emotional tie. This bond can be positive, negative, or distinctly ambivalent, but the patient cannot easily avoid some sort of response. Although this is just a prerequisite for effective therapy and not necessarily a therapeutic element *per se*, it is an essential condition for the successful treatment of individuals with sociopathic traits. In addition, the LSD experience provides effective channels for the discharge and integration of enormous amounts of aggression and destructive feelings underlying antisocial activities. Experiential access to the areas of transcendental feelings and connection with the system of metavalues seems to be even more important in this context. As a result, criminal behavior is often taken out of the narrow context of a revolt against human society and can suddenly be seen as violation of the cosmic order.

Several LSD therapists occasionally described good results in individual patients with antisocial tendencies in the context of larger clinical studies involving a broad range of diagnostic categories. In several instances, researchers conducted special studies focusing on antisocial and criminal populations. Arendsen-Hein (4) treated twenty-one severely-criminal psychopaths with regular LSD sessions using dosages of 50–450 micrograms. After a period of ten to twenty weeks of therapy, twelve were clinically improved and two greatly improved.

In the early sixties, a team of Harvard psychologists headed by Timothy Leary initiated a research program of psychedelic therapy with recidivists at the Concord State Prison in Massachusetts. (55) The drug used in this project was not LSD, but the closely related psilocybin, the active psychedelic principle from the

Mexican sacred mushrooms *Psilocybe mexicana*. The unique aspect of this research was that the psychologists ingested the drug along with the convicts, although a non-drugged "ground control" and supervising psychiatrist were always present. The result of this study, in which over two hundred psychedelic sessions were run with men incarcerated for their antisocial behavior, was a statistically significant reduction in new crimes committed by the group that had had psilocybin experiences. Several years ago, Walter Huston Clark carried out an informal follow-up study, with quite impressive results. At least one interesting attempt has been made to integrate LSD therapy into a complex therapeutic regime under the conditions of maximum security. The results of this experiment conducted at the Maximum Security Division of the Mental Health Center at Penetanguishene, Ontario, have been reported by G.J. Maier, D.L. Tate, and B.D. Paris. (61)

Favorable clinical results have occasionally been described in patients with various sexual abnormalities that are usually very unresponsive to conventional psychotherapy or therapy in general. Among them, individuals showing sadistic and masochistic tendencies seem to have the most favorable prognosis. Once the psychedelic process reaches the perinatal level, powerful channels become available for discharge and integration of enormous amounts of aggressive and self-destructive impulses. Experiences of the death-rebirth sequences offer unique opportunities for the resolution of the intimate perinatal link between sexuality and aggression which underlies sadomasochism. Some other sexual deviations that can respond to psychedelic therapy include fetishism, exhibitionism, and coprophilia. Although favorable results have occasionally been reported for male and female homosexuality, it is difficult to make any generalized statements in this area because of the heterogeneity and complexity of the problems involved. The prognosis of patients in this category is critically dependent on the nature of their problem, their own attitude toward their sexual behavior, and the motivation for therapy. A positive outcome can be expected only when the individual considers the deviation to be a problem, has a strong intrapsychic conflict about it, and shows an active interest in treatment.

Character disorders of various kinds, sometimes even severe and complicated cases, can be considered for LSD therapy if a well-equipped facility with trained personnel is available. Usually, a few exploratory sessions will give the therapist a sufficient indication of the prognosis for a particular individual. In the course of the LSD therapy of character disorders that were originally symptom-free, one can frequently observe temporary manifestations of various neurotic and psychosomatic symptoms in the free intervals between the sessions.

BORDERLINE PSYCHOTIC STATES AND ENDOGENOUS PSYCHOSES

Psychiatric patients with borderline and manifest psychotic conditions need not necessarily be excluded from psychedelic therapy. Although clinical experiences of the treatment of schizophrenic and other psychotic states with LSD are rather limited, it is possible to make certain general conclusions. By and large, the prognosis in psychotic individuals seems to be much better than in certain severely defended neurotics, particularly obsessive-compulsive patients. However, this statement is conditional and needs clarification and specification. LSD work with severely disturbed individuals is a very demanding and intense process which requires special preparation and training. It should not be attempted by anyone who has not had sufficient experience of LSD sessions with "normal" and neurotic individuals. The intervals between the sessions may be characterized by dramatic exteriorization or intensification of various psychotic symptoms. In certain critical stages of the psychedelic process the inner experiences and behavior of the client can be almost entirely focused on the therapist, in the sense of a "transference psychosis." A special treatment unit with trained personnel and 24-hour-a-day supervision is an absolute necessity for this undertaking.

The deepest roots of schizophrenic symptomatology can always be found in the various perinatal matrices and in negative transpersonal experiences. A therapist sharing the complicated journey triggered in the psychotic patient by LSD has to remain grounded and centered during the entire process, which might turn out to be a wild emotional and conceptual roller-coaster. Because of its importance, not only to the LSD therapy for schizophrenia but also for the basic understanding of the dynamics of psychosis, I will illustrate this process with the story of Milada.

Milada was a 38-year-old psychologist who for many years before starting LSD treatment had suffered from a complicated neurotic disorder involving a variety of obsessive-compulsive, organ-neurotic, and hysterical conversion symptoms. She started systematic psychoanalytic treatment, but four months later had to be hospitalized because she developed acute psychotic symptoms. An important part of her clinical symptomatology was an erotomanic delusional system. Milada was convinced that her employer was deeply in love with her and she herself felt irresistible affection and sexual attraction toward him. She sensed a strange erotic and spiritual communion existing between them which they shared intrapsychically, beyond the facade of their rather formal social interaction. Several weeks later she started hallucinating the voice of her imaginary lover. In these hallucinations, she heard him describe in detail his passionate feelings for her, promise a beautiful shared life in the future, and give her advice or specific suggestions. During the evening and night hours Milada experienced powerful sexual sensations which she interpreted as intercourse at a distance, magically performed by her "lover." Although in actual sexual situations she had always been frigid, during these episodes she experienced orgastic feelings of cosmic proportions.

Milada's hospitalization became unavoidable when she started acting under the influence of her delusions and hallucinations. One day in the morning she left her husband, made an attempt to move into her employer's apartment with her children, and got into a physical fight with his wife. She referred to his "voice," which allegedly had told her that divorces had been arranged for both of them and that they could now live together. After many months of unsuccessful treatment with a variety of tranquilizers and antidepressants, as well as individual and group psychotherapy, she was selected for *psycholytic therapy* with LSD.

After twelve LSD sessions, the psychotic symptoms completely disappeared and Milada developed full insight in regard to her irrational behavior in the past. In more than thirty subsequent sessions she worked on a variety of complicated neurotic and psychosomatic problems, reliving traumatic memories from different periods of her life and tracing her present problems to their emotional sources in her unhappy childhood. Much time was spent on her complicated marital situation. Her husband was cruel, insensitive and physically abusive; he was emotionally immersed in the pursuit of a political career and provided no emotional support for her. Both of their children were showing signs of serious emotional disturbances that required professional assistance.

Then the LSD sessions moved into the perinatal realm and Milada experienced the entire spectrum of experiences characteristic of the death-rebirth process. The emotions and physical sensations associated with the reliving of her difficult birth, during which her twin brother had died, were so abysmal that she referred to these sessions as a "psychological Hiroshima." When she finally completed the birth process and experienced the final ego death, I expected a marked improvement, as was the case in most neurotic patients. However, to my great surprise I witnessed a sudden and complete reappearance of the original psychotic symptomatology, which Milada had not shown for many months. The only difference was that this time I became the main target of all the psychotic phenomena; in the process of LSD psychotherapy she had developed a transference psychosis.

At this point Milada believed herself to be under my hypnotic influence and felt in constant rapport with me, in the LSD sessions as well as during the free intervals. She experienced a mutual exchange of thoughts and even verbal communication. It was interesting that in some of these hallucinated interviews we "continued psychotherapy." Milada "discussed" various aspects of her life with me and carried out activities suggested by my illusory voice, such as several hours of bathing and physical training every day and exercises in feminine housework. In these hallucinated conversations I told her that I had decided to drop the therapeutic game and become her lover and husband; I also allowed her to use my last name instead of her husband's name. She was repeatedly assured of my love, was told that her divorce was already arranged, and asked to move with her children into my apartment. It was clear from the context of her LSD sessions that this wishful magical thinking was a transference phenomenon reflecting her early symbiotic relationship with her mother. Among other things Milada talked about the "hypnogamic sessions" she was getting from me in the evening and night hours. Sexual sensations and hallucinations of intercourse were interpreted by her as deliberate lessons in experiencing sex that I had decided to give her in order to accelerate therapy.

At one point, Milada spent many hours a day in bizarre postures that resembled catatonia; however, it was always possible to bring her out of them by talking to her. She would then resume a normal posture, answer questions, and logically explain her behavior. Her emotional and psychosomatic condition at this time was dependent on the position of her body. In some postures she experienced ecstatic bliss, oceanic feelings and a sense of cosmic unity; in others, deep depression, nausea, and metaphysical anxiety. She herself related this phenomenon to the situation during her intrauterine existence where she had to compete physiologically and mechanically with her twin brother.

On the basis of previous experiences with other patients, I continued with regular weekly administrations of LSD despite her persisting psychotic symptoms. These sessions consisted almost entirely of negative experiences of a transpersonal nature. There was an important emphasis on reliving unpleasant intrauterine memories, which she related to the emotional stresses and illnesses of her mother during pregnancy, various embryonal crises, and the mechanical discomfort of being twins in a uterus. She also had some negative karmic sequences and archetypal experiences of a demonic nature.

In the final phase of treatment a most unusual phenomenon occurred: suddenly the LSD had a distinctly paradoxical effect. Under the influence of LSD Milada appeared normal and regained insight and critical judgment; when the effect of the drug was wearing off, the symptoms of transference psychosis recurred. Finally, in her ninetieth session she experienced for several hours profound ecstatic feelings, with cosmic unity as the prevailing pattern. To my surprise, she emerged from this session without the previous psychotic and neurotic symptoms and with a completely restructured personality.

According to her own description, she was now able to experience herself and the world in a way completely different than ever before. She had zest for life, a new appreciation of nature and art, a totally transformed attitude toward her children, and the ability to give up her previous unrealistic ambitions and fantasies. She was able to resume her job and perform it adequately, obtain a divorce from her husband, and live independently while taking care of her two children. To my knowledge, she has not needed any in- or out-patient psychiatric care during the more than twelve years since the termination of her LSD treatment.

In several other schizophrenic patients whom I treated with LSD therapy, the process was similar but less involved and dramatic than the one described above.[3] Kenneth Godfrey, an American psychiatrist also attempted this difficult task and reported successful treatment of psychotic patients with serial LSD sessions. (31)

Even under the best circumstances, patients with marked paranoid tendencies should not be treated by LSD psychotherapy as long as they include the therapist into the paranoid system and see him or her as one of the persecutors. A good therapeutic relationship with a foundation of basic trust seems to be the single most important element for successful psychedelic treatment. Informed consent, active interest, and good cooperation are necessary conditions for a smooth course of therapy. This is very difficult to achieve with paranoid patients; even in milder cases, it requires long and intense drug-free work. If LSD is administered to a paranoid patient, he or she tends to experience the session in total psychological isolation and blame all the emotional and psychosomatic distress on the therapist. The extraordinary nature and scope of the psychedelic experiences can, under these circumstances, not only powerfully reinforce and justify the conviction of the therapist's evil intentions, but magnify his or her image in the patient's eyes into a malefic figure of cosmic proportions.

Psychotic conditions of the manic-depressive type can also be treated by LSD psychotherapy, although special problems might be encountered in this category of patient. A single LSD session can frequently cause a complete remission of the depressive or manic episode. In a similar way, a single administration of the drug can change the phase of the disease, turning depression into mania or vice versa. In this sense, the effect of LSD is comparable to that of electroshock therapy. Within the conceptual framework presented in this book such changes can be understood as COEX or BPM transmodulations—chemically triggered shifts in the dynamic governing systems influencing the patient's ego. It seems that in manic-depressive disorders LSD can precipitate such changes much more easily and more frequently than in other diagnostic categories. This may be because lability and periodicity are typical and intrinsic characteristics of this disease.

The COEX or BPM transmodulations should not be mistaken for a cure of the disease. There is always a possibility that another depressive or manic phase will recur in the future when the dormant negative systems become activated by various physical triggers, specific psychological stresses, or physiological changes within the organism. However, in some cases it seems possible to influence the psychological roots and basic underlying mechanisms of this disorder by systematic intrapsychic work in serial LSD sessions. This procedure has its special risks, the main one being the possibility of triggering deep depressions with suicidal tendencies after some of the sessions. As with borderline psychotic conditions and schizophrenic psychoses, LSD psychotherapy of manic-depressive disorders should be carried out on an in-patient basis, or a suitable facility should at least be available at all times for temporary hospitalization if the condition of the client requires it.

EMOTIONAL DISTRESS AND PHYSICAL PAIN OF DYING INDIVIDUALS

Probably the most interesting and promising indication for LSD psychotherapy is its use in seriously ill people who are facing death. Although this approach has been most systematically explored in cancer patients, it is applicable to persons with other life-threatening diseases. The use of psychedelic therapy in this indication has been discussed in detail in a previous volume[4] and will only be briefly described here.

The original suggestion that psychedelic therapy could be useful for persons with terminal diseases came independently from the American pediatrician of Russian origin, Valentina Pavlovna Wasson, and the writer and philosopher Aldous Huxley. Wasson came to this conclusion on the basis of her experience with the Mexican sacred mushrooms, and Huxley as a result of his psychedelic sessions with mescaline and LSD. The pioneering clinical work with cancer patients was conducted in the early sixties at the Chicago Medical School by Eric Kast who was primarily interested in the possibility of using LSD as an analgesic. A systematic complex study of the effects of psychedelic therapy on cancer patients in relation to their emotional condition, physical pain, concept of death, and attitude toward dying was carried out by the team of the Maryland Psychiatric Research Center. The initiator and original head of this research project was Walter Pahnke; after his death I assumed medical responsibility and completed it in cooperation with William Richards. In this program, over one hundred cancer patients were treated over the years with psychedelic therapy using LSD and a similar short-acting substance, DPT (dipropyltryptamine). Positive changes were observed quite consistently in several different areas. Many patients showed a definite alleviation of various emotional symptoms, such as depression, general tension, sleep disturbances, and psychological withdrawal. LSD therapy also had a striking, although not predictable, effect on severe physical pain. In some patients who had not responded to analgesics or narcotics, pain was alleviated or even completely eliminated for periods of weeks or months after a single LSD session. The most remarkable changes were observed in the patients' concepts of death and attitudes toward dying. Those patients who had perinatal or transpersonal experiences tended to show a marked decrease in fear of death. Their understanding of the process of dying tended to shift in the direction of ancient or non-Western belief systems according to which consciousness or some form of existence continues beyond the time of biological annihilation.

I mentioned earlier that the psychedelic transformation observed after LSD sessions with a transcendental emphasis involves drastic changes in the hierarchy of values. Having experienced death and rebirth and/or feelings of cosmic unity, LSD subjects tend to put less emotional emphasis on the past and future and show an increased appreciation of the present. Preoccupation with the dismal prospects for the future is replaced by concern about the best possible utilization of each day. The ability to draw satisfaction from simple and ordinary things in life is accompanied by acute awareness of the ultimate futility of anxious pursuit of status, power and possessions. It is not difficult to understand that the above changes in values and life strategy can make the situation of the terminally ill more tolerable. Psychological work with the patients and their families also seemed to have a positive influence on the survivors. It not only eased their reaction to dying and to the death of their relative, but helped them to cope with their grief and integrate the loss in a constructive way.

According to the clinical ratings, approximately thirty percent of the cancer patients showed dramatic improvement in the above areas after a single LSD session and an additional forty percent showed a moderate degree of positive change. In the remaining thirty percent there were no manifest differences, positive or negative, from pre- to post-session measurements. The results of DPT-psychotherapy were similar, although less striking and consistent.

Of all the indications for LSD psychotherapy, its use for work with the dying seems to be the most interesting and least controversial or problematic. The possibility of alleviating in a relatively short time the emotional and physical distress of persons facing the ultimate crisis of human life should be of great interest to all of us. Most of the objections raised against the use of LSD are of little relevance here, certainly those concerning heredity and chromosomes. In addition, recent research showing the possible role played by psychological factors in cancer, as well as some of our own observations on the subject, seem to suggest that at least for some cancer patients, LSD psychotherapy could become a factor contributing to healing, and not only a preparation for death.

NOTES

1. The interested reader will find detailed information about the recent convergence of quantum-relativistic physics, mysticism, and modern consciousness-research in books by Itzak Bentov (11), Fritjof Capra (18), Nick Herbert (37), Larry Le Shan (56), Kenneth Pelletier (78), Bob Toben (101), and Arthur Young (105).
2. An example of dramatic and lasting success in a severe case of compulsive neurosis was published in Scandinavia by E. Brandrup and T. Vangaard (16). On page 185 I described striking improvements in a patient with an obsessive-compulsive neurosis that had resisted Freudian psychoanalysis for eighteen years. Unfortunately, our research design did not allow for more than three sessions and the therapy could not be completed.
3. The condensed story of another of these patients, Michael, is presented in my first book, Realms of the Human Unconscious (32), pp. 66 and 235.
4. Stanislav Grof and Joan Halifax: The Human Encounter With Death (34). The bibliography of this book gives all the specific references to original papers in this area.

NON-THERAPEUTIC
USES OF LSD

8

Training Sessions of Mental Health Professionals
Administration of LSD to Creative Individuals
Drug-Induced Religious and Mystical
*   Experiences*
Role of LSD in Personal Growth and
*   Self-Actualization*
Use of LSD in the Development of Paranormal
*   Abilities*

TRAINING SESSIONS OF MENTAL HEALTH PROFESSIONALS

The extraordinary value of LSD for the education of psychiatrists and psychologists became evident at a very early stage of its research. In his pioneering paper, published in 1947, Stoll emphasized that an auto-experiment with this drug gives professionals a unique opportunity to experience first-hand the alien worlds which they encounter in their everyday work with psychiatric patients. During the "model psychosis" phase of LSD research, when the psychedelic state was considered a chemically-induced schizophrenia, LSD sessions were recommended as reversible journeys into the experiential world of psychotics which had a unique didactic significance. The experience was recommended for psychiatrists, psychologists, nurses, social workers, and medical students as a means of acquiring insights into the nature of mental illness. Rinkel (85), Roubíček (90) and other researchers who conducted didactic experiments of this kind reported that a single LSD session can dramatically change the understanding that mental health professionals have of psychotic patients, and result in a more humane attitude toward them.

The fact that the "model psychosis" concept of the LSD state was eventually rejected by most researchers did not diminish the educational value of the psychedelic experience. Although mental changes induced by LSD are obviously not identical with schizophrenia, the ingestion of the drug still represents a very special opportunity for professionals and students to experience many states of mind that occur naturally in the context of various mental disorders. These involve perceptual distortions in the optical, acoustic, tactile, olfactory, and gustatory areas; quantitative and qualitative disturbances of the thought-processes; and abnormal emotional qualities of extraordinary intensity. Under the influence of LSD it is possible to experience sensory illusions and pseudohallucinations, retardation or acceleration of thinking, delusional interpretation of the world, and an entire gamut of intense pathological emotions such as depression, manic mood, aggression, self-destructive craving, and agonizing feelings of inferiority and guilt, or conversely, ecstatic rapture, transcendental peace and serenity, and a sense of cosmic unity. The psychedelic experience can also become a source of revelatory aesthetic, scientific, philosophical, or spiritual insight.

Autoexperimentation with LSD does not exhaust its didactic potential. Another learning experience of great value is participation in the sessions of other subjects. This offers an opportunity for young professionals to observe an entire range of abnormal phenomena and be exposed to and become familiar with extreme emotional states and unusual behavior patterns. This occurs under specially structured circumstances, at a convenient time, and in the context of an existing relationship with the experient. All these factors make this a situation better suited for learning than the admission ward or emergency unit of a psychiatric hospital. In a more specific way, sitting in LSD sessions has been recommended as an unequaled training for future psychotherapists. The intensification of the relationship with the sitters that is characteristic of LSD sessions presents a rare opportunity for a novice professional to observe transference phenomena and learn to cope with them. The use of LSD in the context of a training program for future psychotherapists has been discussed in a special paper by Feld, Goodman, and Guido. (26)

An extensive and systematic study of the didactic potential of LSD sessions was conducted at the Maryland Psychiatric Research Center. In this program, up to three high-dose LSD sessions were offered to mental health professionals for training purposes. Over one hundred persons participated in this program between 1970 when it began, and 1977 when it was ended. Most of these individuals were interested in the psychedelic experience because it was closely related to their own professional activities. Some of them actually worked in crisis intervention units or with patients who had problems related to psychedelic drug use. Others were practitioners of various psychotherapeutic techniques and wanted to compare LSD psychotherapy to their own particular discipline—psychoanalysis, psychodrama, Gestalt therapy, psychosynthesis, or bioenergetics. A few were researchers involved in the study of altered states of consciousness, the dynamics of the unconscious, or the psychology of religion. A small group consisted of professionals who were specifically interested in becoming LSD therapists. They usually spent several months with us, attending staff meetings, watching videotapes of LSD therapy practice, or guiding psychedelic sessions under supervision. They then had the opportunity to undergo their own LSD sessions as part of the training schedule. All the participants in the LSD program for professionals agreed to cooperate in pre- and post-session psychological testing, and complete a follow-up questionnaire six months, twelve months, and two years after the session. The questions in this follow-up form focused on changes which they observed after the

LSD session in their professional work, life philosophy, religious feelings, their emotional and physical condition, and interpersonal adjustment. Although we have much anecdotal evidence of the value of this training program, the data from the pre- and post-session psychological testing and from the follow-up questionnaires has not yet been systematically processed and evaluated.

As I have emphasized earlier, LSD training sessions are an essential qualification for every LSD therapist. Because of the unique nature of the psychedelic state it is impossible to reach a real understanding of its quality and dimensions unless one directly experiences it. In addition, the experience of confronting the various areas in one's own unconscious is absolutely necessary for developing the ability to assist other people with competence and equanimity in their process of deep self-exploration. LSD training sessions are also highly recommended for nurses and all other members of the staff in psychedelic treatment units who come in close contact with clients in unusual states of consciousness.

ADMINISTRATION OF LSD TO CREATIVE INDIVIDUALS

One of the most interesting aspects of LSD research is the relationship between the psychedelic state and the creative process. Professional literature on the subject reflects considerable controversy. Robert Mogar (71), who reviewed the existing experimental data on the performance of various functions related to creative work, found the results inconclusive and contradictory. Thus some studies focusing on instrumental learning demonstrated impairment during the drug experience, while others indicated a definite enhancement of the learning capacity. Conflicting results have also been reported for color perception, recall and recognition, discrimination learning, concentration, symbolic thinking, and perceptual accuracy. Studies using various psychological tests specifically designed to measure creativity usually fail to demonstrate significant improvement as a result of LSD administration. However, how relevant these tests are in relation to the creative process and how sensitive and specific they are in detecting the changes induced by LSD remains an open question. Another important factor to consider is the general lack of motivation in LSD subjects to participate and cooperate in formal psychological testing procedures while they are deeply involved in their inner experiences. In view of the importance of set and setting for the psychedelic experience, it should also be mentioned that many of the above studies were conducted in the context of the "model schizophrenia" approach, and thus with the intention of demonstrating the psychotic impairment of performance.

The generally negative outcome of creativity studies is in sharp contrast to the everyday experience of LSD therapists. The work of many artists—painters, musicians, writers, and poets—who participated in LSD experimentation in various countries of the world has been deeply influenced by their psychedelic experiences.[1] Most of them found access to deep sources of inspiration in their unconscious mind, experienced a striking enhancement and unleashing of fantasy, and reached extraordinary vitality, originality and freedom of artistic expression. In many instances, the quality of their creations improved considerably, not only according to their own judgment or the opinion of the LSD researchers, but by the standards of their professional colleagues. At exhibitions which chronologically show the artist's development, it is usually easy to recognize when he or she had a psychedelic experience. One can typically see a dramatic quantum jump in the content and style of the paintings. This is particularly true of painters who, prior to their LSD experience, were conventional and conservative in their artistic expression.

However, most of the art in the collections of psychedelic therapists comes from subjects who were not professional artists, but had LSD sessions for therapeutic, didactic, or other purposes. Frequently, individuals who did not show any artistic inclinations at all prior to the LSD experience can create extraordinary pictures. In most instances, the intensity of the effect is due to the unusual nature and power of the material that emerges from the depths of the unconscious, rather than the artistic abilities. It is not uncommon, however, for even the technical aspects of such drawings or paintings to be far superior to previous creations by the same subjects. Some individuals actually pursue in their everyday life the new skills they discover in their psychedelic sessions. In exceptional cases, a genuine artistic talent of extraordinary power and scope may emerge during the LSD procedure. One of my patients in Prague, who had loathed drawing and painting all her life and had to be forced to participate in art classes at school, developed a remarkable artistic talent within a period of several months. Her art eventually found enthusiastic acceptance among professional painters and she had successful public exhibitions. In instances like this, one has to assume that the talent already existed in these individuals in a latent form, and that its expression was blocked by strong pathological emotions. The affective liberation through psychedelic therapy had allowed its free and full manifestation.

It is interesting that the LSD experience tends to enhance appreciation and understanding of art in individuals who were previously unresponsive and indifferent. A characteristic observation from psychedelic research is the sudden development of interest in various movements in modern art. Subjects who were indifferent or even hostile toward non-conventional art forms can develop deep insight into suprematism, pointilism, cubism, impressionism, dadaism, surrealism, or superrealism after a single exposure to LSD. There are certain painters whose art seems to be particularly closely related to the visionary experiences induced by LSD. Thus many LSD subjects develop deep empathic understanding of the paintings of Hieronymus Bosch, Vincent van Gogh, Salvador Dali, Max Ernst, Pablo Picasso, René Magritte, Maurits Escher, or H. R. Giger. Another typical consequence of the psychedelic experience is a dramatic change of attitude toward music; many LSD subjects discover in their sessions new dimensions in music and new ways of listening to it. A number of our patients, who were alcoholics and heroin addicts with poor educational background, developed such deep interest in classical music as a result of their one LSD session that they decided to use their meager financial resources for buying a stereo set and starting a record collection of their own. The role of psychedelics in the development of contemporary music and their impact on composers, interpreters, and audiences is so obvious and well-known that it does not require special emphasis here.

Although the influence of LSD on artistic expression is most evident in the fields of painting and music, the psychedelic experience can have a similar fertilizing effect on some other branches of art. Visionary states induced by mescaline and LSD had a profound significance in the life, art and philosophy of Aldous Huxley. Many of his writings, including *Brave New World*, *Island*, *Heaven and Hell*, and *The Doors of Perception* have been directly influenced by his psychedelic experiences. Some of the most powerful poems by Allen Ginsberg were inspired by his self-experimentation with psychedelic substances. The role of hashish in the French art of the *fin de siècle* could also be mentioned in this context. The Canadian-Japanese architect Kiyo Izumi was able to make unique use of his LSD experiences in designing modern psychiatric facilities. (40)

Since LSD mediates the access to the contents and dynamics of the deep unconscious—in psychoanalytic terms, to the primary process—it is not particularly surprising that psychedelic experiences can play an important role in the creative development of artists. However, many observations from psychedelic research indicate that LSD can also be of extraordinary value to various scientific disciplines that are traditionally considered domains of reason and logic. Two important aspects of the LSD effect seem to be of particular relevance in this context. First, the drug can mediate access to vast repositories of concrete and valid information in the collective unconscious and make them available to the experient. According to my observations, the revealed knowledge can be very specific, accurate, and detailed; the data obtained in this way can be related to many different fields. In our relatively limited LSD training program for scientists, relevant insights occurred in such diverse areas as cosmogenesis, the nature of space and time, sub-atomic physics, ethology, animal psychology, history, anthropology, sociology, politics, comparative religion, philosophy, genetics, obstetrics, psychosomatic medicine, psychology, psychopathology, and thanatology.[2]

The second aspect of the LSD effect that is of great relevance for the creative process is the facilitation of new and unexpected syntheses of data, resulting in unconventional problem-solving. It is a well-known fact that many important ideas and solutions to problems did not originate in the context of logical reasoning, but in various unusual states of mind—in dreams, while falling asleep or awakening, at times of extreme physical and mental fatigue, or during an illness with high fever. There are many famous examples of this. Thus, the chemist Friedrich August von Kekulé arrived at the final solution of the chemical formula of benzene in a dream in which he saw the benzene ring in the form of a snake biting its tail. Nikola Tesla constructed the electric generator, an invention that revolutionized industry, after the complete design of it appeared to him in great detail in a vision. The design for the experiment leading to the Nobel prize-winning discovery of the chemical transmission of nerve impulses occurred to the physiologist Otto Loewi while he was asleep. Albert Einstein discovered the basic principles of his special theory of relativity in an unusual state of mind; according to his description, most of the insights came to him in the form of kinaesthetic sensations.

We could mention many instances of a similar kind where a creative individual struggled unsuccessfully for a long time with a difficult problem using logic and reason, with the actual solution emerging unexpectedly from the unconscious in moments when his or her rationality was suspended.[3] In everyday life events of this kind happen very rarely, and in an elemental and unpredictable fashion. Psychedelic drugs seem to facilitate the incidence of such creative solutions to the point that they can be deliberately programmed. In an LSD state, the old conceptual frameworks break down, cultural cognitive barriers dissolve, and the material can be seen and synthesized in a totally new way that was not possible within the old systems of thinking. This mechanism can produce not only striking new solutions to various specific problems, but new paradigms that revolutionize whole scientific disciplines.

Although psychedelic experimentation had been drastically curbed before this avenue could be systematically explored, the study of creative problem-solving conducted by Willis Harman and James Fadiman (36) at the Stanford Research Institute brought enough interesting evidence to encourage future research. The drug used in this experiment was not LSD but mescaline, the active ingredient of the Mexican cactus *Anhalonium Lewinii*, or peyote. Because of the general similarity of the effects of these two drugs, comparable results should be expected with the use of LSD; various accidental observations from our LSD training program for scientists and from the therapeutic use of this drug seem to confirm this. The subjects in the Harman-Fadiman study were twenty-seven males engaged in a variety of professions. The group consisted of sixteen engineers, one engineer-physicist, two mathematicians, two architects, one psychologist, one furniture designer, one commercial artist, one sales manager, and one personnel manager. The objective of the study was to ascertain whether under the influence of 200 milligrams of mescaline these individuals would show increased creativity and produce concrete, valid, and feasible solutions to problems, as judged by the criteria of modern industry and positivistic science. The results of this research were very encouraging; many solutions were accepted for construction or production, others could be developed further or opened new avenues for investigation. The mescaline subjects consistently reported that the drug induced in them a variety of changes which facilitated the creative process. It lowered inhibitions and anxieties, enhanced the fluency and flexibility of ideation, heightened the capacity for visual imagery and fantasy, and increased the ability to concentrate on the project. The administration of mescaline also facilitated empathy with people and objects, made subconscious data more accessible, strengthened the motivation to obtain closure and, in some instances, allowed immediate visualization of the completed solution.

It is obvious that the potential of LSD for enhancing creativity will be directly proportional to the intellectual capacity and sophistication of the experient. For most of the creative insights, it is necessary to know the present status of the discipline involved, be able to formulate relevant new problems, and find the technical means of describing the results. If this type of research is ever repeated, the logical candidates would be prominent scientists from various disciplines: nuclear physicists, astrophysicists, geneticists, brain physiologists, anthropologists, psychologists and psychiatrists.[4]

DRUG-INDUCED RELIGIOUS AND MYSTICAL EXPERIENCES

The use of psychedelic substances for ritual, religious, and magical purposes can be traced back to ancient shamanic traditions and is probably as old as mankind. The legendary divine potion *soma*, prepared from a plant of the same name whose identity is now lost, played a crucial role in the Vedic religion. Preparations from hemp *Cannabis indica* and *sativa* have been used in Asia and Africa for many centuries under different names—hashish, charas, bhang, ganja, kif—in religious ceremonies and folk medicine. They have played an important role in Brahmanism, have been used in the context of Sufi practices, and represent the principal sacrament of the Rastafarians. Religio-magical use of psychedelic plants was widespread in the Pre-Columbian cultures, among the Aztecs, Mayans, Olmecs, and other Indian groups. The famous Mexican cactus *Lophophora williamsii (peyote)*, the sacred mushroom *Psilocybe mexicana (teonanacatl)*, and several varieties of morning glory seeds *(ololiuqui)* were among the plants used. Ritual use of peyote and the sacred mushroom still survives among various Mexican tribes; the peyote hunt and other sacred ceremonies of the Huichol Indians and healing rituals of the Mazatecs using the mushrooms can be mentioned here as important examples. Peyote was also assimilated by many North American Indian groups and about one hundred years ago became the sacrament of the syncretistic Native American Church. South American healers *(ayahuascheros)*, and preliterate Amazonian tribes such as the Amahuaca and the Jivaro use *yagé*, psychedelic extracts from the "visionary vine," the jungle liana *Banisteriopsis caapi*. The best known African hallucinogenic plant is *Tabernanthe iboga (eboga)*, which in smaller dosages serves as a stimulant and is used in large quantities as an initiatory drug. In the Middle Ages, potions and ointments containing psychoactive plants and animal ingredients were widely used in the context of the Witches' Sabbath and the black mass rituals. The most famous constituents of the witches' brews were the deadly nightshade *(Atropa Belladonna)*, mandrake *(Mandragora officinarum)*, thornapple or "jimson weed" *(Datura Stramonium)*, henbane *(Hyoscyamus niger)*, and toad skin. Modern chemical analysis has detected in the skin of toads *(Bufo bufo)*, a substance called *bufotenine* (or *dimethylserotonin*) which has psychedelic properties. The psychedelic plants mentioned above represent only a small selection of those that are most famous. According to ethnobotanist Richard Schultes of the Botanical Department of Harvard University, there exist more than one hundred plants with distinct psychoactive properties.

The ability of psychedelic substances to induce visionary states of a religious and mystical nature is documented in many historical and anthropological sources. The discovery of LSD, and the well-publicized occurrence of these experiences in many experimental subjects within our own culture, has brought this issue to the attention of scientists. The fact that religious experiences could be triggered by the ingestion of chemical agents instigated an interesting and highly controversial discussion about "chemical" or "instant mysticism." Many behavioral scientists, philosophers, and theologians became involved in fierce polemics about the nature of these phenomena, their meaning, validity, and authenticity. The opinions soon crystallized into three extreme points of view. Some experimenters saw the possibility of inducing religious experiences by chemical means as an opportunity to transfer religious phenomena from the realm of the sacred to the laboratory, and thus eventually to explain them in scientific terms. Ultimately, there would be nothing mysterious and holy about religion, and spiritual experiences could be reduced to brain physiology and biochemistry. However, other researchers took a very different stance. According to them, the mystical phenomena induced by LSD and other psychedelic drugs were genuine and these substances should be considered sacraments because they can mediate contact with transcendental realities. This was essentially the position taken by the shamans and priests of psychedelic cultures where visionary plants such as soma, peyote and teonanacatl were seen as divine materials or as deities themselves. Yet another approach to the problem was to consider LSD experiences to be "quasi-religious" phenomena which only simulate or superficially resemble the authentic and genuine spirituality that comes as "God's grace" or as a result of discipline, devotion, and austere practices. In this framework, the seeming ease with which these experiences could be triggered by a chemical entirely discredited their spiritual value.

However, those who argue that LSD-induced spiritual experiences cannot be valid because they are too easily available and their occurrence and timing depend on the individual's decision, misunderstand the nature of the psychedelic state. The psychedelic experience is neither an easy nor a predictable way to God. Many subjects do not have spiritual elements in their sessions despite many exposures to the drug. Those who do have a mystical experience frequently have to undergo psychological ordeals that are at least as difficult and painful as those associated with various aboriginal rites of passage or rigorous and austere religious disciplines.

Most researchers agree that it is not possible to differentiate clearly between spontaneous mystical experiences and "chemical mysticism" on the basis of phenomenological analysis or experimental approaches.[5] This issue is further complicated by the relative lack of specific pharmacological effects of LSD and by the fact that some of the situations conducive to spontaneous mysticism are associated with dramatic physiological and biochemical changes in the body.

Prolonged fasting, sleep deprivation, a stay in the desert with exposure to dehydration and extremes of temperature, forceful respiratory maneuvers, excessive emotional stress, physical exertion and tortures, long monotonous chanting and other popular practices of the "technology of the sacred" cause such far-reaching alterations in body chemistry that it is difficult to draw a clear line between spontaneous and chemical mysticism.

The decision whether chemically induced experiences are genuine and authentic or not thus lies in the domain of theologians and spiritual masters. Unfortunately the representatives of different religions have expressed a wide spectrum of conflicting opinions; it remains an open question who should be considered an authority in this area. Some of these religious experts made their judgments without ever having had a psychedelic experience and can hardly be considered authorities on LSD; others have made far-reaching generalizations on the basis of one session. Serious differences of opinion exist even among leading representatives of the same religion—Catholic priests, Protestant ministers, Rabbis, and Hindu saints—who have had psychedelic experiences. At present, after thirty years of discussion, the question whether LSD and other psychedelics can induce genuine spiritual experiences is still open. Negative opinions of individuals like Meher Baba or R. C. Zaehner stand against those of several Tibetan Buddhist masters, a number of shamans of the psychedelic cultures, Walter Clark, Huston Smith, and Alan Watts.

Whether the experiences produced by LSD are genuine mystical revelations or just very convincing simulations thereof, they are certainly phenomena of great

An experience of unfulfilled religious longing. Groups of people are striving to cross treacherous, swampy waters in imperfect boats in order to reach a deity on the horizon. However, they all sink and drown before reaching their desired goal.

interest for theologians, ministers, and students of religion. Within a few hours, individuals gain profound insights into the nature of religion, and in many instances their purely theoretical understanding and formal belief is vitalized by a deep personal experience of the transcendental realms. This opportunity can be particularly important for those ministers who profess a religion, but at the same time harbor serious doubts about the truth and relevance of what they preach. Several priests and theologians who volunteered for our LSD training program at the Maryland Psychiatric Research Center were skeptics or atheists who were involved in their profession for a variety of external reasons. For them, the spiritual experiences they had in their LSD sessions were important evidence that spirituality is a genuine and deeply relevant force in human life. This realization liberated them from the conflict they had had about their profession, and from the burden of hypocrisy. In several instances, the relatives and friends of these individuals

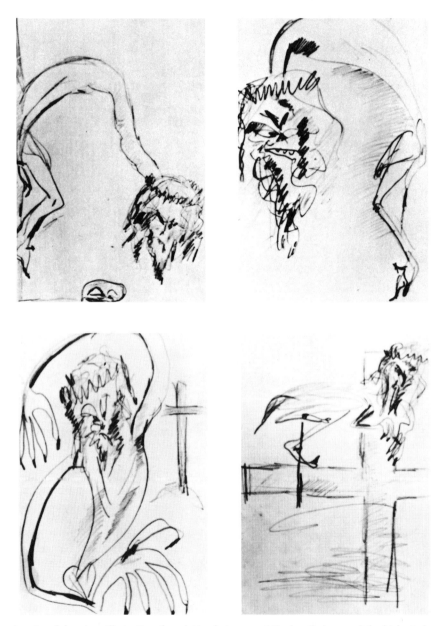

A series of drawings illustrating the relation between spiritual pathology and the biological birth trauma. The first four show images of the most sacred Christian theme—crucifixion—contaminated by what the patient calls "obscene biology". During her session she realized that this confusion reflected not only specific childhood experiences, but particularly the biological trauma of birth.

The sacred event of delivery is inextricably connected with genitals, sexuality, aggression, defecation and urination.

In the final picture the conflict is resolved. The figure of 'Purified Christ' rises above the realm of "obscene biology", separating from it. However, the patient's hands are reaching for the Black Sun which is a symbol of inner reality even beyond Christ, the divine that transcends all forms and limitations.

reported that their sermons following the LSD session showed unusual power and natural authority.

Spiritual experiences in psychedelic sessions frequently draw on the symbolism of the collective unconscious and can thus occur in the framework of cultural and religious traditions other than the experient's own. LSD training sessions are therefore of special interest for those who study comparative religion. Ministers affiliated to a specific church are sometimes surprised when they have a profound religious experience in the context of an entirely different creed. Because of the basically unitive nature of the psychedelic experience, this usually does not disqualify their own religion but places it in a broader cosmic perspective.

ROLE OF LSD IN PERSONAL GROWTH AND SELF-ACTUALIZATION

During the years of intensive LSD research, the major focus was on basic psychopathological investigation, psychiatric therapy, or some quite specific uses, such as enhancement of artistic expression or mediation of a religious experience. Relatively little attention was paid to the value that psychedelic experiences could have for the personal development of "normal" individuals. In the mid-sixties, this issue emerged in an elemental and explosive fashion in a wave of massive non-supervised self-experimentation.

In the atmosphere of national hysteria that ensued, the pros and cons were discussed in a passionate, over-emphatic, and ultimately confusing way. The LSD proselytes presented the drug quite uncritically as an easy and safe panacea for all the problems that beset human existence. Psychedelic self-exploration and personality transformation were presented as the only viable alternative to sudden annihilation in a nuclear holocaust or slow death among industrial waste products. It was recommended that as many people as possible should take LSD under any circumstances and as frequently as they could in order to accelerate the advent of the Aquarian Age. LSD sessions were seen as a rite of passage that should be mandatory for everybody who reached their teens.

Failure to warn the public about the dangers and pitfalls of psychedelic experimentation and to give instructions for minimizing the risks resulted in a large number of casualties. Apocalyptic newspaper headlines describing the horrors of LSD "bummers" and drug-related accidents ignited a witch-hunting response in legislators, politicians, educators, and many professionals. Ignoring the data from almost two decades of responsible scientific experimentation, the anti-drug propaganda switched to the other extreme and presented LSD as a totally unpredictable devil's drug that represented a grave danger to the sanity of the present generation and the physical health of generations to come.

At present, when the emotional charge of this controversy has subsided, it seems possible to take a more sober and objective view of the problems involved. Clinical evidence strongly suggests that "normal" people can benefit most from the LSD process and are taking the least risk when participating in a supervised psychedelic program. A single high-dose LSD session can frequently be of extraordinary value for those persons who do not have any serious clinical problems. The quality of their lives can be considerably enhanced and the experience can move them in the direction of self-realization or self-actualization. This process seems to be comparable in every way to the one that Abraham Maslow described for individuals who had spontaneous "peak experiences."

The official anti-drug propaganda is based on a very superficial understanding of the motivations for psychedelic drug use. It is true that in many instances the drug is used for kicks or in the context of juvenile rebellion against parental authority or the establishment. However, even those who take LSD under the worst circumstances frequently get a glimpse of the drug's real potential, and this can become a powerful force in future use. The fact that many people take LSD in an attempt to find a solution to their emotional dilemmas or from a deep need for philosophical and spiritual answers should not be underestimated. The craving for contact with transcendental realities can be more powerful than the sexual urge. Throughout human history countless individuals have been willing to take enormous risks of various kinds and to sacrifice years or decades of their lives to spiritual pursuits. Any reasonable measures regulating the use of psychedelic drugs should take these facts into consideration.

Very few serious researchers still believe that experimentation with pure LSD represents a genetic hazard. Under proper circumstances the psychological dangers that represent the only serious risk can be reduced to a minimum. In my opinion, there is no scientific evidence that precludes the creation of a network of facilities in which those who are seriously interested in psychedelic self-exploration could engage in it with pure substances and under the best circumstances. Many of these would be subjects who are so deeply motivated that they would otherwise be serious candidates for illegal self-experimentation involving a much higher risk. The existence of government-sponsored centers of this kind would have an inhibiting effect on the immature motivations of people for whom the present strict prohibitions represent a special challenge and temptation. An additional advantage of this approach would be the opportunity to accumulate and process in a systematic way all the valuable information about psychedelics that is otherwise lost in elemental and chaotic unsupervised experimentation. This would also remedy the existing absurd situation in which almost no serious professional research is being conducted in an area where millions of people have been experimenting on their own.

USE OF LSD IN THE DEVELOPMENT OF PARANORMAL ABILITIES

Much historical and anthropological evidence and numerous anecdotal observations from clinical research suggest that psychedelic substances can occasionally facilitate extrasensory perception. In many cultures visionary plants were administered in the context of spiritual healing ceremonies as means to diagnose and cure diseases. Equally frequent was their use for other magical purposes, such as locating lost objects or persons, astral projection, perception of remote events, precognition, and clairvoyance. Most of the drugs used for these purposes have been mentioned earlier in connection with religious rituals. They include the resin or leaves of hemp *(Cannabis indica* or *sativa)* in Africa and Asia; fly-agaric mushrooms among various Siberian tribes and North American Indians; the plant

Tabernanthe iboga among certain African ethnic groups; the snuffs *cohoba (Anadenanthera peregrina)* and *epená (Virola theidora)* of South America and the Caribbean; and the three basic psychedelics of the Pre-Columbian cultures—the peyote cactus (*Lophophora williamsii*), the sacred mushrooms *teonanacatl (Psilocybe mexicana)* and *ololiuqui* or morning glory seeds (*Ipomoea violacea*). Of special interest seems to be *yagé*, a brew prepared from the jungle creeper *Banisteriopsis caapi* and other "vines of the dead" used by South American Indians in the Amazon valley. Harmin, also called yageine or banisterine, one of the active alkaloids isolated from the Banisteriopsis plant, has actually been referred to as *telepathine*. The psychedelic states induced by the extracts of these plants seem to be especially powerful enhancers of paranormal phenomena. The most famous example of the unusual properties of *yagé* can be found in the reports of McGovern, (69) one of the anthropologists who described this plant. According to his description, a local medicine man saw in remarkable detail the death of the chief of a faraway tribe at the time when it was happening; the accuracy of his account was verified many weeks later. A similar experience was reported by Manuel Córdova-Rios (53) who accurately saw the death of his mother in his *yagé* session and was later able to verify all the details. All psychedelic cultures seem to share the belief that not only is extrasensory perception enhanced during the actual intoxication by sacred plants, but the systematic use of these substances facilitates development of paranormal abilities in everyday life.

Much anecdotal material collected over the years by psychedelic researchers supports the above beliefs. Masters and Houston (65) have described the case of a housewife who in her LSD session saw her daughter in the kitchen of their home looking for the cookie jar. She further reported seeing the child knock a sugar bowl from a shelf and spill sugar on the floor. This episode was later confirmed by her husband. The same authors also reported an LSD subject who saw "a ship caught in ice floes, somewhere in the northern seas." According to the subject, the ship had on its bow the name "France." It was later confirmed that the *France* had indeed been trapped in ice near Greenland at the time of the subject's LSD session. The famous psychologist and parapsychological researcher Stanley Krippner (49) visualized, during a psilocybin session in 1962, the assassination of John F. Kennedy which took place a year later. Similar observations were reported by Humphrey Osmond, Duncan Blewett, Abram Hoffer, and other researchers. The literature on the subject has been critically reviewed in a synoptic paper by Krippner and Davidson. (50)

In my own clinical experience, various phenomena suggesting extrasensory perception are relatively frequent in LSD psychotherapy, particularly in advanced sessions. They range from a more-or-less vague anticipation of future events or an awareness of remote happenings to complex and detailed scenes in the form of vivid clairvoyant visions. This may be associated with appropriate sounds, such as spoken words and sentences, noises produced by motor vehicles, sounds of fire engines and ambulances, or the blowing of horns. Some of these experiences can later be shown to correspond in varying degrees with actual events. Objective verification in this area can be particularly difficult. Unless these instances are reported and clearly documented during the actual psychedelic sessions there is a great danger of contamination of the data. Loose interpretation of events, distortions of memory, and the possibility of déja vu phenomena during the perception of later occurrences are a few of the major pitfalls involved.

The most interesting paranormal phenomena occurring in psychedelic sessions are out-of-the-body experiences and the instances of traveling clairvoyance and clairaudience. The sensation of leaving one's body is quite common in drug-induced states and can have various forms and degrees. Some persons experience themselves as completely detached from their physical bodies, hovering above them or observing them from another part of the room. Occasionally, the subjects can lose the awareness of the actual physical setting altogether and their consciousness moves into experiential realms and subjective realities that appear to be entirely independent of the material world. They may then identify entirely with the body images of the protagonists of these scenes, be they persons, animals, or archetypal entities. In exceptional cases the individual may have a complex and vivid experience of moving to a specific place in the physical world, and give a detailed description of a remote locale or event. Attempts to verify such extrasensory perceptions can sometimes result in amazing corroborations. In rare instances, the subject can actively control such a process and "travel" at will to any location or point in time he or she chooses. A detailed description of an experience of this kind illustrating the nature and complexity of the problems involved has been published in my book *Realms of the Human Unconscious*, p. 187. (32)

Objective testing by the standard laboratory techniques used in parapsychological research has generally been quite disappointing and has failed to demonstrate an increase of extrasensory perception as a predictable and constant aspect of the LSD effect. Masters and Houston (65) tested LSD subjects with the use of a special card deck developed in the parapsychology laboratory at Duke University. The deck contains twenty-five cards, each of which has a geometrical symbol: a star, circle, cross, square, or wavy lines. The results of the experiments in which LSD subjects attempted to guess the identity of these cards were statistically nonsignificant. A similar study conducted by Whittlesey (102) and a card-guessing experiment with psilocybin subjects reported by van Asperen de Boer, Barkema and Kappers (6) were equally disappointing, though an interesting finding in the first of these studies was a striking decrease of variance; the subjects actually guessed closer to mean chance expectation than predicted mathematically. Unpublished findings of Walter Pahnke's parapsychological research at the Maryland Psychiatric Research Center suggest that the statistical approach to this problem might be misleading. In this project, Walter Pahnke used a modified version of the Duke University cards in the form of electronic keyboard panels. The LSD subject had to guess the key that had been lit on a panel in an adjacent room either manually or by a computer. Although the results for the entire group of LSD subjects were not statistically significant, certain individuals achieved strikingly high scores in some of the measurements.

Some researchers voiced objections to the uninteresting and unimaginative approach to the study of parapsychological phenomena represented by repetitive card guessing. In general, such a procedure does not have much chance in the competition for the subject's attention as compared to some of the exciting subjective experiences that characterize the psychedelic state. In an attempt to make the task more appealing, Cavanna and Servadio (19) used emotionally-loaded materials rather than cards; photographic color prints of incongruous paintings were prepared for the experient. Although one subject did remarkably well, the overall results were nonsignificant. Karlis Osis (73) administered LSD to a number of "mediums" who were given objects and asked to describe the owners. One medium was unusually successful, but most of the others became so interested in the aesthetic and philosophical aspects of the experience, or so caught up in their personal problems, that they found it difficult to maintain concentration on the task.

By far the most interesting data emerged from a pilot study designed by Masters and Houston (65) who used emotionally charged images with sixty-two LSD subjects. The experiments were conducted in the termination periods of the sessions, when it is relatively easy to focus on specific tasks. Forty-eight of the individuals tested approximated the target image at least two times out of ten, while five subjects made successful guesses at least seven times out of ten. For example, one subject visualized "tossed seas" when the correct image was a Viking ship in a storm. The same subject guessed "lush vegetation" when the image was rain forests in the Amazon, "a camel" when the image was an Arab on a camel, "the Alps" when the picture was the Himalayas, and "a Negro picking cotton in a field" when the target was a plantation in the South.

The study of paranormal phenomena in psychedelic sessions presents many technical problems. In addition to the problems of getting the subject interested and keeping his or her attention on the task, Blewett (12) also emphasized the rapid flow of eidetic imagery that interferes with the ability of the subject to stabilize and choose the response that might have been triggered by the target. The methodological difficulties in studying the effect of psychedelic drugs on extrasensory perception or other paranormal abilities and the lack of evidence in the existing studies cannot, however, invalidate some quite extraordinary observations in this area. Every LSD therapist with sufficient clinical experience has collected enough challenging observations to take this problem seriously. I myself have no doubt that psychedelics can occasionally induce elements of genuine extrasensory perception at the time of their pharmacological effect. On occasion, the occurrence of certain paranormal abilities and phenomena can extend beyond the day of the session. A fascinating observation that is closely related and deserves attention in this context is the frequent accumulation of extraordinary coincidences in the lives of persons who had experienced transpersonal phenomena in their psychedelic sessions. Such coincidences are objective facts, not just subjective interpretations of perceptual data; they are similar to the observations that Carl Gustav Jung described in his essay on synchronicity. (44)

The discrepancy between the occurrence of parapsychological phenomena in LSD sessions and the negative results of specific laboratory studies seems to reflect the fact that an increase in ESP is not a standard and constant aspect of the LSD effect. Psychological states conducive to various paranormal phenomena and characterized by an unusually high incidence of ESP are among the many alternative mental conditions that can be facilitated by this drug; in other types of LSD experiences the ESP abilities seem to be on the same level as they are in the everyday state of consciousness, or even further reduced. Future research will have to assess if the otherwise unpredictable and elemental incidence of paranormal abilities in psychedelic states can be harnessed and systematically cultivated, as it is indicated in shamanic literature.

NOTES

1. The interested reader will find comprehensive discussion of this subject in Robert Masters' and Jean Houston's excellent book *Psychedelic Art* (66). The influence of LSD and psilocybin on the creativity of professional painters has also been uniquely documented in the book *Experimental Psychoses* (90) by the Czech psychiatrist, J. Roubíček. Oscar Janiger's unpublished collection of professional paintings done under the influence of LSD also deserves to be mentioned in this context.

2. Some concrete examples of relevant insights of this kind are described in my book *Realms of the Human Unconscious*. (32)

3. Many additional examples of this phenomenon can be found in Arthur Koestler's book *The Act of Creation*. (48)

4. The interested reader will find more information on the subject in Stanley Krippner's synoptic paper *Research in Creativity and Psychedelic Drugs*. (51)

5. The most interesting study of this kind was Walter Pahnke's (75) Good Friday experiment conducted in 1964 in the Harvard Chapel in Cambridge, Massachusetts. In this study, ten Christian theological students were given 30 milligrams of psilocybin, and ten others who functioned as a control group received 200 milligrams of nicotinic acid as placebo. The assignment to the two groups was done on a double-blind basis. They all listened to a two-and-a-half-hour religious service that consisted of organ music, vocal solos, readings, prayers, and personal meditation. The subjects who were given psilocybin rated very high on the mystical experience questionnaire developed by Pahnke, whereas the response of the control group was minimal.

EFFECTIVE THERAPEUTIC MECHANISMS OF LSD THERAPY

9

Intensification of Conventional Therapeutic
  Mechanisms
Changes in the Dynamics of Governing Systems
Therapeutic Potential of the Death-Rebirth
  Process
Therapeutic Mechanisms on the Transpersonal
  Level

The extraordinary and often dramatic effects of the LSD process on various emotional and psychosomatic symptoms quite naturally give rise to questions about the therapeutic mechanisms involved in these changes. Although the dynamics of some of these transformations can be explained along conventional lines, the majority appear to involve processes as yet undiscovered or unacknowledged by traditional psychology and psychiatry. This does not mean that these phenomena have never been encountered or discussed before. Descriptions of some of these mechanisms are found in the religious literature describing spiritual healing and its effects on emotional or psychosomatic illnesses. Anthropologists may also recognize elements that occur in shamanic practices, aboriginal rites of passage, and various healing ceremonies.

It has already been mentioned that LSD does not have any intrinsic therapeutic properties related simply to its pharmacological effects. It is necessary to structure and approach the experience in a specific way to make the emergence of unconscious material therapeutic rather than destructive. Analysis of the observations from LSD psychotherapy suggests that the therapeutic changes that take place are very complex and cannot be reduced to a single common denominator. The LSD experience appears to involve a variety of factors on many different levels; each has distinct therapeutic potential and can be utilized for effective treatment and personality change. In the following text we will briefly discuss the most important mechanisms of this kind operating in LSD sessions. The richness of opportunities for deep dynamic shifts and transformations that is characteristic of psychedelic states seems to make LSD a very special adjunct to psychotherapy.

INTENSIFICATION OF CONVENTIONAL THERAPEUTIC MECHANISMS

The only factors of therapeutic change available in the initial stages of a psycholytic series are the mechanisms that have been described in the context of traditional psychotherapeutic schools. However, even in superficial psychedelic experiences these mechanisms are greatly intensified. Under these circumstances the defense systems are considerably weakened and psychological resistance decreases. The emotional responses of the subject are dramatically enhanced and one may observe powerful *abreaction* and *catharsis*. Repressed unconscious material, including early childhood memories, becomes easily available, and this may result not only in *enhanced recall* but in genuine age-regression and vivid, complex *reliving of emotionally relevant memories* as well. Unconscious material also frequently apears in the form of various symbolic phenomena with a structure similar to dreams. The emergence of this material and its integration are associated with *emotional and intellectual insights* into the psychodynamics of the patient's symptoms and maladjustive interpersonal patterns.

The therapeutic potential of the reliving of emotionally important episodes from childhood seems to involve two important elements. One of them is a deep release of pent-up energies and their peripheral discharge in the form of emotional and physical abreaction. The second is conscious integration of the content that is now devoid of affective charge. This is made possible by the double orientation or dual role that individuals can assume in the LSD state, either simultaneously or in an alternating fashion. On the one hand, they experience full and complex age-regression to early life periods when the traumatic events took place; on the other hand, they also have access to the position corresponding to their chronological age at the time of the LSD session. In this way, it becomes possible to reevaluate from an adult point of view the relevance of events that were once overwhelming for the immature organism. The replay of early biographical events is thus experienced by a subject who represents an interesting hybrid between a naive, emotionally totally involved child and a more-or-less detached adult observer.

This dual role is also reflected in the therapeutic relationship. The subject can perceive the therapist and interpret objective reality in a way that reflects unresolved material from the past. However, on another level, he or she can also maintain adequate reality-testing and study in detail the origin and mechanism of these distortions. The transference relationship is typically intensified and is experienced in a vivid pictorial form. As indicated in an earlier chapter, the distortions of the therapeutic relationship are frequently exaggerated to the point of caricature, so that the transference nature of the phenomena becomes obvious to both the patient and the therapist. The intensification of the relationship produced by the drug not only facilitates the *transference analysis*, but also offers numerous opportunities for *corrective emotional experiences*. It is essential that the therapist remain understanding, unperturbed, and consistently supportive, without regard to the nature of the emerging material and the patient's behavior. This can have a very powerful therapeutic impact on the patient who frequently has fantasies of disapproval and rejection, or even catastrophic expectations about the therapist's reaction to certain aspects of his or her experience. Any departure from this approach, unless explicitly designed and agreed upon as therapeutic role-playing, can reinforce the impact of the original traumatic situation rather than act in a corrective manner. The demanding and often difficult task of the therapist is somewhat facilitated by the fact that the patient under the influence of LSD is usually less defensive and more open. As a result, he or she may often accept and utilize insights and interpretations that would be impossible or untimely in drug-free psychotherapy.

Suggestibility is usually markedly enhanced and a therapist who uses suggestion in psychotherapy can take advantage of this fact; however, this approach should be used with utmost caution. In my experience any departure from honest and open interaction with the client, or use of various devices and ploys, is ultimately harmful to therapeutic progress.

CHANGES IN THE DYNAMICS OF GOVERNING SYSTEMS

When the dosage is increased or the LSD sessions repeated, new and powerful mechanisms come into action and become available in addition to the above. Many therapeutic changes on deeper levels can be explained as resulting from a chemical intervention in the dynamic interplay of unconscious constellations that have the function of governing systems. The most important of these are the *systems of condensed experience (COEX systems)*, which organize material of biographical nature, and the *basic perinatal matrices (BPM's)*, which have a similar role in relation to the experiential repositories related to the death-rebirth process. The essential characteristics of these two categories of governing systems were described in detail earlier. We could also talk about transpersonal dynamic matrices; however, because of the richness and looser organization of transpersonal realms it would be difficult to describe them in a comprehensive way.

According to the nature of the emotional charge, we can distinguish *negative governing systems* (negative COEX systems, BPM II, BPM III, negative aspects of BPM I, and negative transpersonal matrices) and *positive governing systems* (positive COEX systems, positive aspects of BPM I, BPM IV, and positive transpersonal matrices). The general strategy of LSD therapy is reduction of the emotional charge attached to negative systems and facilitation of experiential access to positive ones. A more specific tactical rule is to structure the termination period of each individual session in a way that facilitates completion and integration of the material that was made available that day. The manifest clinical condition of an individual is not a global reflection of the nature and overall amount of the unconscious material; it is dependent on a specific selective focus and tuning which makes certain aspects of the material experientially available. Individuals who are tuned into various levels of negative psychodynamic, perinatal or transpersonal governing systems perceive themselves and the world in a pessimistic way and experience emotional or psychosomatic distress. Conversely, those persons who are under the influence of positive dynamic governing systems are in a state of emotional well-being and optimal psychosomatic functioning. The specific qualities of the resulting states depend in both instances on the nature of the activated material. For a detailed discussion of the influence of COEX systems, BPM's, and various transpersonal matrices on LSD subjects, see the chapter on post-session intervals. (pp. 230-9)

Changes in the governing influence of dynamic matrices can occur as a result of various biochemical or physiological processes inside the organism, or as a reaction to a number of external influences of a physical or psychological nature. LSD sessions seem to represent a deep intervention in the dynamics of the governing systems and their functional interplay. Detailed analysis of the phenomenology of LSD experiences indicates that in many instances sudden clinical improvement during therapy can be explained as a shift from the psychological dominance of a negative governing system to a state where the individual is under the selective influence of a positive constellation. Such a change does not necessarily mean that all the unconscious material underlying that particular psychopathological state has been worked through. It simply indicates an inner dynamic shift from one governing system to another. This situation can be referred to as *transmodulation*; it can occur on several different levels. A shift among memory constellations involving autobiographical material can be called *COEX transmodulation*. Because of the functional interrelatedness between the COEX systems and the BPMs, most reexperiencing of traumatic childhood memories represents partial and mitigated reliving of a certain facet of the birth trauma. Similarly, positive childhood experiences can be viewed as partial restitution of the pleasant post-natal or intrauterine condition. A comparable dynamic shift from one dominant perinatal matrix to another can be referred to as *BPM transmodulation*. A *transpersonal transmodulation* then involves governing functional systems in the transindividual realms of the unconscious.

A typical *positive transmodulation* has a biphasic course; it involves intensification of the dominant negative system and a sudden shift to the positive. However, if a strong positive system is easily available it can dominate the LSD experience from the very beginning of the session, and the negative system recedes into the background. A shift from one dynamic constellation to another does not necessarily indicate clinical improvement. There is a possibility that a poorly resolved and integrated session will result in *negative transmodulation*—a shift from a positive system to a negative one. This situation is characterized by a sudden occurrence of psychopathological symptoms that were not manifest before the session. Another interesting possibility is a shift from one negative system to another that is also negative in nature. The external manifestation of this intrapsychic event is a remarkable qualitative change in psychopathology from one clinical syndrome to another. Occasionally, this transformation can be so dramatic that the patient moves into a completely different diagnostic category; a clinical illustration of this phenomenon was given earlier in this book (p. 231). Although the resulting condition might appear on the surface to be entirely new, all its essential elements existed in a potential form in the patient's experiential repositories before the dynamic shift occurred. It is thus important to realize that, in addition to working through unconscious material, the LSD procedure can also involve dramatic shifts of focus that change its experiential relevance.

I would like to mention in this context an interesting metaphor which one of my patients used to illustrate her concept of this process. She described the human unconscious as a dark storage house, full of various objects of all kinds, some of them ugly, others beautiful. The LSD process appeared to her to involve not only removing junk and garbage, but also changing the direction of a flashlight illuminating the inside space. Only those of the stored objects that were illumined by the flashlight could be perceived at a particular time. Similarly, only those un-conscious contents that are in the spotlight of conscious awareness can actually be fully experienced.

An issue that deserves special consideration at this point is the relative thera-peutic significance of negative and positive experiences in LSD sessions. The prob-lem whether the emphasis in LSD psychotherapy should be on reliving conflicts and traumatic memories or on achieving transcendental experiences has been one of the most controversial issues between psycholytic and psychedelic therapists. According to my experience, working through the traumatic material and experi-encing ecstatic states are both important and integral parts of the healing process. Moreover, these two aspects of LSD psychotherapy seem to be mutually inter-related in a dialectic fashion. Energetic reduction of negative systems and working through of problematic areas opens the way to deep positive episodes. Conversely, if LSD subjects experience profound transpersonal states in the initial psychedelic sessions, this has a very beneficial influence on the future course of therapy. They transcend the narrow personal framework and see their problems in a cosmic con-text. This results in a generally optimistic attitude that is of great help in dealing with the negative psychodynamic and perinatal material when it emerges during treatment. An individual who has experienced transcendental states has a strong feeling of cosmic identity and knows the ultimate goal of the treatment. The LSD process is seen as work on the barrier that separates him or her from the Self, and not just a blind digging in the *cul-de-sac* of the individual unconscious. A simultaneous emphasis on both aspects of the process with encouragement of its spontaneous course seems to be the best solution to this therapeutic dilemma. However, positive experiences are of fundamental significance to the therapeutic outcome, and every concept of LSD treatment that underestimates them is depriv-ing itself of a powerful therapeutic principle.

THERAPEUTIC POTENTIAL OF THE DEATH-REBIRTH PROCESS

The therapeutic changes associated with experiences on the psychodynamic level seem to be of relatively minor significance compared to those that result from perinatal sequences. The everyday clinical practice of LSD psychotherapy brings repeated evidence of the powerful healing potential of the death-rebirth process. The discovery of this potent therapeutic mechanism, as yet unrecognized and unacknowledged by Western science, represents one of the most surprising find-ings of my LSD research.

Experiential sequences of dying and being born can result in dramatic alleviation of a variety of emotional and psychosomatic problems. Negative peri-natal matrices are an important repository of emotions and physical sensations of extraordinary intensity; they function as a potential experiential source of many psychopathological syndromes. Such crucial symptoms as anxiety, aggression, depression, fear of death, feelings of guilt, a sense of inferiority, helplessness, and general emotional tension seem to have deep roots on the perinatal level. Many aspects of these phenomena and their interrelations make sense if considered in the context of the birth trauma. Similarly, I have also frequently been able to trace a client's preoccupation with various physiological functions or biological material, strange hypochondriacal complaints, and a variety of psychosomatic symptoms to certain aspects of the death-rebirth process. This was particularly true for ordinary or migraine headaches, neurotic feelings, lack of oxygen and suffocation, cardiac distress, nausea and vomiting, various dyskinesias or muscular tensions, pains, and tremors in different parts of the body.

A rather common observation in psycholytic therapy was that patients who had moved beyond the psychodynamic level altogether in their process continued to have difficult LSD experiences and a number of clinical problems in their everyday life. It became evident that certain psychopathological symptoms were rooted in the perinatal level and would not disappear unless and until the underlying material was thoroughly worked through. Thus it was necessary to confront the "no-exit" matrix experientially in order to reach a lasting resolution —not just a temporary remission—of claustrophobia or an inhibited depression. Similarly, the deep roots of an agitated depression were found in the death-rebirth struggle of the third perinatal matrix.

Suicidal urges often disappeared completely when patients worked through and integrated the perinatal material. Several individuals who had completed the death-rebirth process independently reported that their previous suicidal tendencies had actually been unrecognized cravings for the ego death and transcendence. Since this insight was not available to them at the time, they focused psychologically on a situation in objective reality that bore for them a close resemblance to the ego death, namely, physical destruction. The experience of psychological death tends to eliminate or greatly reduce suicidal tendencies and ideation. Powerful aggressive and self-destructive impulses are consumed in the many dramatic experiential sequences of the death-rebirth process. In addition, after completing the process of the ego death individuals consider human existence in a much broader spiritual framework. Consciousness is seen as supraordinated to matter and drastic maneuvers on the material plane appear absurd and ineffective as a remedy for difficulties in individual development. No matter how difficult the life situations and circumstances may be from an objective point of view, suicide somehow no longer appears to be a solution.

In our work with alcoholics and heroin addicts we made some interesting observations that were quite similar to those concerning suicidal individuals. From a certain point of view, alcoholism and heroin addiction can be seen as suicidal behavior extended over a long period of time; the underlying dynamics of suicide and addiction have much in common. LSD patients who had experienced profound feelings of cosmic unity frequently developed a negative attitude toward the states of mind produced by intoxication with alcohol and narcotics. The insights of these patients concerning the nature of their addiction resembled those of persons with suicidal tendencies. After they had discovered and experienced feelings of cosmic unity in their sessions, they realized that the state they had really been craving for was transcendence and not drug intoxication. They recognized a certain superficial similarity and overlap between the alcohol or heroin intoxication and the unitive feelings evoked by LSD, and began to see that their desire for these drugs was based on confusing these two conditions. The elements that the transcendental state has in common with these intoxications are disappearance or diminution of various painful emotions or sensations, emotional indifference toward one's past or future, loosening of the body boundaries, and a fluid, undifferentiated state of consciousness. However, many essential characteristics of the unitive state are not reproduced in the experience of intoxication by alcohol or narcotics. Instead of inducing a state of cosmic consciousness in its totality, these drugs produce its caricature; however, the resemblance is close enough to mislead the individual involved and seduce him or her into systematic abuse. Repeated administrations then lead to biological addiction and irreversible physical, emotional, and social damage.

After experiences of ego death and cosmic unity, abuse of alcohol or narcotics, and suicidal tendencies, are seen as tragic mistakes caused by an unrecognized and misunderstood spiritual craving for transcendence. The presence of strong feelings of this kind, improbable as it might seem in view of the behavior patterns and life style of narcotic addicts and alcoholics, can be illustrated by statistics from psychedelic therapy. In the Spring Grove research, alcoholics and heroin addicts had the highest incidence of mystical experiences of all the groups studied, including neurotics, mental health professionals, and individuals dying of cancer.

Malignant aggression, impulsive behavior and sadomasochistic tendencies also have important roots on the perinatal level. Activation of the destructive and self-destructive potential in the individual is one of the most important aspects of the death-rebirth struggle. Scenes of unbridled aggression and mass destruction, as well as sadomasochistic orgies, are standard components of the perinatal unfolding.[1] In this context, enormous amounts of destructive energy are mobilized and discharged; the result is a dramatic reduction of aggressive feelings and tendencies. The experience of rebirth is typically associated with a sense of love, compassion, and reverence for life.

Perinatal elements also play an important role in the dynamics of various anxiety states and phobias, hysterical conversion symptoms, and certain aspects of obsessive-compulsive neuroses. Many sexual disorders and deviations seem to be anchored on the perinatal level and can be logically explained from certain aspects and facets of the birth trauma. This is true for impotence, frigidity, menstrual cramps, painful vaginal spasms during intercourse (dyspareunia), indulgence in and preoccupation with biological material in a sexual context such as eating feces and drinking urine (coprophilia and urolagnia), clinical sadomasochism, and certain cases of fetishism and homosexuality.

Many important aspects of the schizophrenic process seem to represent perinatal elements in a more-or-less pure form. Here these deep unconscious contents are not mitigated and modified by later biographical material, as is the case in most of the disorders mentioned above. Thus the episodes of diabolic tortures, extreme physical and mental suffering that seems endless, a deep sense of the absurdity of existence, or visions of a monstrous world of cardboard characters and automatons described by many psychotic patients indicate the involvement of BPM II. Sequences involving death, dismemberment, annihilation of the world, cosmic catastrophes, distortions of the aggressive and sexual impulses, preoccupation with biological material, and experiential focus on the birth-sex-death triad are characteristic of BPM III. Messianic delusions, identification with Christ, and experiences of rebirth or of recreation of the world are associated with the transition from the third to the fourth perinatal matrix. Facilitation and completion of the death-rebirth process is associated with the disappearance of many of the above psychotic symptoms.

The perinatal area of the unconscious thus seems to represent a universal, undifferentiated matrix for a number of different psychopathological and psychosomatic symptoms and syndromes. Whether or not pathology develops and what specific form it takes depends on the quality and nature of the individual's postnatal life. This explains why experiences of death and rebirth may be associated with dramatic improvements in a wide variety of clinical conditions and problems. The therapeutic mechanisms available on this level are much more powerful than any known to traditional psychiatry and psychotherapy. The profound changes observed seem to involve a combination of two important therapeutic factors. The first one is release and discharge of enormous amounts of pent-up emotions and physical sensations associated with BPM II and III, which provide energy for clinical symptoms. The second is the healing potential of unitive ecstatic states experienced in the context of BPM IV and I. These experiences have such a profound influence on clinical symptoms of various kinds, on the personality structure, hierarchy of values, and world-view that they deserve special note.

I believe that the experiential content of the perinatal matrices cannot be reduced to the memory of biological birth. However, one way of approaching this new therapeutic principle is to focus on the biological aspects of the perinatal process. Whether or not an actual causal link can be established, experiences of oceanic ecstasy and cosmic union seem to be deeply related to the undifferentiated state of consciousness that an infant experiences in the symbiotic interaction with the maternal organism during undisturbed intrauterine existence and nursing. The association of the feelings of cosmic unity with good womb and good breast experiences offers some clues for the understanding of their far-reaching healing potential. It is a well-established fact of developmental psychology that the blissful egoless states a child experiences during the early period of its life are very important for his or her future emotional development, stability, and mental health.

The experiences of cosmic unity induced in an adult by LSD or by various non-drug techniques seem to be in this sense equivalent to good womb and good breast experiences. They satisfy fundamental psychological and biological needs in the individual and facilitate emotional and psychosomatic healing. The experience of melted ecstasy can thus be seen as a retroactive intervention in the individual's history and an anachronistic satisfaction of basic infantile needs. However, as important as the above mechanism might be, it reflects only one relatively superficial facet of the experience of cosmic unity. To overemphasize the biological side of this phenomenon would be to neglect its philosophical and spiritual dimensions. An individual who has a transcendental experience develops an entirely new image of his or her identity and cosmic status. The materialistic image of the universe in which the individual is a meaningless speck of dust in the vastness of the cosmos is instantly replaced by the mystical alternative. Within the new world-view, the very creative principle of the universe is experientially available to the individual and, in a certain sense, is commensurate and identical with him or her. This is a drastic change of perspective and it has far-reaching consequences for every aspect of life.

In the cultural history of mankind, experiences of this kind have been described in different frameworks for centuries or even millenia. They may occur spontaneously in certain individuals under special circumstances, or be facilitated by various spiritual procedures designed specifically for this purpose. Despite the fact that both the existence of these experiences and their beneficial impact on experients have been known for such a long time, they have hardly ever been mentioned in the context of modern psychotherapy or therapy in general. Until the publication of Abraham Maslow's work, the only framework available in psychiatry for "peak experiences" was that of schizophrenic symptomatology. The healing potential of ecstatic states is of such paramount significance, however, that it suggests an entirely new orientation in psychiatric therapy. We should carefully study the characteristics of these states and develop new methods for their facilitation and induction.

THERAPEUTIC MECHANISMS ON THE TRANSPERSONAL LEVEL

Observations from LSD psychotherapy provide ample evidence that transpersonal experiences are more than just curious phenomena of theoretical interest. In many instances, specific clinical symptoms are anchored in dynamic structures of a transpersonal nature and cannot be resolved on the level of psychodynamic or even perinatal experiences. In order to eliminate a specific emotional, psychosomatic, or interpersonal problem, the patient sometimes has to experience dramatic sequences of a clearly transpersonal nature. Many unusual and interesting observations clearly indicate the need to incorporate transpersonal aspects and approaches into everyday psychotherapeutic practice.

To the surprise of both patient and therapist, seemingly bizarre and unexplainable experiences sometimes have a dramatic impact on certain clinical symptoms and problems. Since the therapeutic process frequently leads into unexplored and uncharted territories, it requires considerable open-mindedness and an adventurous spirit in both the client and the therapist. A therapist who adheres rigidly to conventional paradigms and is unaware of and closed to unfamiliar levels of consciousness will generally be less effective with patients whose problems have a strong transpersonal emphasis. He or she will not encourage them to have experiences that would resolve their symptoms, or might even implicitly and explicitly discourage them from entering transpersonal realms. Such an approach, in addition to being therapeutically less effective, also fails to meet the intense spiritual needs of these patients and give them sensitive guidance.

In some LSD patients difficult emotional symptoms that had not been resolved on the psychodynamic or perinatal level disappeared or were mitigated in connection with various *embryonal experiences*. Reliving attempted abortions, maternal diseases or emotional crises during pregnancy, and fetal experiences of being unwanted ("rejecting womb") can be of great therapeutic value. Particularly dramatic instances of therapeutic change have been observed in connection with *past-incarnation experiences*. Sometimes these occur simultaneously with perinatal phenomena, at other times they are independent thematic gestalts. The subject experiences a sequence set in another country and/or a different historical period, usually with deep emotional involvement and dramatic abreaction. This is associated with a strong sense of reliving an episode from a previous incarnation. A particular emotional, interpersonal or psychosomatic problem is felt to be a meaningful part of a karmic pattern, and disappears when this gestalt is completed. In some instances this may be accompanied by independent synchronistic changes in the lives and specific attitudes of people whom the subject denoted as protagonists in the karmic scene. The following episode is a good illustration of this unusual phenomenon:

Tanya, a 34-year-old teacher and divorced mother of two children, was undergoing LSD psychotherapy for depressions, anxiety states, and a proneness to fatigue. One of her LSD sessions brought an unexpected solution to a severe physical problem which had been considered purely organic in nature. For the previous twelve years she had been suffering from chronic sinusitis with occasional acute flare-ups because of colds or allergies. The sinus troubles had started shortly after her wedding and represented a severe inconvenience in her life. The major manifestations were headaches and strong pains in the cheeks and teeth, low-grade fevers, heavy nasal discharge, and bouts of sneezing and wheezing. On many occasions she was awakened by a coughing attack; some mornings these symptoms lasted three to four hours. Tanya had numerous tests for allergies and was treated by many specialists with antihistamines, antibiotics, and flushing of the sinuses with disinfectant solutions. When all this failed to bring any therapeutic results, the doctors suggested an operation of the sinuses, which Tanya declined.

In one of her LSD sessions, Tanya was experiencing suffocation, congestion and pressure on her head in the context of the birth experience. She recognized that some of these sensations bore a close resemblance to the symptoms associated with her sinus problems; however, they were greatly amplified. After many sequences that were clearly of a perinatal nature, the experience opened fully into a reliving of what appeared to be a past-incarnation memory. In this context, the experiences of oppression, choking and congestion that had earlier been part of the birth trauma became symptoms of drowning. Tanya felt that she was tied to a slanted board and was slowly being pushed under water by a group of villagers. After dramatic emotional abreaction associated with screaming, violent choking, coughing, and profuse secretion of enormous amounts of thick, greenish nasal discharge, she was able to recognize the place, circumstances and protagonists.

She was a young girl in a New England village who had been accused by her neighbors of witchcraft, because she was having unusual experiences of a spiritual nature. A group of villagers dragged her one night to a nearby birch-grove, fixed her to a board, and drowned her head-first in a cold pond. In the bright moonlight, she was able to recognize among her executioners the faces of her father and husband in her present lifetime. At this point, Tanya could see many elements of her current existence as approximate replicas of the original karmic scene. Certain aspects of her life, including specific patterns of interaction with her husband and her father, suddenly appeared to make sense, down to the most specific details.

This experience of the New England drama and all the intricate con-

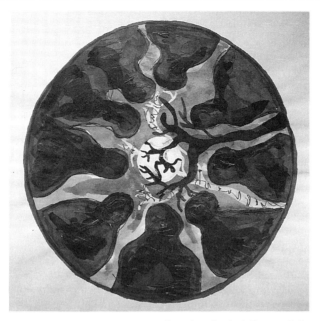

Tanya's experience of a previous incarnation. Above her the dark figures of the crowd form a circle against the night sky and the full moon.

nections Tanya made, convincing though they were on the subjective level, obviously did not constitute proof of the historical validity of the episode and of a causal link between the event and her sinus problems. Nor could her conviction that she was dealing with a karmic pattern be considered evidence for the existence of reincarnation. However, to the astonishment of everybody concerned, this experience cleared the chronic sinus condition that had plagued Tanya for a period of twelve years and had proved completely refractory to conventional medical treatment.

It is interesting to note that this mechanism is not limited to psychedelic states. Many similar observations have been reported by therapists who utilize non-drug techniques, such as hypnosis, gestalt practice or primal therapy. Dennys Kelsey and Joan Grant (45) induce a hypnotic trance in their subjects and suggest that they go back in time to find the source of their emotional or physical problems. Without special programming, many of their subjects relive past-incarnation memories under these circumstances and resolve their symptoms in this context.

One of their clients should be mentioned here because the mechanism involved bears a close resemblance to what I have observed many times during LSD psychotherapy. She suffered from a severe phobia of bird wings and feathers that had resisted conventional psychological treatment for years. Her difficult symptom was resolved after she relived with a dramatic abreaction a scene that had a past-incarnation experiential quality. She experienced herself in a male form, as a

Persian warrior who had been wounded by an arrow and was dying on the battle-field. As he lay there approaching his terminal agony, vultures were gathering around him, awaiting his death. They kept jumping toward him and pecking at him, while hitting his face with their wings. The patient found the roots of her phobia of bird feathers in this horrifying experience; discharge of the emotional energy together with the new insight freed her permanently from the tedious symptom.

Emmett Miller (70) has occasionally made similar observations using a hyp-notic technique which he calls selective awareness. There are psychologists and psychiatrists in the United States who specialize in regressing their clients to the past-incarnation level to find the roots of individual and interpersonal problems. Many past-incarnation experiences have been described in the context of auditing in scientology. The readings of Edgar Cayce also often contain references to karmic levels as the sources of his clients' problems. On occasion, past-incarnation memories emerge spontaneously in everyday life; they can have the same bene-ficial consequences if they are allowed to reach completion. This raises a question as to how many opportunities for effective therapeutic intervention have been missed by Cartesian–Newtonian psychiatrists whose patients reported access to karmic levels. The importance of transpersonal experiences for the therapeutic ap-proach to schizophrenia was illustrated earlier in this book by the history of Milada. (see p. 257)

Ancestral experiences can sometimes play a role similar to past-incarnation memories. In some instances symptoms disappear after patients relive what they feel are memories from the lives of their ancestors. I have also seen patients iden-tify certain intrapsychic problems as internalized conflicts between the families of their ancestors and resolve them on this level. Some psychopathological and psychosomatic symptoms can occasionally be traced back to elements of *plant* or *animal consciousness*. Thus, the complex and seemingly bizarre sensations of a female patient were resolved when she recognized them as states of vegetable con-sciousness and allowed herself to identify with the experience of being a tree. In another patient, unusual physical feelings and symptoms of a severe hay fever were amplified by the effect of the drug and became authentic sensations of being an animal of another species. To illustrate the complexity and fascinating dimen-sions of the problems in question I would like to describe a case that does not in-volve a clear therapeutic outcome but provides most interesting insights.

I was recently contacted by Arthur, a 46-year-old mathematician who had had LSD experiences in the past for didactic purposes and as a means of finding the roots of his neurotic symptoms. Much of the work he had done in his sessions focused on problems of embryonal development and birth. He had to face special complications in these areas owing to the fact that he had a twin sister. In many of his LSD sessions he had visions and experiences of creatures with complex geometrical organization. He felt very emotionally involved in these experiences, although they were strange and did not make any sense. He could not understand why he spent so much time on these bizarre and incomprehensible forms.

Several years later, long after he had discontinued the LSD sessions, he overexerted himself while working on an involved project. For many months he had had little sleep, drank much coffee, and smoked two packs of cigarettes a day. During the convalescence period following a heart attack, he acquired Ernst Haeckel's book *Art Forms in Nature*, (35) a collection of plates depicting various animal forms in the evolutionary pedigree. He was astounded when, looking through the book, he recognized many of the forms that had represented such an important part of his LSD sessions. In an instant he received insights into the nature of the process that he never completed. As a twin, he had to face special problems related to symmetry during his embryological development. His experiences of different stages of his embryological development were associated in the LSD sessions with corresponding animal forms in accordance with Haeckel's biogenetic law.[2] In this context, he recognized that the heart as an asymmetrical organ presents special problems during embryogenesis. It was on this level, in the realm of the basic geometry of nature, that Arthur found the deepest roots of his life-long interest in mathematics, symmetry, and geometrical forms.

In some instances, LSD patients recognized that some of their symptoms, attitudes, and behavior were manifestations of an underlying *archetypal structure*. Full experiential identification with the various archetypal entities can lead to the resolution of such problems. Occasionally, the energy forms involved have such an alien quality that the behavior of the LSD subjects resembles what anthropologists have ascribed to spirit possession. In such cases the therapeutic procedure can have many of the characteristics of exorcism as it was practiced in the medieval church, or the expulsion of evil spirits in aboriginal cultures. Such situations can be very demanding for both patient and therapist. The following story is the most dramatic example of this phenomenon I have ever witnessed; the fact that the patient had amnesia during most of the process distinguishes it from other similar episodes.

While working at the Maryland Psychiatric Research Center, I was invited to a staff conference at the Spring Grove State Hospital. One of the psychiatrists was presenting the case of Flora, a 28-year-old single patient who had been hospitalized by then for more than eight months in a locked ward. All available therapy, including tranquillizers, antidepressants, psychotherapy, and occupational therapy, had been tried but failed, and she was facing transfer to the chronic ward. Flora had one of the most complicated combinations of symptoms and problems I have ever encountered in my psychiatric practice. When she was sixteen years old, she was a member of a gang that conducted an armed robbery and killed a night watchman. As driver of the get-away car, Flora spent four years in prison and was then placed on parole for the rest of her sentence. During the stormy years that followed, she became a multiple drug addict. She was an alcoholic and a heroin addict, and frequently used high doses of psychostimulants and barbiturates. Her severe depressions were associated with violent suicidal tendencies; she frequently had impulses to drive her car over a cliff or collide with another automobile. She suffered from hysterical vomiting which occurred easily in situations where she became emotionally excited. Probably the most agonizing of her complaints was a painful facial cramp, "tic doloreux," for which a Johns Hopkins neurosurgeon had suggested a brain operation consisting in severing the nerves involved. Flora was a lesbian and had severe conflicts and guilt about it; she had never had a heterosexual intercourse in her life. To further complicate the situation, she was court-committed because she had severely wounded her girlfriend and room-mate while trying to clean a gun under the influence of heroin.

At the end of the Spring Grove case conference, the attending psychiatrist asked Dr. Charles Savage and me if we would consider LSD psychotherapy. We found this an extremely difficult decision, especially because this was at the time of the national hysteria concerning LSD. Flora had a criminal record already, she had access to weapons, and had severe suicidal tendencies. We were well aware that the atmosphere was such that if we gave her an LSD session, whatever happened after that point would automatically be blamed on the drug, without regard to her past history. On the other hand, everything else had been tried without success and she was facing a lifetime in a chronic ward. Finally, we decided to take the chance and accept her into the LSD program, feeling that her desperate situation justified the risk.

Flora's first two high-dose LSD sessions were not much different from many others I had run in the past. She faced a number of situations from her stormy childhood and repeatedly relived sequences of the struggle in the birth canal. She was able to connect her violent suicidal tendencies and painful facial cramps to certain aspects of the birth trauma, and to discharge large amounts of intense emotion and physical tension. Despite this, the therapeutic gains seemed to be minimal.

In her third LSD session, nothing extraordinary happened during the first two hours; her experiences were similar to those of the previous two sessions. Suddenly, she started complaining that the painful cramps in her face were becoming unbearable. Before our eyes, the facial spasms were grotesquely accentuated and her face froze into what can best be described as a mask of evil. She started talking in a deep, male voice and everything about her was so different that I could not see any connection between her present appearance and her former self. Her eyes had an expression of indescribable malice and her hands were spastic and looked like claws.

The alien energy that took control over her body and voice introduced itself as the devil. "He" turned directly to me, ordering me to stay away from Flora and give up any attempts to help her. She belonged to him and he would punish anybody who dared to invade his territory. What followed was explicit blackmail, a series of dismal descriptions of what would happen to me, my colleagues, and the program if I would not obey. It is difficult to describe the uncanny atmosphere which this scene evoked; one could almost feel the intangible presence of something alien in the room. The power of the blackmail was further increased by the fact that it involved certain concrete information to which the patient in her everyday life could not have access.

I found myself under considerable emotional stress which had metaphysical dimensions. Although I had seen similar manifestations in some LSD sessions, they were never so realistic or convincing. It was difficult for me to control my fear and a tendency to enter into what I felt would be an active combat with the presence. I found myself thinking fast, trying to choose the best strategy for the situation. At one point, I caught myself thinking that we should have a crucifix in our therapeutic armamentarium. My rationalization for this idea was that this was obviously an archetype that was manifesting and the cross could, under these circumstances, be a specific archetypal remedy.

It soon became clear to me that my emotions, whether of fear or aggression, were making the entity more real. I could not help thinking of scenes from science fiction stories involving alien entities that fed on emotions. Finally, I realized that it was essential for me to remain calm and centered. I decided to put myself into a meditative mood, while I held Flora's cramped hand and tried to relate to her in the form in which I had known her before. At the same time, I tried to visualize a capsule of light enveloping us both, which intuitively seemed to be the best approach. The situation lasted over two hours of clock-time; in terms of the subjective time-sense these were the longest two hours I have ever experienced outside of my own psychedelic sessions.

After this time, Flora's hands relaxed and her face returned to its usual form; these changes were as abrupt as the onset of the peculiar condition. I soon discovered that she did not remember anything of the two hours preceding. Later, in her write-up, she described the first hours of the session and continued with the period following the "possession state." I seriously questioned if I should discuss the time covered by her amnesia with her and decided against it. There did not seem to be any reason to introduce such a macabre theme into her conscious mind.

To my great surprise, this session resulted in an astounding therapeutic breakthrough. Flora lost her suicidal tendencies and developed new appreciation for life. She gave up alcohol, heroin and barbiturates and started zealously attending the meetings of a small religious group in Catonsville. For most of the time she did not have any facial cramps; the energy underlying them seemed to have exhausted itself in the "mask of evil" that she maintained for two hours. The occasional recurrence of the pain was of negligible intensity and did not even require medication. She started experimenting with heterosexual relations and eventually married. Her sexual adjustment was not good, however; she was capable of intercourse, but found it painful and not very pleasant. The marriage ended three months later and Flora returned to lesbian relationships; this time, however, with much less guilt. Her condition was so improved that she was accepted as a taxi driver. Although the following years had their ups and downs, she did not have to return to the psychiatric hospital that could have become her permanent home.

The above discussion and the two examples given represent only a small sample of the observations I have made during twenty years of LSD research which suggest that transpersonal experiences can be of great therapeutic value. Whatever the therapist's professional and philosophical opinion of the nature of transpersonal experiences, he or she should be aware of their therapeutic potential and support clients if their self-exploration takes them into transpersonal realms.

These observations from LSD psychotherapy regarding effective mechanisms of therapeutic change clearly indicate that none of the existing psychological schools covers the entire spectrum of and provides an adequate explanatory framework for all the processes involved. Some of the major psychotherapeutic orientations offer useful formulas in the area of the unconscious on which they focus. Thus Freudian psychoanalysis is of great help while the LSD sessions concentrate on the biographical level. The Rankian framework, with some important modifications, is relevant for understanding the biological aspects of the death-rebirth process. The Reichian and neo-Reichian approaches give important theoretical and practical clues for dealing with the physical and energetic aspects of the biographical or perinatal levels. Jungian psychology has explored and mapped many important experiential realms of the transpersonal domain. Yet each of the above systems is only partially applicable to the psychedelic process, and a rigid adherence to any conceptual framework is ultimately antitherapeutic. In this matter, psychology and psychotherapy can learn an important lesson from modern physics. Recently, theoretical physicist Geoffrey Chew (20) has formulated a revolutionary approach which he calls the *"bootstrap" philosophy of nature*. In this view, the universe is seen not as a gigantic clockwork, an assembly of objects interacting with each other following the principles of Newtonian mechanics, but as an infinitely intricate web of interrelated events. None of the properties of any part of the web is fundamental; they all follow from the properties of the other parts, and the overall consistency of their interrelation determines the structure of the entire web. The way in which various disciplines divide reality is ultimately arbitrary, and all scientific theories are only more or less useful approximations.

In the field of consciousness research the closest parallel to Geoffrey Chew's philosophy is the concept of *spectrum psychology*, formulated by Ken Wilber (103). It suggests that various existing schools accurately describe different levels or bands of consciousness but are not applicable to the psyche in its totality. It is essential for effective LSD psychotherapy to approach the process of self-exploration from the point of view of spectrum psychology and in the spirit of "bootstrap" philosophy. Theoretical models of any kind are only approximate and useful organizations of data about a certain realm available at a certain time. They should not be mistaken for accurate and exhaustive descriptions of the world. To function as a facilitator of scientific progress rather than a hindrance, a conceptual framework has to be tentative and flexible; it should respond or even yield to new observations. Reality is always larger and more complex than the most elaborate and encompassing theory. If the therapist confuses a theoretical system with the "truth" about reality, this will sooner or later interfere with the therapeutic process and create a serious impasse in the treatment of patients whose therapeutic need is for experiences that the system does not include or allow.

My present opinion is that emotional and psychosomatic symptoms indicate blockage of energy and ultimately represent potential experiences in a condensed form, trying to emerge. I believe the role of a therapist should be to help mobilize the energy and facilitate free experiential flow. He or she should not have any conceptual or emotional investment in the nature of the resulting experience and should be willing to support and validate the process as long as it does not involve physical danger to the client or to others. Ultimately it does not seem to make any difference which form the experience takes if the client is true to his or her process and surrenders to it fully. It can be a childhood memory, birth sequence, karmic constellation, phylogenetic episode, or demonic manifestation. The therapist should be sufficiently open-minded to encourage the client to follow the energy flow, regardless of the specific content of the process. Completion of the experiential gestalt brings therapeutic results, whether or not the process has been intellectually understood. After the process is completed, the therapist and the client can make attempts to put the events of the session into a theoretical framework. Depending on the nature and level of the experience, the system that offers the best maps might be Freudian psychoanalysis, Rank's psychology, the theoretical constructs of C. G. Jung, Tibetan Buddhism, alchemy, Kabbalah, or some other ancient cartography of consciousness, the mythology of a particular culture, or a particular spiritual system. However, the intellectual processing should be considered an interesting academic exercise that is not essential for therapeutic progress. Although on the surface this might be seen as intellectual anarchy breeding conceptual chaos, it has a deep logic of its own and can be meaningfully related to a new model of the universe and of human nature. Discussion of this issue has to be reserved for the next volume.

NOTES

1. The possible socio-political implications of this observation have been discussed in detail in my paper, "Perinatal Roots of Wars, Totalitarianism and Revolutions." (33)
2. Ernst Haeckel's biogenetic law states that during its individual development (ontogeny) the organism repeats in a condensed way the history of the species (phylogeny).

EPILOGUE: THE FUTURE OF LSD PSYCHOTHERAPY

In the preceding sections of this book I have tried to express and illustrate my belief that LSD is a unique and powerful tool for the exploration of the human mind and human nature. Psychedelic experiences mediate access to deep realms of the psyche that have not yet been discovered and acknowledged by mainstream psychology and psychiatry. They also reveal new possibilities and mechanisms of therapeutic change and personality transformation. The fact that the spectrum of the LSD experience appears puzzling to most professionals and cannot be accounted for by the existing theoretical frameworks does not mean that the effects of LSD are totally unpredictable. The safe and effective use of this drug requires a fundamental revision of the existing theory and practice of psychotherapy. However, it is possible to formulate basic principles for LSD-assisted psychotherapy which maximize its therapeutic benefits and minimize the risks.

It is very difficult at this point to predict the future of LSD psychotherapy. The fact that it can be used safely and effectively does not automatically mean that it will be assimilated by mainstream psychiatry. This issue is complicated by many factors of an emotional, administrative, political and legal nature. However, we should clearly differentiate between the future of LSD psychotherapy and its contribution to the theory and practice of psychiatry. I mentioned earlier in this volume that LSD is a catalyst or amplifier of mental processes. If properly used it could become something like the microscope or the telescope of psychiatry. Whether LSD research continues in the future or not, the insights that have been achieved in LSD experimentation are of lasting value and relevance.

The theoretical formulations and practical principles that LSD psychotherapy has discovered or validated include a new, expanded cartography of the human mind, new and effective therapeutic mechanisms, a new strategy of psychotherapy, and a synthesis of spirituality and science in the context of the transpersonal approach. In addition, the recent rapid convergence between mysticism, modern consciousness research and quantum-relativistic physics suggests that psychedelic research could contribute in the future to our understanding of the nature of reality.

It is true that psychedelic experimentation has its dangers and pitfalls. But ventures into unexplored areas are never without risk. Wilhelm Conrad Roentgen, the discoverer of x-rays, lost his fingers as a result of his experiments with the new form of radiation. The mortality-rate of the early pilots who paved the way for

today's safe jet travel was allegedly 75 percent. The degree of risk is directly proportional to the significance of the discovery, and its potential; thus the invention
of gun powder involved a different level of risk from the development of nuclear
energy. LSD is a tool of extraordinary power; after more than twenty years of
clinical research I feel great awe in regard to both its positive and negative potential. Whatever the future of LSD psychotherapy, it is important to realize that by
banning psychedelic research we have not only given up the study of an interesting drug or group of substances, but also abandoned one of the most promising approaches to the understanding of the human mind and consciousness.

The present prospects for systematic LSD research and its extensive use in
psychotherapy look rather grim. It is difficult at this point to say whether or not
the situation will change, though there are indications that the general climate
might become more favorable in the years to come.

One of the major problems in LSD psychotherapy was the unusual nature
and content of the psychedelic experience. The intensity of the emotional and
physical expression characteristic of LSD sessions was in sharp contrast to the conventional image of psychotherapy, with its face-to-face discussions or disciplined
free-associating on the couch. The themes of birth, death, insanity, ESP, cosmic
unity, archetypal entities, or past-incarnation memories occurring in psychedelic
states were far beyond the conventional topics of psychotherapy which emphasized biographical data. An average professional at that time felt reluctance
toward or even fear of the experiential realms of this kind because of their association with psychosis. At present, intense emotional outbursts, dramatic physical
manifestations, and various perinatal and transpersonal experiences are much
more acceptable to and less frightening for many therapists because they can be
encountered quite routinely in the context of the new experiential therapies, such as
Gestalt practice, encounter groups, marathon and nude marathon sessions, primal
therapy, and various neo-Reichian approaches. Many modern therapists value
and encourage various dramatic experiences which in the framework of classical
analysis would be seen as dangerous acting-out and considered a reason for discon-
tinuation of treatment or even psychiatric hospitalization. Some modern approaches to schizophrenia actually encourage deep experiential immersion into the
process instead of its chemical inhibition. For new therapists of the above orientation, psychedelics would naturally be the next step to help accelerate and deepen
the process.

LSD entered the scene at the time of the psychopharmacological revolution,
when new tranquillizers and antidepressants had their early triumphs and
generated excessive hope for easy chemical solutions to most of the problems in
psychiatry. At present much of the original enthusiasm in this area has tapered
off. While appreciating the humanization of the mental hospitals and pacification
of psychiatric wards which has brought their atmosphere close to that of general
hospitals, it is becoming increasingly obvious that tranquillizers and antidepressants are, by and large, only symptomatic remedies. They do not solve the problems and in more serious cases lead to a life-long dependence on maintenance
medication. In addition, there is an increasing number of professional papers that
emphasize the dangers of massive use of these drugs—irreversible neurological
symptoms of tardive dyskinesia, degenerative changes in the retina, or actual
physiological addiction with a withdrawal syndrome.

We should also mention important social forces that might play a role in the future changes of policy toward psychedelic research. Many of the young persons who are in or will be moving into various positions of social relevance—as lawyers, teachers, administrators, or mental health professionals—had intense exposure to psychedelics during their student years. Those individuals who had experiences themselves, or had the opportunity to observe the process in close friends and relatives, will have formed an independent image and will not be dependent on second-hand sources for information. Elements of sanity in the new marijuana laws in many states may be the first fruits of this development. The fact that ritualized and responsible use of psychedelics received social sanction in some ancient societies and pre-industrial countries and was meaningfully woven into the social fabric represents a somewhat hopeful precedent.

BIBLIOGRAPHY

1   Abramson, H A: LSD-25 as an Adjunct to Psychotherapy with Elimination of Fear of Homosexuality. *J. Psychol.* 39:127, 1955

2   Abramson, H A, ed.: *The Use of LSD in Psychotherapy*, Josiah Macy Foundation Publications, New York, 1960

3   Anderson, E W; Rawnsley, K: Clinical Studies of LSD-25. *Mschr. Psychiat. Neurol.* 128:38, 1954

4   Arendsen-Hein, G W: LSD in the Treatment of Criminal Psychopaths. *Proc. of the Royal Medico-Psychological Association*, London 1961. Charles C. Thomas, London, 1963

5   Arendsen-Hein, G W: Personal communication

6   Asperen de Boer, S R van; Barkema, P R; Kappers, J: Is It Possible to Induce ESP With Psilocybin? *Internat. J. Neuropsychiat.* 2:447, 1966

7   Bastians, A: Der Mann im Konzentrationslager und der Konzentrationslager im Mann. Mimeographed lecture

8   Becker, A M: Zur Psychopathologie der Lysergsaurediathylamidwirkung *Wien Ztschr. Nervenheilk.* 2:402, 1949

9   Belsanti, R: Modificazioni peuro-psicobiochemiche indotte dalla LSD in schizofrenici e frenastenici. *Acta neurol.* (Napoli), 7:340, 1952

10   Benedetti, G: Beispiel einer strukturanalytischen und pharmakodynamischen Untersuchung an einem Fall von Alkoholhalluzinose, Charakterneurose und psychoreaktiver Halluzinose. *Z. Psychother. med. Psychol.* 1:177, 1951

11   Bentov, I: *Stalking the Wild Pendulum.* E. P. Dutton, New York, 1977

12   Blewett, D: Psychedelic Drugs in Parapsychological Research. *Internat. J. Parapsychol.* 5:43, 1963

13   Bohm, D: Quantum Theory as an Indication of a New Order in Physics. Part A. The Development of New Orders as Shown Through the History of Physics. *Foundations of Physics.* 1:359, 1971
Part B. Implicate and Explicate Order in Physical Law. *Foundations of Physics.* 3:139, 1973

14   Bonny, H; Pahnke, W N: The Use of Music in Psychedelic (LSD) Psycho-
     therapy. *J. Music Therapy* 9:64, 1972

15   Bonny, H; Savary, L M: *Music and Your Mind.* Harper & Row, New York,
     1973

16   Brandrup, E; Vangaard, T: LSD Treatment in a Severe Case of Compulsive
     Neurosis. *Acta Psychiat. Scand.* 55:127, 1977

17   Busch, A K; Johnson, W C: LSD as an Aid in Psychotherapy. *Dis. Nerv.
     Syst.* 11:241, 1950

18   Capra, F: *The Tao of Physics.* Shambhala Publications, Berkeley,
     California, 1976

19   Cavanna, R; Servadio, E: ESP Experiences With LSD-25 and Psilocybin: A
     Methodological Approach. *Parapsychological Monograph No. 5*, 1964

20   Chew, G F: Bootstrap: A Scientific Idea? *Science* 161:762, 1968

21   Condrau, G: Klinische Erfahrungen an Geisteskranken mit LSD-25. *Acta
     Psychiat. Neurol. Scand.* 24:9, 1949

22   Deren, M: *Divine Horsemen: The Living Gods of Haiti.* Thames and Hud-
     son, London, 1953

23   Ditman, K S; Whittlesey, J R B: Comparison of the LSD-25 Experience and
     Delirium Tremens. *Arch. gen. Psychiat.* 1:47, 1959

24   Dubánsky, J et al.: Personal communication

25   Eysenck, H. J; Rachman, S: *The Causes and Cures of Neurosis.* R. R. Knap,
     San Diego, 1965

26   Feld, M; Goodman, J R; Guido, J A: Clinical and Laboratory Observations
     on LSD-25. *J. Nerv. Ment. Dis.* 126:176, 1958

27   Fogel, S; Hoffer, A: The Use of Hypnosis to Interrupt and to Reproduce an
     LSD-25 Experience. *J. Clin. Exper. Psychopathol.* 23:11, 1962

28   Frederking, W; Intoxicant Drugs (Mescaline and LSD-25) in Psycho-
     therapy. *J. Nerv. Ment. Dis.* 121:262, 1953

29   Freud, S; Breuer, J: *Studies in Hysteria.* Translated by A. A. Brill. Nervous
     and Mental Diseases Publishing Co., New York, 1936

30   Giberti, F; Gregoretti, L; Boeri, G: L'impiego della LSD nelle psicone vrosi.
     Sist. nerv. 4:191, 1956

31   Godfrey, K: Personal communication

32   Grof, S: *Realms of the Human Unconscious: Observations from LSD
     Research.* E. P. Dutton, New York, 1976

33   Grof, S: Perinatal Roots of Wars, Totalitarianism and Revolutions. *J.
     Psychohistory* 4:269, 1977

34   Grof, S; Halifax, J: *The Human Encounter With Death.* E. P. Dutton, New
     York, 1977

35   Haeckel, E: *Art Forms in Nature.* Dover Publications, Inc., New York, 1974

36   Harman, W W; Fadiman, J: Selective Enhancement of Specific Capacities Through Psychedelic Training. *In* B Aaronson and H Osmond, eds.: *Psychedelics.* Doubleday Publications, Garden City, New York, 1970, p. 239

37   Herbert, N: *Mind Science: A Physics of Consciousness Primer.* C–Life Institute, Boulder Creek, California, 1979

38   Hofmann, A: The Chemistry of LSD and Its Modifications. *In* D V Sivasankar et al.: *LSD–A Total Study.* PJD Publications Ltd., Westbury, New York, 1975

39   Hugo, V: *Les Misérables.* Fawcett Publishing Co., New York, 1978

40   Izumi, K: LSD and Architectural Design. *In* B Aaronson and H Osmond, eds.: *Psychedelics.* Doubleday Publications, Garden City, New York, 1970, p. 381

41   Jost, F: Zur therapeutischen Verwendung des LSD-25 in der klinischen Praxis der Psychiatrie. *Wien Klin. Wschr.* 69:647, 1957

42   Jost, F; Vicari, R: Zu den Provokationsverfahren in der Medizin (LSD als Provokationsmittel). *Medizinische Nr.* 8:319, 1958

43   Jung, C G: A Review of the Complex Theory. In: *Collected Works of C G Jung.* 8:92. Bollingen Series XX, Princeton University Press, Princeton, N J, 1960

44   Jung, C G: Synchronicity: An Acausal Connecting Principle. In: *Collected Works of C G Jung.* 8:417, Bollingen Series XX, Princeton University Press, Princeton, N J, 1960

45   Kelsey, D; Grant, J: *Many Lifetimes.* Doubleday Publishing Company, Garden City, New York, 1967

46   Koestler, A: The God That Failed. In: *Six Studies in Communism.* Hamish Hamilton, London, 1950

47   Koestler, A: *Arrow in the Blue.* Hamish Hamilton, London, 1952

48   Koestler, A: *The Act of Creation.* Dell Publishing Co., New York, 1964

49   Krippner, S: The Cycle in Deaths Among U.S. Presidents Elected at Twenty-Year Intervals. *Internat. J. Parapsychol.* 145, 1967

50   Krippner, S; Davidson, R: Paranormal Events Occurring During Chemically Induced Psychedelic Experience and Their Implications for Religion. *J. Altered States of Consciousness* 1:175, 1974

51   Krippner, S: Research in Creativity and Psychedelic Drugs. *Internat. J. clin. exp. Hypnosis* 25:274, 1977

52   Laing, R D: *Politics of Experience.* Ballantine Books, New York, 1976

53   Lamb, F B: *Wizard of the Upper Amazon: The Story of Manuel Cordova-Rios.* Houghton Mifflin Co., Boston, 1971

54   Leary, T; Metzner, R; Alpert, R: *The Psychedelic Experience: A Manual Based on the Tibetan Book of the Dead.* University Books, New Hyde Park, N Y, 1954

55   Leary, T et al.: A New Behavior Change Program Using Psilocybin. In: *Psychotherapy: Theory, Research and Practice.* Vol 2: No 2, July, 1965

56   LeShan, L: *The Medium, the Mystic, and the Physicist: Toward a General Theory of the Paranormal.* An Esalen Book, The Viking Press, New York, 1974

57   Leuner, H: *Die experimentelle Psychose.* Springer-Verlag, Berlin, Göttingen, Heidelberg, 1962

58   Levine, J; Ludwig, A M: The Hypnodelic Treatment Technique. *In* H A Abramson, ed.: *The Use of LSD in Psychotherapy and Alcoholism.* The Bobbs-Merrill Co. Inc., New York, 1967

59   Ludwig, A M; Levine, J; Stark, L H: *LSD and Alcoholism: A Clinical Study of Treatment Efficacy.* Charles C. Thomas, Springfield, Ill., 1970

60   MacLean, J R et al.: The Use of LSD-25 in the Treatment of Alcoholism and Other Psychiatric Problems. *Quart. J. Stud. Alcoh.* 22:34, 1961

61   Maier, G J; Tate, D L; Paris, B D: The F Ward LSD Community; The Use of LSD in a Therapeutic Community Within a Maximum Security Setting. Mimeographed paper

62   Martin, A J: LSD Treatment of Chronic Psychoneurotic Patients Under Day-Hospital Conditions. *Internat. J. sos. Psychiat.* 3:188, 1957

63   Maslow, A: *Toward A Psychology of Being.* Van Nostrand, Princeton, N J, 1962

64   Maslow, A: A Theory of Metamotivation: The Biological Rooting of the Value-Life. *In* A Sutich and M A Vich, eds.: *Readings in Humanistic Psychology.* The Free Press, New York, 1969

65   Masters, R E L; Houston, J: *The Varieties of Psychedelic Experience.* Dell Publishing Co., New York, 1966

66   Masters, R E L; Houston, J: *Psychedelic Art.* Grove Press, New York, 1968

67   Masters, R E L; Houston, J: *Mind Games: The Guide to Inner Space.* Dell Publishing Co., 1972

68   McCririck, P: The Importance of Fusion in Therapy and Maturation. Unpublished mimeographed paper

69   McGovern, W: *Jungle Paths and Inca Ruins.* Grosset and Dunlap, New York, 1927

70   Miller, E: *Selective Awareness.* Offset Publication, Menlo Park, 1975

71   Mogar, R E: Current Status and Future Trends in Psychedelic (LSD) Research. *J. Humanistic Psychol.* 4:147, 1965

72   Orr, L; Ray, S: *Rebirthing in the New Age.* Celestial Arts, Milbrae, California, 1977

73   Osis, K: Psychobiological Research Possibilities; & A Pharmacological Approach to Parapsychological Experimentation. In: *Proceedings of Two Conferences on Parapsychology and Pharmacology.* Parapsychology Foundation, New York, 1961

74   Osmond, H: A Review of the Clinical Effects of Psychotomimetic Agents. *Ann. N.Y. Acad. Sci.* 66:418, 1957

75   Pahnke, W: The Good Friday Experiment. Doctoral Dissertation, Harvard University, 1965

76   Pahnke, W N; Richards, W A: *Implications of LSD and Experimental Mysticism. J. Religion and Health* 5:175, 1966

77   Pahnke, W N; Kurland, A A; Unger, S; Savage, C; Grof, S: The Experimental Use of Psychedelic (LSD) Psychotherapy. *J. Amer. Med. Assoc.* 212:1856, 1970

78   Pelletier, K R: *Toward a Science of Consciousness.* A Delta Book, New York, 1978

79   Perls, F: *The Gestalt Approach & Eye Witness to Therapy.* Bantam Books, New York, 1976

80   Perry, J: *The Far Side of Madness.* Prentice-Hall, Englewood Cliffs, N J, 1974

81   Pribram, K: *Languages of the Brain.* Prentice-Hall, Englewood Clifs, N J, 1971

82   Pribram, K: Problems Concerning the Structure of Consciousness. *In* G Globus et al.: *Consciousness and the Brain.* Plenum Publishing Corp, New York, 1976

83   Ram Dass: *Remember, Be Here Now.* Lama Foundation, San Cristobal, New Mexico, 1971, distributed by Crown Publishing, New York

84   Rappaport, M et al.: *Selective Drug Utilization in the Management of Psychosis.* NIMH Grant Report, MH-16445, March, 1974

85   Rinkel, M: The Psychological Aspects of the LSD Psychosis. *In* M Rinkel, ed.: *Chemical Concepts of Psychosis.* McDowell, New York, 1958

86   Robinson, J T et al.: A Controlled Trial of Abreaction With LSD-25. *Brit. J. Psychiat.* 109:46, 1963

87   Roquet, S: *Operación Mazateca: Estudio de hongos y otras plantas allucinogenas Mexicanastratamiento psicoterapeutico de psicosintesis.* Asociacíon Albert Schweitzer, Mexico City, 1971

88   Rothlin, E: Pharmacology of LSD and Some of Its Related Compounds. In: *Psychotropic Drugs.* Elsevier Publishing Co., Amsterdam, 1957

89   Roubíček, J; Srnec, J: "Experimentální psychosa vyvolaná LSD (Experimental Psychosis Induced by LSD). *Čas. Lék čes.* 94:189, 1955

90   Roubíček, J: *Experimentální psychosy (Experimental Psychoses).* Státní zdravotnické nakladatelství, Prague, 1961

91   Sandison, R A; Spencer, A M; Whitelaw, J D A: The Therapeutic Value of LSD-25 in Mental Illness. *J. Ment. Sci.* 100:491, 1954

92   Sandison, R A; Whitelaw, J D A: Further Studies in the Therapeutic Value of LSD-25 in Mental Illness. *J. Ment. Sci.* 103:332, 1957

93   Savage, C; McCabe, O L: Psychedelic (LSD) Therapy of Drug Addiction. *In* C C Brown; C Savage, eds.: *The Drug Abuse Controversy.* Friends Medical Science Research Center, Baltimore, Md., 1971

94   Silverman, J: Acute Schizophrenia: Disease or Dis-Ease? In: *Readings in Psychology Today.* CRM Books, San Francisco, 1972

95   Silverman, J: *Stormy Journey Towards One's Self: On the story of Acute Schizophrenia and Other Dis-eases in Consciousness.* Pending Publication

96   Stewart, K: Dream Theory in Malaya. *In* Charles Tart, ed.: *Altered States of Consciousness.* Anchor Books, Garden City, New York, 1972

97   Stoll, W A: LSD, ein Phantastikum aus der Mutterkorngruppe. *Schweiz Arch. Neurol. Psychiat.* 60:279, 1947

98   Stoll, A; Hofmann, A; Troxler, F: Ueber die Isomerie von Lysergsäure und Isolysergsäure. *Helv. chim. Acta.* 32:506, 1949

99   Tarnas, R: *Prometheus the Awakener.* Pending publication

100   Tart, C: Psychedelic Experiences Associated with a Novel Hypnotic Procedure, Mutual Hypnosis. *Amer. J. Clin. Hypnosis.* 10:65, 1967

101   Toben, B; Sarfatti, J: *Space–Time and Beyond.* E. P. Dutton, New York, 1975

102   Whittlesey, J R B: Some Curious ESP Results in Terms of Variance. *J. Parapsychol.* 24:220, 1960

103   Wilber, K: *The Spectrum of Consciousness.* A Quest Book. The Theosophical Publishing House, Wheaton, Ill., 1977

104   Woolley, D W; Shaw, E: A Biochemical and Pharmacological Suggestion About Certain Mental Disorders. *Proc. Nat. Acad. Sci.* 40:228, 1954

105   Young, A M: *The Reflexive Universe.* Delacorte Press, New York, 1976

APPENDIX:
Crisis Intervention in Situations
Related to Unsupervised Use
of Psychedelics

I

Since the mid-sixties, when experimentation with LSD and other psychedelics moved from psychiatric institutes and clinics to private homes and public places, the role of mental health professionals in regard to these substances has been drastically redefined. Instead of being in the forefront as experimenters and researchers they have become the rescuers and undertakers called upon to deal with the casualties of the psychedelic scene. This development has contributed considerably to the present attitudes of most professionals toward these drugs; the primary focus of psychiatrists and psychologists has shifted from the therapeutic potential of psychedelics to their dangers. In the highly emotional atmosphere created by sensational publicity, professionals have allowed their image of LSD to be shaped by journalists and newspaper headlines rather than scientific data generated by research. Consequently, the casualties and complications of unsupervised experimentation with LSD, instead of being attributed to irresponsible and ignorant use, have been interpreted as reflecting dangers inherent in the drug itself.

Restrictive legislation has practically destroyed scientific research of psychedelic substances, but has not been very effective in curbing unsupervised experimentation. While samples of psychedelic drugs of doubtful quality are readily available in the streets and on college campuses, it is nearly impossible for a serious researcher to get a license for scientific investigation of their effects. As a result of this, professionals are in a very paradoxical situation: they are expected to give expert help in an area in which they are not allowed to conduct research and generate new scientific information. The widespread use of psychedelics and relatively high incidence of drug-related problems are in sharp contrast to the lack of understanding of the phenomena involved; this is true for the general public as well as the majority of mental health professionals.

This situation has very serious practical consequences. Various emergencies associated with psychedelic drug use are handled in a way that is at best ineffective, but more likely counter-productive and harmful. Crisis intervention in psychedelic sessions and treatment of the long-term adverse effects of unsupervised self-experimentation are issues of such medical and social relevance that they deserve special attention. Much of the information that is essential for understanding the problems involved and for an effective approach to this area has been presented in various sections of this book. However, because of the importance of the problem I will briefly review the most pertinent data here and apply them to the area in question.

THE NATURE AND DYNAMICS OF PSYCHEDELIC CRISES

Understanding the dynamics of psychedelic experiences is absolutely necessary for effective crisis intervention. A difficult LSD experience, unless it results from a gross abuse of the individual, represents an exteriorization of a potentially pathogenic matrix in the subject's unconscious. If properly handled, a psychedelic crisis has great positive potential and can result in a profound personality transformation. Conversely, an insensitive and ignorant approach can cause psychological damage and lead to chronic psychotic states and years of psychiatric hospitalization.

Before discussing the difficult experiences that occur in psychedelic sessions, their causes, and the principles of crisis intervention, we will summarize our previous discussions about the nature and basic dynamics of the LSD process. LSD does not produce a drug-specific state with certain stereotypical characteristics; it can best be described as a catalyst or amplifier of mental processes that mediates access to hidden recesses of the human mind. As such, it activates deep repositories of unconscious material and brings their content to the surface, making it available for direct experience.

A person taking the drug will not experience an "LSD state" but a fantastic journey into his or her own mind. All the phenomena encountered during this journey—images, emotions, thoughts and psychosomatic processes—should thus be seen as manifestations of latent capacities in the experient's psyche rather than symptoms of "toxic psychosis." In the LSD state the sensitivity to external factors and circumstances is intensified to a great degree. These extrapharmacological influences involve all the factors usually referred to as "set and setting": the subject's understanding of the effects of the drug and purpose of ingestion, their general approach to the experience, and the physical and interpersonal elements of the situation. A difficult LSD experience thus reflects either a pathogenic constellation in the experient's unconscious, traumatic circumstances, or a combination of the two.

Ideal conditions for an LSD session involve a simple, safe and beautiful physical environment and an interpersonal situation that is supportive, reassuring and nourishing. Under these circumstances, when disturbing external stimuli are absent, negative LSD experiences can be seen as psychological work on the traumatic areas of one's unconscious. It is essential for the good outcome of an LSD session to keep it internalized and fully experience and express everything that is emerging. Psychedelic sessions in which the subject does not stay with the process tend to create a dysbalance in the basic dynamics of the unconscious. The defense system is weakened by the effect of the drug, but the unconscious material that has been released is not adequately worked through and integrated. Such sessions are conducive to prolonged reactions or to subsequent "flashbacks."

The only way to facilitate the completion and integration of an LSD session in which the experiential gestalt remains unfinished is to continue the uncovering work, with or without psychedelics. It is important to emphasize that the effect of LSD is essentially self-limited; the overwhelming majority of difficult psychedelic experiences reach a resolution quite spontaneously. Actually, those states that are most dramatic and stormy tend to have the best outcome. The use of tranquillizers in the middle of a psychedelic session is a grave error and may be harmful. It tends to prevent the natural resolution of the difficult emotional or psychosomatic gestalt and to "freeze" the experience in a negative phase. The only constructive approach is to provide basic protection to the subject, and support and facilitate the process; the least one can do is to not interfere with it.

After this brief introduction, we can return to the problem of complications during unsupervised psychedelic experimentation. Although the basic principles discovered during clinical research with LSD are directly applicable to crisis intervention, it is important to emphasize the basic differences between the two situations. The LSD administered in clinical and laboratory research is pharmaceutically pure and its quality can be accurately gauged; most black market samples do not meet these criteria. Only a small fraction of a "street acid" specimen is relatively pure LSD; the black market preparations frequently contain various impurities or admixtures of other drugs. In some of the street samples that have been analyzed in laboratories, researchers have detected amphetamines, STP, PCP, strychnine, benactyzine, and even traces of urine. There have been instances where alleged LSD samples contained some combination of the above substances and no LSD whatsoever. The poor quality of many of the street specimens is certainly responsible for some of the adverse reactions that occur in the context of unsupervised self-experimentation. In addition, uncertainty about quality and dosage and the resulting fears can have a negative influence on the ability of the subject to tolerate unpleasant experiences, which are then readily interpreted as signs of toxicity or overdose rather than manifestations of the users' unconscious.

However, the quality of drug and the uncertainty about it seem to be responsible for a relatively small fraction of the adverse reactions to LSD. There is no doubt that extrapharmacological elements, such as the personality of the subject and the set and setting, are by far the most important factors.

In order to understand the frequency and seriousness of psychedelic crises that occur in the context of unsupervised self-experimentation, it is important to take into consideration the circumstances under which many people tend to take LSD. Some of them are given the drug without any prior information about it, without adequate preparation, and sometimes even without forewarning. The general understanding of the effects of LSD is poor, even among experienced users. Many of them take LSD for entertainment and have no provisions in their conceptual framework for painful, frightening and disorganizing experiences. Unsupervised experimentation frequently takes place in complex and confusing physical and interpersonal settings that can contribute many important traumatic elements. The hectic atmosphere of large cities, busy highways in the rush hour, crowded rock concerts or discos, and noisy social gatherings are certainly not settings conducive to productive self-exploration and safe confrontation with the difficult aspects of one's unconscious.

Personal support and a relationship of trust are absolutely crucial for a safe and successful LSD session, and these are seldom available under these circumstances. Not infrequently the person under the influence of LSD is surrounded by total strangers. In some other instances good friends may be present, but they are themselves under the influence of the drug or are unable to tolerate and handle intense and dramatic emotional experiences. When a group of people take LSD together, the painful experiences of one person can create a negative atmosphere which contaminates the sessions of others. There have even been episodes in which persons who took LSD or were given the drug were, for a variety of reasons, exposed to deliberate psychological abuse. It is easy to understand that such toxic circumstances are highly conducive to adverse reactions.

PROFESSIONAL CRISIS INTERVENTION AND THE SELF-HELP APPROACHES

The present intervention offered by professionals in psychedelic crises is based on the medical model and usually creates more problems than it solves. The steps typically taken under these circumstances reflect a serious lack of understanding of the nature of the psychedelic experience, and are conducive to long-term complications. This is further complicated by the numerous demands on the time of a mental health practitioner and a lack of adequate facilities for handling casualties from the psychedelic scene. The tranquillizers that are routinely administered under these circumstances tend to prevent effective resolution of the underlying conflict and thus contribute to the incidence of chronic emotional and psychosomatic difficulties after the session. Instant transfer of the individual to a psychiatric facility in the middle of the LSD experience is not only unnecessary, but represents a dangerous and harmful practice. It disregards the fact that the LSD state is self-limiting; in most instances, a dramatic negative experience if properly handled will result in a beneficial resolution and the subject will not need any further treatment. The "emergency transfer" to a psychiatric facility, particularly if it involves an ambulance, creates an atmosphere of danger and urgency that contributes considerable additional trauma for a person who is already extremely sensitized by the psychedelic state and the painful emotional crisis. The same is true of the admission procedure in the psychiatric facility and the atmosphere of the locked ward which is the final destination of many psychedelic casualties.

Exposure to the routines of the psychiatric machinery while under the influence of LSD can cause a life-long trauma. The fact that psychiatric diagnosis and hospitalization may often represent a serious social stigma is another important factor to consider before proceeding with an unnecessary transfer and admission. Moreover, if the LSD process does not reach a satisfactory resolution, contemporary psychiatric care applies continued medication with tranquillizers instead of the uncovering therapy that is the preferred treatment under these circumstances.

The basic points of the above discussion can be illustrated with the following example:

When I was working in the Psychiatraic Research Institute in Prague,

Czechoslovakia, I was asked as consultant to see two employees of the pharmaceutical laboratories that were involved in the production of LSD. They had both suffered delayed adverse effects of an accidental intoxication with LSD, while synthesizing the drug. One of them, a man in his forties who was heading the department, showed symptoms of deep depression with occasional bouts of anxiety, a sense of meaninglessness of existence, and doubts about his sanity. He dated these symptoms to the time of his intoxication with LSD and subsequent brief hospitalization in a psychiatric facility. His assistant, a woman in her twenties who had experienced accidental intoxication with LSD several months after he did, complained about bizarre sensations in her scalp; she was convinced that she was rapidly losing her hair, although there were no objective signs to support this.

During the diagnostic interviews with them I tried to reconstruct the circumstances of their LSD experiences and the dynamics of the problems they presented. The story that I heard, although unbelievable of LSD therapists or people familiar with the nature of psychedelic states, is unfortunately a typical example of crisis intervention based on the conventional medical and psychiatric models. The pharmaceutical laboratories that were involved in the production of LSD were situated approximately two hundred miles from Prague, where most of the clinical and laboratory research with psychedelics was happening at that time. When the management received the order to start the synthesis of Czechoslovakian LSD, it was felt that, because of the nature of the substance, the staff should be informed about its effects and instructed about the necessary measures in case of accidental intoxication. The director invited from the nearby state mental hospital a psychiatrist who had no personal or professional experience of LSD and prepared himself by reading a few papers on the "model psychosis" approach to schizophrenia. During the seminar with the staff, this superficially informed psychiatrist managed to paint an apocalyptic picture of LSD. He told them that this colorless, odorless and tasteless substance could insidiously enter their system, as had happened to Dr. Albert Hofmann, and induce a state of schizophrenia. He suggested that they should keep a supply of Thorazine in their first-aid kit and in case of accidental intoxication bring the tranquilized victim without delay to the psychiatric hospital.

As a result of these instructions, both laboratory workers received Thorazine shortly after they had started to feel the effects of the drug, and were rushed in an ambulance to the locked ward of the state mental hospital. There they spent the rest of the intoxication period and a few following days in the company of psychotic patients. While under the influence of the LSD-Thorazine combination, the department chief witnessed several *grand mal* seizures and had a long discussion with a patient who was showing him his wounds after a suicide attempt. The fact that he was put by mental health experts in the company of severely disturbed patients contributed considerably to his fear that he might himself be developing a similar condition. Analysis of his LSD state, which was only incompletely truncated by the Thorazine medication, showed that he was experiencing elements of BPM II, and the confinement in the locked ward and his adventures there represented a powerful reinforcement of his desperate state.

The experience of his research assistant was more superficial; her reaction to the atmosphere of the locked ward was to pull herself together and maintain control at any cost. Retrospective analysis of her experience showed that she was approaching a traumatic childhood memory, but because of the external circumstances she suppressed it and prevented it from surfacing. Her feeling of losing her hair turned out to be a symptom related to this deep psychological regression; the infantile body image corresponding to the age when she experienced the traumatic event involved hairlessness as a natural condition.

During their visit to the Psychiatric Research Institute in Prague these two pharmaceutical workers were able not only to work on their symptoms, but also to change their image of LSD and the negative feelings associated with it. We explained to them the nature of the LSD state and discussed with them our therapeutic program and the principles of conducting sessions. Before they left they had ample opportunity to discuss the effects of LSD with patients undergoing psycholytic treatment who had experienced their sessions under substantially different circumstances. I assured them that there was no reason for alarm if someone was intoxicated by LSD; as a matter of fact, we were producing situations like that routinely in our program. They were advised to have a special, quiet room where the intoxicated individual could spend the rest of the day listening to music in the company of a good friend.

Several months later, I received a call from the department chief. He told me that they had had another "accident"; a nineteen-year-old laboratory assistant had experienced a professional intoxication. She spent the day in a comfortable room adjacent to her laboratory in the company of her friend and "had the time of her life." She found her experience very pleasant, interesting and beneficial.

The avoidance techniques developed by the self-help movement, although less harmful than the approach based on the medical and psychiatric model, are also counterproductive. Attempts to engage the subject in superficial conversations ("talking them down"), to distract them by showing them flowers and beautiful pictures, or taking them for a walk does not solve the underlying problem. This can be seen at best as playing for time—keeping the individual occupied with distracting maneuvers until the crisis subsides or diminishes with the waning of the pharmacological effect of the drug. These approaches are based on the erroneous assumption that the drug has created the problem. Once we realize that we are dealing with the dynamics of the unconscious, not a pharmacological state, the short-sightedness of this approach becomes obvious. The danger in using techniques that encourage avoidance lies in the failure to confront and resolve the unconscious material that underlies the emotional and psychosomatic crisis. LSD sessions in which the emerging gestalt is not completed are conducive to prolonged reactions, negative emotional and physical aftereffects, and "flashbacks".

COMPREHENSIVE CRISIS INTERVENTION
IN PSYCHEDELIC EMERGENCIES

Having discussed the factors that contribute to the development of emergencies in unsupervised LSD sessions and described the harmful practices that characterize most professional and lay interventions, I would like to outline what I consider the optimal approach to psychedelic crises, based on the understanding of their dynamics. What constitutes an emergency in an LSD session is highly relative, and depends on a variety of factors. It reflects an interplay between the subject's own feelings about the experience, the opinions and tolerance of the people present, and the judgment of the professional called upon to offer help. This last is a factor of critical importance; it depends upon the therapist's degree of understanding of the processes involved, his or her clinical experience with unusual states of consciousness, and his or her freedom from anxiety. In psychedelic crisis intervention, as in psychiatric practice in general, drastic measures frequently reflect the helpers' own feelings of threat and insecurity, not only vis à vis possible external danger, but also in relation to their own unconscious. The experience from LSD therapy and the new experiential psychotherapies clearly indicates that exposure to another person's deep emotional material tends to shatter psychological defenses and to activate corresponding areas in the unconscious of the persons assisting and witnessing the process, unless they have confronted and worked through these levels in themselves. Since traditional psychotherapies are limited to work on biographical material, even a professional with full training in analysis is inadequately prepared to deal with powerful experiences of a perinatal and transpersonal nature. The prevailing tendency to put all such experiences into the category of schizophrenia and suppress them in every way reflects not only a lack of understanding, but also a convenient self-defense against the helpers' own unconscious material.

As the sophistication and clinical experience of LSD therapists has increased, it has become more and more evident that negative episodes in psychedelic sessions should not be seen as unpredictable accidents, but intrinsic and lawful aspects of the therapeutic work with traumatic unconscious material. From this point of view the colloquial term "bummer" or "bad trip" does not make sense. To an experienced LSD therapist an unsuccessful psychedelic session is not one in which the subject experiences panic anxiety, self-destructive tendencies, abysmal guilt, loss of control, or difficult physical sensations. If properly handled, a painful and difficult LSD session can bring about an important therapeutic breakthrough. It can facilitate resolution of problems that have plagued the subject in subtle ways for many years and contaminated his or her everyday life. An unsuccessful session, however, is one in which difficult feelings begin to emerge, the subject does not fully surrender to the process and the gestalt remains unresolved. From this point of view, all psychedelic experiences in which the process is thwarted by the administration of tranquillizers and external distractions such as transfer to a psychiatric hospital are not failures because of the nature of the psychological process involved, but because the crisis management has interfered with a positive resolution.

Although LSD can induce difficult experiences even under the best circumstances, it would be a mistake to attribute all "bad trips" to the drug itself. The psychedelic state is determined by a variety of non-drug factors; the incidence of serious complications depends critically on the personality of the subject, and the elements of set and setting. This can be illustrated by comparing the incidence of complications during the early supervised experimentation with LSD, and the psychedelic scene of the sixties. In 1960, Sidney Cohen published a paper entitled, *LSD: Side Effects and Complications. J. Nerv. Ment. Dis. 130:30, 1960.* It was based on reports from forty-four professionals who had administered LSD and mescaline to about five thousand persons over twenty-five thousand times; the number of sessions per person ranging between one and eighty. In the group of normal volunteers, the incidence of attempted suicides after the session was less than one in a thousand cases, and that of prolonged reactions lasting over forty-eight hours was 0.8 per thousand. The numbers were somewhat higher when psychiatric patients were used as subjects; in every thousand patients there were 1.2 suicide attempts, 0.4 completed suicides and 1.8 prolonged reactions lasting over forty-eight hours. In comparison with other methods of psychiatric therapy, therefore, LSD appeared to be unusually safe, particularly when contrasted with other procedures used routinely in psychiatric treatment at that time, such as electroshocks, insuline comas, and psychosurgery. These statistics contrast sharply with the incidence of adverse reactions and complications associated with unsupervised experimentation. During my visit to the Haight-Ashbury clinic in San Francisco in the late sixties, I was told by its director David Smith that they were treating an average of fifteen "bad trips" a day. Although this does not necessarily mean that all these clients had long-lasting adverse effects from their psychedelic experiences, it illustrates the issue in question.

The experience and sophistication of psychiatrists and psychologists in relation to psychedelics was certainly not great during the early years and the settings were far from ideal. However, the sessions reported in Dr. Cohen's paper were conducted in protected environments, under reasonable supervision and by responsible individuals. In addition, those who had difficult experiences were in a place that was equipped to provide help in case of need and they did not have to be subjected to the absurd ordeal of transfer to a psychiatric facility.

The psychedelic crisis is caused by a complicated interplay of internal and external factors. The therapist has to distinguish which of the two sets of influences is more important and proceed accordingly. The first and most important step in handling a psychedelic crisis is to create a simple, safe and supportive physical and interpersonal environment for the subject. In cases where external factors seem to have played a crucial role, it is important to remove the individual from the traumatic situation or change it by active intervention. If the crisis occurred in a public locale, he or she should to be taken to a quiet, secluded place. If the incident happens during a party in a private residence, it is important to simplify the situation by moving to a separate room or asking the guests to leave. A few close friends who appear sensitive and mature may be asked to assist in the process. They can provide group support or help the subject to actively work through the underlying problem during the termination period of the session. The techniques of group involvement in psychedelic sessions have been discussed earlier in this book (p. 145).

After creating a safe environment the next important task is to establish good contact with the subject. A relationship of trust is probably the most significant prerequisite for the positive outcome of a psychedelic session in general and for successful handling of a crisis in particular. A person asked to intervene in a crisis triggered by LSD is at a great disadvantage as compared to an LSD therapist facing a similar situation in the course of psychedelic treatment, because the therapeutic session is preceded by a drug-free preparation period during which there is enough time to establish good contact and a relationship of trust. If a difficult situation arises in the course of an LSD series, the client can also draw on his or her memories of previous sessions where painful experiences had been successfully worked through and integrated with the help of the therapist.

In contrast, the professional dealing with a crisis outside of the therapeutic context walks into the emergency situation as a stranger, usually without any previous contact with the subject and other persons involved. Trust and cooperation have to be established in a very short time and often under dramatic circumstances. Freedom from anxiety, an ability to remain centered, deep empathy, and intimate knowledge of the dynamics of psychedelic states are the only means of generating trust under these circumstances.

It is essential to convey a sense of safety and security by emphasizing the self-limiting nature of the LSD experience. No matter how critical the condition appears to be, in most instances it will be resolved spontaneously five to eight hours after the ingestion of the drug. This time limit should be clearly communicated to the subject and other people present; until that time there is absolutely no reason to panic or worry, however dramatic the emotional and psychosomatic manifestations might be. It is also of great advantage to keep the subject in a reclining position, but this should be attained without using physical force and open restraint. With a little experience, one can develop a technique with which it is possible to effectively restrain the individual using a context of support and cooperation rather than conflict.

When adequate contact has been established, a positive framework should be offered for the difficult LSD experience. It is essential to present it as an opportunity to face and work through certain traumatic aspects of one's unconscious rather than as an unfortunate and tragic accident. A person assisting in a psychedelic crisis should make consistent attempts to internalize the experience of the LSD subject and encourage him or her to face the critical issues involved. The LSD subject should be encouraged to keep his or her eyes closed and confront the experience, whatever it is. The therapist should repeatedly communicate to the subject that the quickest way out of this difficult state is through surrendering to the emotional and physical pain, experiencing it fully and finding appropriate channels to express it. This process of surrendering can be greatly facilitated by music. If a good high-fidelity stereo set is available, and the subject is open to it, music should be introduced into the situation as soon as possible.

When good rapport has been established, it is possible to offer active assistance using comforting physical contact, elements of playful struggle, and pressure on or massage of the parts of the body where the energy appears to be blocked. This should not be done if the trust bond is precarious or absent; it is absolutely contraindicated if the subject is paranoid and includes the people present among his or her persecutors. In some instances simply being with the client and playing for time might be the only solution. Under such circumstances, it is essential to use any possible means and existing resources to keep the LSD subject from hurting himself or others and causing serious material damage. While following this basic rule, occasional attempts should be made to establish rapport and gain the individual's cooperation.

If the gestalt of the experience remains unfinished when the effect of the drug is subsiding, psychological and physical activity should be used to facilitate integration. Ideally, the subject should complete the session feeling comfortable and relaxed, without any residual emotional or psychosomatic symptoms. The two techniques that have proven useful in this context—the abreactive approach and the cleansing hyperventilation—have been discussed earlier in this book (pp. 144-5, 147-8). After the subject reaches a psychologically and physically comfortable state, it is important to create a safe and nourishing atmosphere for the rest of the day and night. Ideally, a person who has been through a psychedelic crisis should not be left alone for at least twenty-four hours after the ingestion of the drug. After this time the therapist should see the client again, reevaluate the situation and, depending on his or her condition, choose the future strategy. In most instances no further provisions are necessary if the crisis was properly handled. It is useful to discuss the LSD experience in detail and facilitate its integration into the client's everyday life. If significant emotional and psychosomatic complaints have appeared as a result of the LSD experience, arrangements should be made for follow-up uncovering therapy and body work. An individualized selection of meditation techniques, Gestalt practice, neo-Reichian approaches, guided imagery with music, controlled breathing, polarity massage or rolfing should be offered to the client.

Where the clinical condition remains precarious despite all the uncovering work, this treatment may have to be continued on an in-patient basis. If all the above approaches prove ineffective, integration can be facilitated by chemical means. Ideally, a supervised psychedelic session should be scheduled after adequate preparation. This approach might seem paradoxical to the average mental health professional, since it involves administration of the same drug or category of drugs that apparently brought the client trouble in the first place. Yet judicious use of psychedelics under these circumstances is the preferred treatment. Clinical experiences have shown that it is extremely difficult to restore defenses by the use of covering techniques such as tranquillizers, once the unconscious has been opened by a powerful psychedelic substance. It is much easier to continue the uncovering strategy and facilitate completion of the unfinished gestalt.

Psilocybin, methylene-dioxy-amphetamine (MDA), tetrahydrocannabinol (THC), and dipropyltryptamine (DPT) are viable alternatives to LSD. They have the same general effects and are less contaminated by bad publicity. MDA and THC seem to be particularly useful in this context, because of their gentle effect and selective affinity to positive governing systems in the unconscious. Effective psychological work with these substances involves less emotional and psychosomatic pain than when LSD is used.

Since the above psychedelics are not readily available, and obtaining permission to use them involves tedious administrative procedures, a session with Ritaline (100–200 milligrams) or Ketalar (100–150 milligrams) might be a more feasible approach. Tranquillizers should not be used in any condition related to the use of psychedelic drugs until all the above uncovering approaches have been tried and have failed.

Powerful non-drug approaches could also be used in lieu of tranquillizers in all those cases where a poorly resolved LSD experience results in a long-term psychotic condition and psychiatric hospitalization lasting months or years. If these do not bring about sufficient clinical improvement, psychedelic therapy, using the substances mentioned above, is the next logical choice. Ketalar, a drug that is legally available and has been used in a medical context for general anesthesia could prove promising in these otherwise desperate cases.

I would like to conclude this discussion of psychedelic crisis intervention with a description of the most dramatic situation of this kind I have encountered in my professional career.

In my third year in Big Sur, California, I was awakened at 4:30 one morning by a telephone call. It was the night guard from the nearby Esalen Institute asking for help. A young couple called Peter and Laura, who were traveling down the coast, had parked their VW camper on coastal route 1 in the vicinity of the Esalen Institute and had decided to take LSD together. They rolled out the bed in their car and shortly after midnight both of them ingested the drug. Laura's experience was relatively smooth, but Peter progressively developed an acute psychotic state. He became paranoid and violent, and after a period of verbal aggression he started throwing things around and demolishing the car. At this point Laura panicked, locked him in the car and sought help at Esalen. She appeared at the guard shack completely naked, holding the car keys in her hand. The night guard knew about my previous work with psychedelics and decided to give me a call; he also woke up Rick Tarnas, a resident psychologist who had done his dissertation on psychedelic drugs.

While the guard was taking care of Laura, who calmed down and had a pleasant, uncomplicated LSD experience, Rick and I walked to the camper. As we approached the car we heard loud noises and shouting; when we came closer we noticed that several of the windows were broken. We unlocked the car, opened the door and started talking to Peter. We introduced ourselves and told him that we had had considerable experience with psychedelic states and had come to help him. I tentatively stuck my head inside the door and looked into the camper; a half-gallon bottle missed me by about four inches and landed on the dashboard. I repeated this several times, and two more objects came flying in my direction. When we felt that Peter had nothing more to throw, we quickly moved into the camper and lay down on the roll-out bed on either side of him.

We continued talking to Peter, reassuring him that everything would be all right in an hour or two; knowing that he and his girlfriend had taken LSD after midnight, we could give him this definite time limit. It became obvious that he was in a paranoid state and saw us as hostile FBI agents who had come to fetch him. We held his arms in a comforting and reassuring way, changing this into a firm grip whenever he made an attempt to escape, but avoiding real physical antagonism and struggle. All the while, we kept talking about having had difficult experiences ourselves, and finding them retrospectively useful. His condition oscillated for about an hour between mistrust with anxiety-laden aggressive impulses, and episodes of relief when it was possible to connect with him.

As time went by and the LSD state became less intense, Peter slowly developed trust. He was more and more willing to keep his eyes closed and face the experience, and we were even able to start working carefully on the blocked parts of his body, encouraging full emotional expression. By seven o'clock all negative elements completely disappeared from Peter's LSD experience. He felt cleansed and reborn, and was thoroughly enjoying the new day. His previous hostility turned into deep gratitude and he kept repeating how much he appreciated our intervention.

At about half-past-seven Laura appeared at the camper and joined us; she was herself in very good condition, but was naturally concerned about Peter. Rick and I helped dispel the negative aftermath of the dramatic events of the night and facilitated their reunion. We advised them strongly against driving that day. They spent a leisurely day by the Pacific Ocean and the next day continued their journey south. They were both in good spirits, although somewhat worried about the bill for the repair of their damaged camper.

APPENDIX:
The Effects of LSD on Chromosomes, Genetic Mutation, Fetal Development and Malignancy

II

In the last decade, a serious new dimension has been added to the LSD controversy. A number of scientific papers have been published indicating that LSD might cause structural changes in the chromosomes, genetic mutations, disturbances of embryonic development, and malignant degeneration of cells. However, a comparable number of publications question the accuracy of these allegations. Some are independent experimental studies which have yielded negative results, others criticize the original papers for serious conceptual and methodological inadequacies. Despite all the experimental work done in this area, and the vast expenditure of time and energy, the results are ambiguous and contradictory. It seems appropriate to include in this book a critical review of all the relevant research because the issue is extraordinarily important to the future of LSD psychotherapy.

The following discussion is based almost exclusively on careful study of the existing literature. I have limited firsthand research experience in this area, and genetics is not my primary field of interest and expertise. In the LSD study conducted in the Psychiatric Research Institute in Prague we did not examine the effect of LSD on the chromosomes or its implications for heredity; there were at that time no experimental or clinical observations that would suggest the need for such studies. The first paper that attracted the attention of scientists to this area did not appear until the late 1960's. (22)* After my arrival in the United States, I participated in a major study concentrating on structural changes of the chromosomes in the white blood cells following LSD administration. This was one of the few genetic studies using pure pharmaceutical LSD, a double-blind approach, and comparison of the samples before and after the administration of the drug. (106)

The material discussed in this review will be divided into several thematic groups. The first group includes papers describing structural changes of the chromosomes produced by LSD *in vitro*†; in these experiments various concentrations of LSD are added to cultures of cells from human, animal, or plant tissues in a test-tube. The second group involves *in vivo*† studies of LSD; in this type of

---

*Numbers apply to references that appear after this Appendix.
†*In vitro* literally means in glass, and refers to experiments conducted in test-tubes; *in vivo* is a medical term for experiments in living organisms.

research the effect of LSD is studied after the substance has been ingested by or injected into animals or humans. The papers in the third group describe the results of experiments studying the influence of LSD on the genes, and its mutagenic effects. It includes a small number of papers dealing with the detailed mechanism of the action of LSD on the deoxyribonucleic acid (DNA), the most important constituent of the chromosomes. The fourth group consists of publications describing the consequences of LSD administration on the growth, development and differentiation of human and animal embryos. Finally, the fifth group comprises papers focusing on the possible link between LSD and the development of malignant changes in cells, especially in the case of leukemia.

In the following sections, the most relevant findings in these five thematic categories will be briefly reviewed and critically evaluated.

THE EFFECT OF LSD ON CHROMOSOMAL STRUCTURE

The possibility of inducing structural changes in the chromosomes by exogenous agents such as radiation, viruses, and a variety of chemicals, has been a subject of great scientific interest for a long time. The genetic controversy about LSD started in 1967 when *Cohen, Marinello and Back* (22) published a paper suggesting that LSD should be added to the list of substances capable of causing abnormalities in the chromosomes. Because of the widespread use of LSD, this information created vivid interest in scientific circles, and a number of investigators focused their attention on this area. Two major approaches were used in these studies; in some the effect of LSD on the chromosomes was studied in the test tube (*in vitro*), in others in the living organism (*in vivo*). The cells studied were in most cases human white blood cells (lymphocytes).

In the *in vitro* studies, the blood samples were drawn from normal, healthy persons with no history of prior drug injection, radiation exposure, or recent viral infection. After incubation at 37° centigrade in appropriate media, colcemide was added to stop the cell division at the stage of metaphase. The cells were then harvested, made into specifically stained cytological preparations and examined with phase contrast microscopy. During the period of incubation, LSD dissolved in sterile distilled water was added to the experimental cultures in various concentrations.

In the *in vivo* studies, the blood samples were drawn from subjects who had been exposed to either "street acid" (illicit material allegedly containing LSD) or pharmaceutically pure LSD. In most of these studies, the chromosomes were examined after the exposure to LSD (retrospective approach); in a minority of these studies, the checkups were done both before and after the administration of the drug (prospective approach). The technical procedure employed in the *in vivo* studies did not differ significantly from that described for the *in vitro* approach. A special and rather important subgroup of the *in vivo* studies are reports about the influence of LSD on the chromosomes of the germinal cells (meiotic chromosomes).

IN VITRO STUDIES

Cohen, Marinello and Back (22) added LSD to cultured human leucocytes obtained from two healthy individuals. They used five concentrations ranging from 0.001 to 10.0 micrograms of LSD per cubic centimeter (cc), and the time of exposure was 4, 24, and 48 hours. The incidence of chromosome breaks for treated cells was at least twice that of control cells for all treatments, except at the lowest concentration and time (0.001 micrograms of LSD per cc for four hours) where no difference existed between treated and control cells. There was no simple linear relationship between the frequency of these aberrations and the LSD dosage or duration of exposure. In a later study, *Cohen, Hirschhorn and Frosch* (20) described the results of a larger study in which they used peripheral leucocyte cultures from six normal, healthy persons; the concentrations of LSD and the times of exposure were the same as in the original study. They found a significant inhibition of cellular division (mitosis) on addition of the drug in any concentration. The suppression of mitosis was directly proportional to the duration of exposure. The lowest frequency of chromosomal breakage among the controls was 3.9 percent of cells; among the treated cultures, the lowest frequency was almost twice the control (7.7 percent) and ranged to over four times the control value (17.5 percent).

In 1968, *Jarvik et al.* (63) tried to replicate some of the *in vitro* experiments of Cohen's group. In addition to LSD, they used as testing substances ergonovine (a drug commonly used in obstetric practice), aspirin, and streptonigrine. They found a higher incidence of chromosome breaks in the LSD samples (10.2 percent with the range 0.0–15.0) as compared to the control samples (5.2 percent with the range from 0.0–9.0). They found, however, approximately the same breakage rate with aspirin (10.0 percent) and ergonovine (9.6 percent). The concentration of LSD in blood used in this study approximates the level reached one to four hours after injection of 1,000 micrograms of LSD. On the other hand, the level of aspirin used was considerably below the common therapeutic level. Streptonigrine, a substance with a well-known dramatic effect on the chromosomes, induced chromosome breakage in 35 percent of the examined cells. It is interesting to note that two of the eight cases described in this paper did not respond to LSD with an increase in chromosome breaks.

Corey et al. (24) performed an *in vitro* study in ten individuals; 1 microgram per cc of LSD was added to the culture during the last twenty-four hours of incubation. The authors found an increase in chromosome breaks in all ten subjects. Although the *in vitro* concentration of LSD was much greater than any known comparable ingested dosage, the mean increase of 4.65 breaks per 100 cells was small compared to the range of frequencies (0.0–15.2) observed in the untreated cultures.

In this connection it is interesting to mention that *Singh, Kalia and Jain* (92) found an increased incidence of chromosome breakage in the cells of barley root as a result of exposure to LSD in the concentration 25 micrograms per cc. On the other hand, *MacKenzie and Stone* (73) reported negative results of experiments on lymphocytes, hamster fibroblasts and on the plant *Vicia faba*.

The above-mentioned findings of structural changes in chromosomes following LSD administration became the basis of speculations concerning the possible influence of this drug on genetic mutations, fetal development and malignancy. In the atmosphere of national hysteria then existing, the original report of *Cohen,*

Marinello and Back (22) was widely publicized by the mass media. As a result, the significance of their findings was considerably over-emphasized, and many premature conclusions were drawn for which there was not sufficient scientific justification.

Several important facts have to be taken into consideration before we can draw any substantial conclusions from the findings of increased chromosome breakage associated with LSD in the *in vitro* experiments. It must be emphasized that the findings themselves were not completely consistent. In several studies there were no indications of increased chromosome breakage following the exposure to LSD. (27, 73, 105). In addition, the concentrations of LSD and durations of exposure used in these studies were usually much greater than those occurring in the human organism after the ingestion of LSD in the commonly used dosages. *Cohen, Marinello and Back* (22) themselves did not find increased breakage of chromosomes at the lowest concentration and time (0.001 micrograms of LSD per cc for four hours). *Loughman et al.* (70) emphasized that it is precisely the lowest concentration and duration of exposure used in this study that most closely approximates the expected concentration in blood, liver and other organs after a dose of 100 micrograms of LSD ingested by a man weighing 70 kg. If the metabolic degradation of LSD is considered, then the effective concentration *in vivo* of unchanged LSD would be considerably less than this, approximating 0.0001 micrograms per cc—a concentration used only by *Kato and Jarvik*, (65) who found no increase in breakage at this dosage.

In general, special caution is required in extrapolating the *in vitro* findings to the situation in the living organism. The intact human organism differs from isolated cells in the test tube in its enormous complexity and in its ability to detoxify and excrete noxious compounds. Substances that are toxic *in vitro* do not necessarily have the same effect *in vivo*. In addition, some of the techniques used in the *in vitro* studies can create an artificial situation and introduce factors that do not exist in the living organism. This issue has been discussed in detail in an excellent review on LSD and genetic damage by *Dishotsky et al.* (28) These authors point to the fact that all the studies on cultured lymphocytes have used modifications of a technique in which the lymphocytes are stimulated by phytohemagglutinin to enter the reproductive cell cycle. In the normal state *in vivo*, small lymphocytes are in a phase of growth which precedes DNA synthesis; they do not grow, divide or enter the cell cycle. Thus, in the studies *in vitro*, lymphocytes are exposed to chemical agents during developmental stages of the cell cycle, including the synthesis of DNA, which do not normally occur in these cells in the body. Damage to a lymphocyte in this phase generally will not manifest itself as chromatid-type change in a subsequent division. Most, if not all chromatid-type changes are initiated by technical procedures, and the great majority of lesions reported in the *in vitro* and *in vivo* studies were of the chromatid type. The findings of an increased rate of chromosomal breakage in lymphocytes exposed to LSD *in vitro* must therefore be interpreted with great caution.

Many recent studies concerning the structural changes caused in chromosomes by LSD gave the impression that this effect was something specific and unique. Most of these reports have silently bypassed a fact that would have made the issue much less interesting and sensational. The changes in chromosomal structure described are not exclusively caused by LSD; they can be induced by a variety of other conditions and substances. Factors that have been known to cause chromosomal breakage *in vitro* include radiation, changes in temperature, variations in oxygen pressure, impurities in tap water unless it is distilled twice, and a variety of common viruses. The long list of chemical substances that increase the chromosomal breakage rates contains many commonly used drugs, including aspirin and other salicylates, artificial sweeteners, the insecticide DDT, morphine, caffeine, theobromine, theophylline, tranquillizers of the phenothiazine type, some vitamins and hormones, and many antibiotics such as aureomycin, chloromycetin, terramycin, streptomycin and penicillin.

In this connection it is interesting to quote *Sharma and Sharma*, (91) who have written an extensive summary of the literature on chemically induced chromosome breaks: "Since the first induction of chromosomal mutations by chemicals and the demonstration of definite chromosome breakage by Oehlkers, such a vast multitude of chemicals have been shown to possess chromosome breaking properties that the problem has become increasingly complex." *Jarvik*, (61) discussing the paper by *Judd, Brandkamp and McGlothlin*, (64) was even more explicit: ". . . and it is likely that any compound added at the appropriate time, in the appropriate amount, to the appropriate cell type, will cause chromosome breaks."

IN VIVO STUDIES

Because of the limitations of the *in vitro* approach, *in vivo* studies are preferred for assessing the possible genetic dangers associated with administration of LSD. Unfortunately, of the twenty-one reports that have been published by seventeen laboratories many have serious methodological shortcomings and are more or less inadequate, while individual reports contradict each other and their overall results are inconclusive. Two major approaches have been used in the *in vivo* studies. In fourteen of these projects, subjects were exposed to illicit substances of unknown composition and potency, some of which were alleged to be LSD. In eleven studies, individuals were exposed to known quantities of pharmaceutically pure LSD in experimental or therapeutic settings.

Dishotsky et al (28) published a review in which they presented a synopsis of the studies of this kind conducted prior to 1971. According to this review, of a total of 310 subjects studied, only 126 were treated with pure LSD; the other 184 subjects were exposed to illicit or "alleged" LSD. Eighteen of the 126 subjects (14.29 percent) in the group given pure LSD showed a higher frequency of chromosome aberration than the controls. In contrast, 89 of the 184 subjects (48.9 percent) in the group taking illicit LSD showed an increased incidence of aberrations—more than three times the frequence reported for subjects given pharmacologically pure LSD. Only 16.67 percent (18 of 108) of all the subjects reported to have chromosome damage, were given pure LSD. There is, therefore, good reason to discuss the two categories of *in vivo* studies, those with pure and those with "alleged" LSD, separately.

Illicit LSD and Chromosomal Damage
The initial findings of chromosomal damage in illicit LSD users were reported by *Irwin and Egozcue*. (57) They compared a group of eight illicit LSD users with a group of nine controls. The users had a mean breakage rate of 23.4 percent, more

than double the 11.0 percent rate in the controls. Only two of the eight users did not have increased breakage rates. In a later and more extensive study carried out by *Egozcue, Irwin and Maruffo*, (33) the mean breakage rate in forty-six illicit LSD users was 18.76 percent (with a range between 8 and 45 percent); this was more than double the rate of 9.03 percent found in control cells. Only three of the forty-six users did not have a breakage rate higher than the mean control rate. In addition, the authors studied the chromosomes of four infants exposed to LSD *in utero*. All four showed breakage rates above the mean control value. There was no evidence of disease or physical malformation in any of these children.

These findings were supported by *Cohen, Hirschhorn and Frosch*, (20) who studied eighteen subjects exposed to illicit LSD. They described an increased chromosomal breakage in this group (mean 13.2 percent) which was more than triple that of the control group (3.8 percent). The authors also examined the chromosomes of four children born to three mothers who took LSD during pregnancy. The frequency of chromosome breaks was elevated in all four, and was greater in the two children who were exposed to LSD during the third and fourth months of pregnancy than in the two infants exposed to low doses of LSD late in pregnancy.

In a later paper, *Cohen et al.* (21) reported that thirteen adults exposed to illicit LSD showed chromosome breakage rates that were above the control mean. In nine children exposed to illicit LSD *in utero*, they found a mean breakage of 9.2 percent, as compared with 4.0 percent in four children whose mothers had used illicit LSD before but not during pregnancy. The breakage rate in the control group was 1.0 percent. All but two children had been exposed to other drugs during pregnancy; all were in good health and showed no birth defects.

Nielsen, Friedrich and Tsuboi (82) found that their ten subjects exposed to illicit LSD had a mean breakage rate of 2.5 percent; this was significantly higher than that of the control group (0.2 percent). However, the allegedly pathological 2.5 percent rate is lower than that of the controls in other positive studies.

A number of investigators have not been able to demonstrate increased chromosome breakage in LSD users. The synoptic paper by *Dishotsky et al.* (28), quotes nine groups of researchers who reported negative results of similar studies. At the present time, therefore, the results of the *in vivo* studies are considered rather controversial and at best inconclusive.

Many investigators have attempted to offer explanations for the existing discrepancies between positive and negative reports. Some have criticized the breakage rate for controls in the studies by *Cohen et al.* (21) (3.8 percent) and *Irwin and Egozcue* (57) (11.9 percent and 9.03 percent) as being unusually high. Others have suggested that the high control values could have resulted from viral contamination of the cultures, insufficiently fortified media interfering with chromosome repair, technical variation in cell culturing, and the approach to chromosome evaluation. It was also pointed out that in these studies, chromosome-type and chromatid-type changes were not reported separately but were combined and then converted to "equivalent numbers of breaks." Combining the two types of aberrations in a single index obscures the distinction between real chromosome damage occurring *in vivo* and damage arising in the course of cell culture.

However, these factors cannot account for the discrepancies between the findings of various teams of investigators. If they did, the aberrations resulting from these effects would be randomly distributed between groups exposed to illicit LSD and control groups. Since the distribution is uneven, these factors do not explain the significantly elevated breakage rates in eighty of the eighty-six subjects exposed to illicit LSD studied by *Cohen et al.* and by *Irwin and Egozcue.*

A much more important clue to the understanding of this controversy seems to be related to certain characteristics of the group of the "LSD users." In this type of research, the investigators depend on the recall and reliability of the subjects in determining the type of drugs they have used in the past, the number and frequency of exposures, the alleged dosages, and interval since last exposure. Even in cases where the reports are accurate, the subjects usually do not know the content and the quality of the samples they are using. The content of pure LSD in the illicit LSD samples is almost always questionable, and various impurities and admixtures rather frequent. The samples analyzed in the past have been demonstrated to contain amphetamines, mescaline, DOM (4–methyl–2, 5–dimethoxyamphetamine, also called STP), phencyclidine (phenylcyclohexylpiperidine, PCP or "angel dust"), benactyzine and even strychnine. In addition, all the subjects tested used or abused drugs other than street LSD. These drugs included, among others, Ritaline, phenothiazines, alcohol, amphetamines, cocaine, barbiturates, heroin and other opiates, and various psychedelic substances such as marihuana, hashish, psilocybin, mescaline, STP, methylenedioxyamphetamine (MDA), and dimethyltryptamine (DMT). Under the circumstances, one questions the logic of referring to this group in scientific papers as "LSD users." Most of these subjects were actually multiple-drug users or abusers exposed to a variety of chemicals of unknown composition, quality and potency.

In addition, it has been repeatedly reported that this population suffered from malnutrition and had very high rates of venereal disease, hepatitis and various other viral infections. It was mentioned above that viruses are one of the most common factors causing chromosomal damage; the possible role of malnutrition remains to be evaluated. *Dishotsky et al.* (28) conclude their review of the *in vivo* studies involving illicit LSD by relating the findings of increased chromosome breakage to a combination of factors such as long term excessive exposure to illicit chemical agents, the presence of toxic contaminants, the intravenous route of administration, and the physical debility of many drug abusers. According to them, positive results, when found, are related to the more general effects of drug abuse and not, as initially reported, specifically to the use of LSD.

Pure LSD and Chromosomal Damage
Chromosomal studies of persons who received pharmaceutically pure LSD in an experimental or therapeutic framework are much more relevant and reliable as a source of information than the studies of illicit drug users. In these studies, there is no uncertainty concerning purity, dosage, frequency of exposure and the interval between the latest exposure and blood sampling. Two different approaches can be distinguished in the chromosome studies using pure LSD. The studies of the first type are *retrospective* and use a "post hoc" design; they examine the chromosomal changes in subjects who were exposed to pure LSD in the past. The studies of the second type are *prospective*; the chromosomal patterns are examined both before and after the exposure to LSD, and each subject serves as his own control.

Retrospective Studies of Chromosomal Changes in Pure LSD Users. A review of the studies in this category reveals that only two groups of investigators have reported an increased rate of chromosome breakage in their subjects. Five other teams failed to confirm these positive findings.

Cohen, Marinello and Back (22) reported in their initial study that they found chromosomal damage in the white blood cells of one paranoid schizophrenic patient who had been treated fifteen times in the past with LSD in dosages between 80 and 200 micrograms. *Nielsen, Friedrich and Tsuboi* (80) examined the chromosomes of five persons treated with LSD and found "no correlation between any specific drug and the frequency of gaps, breaks, and hyperdiploid cells." The authors later regrouped their data, forming smaller groups on the basis of age and sex. (81) After this revision of the original material, they concluded that LSD induced chromosomal damage. *Tjio, Pahnke and Kurland* (106) criticized this study on the basis of the insufficient number of cells analyzed for a reliable determination of breakage rates. Three of the five LSD subjects studied had no chromosomal aberrations, and the two remaining subjects accounted for all six breaks found. In addition, the 1.7 percent breakage rate is still within the values reported for the general population. Another study by *Nielsen, Friedrich and Tsuboi* (82) which reported an increased breakage rate of 4.3 percent in a group of nine former LSD users has been criticized by *Dishotsky et al.* (28) on the basis of its unusual approach to data analysis.

Sparkes, Melnyk and Bozzetti (99) did not find an increase in chromosomal breakage in four patients treated with LSD in the past for medical reasons. Negative results were also reported by *Bender and Siva Sankar,* (11) who examined the chromosomes of seven schizophrenic children who had been treated in the past by prolonged administration of LSD. These children received LSD daily in two divided dosages of 100 to 150 micrograms for a period of weeks or months. The frequency of chromosome breakage in this group was less than 2 percent and did not differ from that of the control group.

Siva Sankar, Rozsa and Geisler (93) studied the chromosome patterns in fifteen children with psychiatric problems who had been given LSD, UML or a combination of both. LSD was administered daily; the average dose for the whole group was 142.4 micrograms per day per patient, and the duration of therapy varied from 2 to 1,366 days. The breakage rate for the group treated with LSD was 0.8 percent, for the group treated with both LSD and UML 1.00 percent. This was not significantly higher than the rate of breakage in the controls. The patients in this study received LSD two to four years prior to the chromosome studies. The authors admitted that the effects of LSD on the leucocyte chromosomes might have been rectified over such a long period of time. In any case, this would indicate that LSD therapy has no long-lasting effects on the chromosomes.

Tjio, Pahnke and Kurland (106) published the results of chromosome analysis of a group of eight "normal" subjects who had received pure LSD in research experiments one to twenty-six times, two to fifteen months prior to giving the blood sample. The mean total chromosomal aberration rate for this group was 2.8 percent, and the individual rate in none of them exceeded the pre-LSD mean of 4.3 percent found in the patient sample.

Corey et al. (24) reported the result of a retrospective chromosomal study of sixteen patients, five of whom had been treated with LSD only, five with mescaline only, and six with LSD plus mescaline. In the eleven individuals who were clinically treated with LSD dosages ranging from 200 micrograms to 4,350 micrograms, frequency of chromosome breaks did not differ from that found in the thirteen controls. The respective frequencies were 7.8 percent for LSD, 5.6 percent for mescaline, 6.4 percent for LSD plus mescaline, and 7.0 percent for the control group.

In an unpublished study, *Dishotsky et al.* examined the chromosomes of five subjects exposed in the past to pure LSD. The mean breakage rate in this group (0.40 percent) was not significantly different from that of the eight control persons (0.63 percent). In their review paper, *Dishotsky et al.* (28) indicate that fifty-eight of seventy (82.9 percent) of the subjects studied after treatment with pure LSD did not have chromosome damage. Because of incomplete data on nine of the remaining twelve subjects, they were not able to compute the precise percentage of subjects with elevated breakage rates. However, they estimated that this figure would range between 17.1 percent and 4.9 percent. All but one of the twelve subjects were reported by a single team of investigators. The authors concluded that in view of the procedures, incomplete data, questionable re-analysis of the data, and low breakage rates reported, there is no definite evidence from this type of experiment that pure LSD causes chromosome damage.

Prospective Studies of Chromosomal Changes in Pure LSD Users. The studies comparing the chromosomal changes before and after exposure to pure LSD represent the most adequate scientific approach to the problem from the methodological point of view, and are the most reliable source of scientific information. The first report in this category was published in 1968 by *Hungerford et al.* (55) who examined the chromosomes of three psychiatric patients before and after repeated therapeutic administrations of LSD. Blood samples were taken from all patients before any LSD therapy, one hour before and one and fourteen hours after each dose; follow-up samples were taken at intervals of one to six months. An increase in chromosome aberrations was observed after each of three intravenous injections of LSD. The increase was small in two of the three subjects; however, dicentric and multiradial figures appeared only after treatment, and acentric fragments appeared more frequently after treatment. In the follow-up study, a return to earlier levels was observed in all three patients. The data from this study indicated that pure LSD may produce transitory increases of chromosome abnormalities, but that these are no longer evident one month after administration of the final dose. The results were slightly complicated by the administration of chlorpromazine (Thorazine), which in itself can produce chromosomal aberrations. It is interesting to note that Hungerford's study is the only one in which LSD was administered intravenously.

Tjio, Pahnke and Kurland (106) reported the results of a study of thirty-two hospitalized alcoholic or neurotic patients treated with LSD in the framework of a double-blind controlled study at the Maryland Psychiatric Research Center. The dosage of LSD was 50 micrograms in eleven patients and 250–450 micrograms in twenty-one patients. The number of cells observed in this study (22,500) was more than twice the total number of cells observed in all other studies of pure LSD users. The amount of breakage was not directly proportional to the dosage; actually those in the low-dose range showed greater increases than those on high dosage. The authors also examined a group of five persons who had taken illicit LSD from four to thirty-six times before the study. In these subjects, blood samples were drawn for seven to ten consecutive days before, during and after treatment with pure LSD either two or three times. Statistical analysis revealed no significant difference in the chromosomal aberration before and after LSD. In another prospective study, *Corey et al.* (24) examined the chromosomes of ten persons before and after the administration of 200–600 micrograms of pure LSD. The authors found no significant difference in the rate of chromosome breakage between the pre- and post-samples and confirmed the negative findings of the previous study.

It is interesting to mention in this connection two prospective studies of LSD-related chromosomal damage which were conducted in Rhesus monkeys (*Macaca mulatta*); the results of both studies were rather inconclusive. *Egozcue and Irwin* (32) administered high dosages of LSD (40 micrograms per kg.) four times at ten day intervals. Two of their animals showed increased chromosomal breaks, whereas the other two stayed within normal values. *Kato et al.* (66) described transitory changes in chromosomes after multiple, subcutaneous injections of LSD in high doses (125–1000 micrograms per kg. per injection) in Rhesus monkeys. The authors have not provided a statistical evaluation of the results; *Dishotsky et al.*, (28) who later analyzed their data, found them statistically nonsignificant.

Dishotsky et al. (28) also offered a synoptic evaluation of the prospective LSD studies. According to them, only six of the fifty-six patients (10.7 percent) studied before and after treatment with pure LSD had elevated breakage rates; of these, three received LSD intravenously and one had a viral infection. Of these six subjects, one individual was not available for follow-up determinations; in the remaining five, breakage returned to that observed before treatment. From the total number of subjects studied before and after treatment, 89.3 percent did not have chromosome damage. The results of the prospective LSD studies are thus in agreement with the negative conclusion of five of the seven teams that studied subjects only after LSD treatment.

Chromosomal Changes in Germinal Cells
In the past, the positive findings of some chromosomal studies have been used as a basis for far-reaching speculations concerning the hereditary dangers associated with LSD. Journalists, and also several scientific workers, described their rather apocalyptic visions of the offspring of LSD users. Such speculations were rather premature, and insufficiently substantiated by experimental data. The reasoning that refers to structural abnormalities of the chromosomes as "damage" and relates them automatically to genetic hazards has serious gaps in its logic. In reality, it is not quite clear whether or not the structural changes in the chromosomes of the white blood cells have any functional significance, and whether they are associated with genetic abnormalities. There exist many chemical substances that cause chromosomal breaks but have no adverse effects on genetic mutation or fetal development. The complexity of this problem can be illustrated by the case

of viruses. A variety of virus diseases (such as herpes simplex and shingles, measles, chicken pox, influenza, yellow fever, and possibly mumps) induce marked chromosomal damage without causing fetal malformations. According to *Nichols*, (79) one of the exceptions is rubella (German measles), a disease that is notorious for causing severe fetal malformations when acquired by the mother in the first trimester of pregnancy.

In addition to the methodological problems involved and the inconsistency of the findings discussed above, one more important fact has to be taken into consideration. In all the studies quoted, the effect of illicit or pure LSD, *in vitro* or *in vivo*, was assessed in the chromosomes of the white blood cells. No direct conclusions about the hereditary dangers associated with the administration of LSD can be drawn on the basis of these studies since the lymphocytes are not involved in the reproductive processes. Speculations about such dangers could be made only on the basis of chromosomal findings in germ cells such as the spermatozoids and ova, or their precursor cells. Unfortunately, the few existing studies of the chromosomes of germinal cells (the so-called meiotic chromosomes) yielded as inconclusive results as the studies of the chromosomes of somatic cells.

Skakkebaek, Phillip and Rafaelsen (95) studied meiotic chromosomes from six healthy male mice injected with large dosages of LSD (1,000 micrograms per kg); the number of injections and intervals between exposures varied. Several chromosomal breaks, gaps and unidentifiable fragments were found in the treated animals but, with a few exceptions, not in the control animals. The authors consider their finding tentative evidence that high doses of LSD may influence meiotic chromosomes in mice. They admitted that the number of abnormalities was small and technical errors could not be excluded, but concluded that the changes found could have influence on fertility, size of the litter, and the number of congenital malformations. In a later study, *Skakkebaek and Beatty* (94) injected four mice subcutaneously with dosages of 1,000 micrograms per kg of LSD twice a week for five weeks. Analysis carried out on a blind basis showed a high frequency of abnormalities in two of the treated mice. In addition, the spermatozoa of LSD-treated mice also showed morphological differences, with a more rounded convex side of the head and broader heads in general. The practical significance of these findings is considerably reduced by the fact that the dosages used far exceed anything used in clinical practice. A comparable dose in humans would come to 60,000–100,000 micrograms per person, which is 100 to 1,000 times more than the dosages commonly used in experimental and clinical work with LSD.

Another positive finding of meiotic chromosome damage induced by LSD was reported by *Cohen and Mukherjee.* (23) These authors injected thirteen male mice with a single dose of LSD at a concentration of 25 micrograms per kg. In this study the meiotic cells were apparently less vulnerable than somatic cells. However, there was an obvious tenfold increase in chromosome damage among the mice treated with LSD. This reached a maximum between two and seven days after injection, with a subsequent decrease and return to almost normal levels after three weeks. On the basis of evidence from clinical human cytogenetic studies, the authors concluded that chromosome anomalies of this type may lead to reduced fertility, congenital abnormalities and fetal wastage.

The other existing studies of the effect of LSD on meiotic cells brought essentially negative results. *Egozcue and Irwin* (32) studied the effects of LSD administration in mice and Rhesus monkeys. The mice in this study received 5 micrograms per kg of LSD daily in a number of injections increasing from one to ten. Four adult male Rhesus macaques ingested doses of either 5, 10, 20 or 40 micrograms per kg of LSD. Six months after their single dose of LSD, three of the monkeys received four doses each, at ten-day intervals, of 40 micrograms per kg of LSD per dose. The authors reported essentially negative results in both the mice and the monkeys. In mice, occasional chromosomal breaks and fragments were observed in similar proportions in the control and the experimental groups. In the Rhesus monkeys, no significant differences were found before or after acute or chronic treatment.

Jagiello and Polani (60) published the results of a detailed and sophisticated study of the effect of LSD on mouse germ cells. They performed acute and chronic experiments on both male and female mice. The dosage of LSD in the chronic experiments ranged between 0.5–5.0 micrograms; in the acute experiments a single subcutaneous dose of 1,000 micrograms per kg of LSD was administered. The results of this study were essentially negative. The authors attributed the discrepancies with other studies to mode of administration, dosage and the animal strain involved.

In two of the existing studies, the effects of LSD on the meiotic chromosomes were tested in the banana fly, *Drosophila melanogaster*, an organism that has played an important role in the history of genetics. In one of these studies, *Grace, Carlson and Goodman* (44) injected male flies in concentrations of 1, 100 and 500 micrograms per cc. The dosage used is equivalent to approximately one liter of the same solution in humans (1,000, 100,000 and 500,000 micrograms respectively). No chromosomal breaks were observed in premeiotic, meiotic or postmeiotic sperm. The authors concluded that LSD is in a class quite distinct from that of ionizing radiation and mustard gas. If it is a mutagenic or radiomimetic agent in human chromosomes, it is not a very powerful one. In another study, *Markowitz, Brosseau and Markowitz* (74) fed LSD to male fruit flies in a 1 percent sucrose solution for twenty-four hours; the concentrations used were 100, 5,000, and 10,000 micrograms per cc. In these experiments, LSD had no detectable effect on chromosome breakage. The authors concluded that LSD is a relatively ineffective chromosome breaking agent in *Drosophila*.

Considerable caution is required in extrapolating the data about the effect of LSD on meiotic chromosomes obtained from animal experiments to humans, because of rather wide interspecies variability. The only report about the effect of LSD on human germ cells was published by *Hultén et al.* (54) These authors examined the testicular biopsy in a patient who had used massive doses of illicit LSD in the past, up to an alleged 1,000 micrograms. For a period of four weeks he practiced the administration of these dosages daily. There was no evidence of an increased frequency of structural chromosome aberrations in the germinal tissue of the testicles.

Concluding this discussion of the effects of LSD on chromosomal structure, we can say that the results of the existing studies are inconclusive despite the fact that the dosages used in many experiments far exceed the doses used in clinical practice. Whether LSD causes structural changes in the chromosomes or not remains an open question. If it does, the circumstances and dosage range in which these occur have not been established, and the interpretation of these changes and their functional significance is even more problematic. This question could not be answered even on the basis of results of methodologically perfect chromosomal studies. In future research, much more emphasis should be put on the study of the effect of LSD on genetic mutation and embryonal development.

MUTAGENIC EFFECTS OF LSD

In the past, the classic experimental animal for the study of genetic mutations has been the banana fly, *Drosophila melanogaster*. Several studies exist in which the effect of LSD on genetic mutation has been observed in this fly. *Grace, Carlson and Goodman* (44) studied the mutagenic effects of intra-abdominal injections of LSD in concentrations ranging from 1 to 500 micrograms per cc. They have not found an increase in induced mutations in the LSD-treated group. On the basis of these negative findings, the authors consider it improbable that LSD induces mutation in humans. *Markowitz, Brosseau and Markowitz* (74) fed LSD to male flies in concentrations of 100, 5,000 and 10,000 micrograms per cc. In this experiment, LSD produced a significant increase in the frequency of sex-linked recessive lethal mutations. The authors concluded that LSD at high concentrations is a weak mutagen in *Drosophila*.

In several studies performed in Drosophila flies, lower concentrations of LSD had no mutagenic effects, but an increased frequency of induced mutations was observed after excessive dosages. *Vann* (111) reported that dosages of 24,000 micrograms per kg produced no significant increase in the frequency of recessive lethals, whereas a dosage of 470,000 micrograms per kg did. *Browning* (15) administered intraperitoneal injections of 0.3 microliters of a solution containing 10,000 micrograms per cc of LSD; this dosage corresponds to about 4,000,000 micrograms per kg of body weight. Out of seventy-five flies, only fifteen survived this procedure, and ten were fertile. Under these circumstances, a significant increase in recessive lethal mutations in the X-chromosome of male flies was observed by the author. A 1:1 dilution of the original solution, when injected into one hundred males, resulted in thirty-five survivors of which thirty were fertile; the frequency of mutations markedly dropped. *Šrám* (101) concluded on the basis of his experiments with LSD in the Drosophila fly that LSD is a weak mutagen producing gene and chromosome mutations only when used in very high concentrations; this finding is in basic agreement with the existing literature on the mutagenic effects of LSD.

The effects of LSD were also tested on another standard genetic system, namely the fungus *Ophistoma multiannulatum*. *Zetterberg* (118) exposed the cells of this fungus to 20–50 micrograms per cc of LSD; he did not find any difference between treated and control cells. The data on Drosophila flies and fungi suggest that LSD is a weak mutagenic agent that is effective only in doses far exceeding those commonly used by human subjects.

There are several interesting studies focusing on the interaction of LSD with deoxyribonucleic acid (DNA) and ribonucleic acid (RNA); these studies could contribute to our understanding of the mechanism of interaction between LSD and the chromosomes or genes. *Yielding and Sterglanz* (115), using spectrophotometric methods, were able to demonstrate binding of LSD, its inactive optical isomer, and its inactive brominated analogue by helical DNA of the calf thymus. Binding did not take place with yeast RNA or nonhelical DNA, suggesting that this binding is specific for helical DNA.

Wagner (112) concluded on the basis of his experiments that LSD interacts directly with purified calf thymus DNA, probably by intercalation, causing conformational changes in the DNA. According to him, it is unlikely that this could influence the internal stability of the DNA helix enough to cause chromosomal breakage. However, it may lead to the dissociation of histones, which could render DNA susceptible to enzymatic attack. *Smythies and Antun* (98) performed similar experiments and arrived at the conclusion that LSD binds to nucleic acids by intercalation. According to *Dishotsky et al.*, (28) this evidence of LSD intercalation into the DNA helix provides a clue to the physical mechanism involved in the mutagenic effects of high doses of LSD in Drosophila and the fungus, as reviewed above.

Nosal (83) investigated the effects of LSD on the Purkinje cells of the cerebellum of growing rats. These studies were specifically focused on the action of the ribonucleoproteins (RNP) of the differentiating nucleus-ribosome system. Only large doses of LSD (100–500 micrograms per kg) seemed to induce changes in the structure and staining properties of this cellular system.

Obviously, much more research is needed for the final clarification of the interesting interaction between LSD and various chemical substances involved in the genetic mechanisms.

TERATOGENIC EFFECTS OF LSD

It has been frequently hypothesized in the past that LSD may be a potential cause of abortions, fetal wastage and congenital malformations. The actual experimental studies of the effect of LSD on embryonic development have been made primarily in rodents. Since free transplacental transfer of LSD has been demonstrated in an autoradiographic study performed by *Idanpään-Heikkilä and Schoolar*, (56) it is conceivable that it might influence the developing fetus. In this study, the injected LSD rapidly passed the placental barrier into the fetus; however, according to the authors, the relatively high affinity of LSD for the maternal organs seemed to diminish the amount of the drug available for transfer into the fetus itself.

The experimental data from mice, rats and hamsters have been rather controversial. *Auerbach and Rugowski* (10) reported a high rate of embryonal malformations in mice following relatively low doses of LSD administered early in pregnancy. In all cases the induced malformations involved characteristic brain defects. Abnormalities of the lower jaw, shifts in the position of the eyes, and modifications of the facial contour were frequently associated with these defects. There was no observable effect on the embryonic development if the LSD exposure occurred later than the seventh day of gestation. These findings were partially supported by *Hanaway* (47) who experimented with LSD in mice of a different strain. Using comparable dosages, he described a high incidence of lens abnormalities; however, he was unable to discover any malformation of the central nervous system, even on histological examination. *DiPaolo, Givelber and Erwin* (27) administered LSD to pregnant mice and hamsters. The total amount of LSD injected in mice ranged from 0.5 micrograms to 30 micrograms per pregnant animal; Syrian hamsters were injected with a single dose ranging between 10 and 300 micrograms. The authors concluded that their investigation failed to demonstrate that LSD is teratogenic for mice and Syrian hamsters. They interpreted the increased frequency of malformed embryos in some of the experiments as an indication of a potentiating effect of LSD on individual threshold differences. It is necessary to emphasize that the doses used in this study were 25 to 1,000 times the human dosage. *Alexander et al.* (4) administered 5 micrograms per kg of LSD to pregnant rats. They described a significantly increased frequency of stillbirth and stunting in two of their experiments where LSD was administered early in pregnancy. In the third experiment, where the animals received similar single injections of LSD late in pregnancy, there was no obvious effect on the offspring. *Geber* (42) reported a study in pregnant hamsters in which he administered LSD, mescaline and a brominated derivative of LSD. He described a markedly increased frequency of runts, dead fetuses and reabsorbed fetuses in the experimental groups. In addition, he observed a variety of malformations of the central nervous system such as exencephaly, spina bifida, interparietal meningocele, omphalocele, hydrocephalus, myelocele and hemorrhages of local brain areas, as well as edema along the spinal axis and in various other body regions. The dosages of LSD used in this experiment ranged between 0.8 micrograms per kg and 240 micrograms per kg. However, there was no correlation between the dose and the percentage of congenital malformation. LSD and mescaline produced similar malformations; mescaline appeared to be a less potent teratogen, as judged by the dose.

There exist a number of studies in which negative results were reported in all the species mentioned. *Roux, Dupuis and Aubry* (88) administered LSD in dosages from 5–500 micrograms per kg per day to mice, rats and hamsters. There was no increase in fetal mortality or decrease in the mean weight of the fetuses for any group of experimental animals. There was no significant increase in the incidence of external malformations, and sections performed in approximately 40 percent of the experimental animals showed no visceral malformations. The authors concluded, on the basis of the results, that in the three species studied, no abortificient, teratogenic or embryonic growth-depressing factors were observed, even after enormous doses.

At least four studies of the teratogenic effect of LSD carried out on rats brought negative results. *Warkany and Takacz* (113) found no abnormalities in their experimental Wistar rats, despite the fact that they used large doses of LSD (up to eighty times those given by *Alexander et al.*). (4) The only finding was a reduction in size in one of the young. *Nosal* (83) administered LSD to pregnant rats in dosages of 5, 25, and 50 micrograms per kg on the fourth and seventh days of gestation. He did not observe any external malformations of the head, vertebral column and extremities, or macroscopic lesions of the central nervous system and viscera. There were no differences from the controls as to mortality and fetal resorption or reduced number and size of the offspring, even with higher dosages. Negative results were also obtained in two studies performed and published by *Uyeno*. (109, 110)

Fabro and Sieber (35) studied the effect of LSD and thalidomide on the fetal development of white rabbits. Thalidomide had a marked embryotoxic effect and produced an increased incidence of resorptions, decreased the mean fetal weight, and induced malformations of fetuses. Pregnant rabbits given LSD in a dosage of 20 or 100 micrograms per kg of body weight produced litters which were not significantly different from the controls. Decrease of the mean fetal weight at twenty-eight days was the only effect which could be detected in the litters of does treated with daily doses as high as 100 micrograms per kg.

As emphasized by *Dishotsky et al.*, (28) an overall view of the rodent studies indicates a wide range of individual, strain, and species susceptibility to the effects of LSD. The effect, when found, occurs at a highly specific time early in gestation; no effect was reported with exposures occurring late in pregnancy. Extreme caution is required in extrapolating results from the rodent studies to the human situation, since fetal development and growth in these species is markedly different. Rodents lack the chorionic villi in the placenta, so that the fetal blood is separated from the maternal sinuses only by endothelial walls. This makes the rodents much more sensitive than humans to the teratogenic potential of any given substance.

In the only existing experimental study in primates, *Kato et al.* (66) administered multiple subcutaneous injections of LSD to pregnant Rhesus monkeys. Of four animals treated, one delivered a normal infant, two were stillborn with facial deformities and one died at one month. The two control animals delivered normal offspring. The dosage used in this study was more than 100 times the usual experimental dose for humans. The authors themselves concluded that the small size of their sample made it impossible to draw any definite conclusion.

The information about the influence of LSD on the development of human embryos is scanty and exists only in the form of clinical observations. For obvious reasons, this problem cannot be approached in an experimental manner in humans. There are six reported cases of malformed infants born to women who ingested illicit LSD prior to or during pregnancy. *Abbo, Norris and Zellweger* (2) described a child born with a congenital limb anomaly. Both parents of the child had taken alleged LSD of unknown purity and amount from an unidentified source on an indefinite number of occasions. The mother took LSD four times during pregnancy, twice during the first three months, which is the time at which the limbs are differentiated. *Zellweger, McDonald and Abbo* (117) reported the case of a child born with a complex unilateral deformity of the leg. This anomaly, the so-called fibular aplastic syndrome, includes absence of fibula, anterior bowing of the shortened tibia, absence of lateral rays of the foot, shortening of the femur, and dislocation of the hip. The parents of this child took illicit LSD, the mother on the 25th day and three times between the 45th and 98th day after her last menstrual period. The authors emphasized the fact that the seventh week of gestation is the period of most active differentiation of the lower limbs; this was also established for the thalidomide embryopathy. *Hecht et al.* (49) observed malformation of the arm in the case of a child whose parents had taken LSD and smoked marijuana. The mother took unknown amounts of LSD before and during early pregnancy. The authors concluded that the relation of the deformity to LSD in this case is unclear. *Carakushansky, Neu and Gardner* (16) reported a similar case. It involved an infant with a terminal transverse deficit of portions of fingers on the left hand and syndactyly of the right hand with shortened fingers. This malformation is characterized by a failure of the fingers to separate and function independently. The mother was believed to have been exposed to LSD and cannabis during pregnancy. *Eller and Morton* (34) gave a report of a severely deformed baby with an anomaly involving defective development of the thoracic part of the skeleton (spondylothoracic dysplasia). This rare condition had previously been described only in infants of Puerto Rican parents. The mother in this case happened to take LSD once around the time of conception. The authors question the causal relationship between LSD and the deformity. Finally, *Hsu, Strauss and Hirschhorn* (53) published the report of a female infant born with multiple malformations, to parents who were both LSD users prior to conception. During pregnancy the mother also took marijuana, barbiturates and methedrine. The malformations in this case were associated with chromosomal aberrations indicating the so-called trisomy 13 syndrome.

Berlin and Jacobson (12) studied 127 pregnancies in 112 women where one or both of the parents admitted taking LSD before or after the infant's conception. According to the authors, sixty-two pregnancies resulted in live birth, six of these infants had congenital abnormalities, with one neonatal death. One of the fifty-six normal newborns died from an intrapulmonary hemorrhage. Sixty-five pregnancies were terminated by abortion; seven abortions were spontaneous and four of these fetuses were abnormal. Out of fourteen therapeutic abortions, there were four abnormal fetuses. The rate of defects of the central nervous system was about sixteen times that in the normal population. One of the findings in all the abortion specimens was failure of fusion of the cortex. Three of the six abnormal children born alive had myelomeningocele and hydrocephalus; one had hydrocephalus only. The authors themselves emphasized that the mothers in this study were a very high risk obstetric population for many reasons. In addition to ingestion of alleged LSD, there was multiple drug use (15 percent used narcotics), infectious diseases and malnutrition. Most of the therapeutic abortions were done for psychiatric reasons. Thirty-six percent of the women had undergone extensive radiological investigations for abdominal complaints.

Berlin and Jacobson's study, as well as all the previously mentioned case reports of fetal abnormalities, involve infants born to parents who ingested illicit substances of unknown dosage and origin that were considered to be LSD; to date there is no report of congenital malformations in human offspring exposed to pure LSD. In addition, as *Blaine* (13) pointed out in his rather bitter and emphatic criticism of the paper by *Eller and Morton*, (34) there is no scientific evidence in these individual case histories of a causal relation between the ingestion of illicit substances and the subsequent development of the embryonal malformation. The findings could represent pure coincidences and be related to any number of situations that contribute to congenital abnormalities, such as maternal nutrition, physiological, psychological and pathological states, socio-economic circumstances, or various cultural practices. Differences in type and severity of malformations may be due to genetic factors, both embryonic and parental.

There exists a considerable amount of clinical evidence contradicting or limiting the above findings. Three studies focusing primarily on the frequency of chromosome breaks in children exposed to illicit LSD *in utero* reported elevated breakage rates of the chromosomes. (27, 33, 54) However, all fourteen infants studied were in good health and had no indications of birth defects. It is interesting to note in this context that the hypothesis of the possible teratogenic action of LSD was originally derived from observations of increased chromosomal breakage. In the majority of the reported cases of actual congenital malformations attributed to LSD, the chromosomal findings were normal. Conversely, the children exposed to LSD *in utero* and reported as having chromosome damage did not show any physical abnormalities. Although it is not common, for obvious reasons, to publish case histories with negative results, *Sato and Pergament* (89) presented one in their discussion of the case of *Zellweger et al..* (117) They described a newborn whose mother had taken LSD before and during early pregnancy six times. The pregnancy was uneventful, and she gave birth to a full-term, healthy girl. The doses of alleged LSD taken by the mother were sufficient to produce a psychedelic effect. She took LSD during the critical stage for production of limb deformities, as in Zellweger's case, but no fetal deformities developed.

Aase, Laestadius and Smith (1) observed a group of ten pregnant women who were ascertained as having ingested LSD in hallucinatory dosages. These women subsequently delivered ten living and healthy children. There was no evidence of teratogenic effects or chromosomal damage in any of these ten babies considered to have been exposed to LSD *in utero*. The authors point out a most interesting fact, that all of the delivered children were girls. The low probability of this being a random event suggests that LSD may have an influence on the sex ratio. *Healy and Van Houten* (48) calculated that the probability of the entire series of ten pregnancies resulting in children of the same sex is 1:1024. They suggested that LSD might enhance the basic immunological incompatibility between male fetuses and their maternal hosts; this results in the detection of the fetal tissue as antigenic. A similar hypothesis was offered in the past as an explanation of the observation that women who became schizophrenic within one month of conception gave birth to female offspring only.

McGlothlin, Sparkes and Arnold (76) studied 148 human pregnancies following ingestion of LSD; this was part of a larger study of 300 persons randomly drawn from a population of 750 who received LSD orally in either an experimental or psychotherapeutic setting. The number of sessions ranged between one and eighty-five, and the usual dosages were 25–400 micrograms. For twenty-seven pregnancies, there was additional use of LSD under non-medical conditions. In a small percentage marihuana (8 percent) and strong psychedelics such as peyote, mescaline and psilocybin were also used. The authors found no evidence that the use of LSD in reasonable doses by men before intercourse leading to conception, is related to an increase in the rate of abortions, premature births or birth defects. However, they found some evidence that the use of LSD by women prior to conception may increase the incidence of spontaneous abortions; the causal connection between these two events is not clear and requires further research. There was little to suggest that exposure of either parent to LSD prior to conception and in the amounts described in this study increased the risk of having a child with a congenital defect. The only increased risk observed in this study, therefore, was a possible higher incidence of spontaneous abortions among women exposed to LSD. Spontaneous abortions occurred significantly more often when the mother had taken LSD than when the father only had taken it. The authors offered two explanations for this finding: (1) The period required for the maturation process of the ova is very long; it takes several years, as compared to a few weeks for the spermatozoa. (2) In one-half of the cases the mothers were given medical LSD for therapeutic purposes. It is a well-known fact that greater emotional stress in neurotic patients increases the incidence of abortions, and this suggests that the connection found in this survey between LSD and abortion might not be causal at all, but purely coincidental.

Arendsen-Hein (7) presented at the Congress of the European Medical Association for Psycholytic Therapy at Würzburg in 1969 data about the offspring of 4,815 former LSD patients from several European countries, including England. Of 170 children born to these patients after they had completed LSD therapy, frequently involving multiple exposures, only two showed congenital anomalies. One child had a dislocation of the left hip joint; another child, born to a couple where the father used LSD, had the little finger and ring finger on one hand grown together (syndactyly). Two women from this sample took LSD within fourteen days after conception (in one case 400 micrograms), and both children were normal. Thus, out of 170 infants, only two showed pathology; the author felt that even in these two cases the anomalies were of a common kind and could not be attributed to LSD for any sound reason.

The experimental and clinical evidence for the teratogenic effects of LSD can be summarized as follows. Increased incidence of congenital malformation has been reported in mice, rats and hamsters; however, there exist a number of papers contradicting these findings. The information from experiments on lower primates, although preliminary, suggests a possible teratogenic effect and deserves further investigation. There exist several case reports of malformed children born to users of illicit LSD, and one study suggesting a high incidence of birth defects and abortions in this group. The causal relation of these malformations to the use of LSD is not established. The unknown chemical composition of the samples of alleged LSD, as well as the existence of many other important variables characterizing the group of "LSD users" (such as infections, malnutrition, multiple drug use, and emotional disorders) leave all the conclusions open to question. There are indications of an increased risk of spontaneous abortions related to the use of LSD. There is no evidence at present that pure LSD causes birth defects or fetal wastage in humans. However, for practical clinical purposes pregnancy should be considered a contraindication for the administration of LSD. This is not something unique and specific to LSD; similar caution is required in regard to many other substances. The balance between the maternal organism and the developing fetus, especially in the first trimester of pregnancy, is very precarious and can be disturbed by a wide variety of external influences.

CARCINOGENIC EFFECTS OF LSD

It has repeatedly been mentioned in the literature that LSD might have carcinogenic potential. This speculation appeared for the first time in the paper by *Cohen, Marinello and Back.* (22) The authors drew this conclusion from their findings of a markedly increased frequency of chromosomal breakage and a quadriradial chromosome exchange figure in a patient with paranoid schizophrenia who had undergone extensive LSD psychotherapy. This is a combination occurring in three inherited disorders: Bloom's syndrome, Fanconi's anemia and ataxia teleangiectatica. These disorders are connected with a high incidence of leukemia and other neoplastic diseases. The authors also pointed out that cells of neoplastic origin show a variety of chromosomal aberrations, many of which are not unlike those they had found in subjects after ingestion of LSD. In addition, some of the agents known to produce similar chromosome aberrations, such as radiation and various viruses, are known carcinogens.

The carcinogenic hypothesis was supported by the finding of *Irwin and Egozcue* (57) that nine subjects who had taken illicit LSD had chromosomal fragments resembling the so-called Philadelphia (Ph₁) chromosome, often associated with chronic granulocytic leukemia. *Grossbard et al.* (46) found a Ph₁-like chromosome in all thirty-five peripheral leucocytes from an individual who had used illicit LSD and other drugs and who later developed acute leukemia.

Several serious objections can be raised against this hypothesis. First, the evidence that pure LSD causes chromosomal aberrations is rather problematic and inconclusive. Second, the cause of the chromosomal lesions in the above mentioned inherited disorders is not known, nor has it been established whether these lesions have any relation to subsequent neoplastic developments. There exist many chromosome breaking agents which are not associated with leukemia, and quadriradial and other rearrangement figures have also been found in the white blood cells of normal individuals. Third, Cohen's comparison of the effects of LSD with those of radiation does not seem to be well substantiated by experimental and clinical findings. According to *Dishotsky et al.*, (28) long-term chromosomal damage following LSD injection has been reported in three retrospective studies. In two reports of subjects studied before and after they took LSD (prospective approach), the occasional damage that was found was without exception transitory, suggesting a reversibility of effect unlike that associated with radiation. Fourth, the Ph₁-like chromosome was reported in only two studies; in both of them it was found in peripheral leucocytes. In chronic granulocytic leukemia, the Ph₁ chromosome is characteristic only of myeloid and erythroid cells, which normally do not divide in peripheral blood. *Dishotsky et al.* (28) quote *Nowell and Hungerford* (84) who initially described this lesion: "A chromosome compatible with the Ph₁ would have to be observed in blood cells other than lymphocytes to be relevant to the question of chronic granulocytic leukemia."

Only two cases of leukemia have been reported in individuals who were treated in the past with pure LSD. (41, 108) In both of them it remains to be established whether the association represents a causal relation or a coincidence. In one of these cases, reported by *Garson and Robson*, (41) there was a "remarkable incidence of childhood malignancies strongly suggestive of a familial predisposition to malignant disease." At the present time the carcinogenic hypothesis seems to be rather poorly supported by experimental and clinical data and remains in the realm of pure speculation. There appears to be no definite evidence that LSD is a carcinogenic agent.

SUMMARY AND CONCLUSION

Two-thirds of the existing *in vitro* studies have reported some degree of increased chromosomal breakage following exposure to illicit or pure LSD. With one exception, these changes were observed with concentrations of LSD and durations of exposure that far exceeded the dosages commonly used in humans. In none of the studies was there a clear dosage-response relationship. Since similar findings have been reported with many commonly used substances, including artificial sweeteners, aspirin, caffeine, phenothiazine tranquillizers and antibiotics, there is no reason why LSD should be singled out and put in a special category. There is no justification for referring to the structural changes of the chromosomes as "chromosomal damage"; their functional relevance and relation to heredity remains to be established. In addition, the fact that the *in vitro* experiments bypass the excretory and detoxifying systems present in the integral organism casts doubt on the overall relevance of the *in vitro* results.

In the *in vivo* chromosomal studies, the majority of positive findings was reported in persons who had been exposed to illicit, "alleged" LSD. *Dishotsky et al.* (28) in their excellent synoptic review of the chromosomal studies made in the past, summarized the existing evidence in the *in vivo* papers as follows: "In twenty-one *in vivo* chromosomal studies, a total of 310 subjects were reported. Of these, 126 were treated with pure LSD; the other 184 were exposed to illicit, alleged LSD. Only 18 of 126 (14.3 percent) of the subjects in the pure LSD group were reported to have chromosomal aberration frequencies above mean control rates. In contrast, 89 of 184 (48.9 percent) of the subjects in the illicit LSD group had elevated aberration frequencies. Of all the subjects reported to have chromosomal damage, only 18 of 108 (16.7 percent) were exposed to pure LSD. The frequency of individuals with chromosomal damage reported among illicit drug users was nearly triple that associated with the use of pharmacologically pure LSD." These findings indicate that chromosomal aberrations when found were related to the more general effects of drug abuse and not to LSD *per se*; it is highly improbable that pure LSD ingested in moderate dosages produces chromosomal aberrations in the white blood cells.

The positive findings in some of the chromosomal studies using human leucocytes were interpreted as indicating genetic damage and danger to future generations. To be of direct genetic relevance, however, the chromosomal damage would have to be demonstrated in the germinal cells, the sperms and ova, or their precursor cells. Several existing studies of the effect of LSD on the meiotic chromosomes have been inconclusive despite the use of excessive dosages. The mutation studies in *Drosophila melanogaster* indicate no mutagenic effect from 0.28 to 500 micrograms of LSD per cc and a definite mutagenic effect from 2,000–10,000 micrograms of LSD per cc. The fact that truly astronomic dosages have to be used to induce mutations in Drosophila shows LSD as a rather weak mutagen that is unlikely to be mutagenic in any concentration used by human subjects.

In some of the early studies, LSD was implicated as a potential cause of congenital malformations, abortions and fetal wastage. The original reports of teratogenic effects in hamsters, rats and mice have not been confirmed by later studies. The experiments in rodents indicated a rather wide range of individual strain and species susceptibility to the effects of LSD. It is highly questionable whether and to what extent the results of such investigations can be extrapolated to the situation in humans. There have been six individual cases reported of malformed children born to parents who have used illicit LSD. Only one team of workers reported an increased frequency of congenital malformations in the offspring of illicit LSD users. In regard to the high frequency of unexplained "spontaneous" birth defects and the wide-spread abuse of LSD, the above observations may be coincidental. The increased occurrence of malformations in the LSD users réported in one of the studies may be explained by many other variables characterizing this group, and there is no logical reason to implicate LSD as the single or most important factor. At the present time there is no clear evidence that pure LSD is teratogenic in humans. However, in view of the high vulnerability of the developing fetus to a great variety of substances and conditions, the administration of LSD is contraindicated for the gestation period.

There is no clinical or experimental data demonstrating that LSD has carcinogenic properties, as suggested by some of the early studies. No increase in the incidence of tumors among LSD users has ever been detected. Case reports of leukemia and malignant tumors in the population of LSD users have been exceedingly rare. In the three existing case reports of leukemia, there has been no proof or even indication of a causal relationship, and the association of leukemia with LSD use may have been merely a coincidence.

As this review shows, no convincing experimental or clinical evidence exists to prove that the commonly used dosages of pure LSD produce genetic mutations, congenital malformations or malignant growths. As far as illicit LSD is concerned, the situation is much more complex, and the results of the studies of illicit LSD users should not be considered relevant to the question of the biological dangers of LSD. Uncertainties about the dosage, and the contamination of black-market samples of psychedelic drugs by various impurities and additives contribute a very important dimension to the already serious psychological hazards associated with unsupervised self-experimentation.

There is absolutely no indication in the research data currently available that responsible experimental and therapeutic use of LSD by experienced professionals should be discontinued.

UPDATE TO 2008 EDITION

No new developments have occurred in this area. A 1998 review examining the developmental toxicity of psychoactive drugs addressed LSD only briefly and confirmed that normal [recreational or therapeutic] doses of LSD do not produce any chromosomal damage.

Li, J.H., Lin, L.F., Genetic toxicology of abused drugs: a brief review. *Mutagenesis* 13: 557-565, 1998.

REFERENCES

This list includes works cited in the text and other related works consulted by the author for this critical review.

1 Aase, J. M., Laestadius, N., Smith, D. W.: Children of Mothers who Took LSD in Pregnancy. *Lancet* II: 100, 1970.

2 Abbo, G., Norris, A., Zellweger, H.: Lysergic Acid Diethylamide (LSD-25) and Chromosome Breaks. *Humangenetik* 6:253, 1968.

3 Aghajanian, G. K., Bing, O. H.: Persistence of Lysergic Acid Diethylamide in the Plasma of Human Subjects. *Clin. Pharmacol. Ther.* 5:611, 1964.

4 Alexander, G. J., Miles, B. E., Gold, G. M., Alexander, R. B.: LSD: Injection Early in Pregnancy Produces Abnormalities in Offspring of Rats. *Science* 157:459, 1967.

5   Alexander, G. J., Gold, G. M., Miles, B. E., Ennes, B., Alexander, R. B.:
     Lysergic Acid Diethylamide Intake During Pregnancy: Fetal Damage in
     Rats. *J. Pharmacol. Exp. Ther.* 173:48, 1970.

6   Aptekar, R. G.: Possible Effects of LSD. *New Eng. J. Med.* 283:765, 1970.

7   Arendsen-Hein, G. W.: Presentation at the Congress of the European
     Medical Association for Psycholytic Therapy at Wurzburg, W. Germany,
     1969.

8   Assemany, S. R., Neu, R. L., Gardner, L. I.: Deformities in a Child Whose
     Mother Took LSD. *Lancet* I:1290, 1970.

9   Auerbach, R.: LSD: Teratogenicity in Mice. *Science* 170:558, 1970.

10   Auerbach, R., Rugowski, J. A.: Lysergic Acid Diethylamide: Effect on
     Embryos. *Science* 157:1325, 1968.

11   Bender, L., Siva Sankar. D. V.: Chromosome Damage Not Found in
     Leukocytes of Children Treated with LSD-25. *Science* 159:749, 1968.

12   Berlin, C. M., Jacobson, C. B.: Link Between LSD and Birth Defects
     Reported. *JAMA* 212:1447, 1970.

13   Blaine, J. D.: Inculpation of LSD Challenged. *New Eng. J. Med.* 283:1231,
     1970.

14   *Brit. Med. J.*: LSD and Chromosomes. II:778, 1968.

15   Browning, L. S.: Lysergic Acid Diethylamide: Mutagenic Effects in Droso-
     phila. *Science* 161:1022, 1968.

16   Carakushansky, G., Neu, R. I., Gardner, L. I.: Lysergide and Cannabis as
     Possible Teratogens in Man. *Lancet* II:150, 1969.

17   Cohen, H. P., Turner, W. J., Merlis, S.: A Study of Drug Effects on
     Chromosomes. Mimeographed copy.

18   Cohen, M. M.: LSD and Chromosomes. *Science J.*, p. 76, Sept., 1968.

19   Cohen, M. M.: The Interaction of Various Drugs with Human Chromo-
     somes. *Can J. Genet. Cytol.* II:1, 1969.

20   Cohen, M. M., Hirschhorn, K., Frosch, W. A.: *In Vivo* and *In Vitro*
     Chromosomal Damage Induced by LSD-25. *New Eng. J. Med.* 277:1043,
     1967.

21   Cohen, M. M., Hirschhorn, K., Verbo, S., Frosch, W. A., Groeschel,
     M. M.: The Effect of LSD-25 on the Chromosomes of Children Exposed *In
     Utero*. *Pediat. Res.* 2:468, 1968.

22   Cohen, M. M., Marinello, M. J., Back, N.: Chromosomal Damage in
     Human Leukocytes Induced by Lysergic Acid Diethylamide. *Science* 155:
     1417, 1967.

23   Cohen, M. M., Mukherjee, A. B.: Meiotic Chromosome Damage Induced
     by LSD-25. *Nature* 219:1072, 1968.

24   Corey, M. J., Andrews, J. C., McLeod, M. J., MacLean, J. R., Wilby,
     W. E.; Chromosome Studies on Patients (*In Vivo*) and Cells (*In Vitro*)
     Treated with Lysergic Acid Diethylamide. *New Eng. J. Med.* 282:939,
     1970.

25 Court Brown, W. M.: Is Lysergide a Teratogen? *Lancet* I:1154, 1967.

26 Denson, R.: Effects of LSD on Chromosomes. *Canad. Med. Ass. J.* 98:609, 1968.

27 DiPaolo, J. A., Givelber, H. M., Erwin, H.: Evaluation of Teratogenicity of Lysergic Acid Diethylamide. *Nature* 220:490, 1968.

28 Dishotsky, N. I., Loughman, W. D., Mogar, R. E., Lipscomb, W. R.: LSD and Genetic Damage. *Science* 172:431, 1971.

29 Dixon, A. K.: Evidence of Catecholamine Mediation in the 'Aberrant' Behavior Induced by Lysergic Acid Diethylamide (LSD) in the Rat. *Experientia* 24:743, 1968.

30 Dorrance, D. L.: Chromosomal and Teratogenic Effects of LSD: A Literature Review. *The New Physician* 18:7, 1969.

31 Dorrance, D., Janiger, O., Teplitz, R. L.: *In Vivo* Effects of Illicit Hallucinogens on Human Lymphocyte Chromosomes. *JAMA* 212:1488, 1970.

32 Egozcue, J., Irwin, S.: Effect of LSD-25 on Mitotic and Meiotic Chromosomes of Mice and Monkeys. *Humangenetik* 8:86, 1969.

33 Egozcue, J., Irwin, S., Maruffo, C. A.: Chromosomal Damage in LSD Users. *JAMA* 204:122, 1968.

34 Eller, J. L., Morton, J. M.: Bizarre Deformities in Offspring of Users of Lysergic Acid Diethylamide. *New Eng. J. Med.* 283:395, 1970.

35 Fabro, S., Sieber, S. M.: Is Lysergide a Teratogen? *Lancet* I:639, 1968.

36 Finoganova, S. A.: The Cytogenetic and Teratogenic Effects of LSD-25. *Zh. Neuropat. Psikhiat. Korsakov.* 70:770, 1970.

37 Fitzgerald, P. H., Dobson, J. R. E.: Lysergide and Chromosomes. *Lancet* I:1036, 1968.

38 Fitzgerald, P. H., Dobson, J. R. E.: Radiomimetic Properties of LSD. *New Eng. J. Med.* 278:1404, 1968.

39 Fort, J., Metzner, R.: LSD, Chromosomes, and Sensationalism. *Psyched. Rev.* 10, 1968.

40 Friedrich, U., Nielsen, J.: Lithium and Chromosome Abnormalities. *Lancet* II:435, 1969.

41 Garson, C. M., Robson, M. K.: Studies in a Patient with Acute Leukemia After Lysergide Treatment. *Brit Med. J.* 2:800, 1969.

42 Geber, W. F.: Congenital Malformations Induced by Mescaline, Lysergic Acid Diethylamide, and Bromolysergic Acid in the Hamster. *Science* 158:265, 1967.

43 Geber, W. F.: Mechanism of Teratogenesis by Psychotomimetic Compounds. *Fed. Proc.* 27:220, 1968.

44 Grace, D., Carlson, E. A., Goodman, P.: *Drosophila Melanogaster* Treated with LSD: Absence of Mutation and Chromosome Breakage. *Science* 161:694, 1968.

45 Greenblatt, D. J., Shader, R. I.: Adverse Effects of LSD: A Current Perspective. *Connecticut Med.* 34:895, 1970.

46   Grossbard, L., Rosen, D., McDelvray, E., DeCapra, A., Miller, O., Bank, A.: Acute Leukemia with Ph₁-Like Chromosome in an LSD User. *JAMA* 205:167, 1968.

47   Hanaway, J. K.: Lysergic Acid Diethylamide: Effects on the Developing Mouse Lens. *Science* 164:574, 1969.

48   Healy, J. M., Van Houten, P. L.: Effect of Psychotomimetic Agents on Sex Ratio? *Lancet* II:574, 1970.

49   Hecht, F., Beals, R. K., Lees, M. H., Jolly, H., Roberts, P.: Lysergic Acid Diethylamide and Cannabis as Possible Teratogens in Man. *Lancet* II:1087, 1968.

50   Hirschhorn, K., Cohen, M. M.: Nonpsychic Effects of Lysergic Acid Diethylamide. *Ann. Int. Med.* 67:1109, 1967.

51   Hoey, J.: LSD and Chromosome Damage. *JAMA* 212:1707, 1970.

52   Houston, B. K.: Review of the Evidence and Qualification Regarding the Effects of Hallucinogenic Drugs on Chromosomes and Embryos. *Amer. J. Psychiat.* 126:137, 1969.

53   Hsu, L. Y., Strauss, L., Hirschhorn, K.: Chromosome Abnormality in Offspring of LSD User, D. Trisomy with D/D Translocation. *JAMA* 211:987, 1970.

54   Hultén M., Lindsten, J., Lidberg, L., Ecklund, H.: Studies on Mitotic and Meiotic Chromosomes in Subjects Exposed to LSD. *Annales de Génétique* II:201, 1968.

55   Hungerford, D. A., Taylor, K. M., Shagass, C., LaBadie, G. V., Balaban, G. B., Paton, G. R.: Cytogenetic Effects of LSD-25 Therapy in Man. *JAMA* 206:2287, 1968.

56   Idanpään-Heikkilä, J. E., Schoolar, J. C.: LSD Autoradiographic Study on the Placental Transfer and Tissue Distribution in Mice. *Science* 164:1295, 1969.

57   Irwin, S., Egozcue, J.: Chromosomal Abnormalities in Leukocytes from LSD-25 Users. *Science* 157:313, 1967.

58   Irwin, S. Egozcue, J.: Chromosomal Damage Among LSD-25 Users. *Science* 159:749, 1968.

59   Jacobson, C. B., Magyar, V. L.: Genetic Evaluation of LSD. *Clin. Proc. Child. Hosp.*, 24:153, 1968.

60   Jagiello, G., Polani, P. E.: Mouse Germ Cells and LSD-25. *Cytogenetics* 8:136, 1969.

61   Jarvik, L. F.: Contradictions in LSD Research. *Science* 162:621, 1968.

62   Jarvik, L. F., Kato, T.: Is Lysergide a Teratogen? *Lancet* I:250, 1968.

63   Jarvik, L. F., Kato, T., Saunders, B., Moralishvili, E.: LSD and Human Chromosomes. *Psychopharmacology, A Review of Progress* 1957–1967, Pub. Health Service Pub. No. 1836, p. 1247, 1968.

64   Judd, L. L., Brandkamp, W. W., McGlothlin, W. H.: Comparison of the Chromosomal Patterns Obtained from Groups of Continued Users, Former Users, and Nonusers of LSD-25. *Amer. J. Psychiat.* 126:626, 1969.

65 Kato, T., Jarvik, L. F.: LSD-25 and Genetic Damage. *Dis. Nerv. Syst.* 30:42, 1969.

66 Kato, T. Jarvik, L. F., Roizin, L., Moralishvili, E.: Chromosome Studies in Pregnant Rhesus Macaque Given LSD-25. *Dis. Nerv. Syst.* 31:245, 1970.

67 Kruskal, W. H., Haberman, S.: Chromosomal Effect and LSD: Samples of Four. *Science* 162:1508, 1968.

68 Kurland, A. A., Pahnke, W. N., Unger, S., Savage, C., Grof, S.: Psychedelic LSD Research, in *Psychotropic Drugs in the year 2000*, Wayne Evans and Nathan Kline, eds. Charles C. Thomas, Springfield, Ill., 1971.

69 Legator, M. S., Jacobson, C. B.: Chemical Mutagens as a Genetic Hazard. *Clin. Proc. Child. Hosp.*, 24:184, 1968.

70 Loughman, W. D., Sargent, T. W., Israelstam, D. M.: Leukocytes of Humans Exposed to Lysergic Acid Diethylamide: Lack of Chromosomal Damage. *Science* 158:508, 1967.

71 Loughman, W. D., Sargent, T. W.: Answer to "Chromosome Damage by LSD" by H. M. Slatis. *Science* 159:1493, 1968.

72 Lucas, G. J., Lehrnbecher, W.: Evaluation of Chromosomal Changes. *New Eng. J. Med.* 281:1018, 1969.

73 MacKenzie, J. B., Stone, G. E.: Chromosomal Abnormalities in Human Leukocytes Exposed to LSD-25 in Culture. *Mamm. Chromosome Newsl.* 9:212, 1968.

74 Markowitz, E. H., Brosseau, G. E., Jr., Markowitz, E.: Genetic Effects of LSD Treatment on the Post-Meiotic Stages of Spermatogenesis in *Drosophila Melanogaster*. *Mut. Res.* 8:337, 1969.

75 Markowitz, E., Klotz, J. H.,: LSD and Chromosomes. *JAMA* 211:1699, 1970.

76 McGlothlin, W. H., Sparkes, R. S., Arnold, D. O.: Effect of LSD on Human Pregnancy. *JAMA* 212:1483, 1970.

77 Monti, W.: Teratogenic Effects of LSD. *Riv. Ostet. Ginec.* 23:395, 1968.

78 Myers, W. A.: LSD and Marihuana: Where are the Answers? *Science* 160:1062, 1968.

79 Nichols, W. W.: Studies on the Role of Viruses in Somatic Mutation. *Hereditas* 55:1, 1966.

80 Nielsen, J., Friedrich, U., Tsuboi, T.: Chromosome Abnormalities and Psychotropic Drugs. *Nature* 218:488, 1968.

81 Nielsen, J., Friedrich, U., Tsuboi, T., Jacobsen, E.: Lysergide and Chromosome Abnormalities. *Brit. Med. J.* II:801, 1968.

82 Nielsen, J., Friedrich, U., Tsuboi, T.: Chromosome Abnormalities in Patients Treated with Chlorpromazine, Perphenazine, and Lysergide. *Brit. Med. J.* II:634, 1969.

83 Nosal, G.: Complications and Dangers of Hallucinogenic Drugs: Cytopharmacologic Aspects. *Laval Med.* 40:48, 1969.

84   Nowell, P. C., Hungerford, D. A.: Chromosome Studies on Normal and Leukemic Human Leukocytes. *J. Nat. Cancer Inst.* 25(1):85, 1960.

85   Ostertag, W., Duisberg, E., Sturmann, M.: The Mutagenic Activity of Caffeine in Man. *Mut. Res.* 2:293, 1965.

86   Prince, A. M.: LSD and Chromosomes. *Psyched. Rev.* 9:38, 1967.

87   Retterstol, N.: What do we Know Today About the Effect of LSD on Chromosomes and About its Teratogenic Effects? *T. Norsk. Laegeforen* 90:122, 1970.

88   Roux, C., Dupuis, R., Aubry, M.: LSD: No Teratogenic Action in Rats, Mice and Hamsters. *Science* 169:588, 1970.

89   Sato, H., Pergament, E.: Is Lysergide a Teratogen? *Lancet* I:639, 1968.

90   Schmickel, R.: Chromosome Aberrations in Leukocytes Exposed *In Vitro* to Diagnostic Levels of X-Rays. *Amer. J. Hum. Genet.* 19:1, 1967.

91   Sharma, A. K., Sharma, A.: Spontaneous and Chemically Induced Chromosome Breaks. *International Review of Cytology*, G. H. Bourne and J. F. Danielli, eds., vol. 10, p. 101 ff, Academic Press, New York, 1960.

92   Singh, M. P., Kalia, C. S., Jain, H. K.: Chromosomal Aberrations Induced in Barley by LSD. *Science* 169:491, 1970.

93   Siva Sankar, D. V., Rozsa, P. W., Geisler, A.: Chromosome Breakage in Children Treated with LSD-25 and UML-491. *Compreh. Psychiat.* 10:406, 1969.

94   Skakkeback, N. E., Beatty, R. A.: Studies on Meiotic Chromosomes and Spermatozoan Heads in Mice Treated with LSD. *J. Reprod. Fertil.* 22:141, 1970.

95   Skakkebaek, N. E., Phillip, J., Rafaelsen, O. J.: LSD in Mice; Abnormalities in Meiotic Chromosomes. *Science* 160:1246, 1968.

96   Slatis, H. M.: Chromosome Damage by LSD. *Science* 150:1492, 1968.

97   Smart, R. G., Bateman, K.: The Chromosomal and Teratogenic Effects of Lysergic Acid Diethylamide: A Review of the Current Literature. *Canad. Med. Ass. J.* 99:805, 1968.

98   Smythies, J. R., Antun, F.: Binding of Tryptamine and Allied Compounds to Nucleic Acids. *Nature* 233:1063, 1969.

99   Sparkes, R. S., Melnyk, J., Bozzetti, L. P.: Chromosomal Effect *In Vivo* of Exposure to Lysergic Acid Diethylamide. *Science* 160:1343, 1968.

100   Sparkes, R. S., Thomas, D., Melnyk, J., Bozzetti, L. P.: Chromosomal Effect and LSD: Samples of Four. *Science* 162:1509, 1968.

101   Šrám, R. J.: Mutagenic Effect of LSD in *Drosophila Melanogaster*. *Activ. Nerv. Super.* (Praha), 12:265, 1970.

102   Stenchever, M. A., Jarvis, J. A.: Lysergic Acid Diethylamide (LSD): Effect on Human Chromosomes *In Vivo*. *Amer. J. Obstet. & Gyn.* 106:485, 1970.

103   Stoll, A., Rothlin, E., Rutschmann, J., Schlach, W. R.: Distribution and Fate of 14C-Labeled LSD-25 in the Animal Body. *Experientia* 11:396, 1955.

104   Stubbs, V., Jacobson, C. B.: LSD and Genetic Damage. *George Wash. Univ. Magazine*, 5:26, 1969.

105   Sturelid, S., Kihlman, B. D.: Lysergic Acid Diethylamide and Chromosome Breakage. *Hereditas* 62:259, 1969.

106   Tjio, J. H., Pahnke, W. N., Kurland, A. A.: LSD and Chromosomes, A Controlled Experiment. *JAMA* 210:849, 1969.

107   Tjio, J. H., Pahnke, W. N., Kurland, A. A.: Pre- and Post-LSD Chromosomal Aberrations: A Comparative Study. In: *Advances in Biochemical Psychopharmacology*, (E. Costa and P. Greengard, eds.) vol. 1, p. 191, Raven Press, New York, 1969.

108   Tylden, E.: Problems Associated with LSD. *Brit. Med. J.* II:704, 1968.

109   Uyeno, E. T.: Lysergic Acid Diethylamide in Gravid Rats. *Proc. West. Pharmacol. Soc.* 13, 1970.

110   Uyeno, E. T.: Effects of Prenatally Administered Lysergic Acid Diethylamide on the Viability and Behavioral Development of Rat Offspring. Report of the 32nd. Annual Meeting of the Committee on Problems of Drug Dependence, Feb., 1970, Washington, D.C.

111   Vann, E.: Lethal Mutation Rate in *Drosophila* Exposed to LSD-25 by Injection and Ingestion. *Nature* 223:95, 1969.

112   Wagner, T. E.: *In Vitro* Interaction of LSD with Purified Calf Thymus DNA. *Nature* 222:1170, 1969.

113   Warkany, J., Takacz, E.: Lysergic Acid Diethylamide (LSD): No Teratogenecity in Rats. *Science* 159:731, 1968.

114   Whitmore, F. W.: Chromosomal Effect and LSD: Samples of Four. *Science* 162:1508, 1968.

115   Yielding, K. L., Sterglanz, H.: Lysergic Acid Diethylamide (LSD) Binding to Deoxyribonucleic Acid (DNA) (33203). *Soc. exp. Biol. Med.* 128:1096, 1968.

116   Zellweger, H., McDonald, J. S., Abbo, G.: Is Lysergic Acid Diethylamide a Teratogen? *Lancet* II:1066, 1967.

117   Zellweger, H., McDonald, J. S., Abbo, G.: Is Lysergide a Teratogen? *Lancet* II:1306, 1967.

118   Zetterberg, G.: Lysergic Acid Diethylamide and Mutation. *Hereditas* 62:262, 1969.

INDEX

STANISLAV GROF RECEIVES THE DAGMAR AND VÁCLAV HAVEL FOUNDATION VISION 97 AWARD

By R.M. Crockford
October 2007

ANOTHER CHAPTER in Prague's history as a city of unusual wonder was recorded on October 5, when the Dagmar and Václav Havel Foundation VISION 97, created by playwright and former Czech President, Václav Havel, presented a lifetime achievement award to Dr. Stanislav Grof, one of the world's leading psychedelic researchers. Dr. Grof, who was born near Prague in 1931, pioneered LSD-assisted psychotherapy in Czechoslovakia until he immigrated to the United States in 1967.

The ceremonies took place at the Prague Crossroads, a deconsecrated 10th-century church converted into a spiritual and meeting center by Mr. Havel's foundation. The day began with Dr. Grof signing copies of New Perspectives in Psychiatry and Psychology, a collection of his recent writings in Czech, and then joining a two-hour panel discussion about his work and the challenges of trying to reconcile mystical experiences with organized religion and modern psychiatry. The discussions, open to the public, were attended by about 100 well-wishers – a local magazine recently named Dr. Grof one of the 20 most important spiritual leaders in the Czech nation's history – along with several Czechs trained in holotropic breathwork, a drug-free method to induce non-ordinary states of consciousness that Dr. Grof developed with his wife Christina.

"Many addicts are on a journey to find something, and they had several mystical experiences, but most of them were not able to integrate them," said Dr. Stanislav Kudrle, a Czech psychiatrist who has used breathwork to treat drug and alcohol dependent individuals for 18 years. "What Stan Grof did is, he brought the maps, he brought the model and the method which makes it possible to support these people on their quest."

Not everyone was pleased about the awarding of the Havel prize to Dr. Grof. Priests and psychiatrists were quoted in a Prague newspaper that day saying the Foundation had made an "embarrassing mistake," and a Czech skeptics society accused Dr. Grof of "propagating absurd ideas" by claiming that breathwork enables participants to re-experience past lives and their own birth. But President Havel himself dismissed such criticisms later in the evening, in his speech to the packed auditorium.

"This prize is for visionaries, for explorers, for people who overstep boundaries and notice new and unpredictable connections," said Havel. Such researchers take risks, he noted, because they're often attacked by "hard traditionalists who can't imagine that science could step beyond its own limits. These people can even be fanatical opponents to anything that is outside traditional thinking. In the name of rationality, they sometimes actually fight against new ideas."

"I've always believed that what happened once can't be erased, that the whole history of our planet, and the cosmos, is being written somewhere – that Being has its own memory," Havel continued. "The work of Dr. Grof showed me that sometimes, something can return from this greater memory to our own consciousness. And that we can surprisingly experience, maybe only for a few minutes, something that happened a long time ago, or in faraway places, that we couldn't know by other means."

Havel and his wife Dagmar presented Dr. Grof with a stylized Crutch of St. Vojtech (Adalbert), the patron saint of Bohemia. Afterwards, Dr. Grof said he was deeply moved by the ceremony. It brought his work back to his birthplace, he noted, and it was an honor to be recognized by a statesman and philosopher he greatly admires.

"And then [there was] the tremendous surprise that Václav Havel had the courage to appreciate research in something that's so controversial. It's extremely important in terms of other people taking a second look, because of whom he is. I hope that it can ultimately help the field."

R.M. Crockford is a Canadian writer researching the psychiatric use of LSD in Czechoslovakia in the 1960s. eskelsd@hotmail.com

Dr. Stanislav Grof receiving Václav Havel's Vision Award at the ceremony on October 5, 2007 in Prague. President Havel is giving him the Crutch of St. Vojtech (a symbol associated with the Czech holy patron) and a diploma, with the orchestra in the background.

Havel's Description of the Award:

TO THINKERS whose scientific work returns science into the framework of general culture, transcends the dominant concepts of knowledge and being, reveals unknown, surprising, or overlooked connections, and touches in a new way the mysteries of the universe and of life. It is thus an Award by which we would like to bring the attention of the public to spiritual achievements, which in the best sense of the word do not meet the criteria of the established ways of exploring reality.

Previous winners of the award include Karl Pribram, Umberto Eco, Robert Reich, and Joseph Wiezenbaum.

Stanislav Grof: On the occasion of the Dagmar and Václav Havel Foundation VISION 97 Award

Prague Crossroads 5 October 2007

Dear Mrs. Havel, Dear President Havel, Ladies and Gentlemen:

It is a great pleasure for me to return to Prague, where I was born, spent my childhood, grew up, and received my basic training. An even greater source of pleasure than my visit to this city that I love so much are the extraordinary circumstances that brought me to Prague this time. I would like to thank wholeheartedly President Havel, Mrs. Havel, and the board of consultants of the Dagmar and Václav Havel Foundation for granting me the prestigious Vision 97 Award for my work in the area of research of consciousness and the human psyche. It is for me an immense honor and also a great surprise after fifty years of struggle with the "public anonym" in science, described in such an articulate way by Professor Vopenka in his 2004 acceptance speech, after he himself received the Vision 97 Award.

An important reason why the Vision 97 Award means so much to me is my profound admiration and respect for President Havel as artist, philosopher, and statesman with a broad spiritual vision and as a man of extraordinary personal values. My admiration is shared by many of my American friends, who have repeatedly expressed to me their wish to have in the present difficult situation a president with the intellectual, moral, and spiritual qualities of Václav Havel. And during my journeys to different countries, I often had the opportunity to find out that similar feelings are shared by many people all over the world. I cannot imagine another appreciation of my work that would be for me personally more meaningful. Today's ceremony falls on President Havel's birthday, and I would like to use this opportunity to congratulate him on this important anniversary and wish him much happiness, inner peace, personal satisfaction, and good health in the years to come.

It seems to be my destiny – or karma if you wish – to be involved in research of areas that are subjects of great controversy in science and society. My unconventional professional career started here in Prague more than fifty years ago when I volunteered as a beginning psychiatrist for a session with LSD-25, diethylamid of lysergic acid. My preceptor, Docent Roubíček, received this fascinating experimental substance from the Swiss pharmaceutical company, Sandoz. The incredibly powerful psychedelic effects of this ergot alkaloid had been discovered by Dr. Albert Hofmann, who accidentally intoxicated himself while working on its synthesis.

The research project of Docent Roubíček required a combination of the pharmacological effect of LSD with exposure to a powerful stroboscopic light oscillating at various frequencies. This combination evoked in me a powerful mystical experience that has radically changed my personal and professional life. It had such a profound effect on me that research of the heuristic, therapeutic, transformative, and evolutionary potential of non-ordinary states of consciousness has become my profession, vocation, and personal passion for the rest of my life.

During approximately half of this period, my interest focused on clinical research of psychedelic substances, first at the Psychiatric Research Institute in Prague-Bohnice and later at the Maryland Psychiatric Research Center in Baltimore, Maryland, where I headed for several years the last surviving official psychedelic research in the United States. During the second half of this period, my wife Christina and I developed jointly the method of Holotropic Breathwork, which induces deep non-ordinary states of consciousness with the use of very simple means, such as accelerated breathing, evocative music, and a certain kind of bodywork. Over the years, we have also worked with many people undergoing spontaneous episodes of non-ordinary states of consciousness – psychospiritual crises or "spiritual emergencies" as we call them.

Research of non-ordinary states of consciousness (or their important subgroup, for which I coined the term "holotropic") has been for me a source of countless surprises and conceptual shocks, requiring radical changes in understanding consciousness, the human psyche, and the nature of reality. After many years of daily encounters with "anomalous phenomena," which contemporary science was unable to explain and the existence of which was in conflict with its fundamental metaphysical assumptions, I came to the conclusion that careful study of holotropic states and various phenomena, which are associated with them, such as statistically highly improbable meaningful coincidences (Jung's "synchronicities") shows the inevitability of a radical revision of thinking in psychology and psychiatry.

Conceptual changes required in these disciplines would in their nature, depth, and scope resemble the revolution that the physicists experienced in the first three decades of the twentieth century, when they had to move from Newtonian mechanics to theories of relativity and later to quantum physics. It is even possible to say that – in a certain sense – this conceptual revolution would be a logical completion of the radical changes, which many years ago already occurred in physics.

The changes in the understanding of consciousness and of the human psyche in health and disease that naturally follow from the research of holotropic states fall into several categories. This research has shown the necessity to expand the traditional model of the psyche, limited to postnatal biography and the Freudian individual unconscious by two vast areas – perinatal (which has a close connection with the memories of biological birth) and transpersonal (mediating experiences of identification with other people, animals, and the botanical realm and with human and animal ancestors, as well as experiences of the historical and archetypal collective unconscious, as described by C.G. Jung). Traditional psychiatry sees the beginnings of "psychogenic" disorders – those that do not have any demonstrable biological causes – in infancy and childhood. The work with holotropic states shows clearly that these disorders have additional deep roots in the perinatal and transpersonal realms of the unconscious. This finding might seem – in and of itself – very pessimistic, but it is outweighed by the discovery of new effective therapeutic mechanisms, which operate on these deep levels of the unconscious.

The goal in traditional psychotherapies is to reach intellectual understanding of how the human psyche functions, what are its basic motivating forces, why symptoms develop and what is their meaning. This understanding then forms the basis for the development of techniques that psychotherapists use for the treatment of their clients. A serious problem associated with this strategy is a striking lack of agreement among psychologists and psychiatrists concerning the most fundamental theoretical problems and, consequently, an astonishing number of competing schools of psychotherapy. The work with holotropic states offers a surprising, radical alternative – mobilization of the deep inner healing intelligence of clients that is capable of governing the process of healing and transformation.

Materialistic science does not have a place for any form of spirituality and considers it to be essentially incompatible with the scientific worldview. It perceives any form of spirituality as an indication of lack of education, superstition, gullibility, primitive magical thinking, or a serious psychopathological condition. Modern consciousness research shows that spirituality is a natural and legitimate dimension of the human psyche and of the universal order of things. However, it is important to emphasize that this statement refers to direct authentic spirituality based on personal experience and not to the ideology and dogmas of organized religions.

New observations show that consciousness is not an epiphenomenon of matter – a product of complex neurophysiological processes in the brain – but a fundamental primary attribute of existence, as it is described in the great spiritual philosophies of the East. As suggested by the Swiss psychiatrist C.G. Jung, the psyche is not enclosed in the human skull and brain, but permeates all of existence (as anima mundi). The individual human psyche is an integral part of this cosmic matrix and can under certain circumstances experientially identify with its various aspects.

This new understanding of the human psyche has important sociopolitical implications. Medical anthropologists have shown that the striking physical differences between various human groups disappear when the scientific research of Homo sapiens penetrates the thin layers of the epidermis; the basic anatomical, physiological, and biochemical characteristics are shared by all of humanity. Modern consciousness research complemented this observation by similar findings related to the human psyche. On the postnatal biographical level exist large individual and cultural differences; the conditions of life differ radically from person to person from family to family, and from culture to culture. However, these differences begin to disappear as soon as experiential self-exploration in holotropic states of consciousness reaches the perinatal level. All members of the human species share the experiences of prenatal life and birth; the differences in this area are inter-individual rather than specific for various racial groups. And when the process of deep experiential probing reaches the transpersonal level, all differences disappear.

Our observations have shown that people from all human groups with whom Christina and I have worked in various parts of the world – in Europe, India, Japan, Taiwan, Australia, South, Central, and North America, Australia, and Polynesia – had in their holotropic experiences access to the entire collective unconscious as described by C.G. Jung, both in its historicaland archetypal-mythological realms, without regard to their own racial, national, and cultural background. These experiences have even frequently bridged gender differences – many karmic, ancestral, and racial experiences contained convincing identification with members of the opposite sex. Equally frequent were identifications with representatives of other animal species. Observations of this kind provide strong evidence for something that traditional materialistic scientists would consider impossible and utterly absurd – that the entire history of humanity and life on this planet are permanently recorded in an immaterial field to which each of us has under certain circumstances experiential access. Hungarian/Italian system theorist, Ervin Laszlo, has been able to define scientifically such a field and gave it the name the "psi field;" more recently, he renamed it as the "akashic field" by linking it explicitly to the spiritual traditions.

Perinatal and transpersonal experiences have profound psychological implications. When the content of the perinatal level of the unconscious surfaces into consciousness and is adequately processed and integrated, it results in a radical personality change. The individual experiences a considerable decrease of aggressive tendencies and becomes more tolerant and compassionate toward others. The experience of psychospiritual death and rebirth and conscious connection with positive postnatal and prenatal memories, reduces irrational ambitions and urges and increases élan vital and joi d'vivre – the ability to enjoy life and draw satisfaction from simple situations such as everyday activity, eating, love-making, nature, and music.

The process of spiritual opening and transformation typically deepens further as a result of transpersonal experiences. Feelings of oneness with the universe and its creative principle lead to identification with all sentient beings and bring a sense of awe, wonder, love, compassion, and inner peace. Spirituality that results from this process is universal, all-encompassing, transcending all organized religions; it resembles the attitude to the Cosmos found in the mystics of all ages. It is extremely authentic and convincing, because it is based on deep personal experience. It is therefore capable of competing successfully with the dogmas of organized religions, as well as the monistic-materialistic worldview of Western science.

People, who are experientially connected with the transpersonal dimensions, have a tendency to appreciate existence and feel reverence for all creation. One of the most remarkable consequences of various forms of transpersonal experiences is spontaneous emergence and development of genuine humanitarian and ecological interests and need to take part in activities aimed at peaceful coexistence and well-being of humanity. This is based on an almost cellular understanding that any boundaries in the Cosmos are relative and arbitrary and that each of us is, in the last analysis, identical and commeasurable with the entire fabric of existence. As a result of these experiences, individuals tend to develop feelings that they are planetary citizens and members of the human family before belonging to a particular country or a specific racial, social, ideological, political, or religious group. It seems obvious that transformation of this kind could significantly increase our chances of survival, if it could occur on a sufficiently large scale.

It seems that we are involved in a dramatic race for time, which has no parallel in human history. What is at stake is nothing less than the future of humanity and the fate of life on our planet. If we continue using the old strategies that have caused the current global crisis and which are in their consequences destructive and self-destructive, it might lead to annihilation of modern civilization and possibly even the human species. However, if a sufficient number of people undergo a process of inner psychospiritual transformation and attain a higher level of awareness, we might in the future reach a situation when we will deserve the name, which we have so proudly given to our species: Homo sapiens sapiens.

In closing, I would like to express my deep gratitude to Christina, my wife, best friend, and co-worker, for everything that she contributed over the years to the research, which has today received such an extraordinary appreciation.

AFTERWORD:
THE PSYCHEDELIC RESEARCH RENAISSANCE —
A REVIEW OF RECENT PSYCHEDELIC
PSYCHOTHERAPY RESEARCH

By: L. Jerome, Ph.D., Valerie Mojeiko, Rick Doblin, Ph.D.

IT IS NOW 2008, and this is the fourth time that LSD Psychotherapy by Dr. Stanislav Grof has gone to press. Since the third edition was published seven years ago, more progress has been made in the field of psychedelic therapy than in the previous twenty-one years since its original publication. There are currently patients being treated around the globe with psilocybin, MDMA, ibogaine, and soon LSD, as part of legitimate "above-ground" research investigations. The renewal of LSD-assisted psychotherapy research marks the culmination of the initial period of the renaissance of psychedelic research. Indeed, LSD is perhaps the most controversial of all the psychedelics due to its widespread non-medical use in the 1960s and its association with political protest groups, most notably the anti-Vietnam War movement. This afterward aims to summarize the tremendous accomplishments that have enabled the pioneering research of Dr. Grof and many others to return to the laboratory in mainstream Western society.

Three American organizations have been instrumental in sponsoring and funding the resurgence of research: the Multidisciplinary Association for Psychedelic Studies (MAPS; www.maps.org) (the publisher of this book), the Heffter Research Institute (HRI; www.heffter.org), and the Council on Spiritual Practices (www.csp.org). All three organizations are located and sponsor research in the United States. MAPS also sponsors research in Europe, Israel, Canada, and Mexico, and HRI sponsors research in Switzerland. In Switzerland, the Swiss Association for Psycholytic Therapy (SAePT) has also played over the years, and continues to play, a role in keeping the torch burning and in co-sponsoring research.

After thousands of psychedelic research studies were conducted from the 1940s to the late 1960's, nearly all human studies of LSD, psilocybin, and other psychedelics ceased in 1972 in the US and around the world as a result of political suppression. However, after almost twenty-years of hiatus, with the approval of a new generation of regulators, a new generation of researchers began cautiously studying psychedelic drugs and MDMA in the context of research into the correlates of consciousness and basic psychopharmacology, and the potential of these substances as psychotherapeutic agents. Kicking off this new paradigm in 1990, Dr. Rick Strassman investigated the physiological and subjective effects of N,N-5,5-dimethyltryptamine (DMT), assessing subjective and physiological effects after injections of up to 0.4

mg/kg DMT (Strassman 1994; Strassman 1996; Strassman and Qualls 1994).

There are currently seven basic areas of clinical research into the uses of psychedelics that will be discussed in more detail below:

1) Psychedelic (psilocybin, LSD, and MDMA)-assisted psychotherapy in subjects with anxiety associated with end-of-life issues
2) Psilocybin in the treatment of obsessive-compulsive disorder (OCD),
3) LSD, lysergic acid amide (LSA), and psilocybin in the treatment of cluster headaches (CH),
4) Psilocybin in catalyzing spiritual experiences,
5) MDMA-assisted psychotherapy in subjects with posttraumatic stress disorder (PTSD)
6) Ketamine-assisted psychotherapy and ibogaine use in the treatment of alcoholism and opiate dependence
7) Basic scientific studies with various psychedelics

Many of the psychotherapy studies described below involve psychotherapy that is either directly based upon or borrows elements from the psychotherapeutic methods of Dr. Grof. These elements include: performing therapy in a setting specifically designed for comfort and introspection, treatment by a male/female pair of co-therapists, the use of musical programs, and encouraging patients to confront whatever feelings arise while the therapists serve as supportive guides in the experience. Even when not seeking to replicate Grof's techniques, people studying psychedelic-assisted psychotherapy have been influenced by the LSD-assisted psychotherapy performed by Dr. Grof.

PSILOCYBIN/LSD/MDMA PSYCHOTHERAPY IN SUBJECTS WITH END-OF-LIFE RELATED ANXIETY

Researchers interested in studying this therapeutic potential of psychedelic drugs began conducting studies during the early 2000s. Many of these studies are based on at least some features of Dr. Grof's original format for LSD therapy. In April 2004, Charles S. Grob, M.D. began a pilot study at the Los Angeles Biomedical Research Institute at Harbor-UCLA Medical Center examining psilocybin-assisted psychotherapy as a potential treatment for anxiety in 12 subjects diagnosed with advanced-stage cancer (Grob 2005). The study aims to test whether psilocybin might be effective in reducing anxiety, depression, and physical pain, thereby improving the quality of life for these patients. Dr. Grob wished to follow the model and research first laid down by Grof (Grob 2007 (personal communication)). At the time of this writing, 11 of 12 subjects in this study, sponsored by HRI, have completed the treatment. Study results have not yet been published.

A MAPS-funded study under development will examine the safety and efficacy of psilocybin-assisted psychotherapy in treating nine subjects with anxiety associated with Stage IV melanoma. This investigation will take place at the Mt. Sinai Comprehensive Cancer Center (MSCCC) in Miami, Florida, and the principal investigator is Sameet Kumar, Ph.D., Clinical Psychologist in MSCCC's Department of Psychosocial Services. The FDA has reviewed the protocol favorably, which at the time of this writing is under review with the Institutional Review Board (IRB) at MSCCC. The study is expected to commence in early 2008.

MAPS and SAePT are co-sponsoring a similar study of illness-related anxiety using LSD rather than psilocybin, studying people with any life-threatening diagnosis in addition to diagnoses of advanced-stage cancer. This study is to take place in Solothurn, Switzerland, under the direction of Peter Gasser, M.D. (Gasser 2007). Though there has been prior research with LSD in cancer patients with anxiety that demonstrated safety and some degree of efficacy (Grof et al. 1973; Kast 1967; Kast and Collins 1964; Pahnke et al. 1971), no researchers have been able to follow up on these findings during the past 35 years. Dr. Gasser's study has been approved by both a Swiss Ethics Committee and SwissMedic. This study is also expected to commence in early 2008.

MAPS was instrumental in initiating a study at Harvard Medical School's McLean Hospital investigating MDMA-assisted psychotherapy in the treatment of anxiety associated with a diagnosis of advanced-stage cancer (Halpern 2006). Principal investigator John H. Halpern, M.D. plans to enroll 12 participants and has begun to recruit people for this study. This is the first clinical study of any psychedelic to take place at Harvard Medical School since 1965.

Psilocybin in Subjects with Obsessive Compulsive Disorder

Beyond the indications that Dr. Grof outlined in this seminal text, anecdotal reports have led researchers to examine the potential applications of psychedelics to the treatment of other conditions. Dr. Francisco Moreno and colleagues recently investigated psilocybin as a potential treatment for nine patients suffering from OCD (Moreno et al. 2006). Dr. Moreno's team conducted their research on the basis of previous medical case reports of efficacy (Hanes 1996; Leonard and Rapoport 1987; Moreno and Delgado 1997). Subjects in the study received four different doses of psilocybin ranging from sub-psychedelic to frankly psychedelic. Marked decreases in OCD symptoms of variable degrees were observed in all subjects during one or more of the treatment sessions.

LSD, LSA, and Psilocybin in Subjects with Cluster Headache

CH is an extremely painful and often treatment-resistant type of headache. However, a group of individuals suffering from cluster headaches discovered a potential application of psychedelics in the treatment of this debilitating disorder. Clusterbusters (clusterbusters.com), an organization founded by people with CH, is sponsoring research with some support from MAPS that will examine the safety and efficacy of using LSD, psilocybin, or LSA-containing "morning glory" seeds to interrupt CH cycles or to prevent future CH attacks from occurring. This research grew out of the experience of Clusterbuster members, and is supported by a case series (Sewell et al. 2006). All three psychedelic compounds seem to help people with CH, with preliminary evidence suggesting that LSD is the most effective treatment. Research will also be important to confirm safety from ergotism, which is a potential complication from repeated and/or high-dose exposures to most botanical sources of LSA as a result of containing other ergolines (Chao and Der Marderosian 1973). Protocols to study the use of LSD and psilocybin in the treatment of CH are currently in the protocol development and approval stage at McLean Hospital, Harvard Medical School, under the direction of principal investigator Dr. Halpern.

Psilocybin in Catalyzing Spiritual Experiences

Research examining the effects of psilocybin and other psychedelics has provided the basis for a recent study investigating spiritual experiences arising from the use of psilocybin. A study supported by the Council on Spiritual Practices showed psilocybin to be a catalyst for peak or spiritual experiences when administered to people with established religious or spiritual practices (Griffiths et al. 2006). This study garnered significant media attention, and that attention has made it easier for other studies to take place, most notably the study of psilocybin-assisted psychotherapy under development with Dr. Kumar at MSCCC.

MDMA Research

The renewal of formal psychedelic research began primarily with MDMA, which was legal until 1985 and which is milder and shorter-acting than the traditional psychedelics such as LSD and psilocybin.

George Greer, M.D. and Requa Tolbert, R.N., M.S.N. (1986) conducted an uncontrolled study of then legal MDMA-assisted psychotherapy. This work was inspired in part by attending a seminar that Dr. Grof conducted at Esalen on psychedelic psychotherapy in 1975 (Greer 2007). Greer and Tolbert used psychotherapeutic methods largely adapted from those found in *LSD Psychotherapy*. After MDMA was criminalized in the US in 1985, the FDA initially refused to permit clinical research.

In 1985, the World Health Organization (WHO) Expert Committee on Drug Dependence issued its 22nd Report, in which MDMA was recommended for criminalization around the world. This recommendation was made over the objection of the Chairman, Dr. Paul Grof (Stan Grof's brother), who managed to persuade the Committee to conclude its recommendation with a statement urging "countries to use the provisions of article 7 of the Convention of Psychotropic Substances to facilitate research on this interesting substance."

In 1988, based in part on the justification provided by this sentence, the Swiss Ministry of Health authorized a small group of psychiatrists to administer MDMA and LSD to their patients. No formal research was required but permission was withdrawn in 1993. In order to gather some data, self-report questionnaires were mailed to patients asking them to evaluate the outcomes of their therapy (Gasser, 1994).

In 1992, the FDA approved the first human research with MDMA, permitting Dr. Charles Grob to conduct a MAPS-sponsored Phase I dose-response study. In 1996, Dr. Grob and colleagues published their results (Grob et al. 1996).

Interest in the effects of MDMA and psychedelic drugs continued to grow throughout the 1990s. Franz Vollenweider, M.D. and colleagues at the University of Zurich took up two programs of research in the mid-1990s, one studying psilocybin and the other MDMA. The Zurich team conducted brain imaging and reported on the metabolism and subjective effects of psilocybin (Hasler et al. 1997; Vollenweider et al. 1998a; Vollenweider et al. 1997; Vollenweider et al. 1998b). They continued this research with a number of studies into the effects of psilocybin on brain function and some of the receptor systems involved in producing these effects (Umbricht et al. 2003; Vollenweider et al. 1999). The Zurich team also conducted studies on the subjective, physiological, and neuroendocrine effects of MDMA in humans

(Vollenweider et al. 1998a), and they performed imaging and EEG studies, as well (Frei et al. 2001; Gamma et al. 2000). This team conducted studies with 74 participants and included evaluation of neurotransmitter systems involved in the acute effects of MDMA (Liechti et al. 2001; Liechti and Vollenweider 2001). Euphrosyne Gouzoulis-Mayfrank, M.D. and colleagues at the University of Aachen, Germany began performing studies with psilocybin and the MDMA relative, 3,4-methylenedioxyethylamphetamine (MDE) at approximately the same time as the Zurich team (Gouzoulis et al. 1992; Spitzer et al. 1996), culminating in studies comparing these drugs with the psychostimulant methamphetamine (Gouzoulis-Mayfrank et al. 1999a; Gouzoulis-Mayfrank et al. 1999b).

Only a few years later, a team of researchers in Barcelona, Spain began studying the effects of MDMA in male volunteers (Cami et al. 2000; Mas et al. 1999). In 2000, a MAPS-sponsored Spanish researcher, José Carlos Bouso, Ph.D., began a pilot study of MDMA-assisted psychotherapy in women with PTSD related to sexual assault; his studies were halted in 2002 for political reasons after media coverage of the study (Bouso 2003). With the exception of the work of Greer and Tolbert and this preliminary work in Spain, which remains unpublished to date (Bouso et al. 2008), these initial studies did not consider the therapeutic potential of psychedelic drugs, but their findings supported the safety of human trials.

Researchers at the University of California-San Francisco studied the physiological, subjective, and neuroendocrine effects of MDMA (Harris et al. 2002; Lester et al. 2000), with funding from the US National Institute on Drug Abuse (NIDA). Around the same time, addiction researchers at Wayne State University began NIDA-funded studies on MDMA that included investigations of desirable drug effects ("reinforcing effects") and neurotransmitter systems involved in producing MDMA effects (Tancer and Johanson 2001; Tancer and Johanson 2003).

MDMA-Assisted Psychotherapy in Subjects with Posttraumatic Stress Disorder

Researchers are also picking up where Greer and Tolbert left off with respect to MDMA-assisted psychotherapy. Not long after Dr. Grob had begun the study of psilocybin-assisted psychotherapy, the FDA reviewed and the IRB approved the first study of MDMA-assisted psychotherapy. In March 2004, Michael Mithoefer, M.D. and Ann Mithoefer, B.S.N. became the first legal MDMA psychotherapy researchers in the United States when they began using MDMA in survivors of sexual or other physical assault with treatment-resistant PTSD (Mithoefer 2004; 2006). The study, which is taking place in Charleston, South Carolina, recently recruited its 20th subject, and the investigators will be analyzing final results in the middle of 2008. Study criteria were expanded over the course of the recruitment period to include subjects with war and terrorism-related PTSD, and there are two veterans of the war in Iraq enrolled in the study. The second vet (Subject #21, the final subject in the study) required FDA and IRB approval prior to enrollment. Though classified as disabled by the VA, he was not offered individual psychotherapy and was thus not a treatment failure. Results from this Phase II study will be submitted to the FDA as the basis for a larger Phase III study that will be designed to generate data under an investigational new drug application (IND) seeking eventual approval

366

of MDMA-assisted psychotherapy as a legal pharmaceutical treatment.

This was the flagship study for several more of its kind, all sponsored by MAPS in an effort to develop MDMA as a prescription medicine. A Phase II, MDMA/PTSD pilot study taking place in Switzerland under the direction of Peter Oehen, M.D. and Verena Widmer, R.N. began in 2006 and has currently treated four (one dropped out) out of an eventual 12 subjects, under a similar protocol and subject population as the study in the US (Oehen 2006). The data from this Swiss study will be submitted to the European Medicines Agency (EMEA) in addition to the US FDA. A study is also underway in Israel at Beer Yaakov Mental Health Center investigating MDMA's efficacy in treating subjects with war and terrorism-related PTSD (Mojeiko 2006). Principal investigator Moshe Kotler, M.D. is former chief psychiatrist of the Israeli Defense Forces and is the current chair of the Department of Psychiatry at Tel Aviv University's Sackler School of Medicine. This data will also go toward approval by both the US FDA and EMEA.

Ibogaine Research in Subjects with Opiate Dependence

A myriad of ibogaine clinics have sprung up all over North America and Europe to treat people with addictions. This work is in line with anecdotal reports and research findings in non-human subjects suggesting that ibogaine is effective at eliminating or reducing the signs of opiate withdrawal (Alper 2001). MAPS is currently sponsoring two observational case series, one now underway and another in development, that will study the long-term effectiveness of ibogaine in treating dependence to opiates and other drugs. These observational studies will survey people who are already receiving treatment from existing clinics for up to 12 months after being administered ibogaine. Along the line of Dr. Grof's work in the use of LSD to treat addictions, these studies will pay particular attention to the content of the psychedelic experience and how it relates to recovery rates.

Ketamine-Assisted Psychotherapy in Alcoholics and Opiate Dependent Subjects

Evgeny Krupitsky, M.D., a Russian researcher, has reported promising findings from treating people with dependence to alcohol and heroin through the use of the dissociative psychedelic ketamine (Krupitsky et al. 2002; Krupitsky et al. 2001; Krupitsky and Grinenko 1997). In a MAPS and HRI co-sponsored study, Dr. Krupitsky found that the subjects in the experimental group who received a high, psychedelic dose of ketamine had a significantly greater rate of abstinence in a two year follow-up period than people who received a low, sub-psychedelic dose of ketamine. He has also found that multiple ketamine-assisted psychotherapy sessions are more effective than a single session, demonstrating that the one-dose miracle cure model needs to be replaced by the more realistic model of repeated sessions over time (Krupitsky et al. 2007). Unfortunately, Dr. Krupitsky has been blocked from conducting further studies due to the rise of the non-medical use of ketamine in Russia and the heavy-handed refusal of the Russian authorities to permit continued scientific research into ketamine's therapeutic uses in the treatment of addiction.

367

Basic Science with Psilocybin, DMT, Ayahuasca, MDMA

Scientists studying perception, attention, and cognition continue to examine the effects of psilocybin, ayahuasca (the South American psychedelic brew and its constituent DMT) and MDMA in humans. Working with Dr. Vollenweider's research team at the University of Zurich, Dr. Olivia Carter and colleagues have studied and published findings on the effects of psilocybin on visual perception (Carter et al. 2005; Carter et al. 2007; Carter et al. 2004; Wittmann et al. 2007). The Zurich team has also continued publishing papers on the subjective and physiological effects of different doses of psilocybin (Hasler et al. 2004). In Spain, Jordi Riba, Ph.D. and colleagues have studied the physiological, electroencepha-lographic, and subjective effects of freeze-dried ayahuasca (Riba et al. 2004; Riba et al. 2002a; Riba et al. 2002b; Riba et al. 2001). Continuing in the vein of her earlier research, Dr. Gouzoulis-Mayfrank and colleagues are now comparing and contrasting the acute subjective, and cognitive effects of DMT with those of ketamine, using within-subject designs (Gouzoulis-Mayfrank et al. 2006; Gouzoulis-Mayfrank et al. 2005; Heekeren et al. 2007). Meanwhile, in the Netherlands, Kim P.C. Kuypers, Ph.D. and colleagues are studying the acute effects of MDMA upon skills employed in driving vehicles, including visual attention, perception, and impulsivity (Kuypers and Ramaekers 2005; 2007; Kuypers et al. 2007; Ramaekers and Kuypers 2006). Only now are these studies taking up the promise that psychedelic compounds offer in understanding perception, cognition, and the correlates of consciousness.

Conclusion

After over thirty years of quiescence, psychiatric and psychological research has rediscovered the potential of psychedelic compounds. The current group of studies is more sophisticated than its predecessors, and some have even taken up the challenge of investigating psychedelic-assisted psychotherapy. In a climate where the US Supreme Court recently ruled to stay the hand of the federal government in further prosecuting a religion for using ayahuasca tea (Gonzales v. O Centro Espirita Beneficente União Do Vegetal, 2006), research into the therapeutic uses of psychedelics is finally thriving. Western culture is once again opening up to the idea of using psychedelics as medicines and beginning the healing of the deep traumas of our society, a fitting tribute to the power of the ideas and data presented by Dr. Stanislav Grof in *LSD Psychotherapy*.

References for Afterword

Alper KR (2001) Ibogaine: a review. Alkaloids Chem Biol 56: 1-38

Bouso JC (2003) MDMA/PTSD research in Spain: An update. MAPS Bulletin 13: 7-8

Bouso JC, Doblin R, Farre M, Alcazar MA, Gomez-Jarabo G (2008) 3,4-Methylene-dioxymethamphetamine (MDMA)-assisted psychotherapy, using low doses, in a small sample of women with chronic Posttraumatic Stress Disorder (PTSD). J Psychoactive Drugs, in press

Cami J, Farre M, Mas M, Roset PN, Poudevida S, Mas A, San L, de la Torre R (2000) Human pharmacology of 3,4-methylenedioxymethamphetamine ("ecstasy"): psychomotor performance and subjective effects. J Clin Psychopharmacol 20: 455-66

Carter OL, Burr DC, Pettigrew JD, Wallis GM, Hasler F, Vollenweider FX (2005) Using psilocybin to investigate the relationship between attention, working memory, and the serotonin 1A and 2A receptors. J Cogn Neurosci 17: 1497-508

Carter OL, Hasler F, Pettigrew JD, Wallis GM, Liu GB, Vollenweider FX (2007) Psilocybin links binocular rivalry switch rate to attention and subjective arousal levels in humans. Psychopharmacol (Berl)

Carter OL, Pettigrew JD, Burr DC, Alais D, Hasler F, Vollenweider FX (2004) Psilocybin impairs high-level but not low-level motion perception. Neuroreport 15: 1947-51

Chao JM, Der Marderosian AH (1973) Ergoline alkaloidal constituents of Hawaiian baby wood rose, Argyreia nervosa (Burm. f.) Bojer. J Pharm Sci 62: 588-91

Frei E, Gamma A, Pascual-Marqui R, Lehmann D, Hell D, Vollenweider FX (2001) Localization of MDMA-induced brain activity in healthy volunteers using low resolution brain electromagnetic tomography (LORETA). Hum Brain Mapp 14: 152-65

Gamma A, Buck A, Berthold T, Liechti ME, Vollenweider FX (2000) 3,4-Methylene-dioxymethamphetamine (MDMA) modulates cortical and limbic brain activity as measured by [H(2)(15)O]-PET in healthy humans. Neuropsychopharmacol 23: 388-95

Gasser P (1994) Psycholytic therapy with MDMA and LSD in Switzerland. MAPS Bulletin 5: 3-7

Gasser P (2007) Update: LSD-assisted psychotherapy in persons suffering from anxiety associated with advanced-stage life-threatening illness: a Phase 2, double-blind, placebo-controlled dose-response pilot study. MAPS Bulletin 17: 17

Gouzoulis-Mayfrank E, Heekeren K, Neukirch A, Stoll M, Stock C, Daumann J, Obradovic M, Kovar KA (2006) Inhibition of return in the human 5HT2A agonist and NMDA antagonist model of psychosis. Neuropsychopharmacol 31: 431-41

Gouzoulis-Mayfrank E, Heekeren K, Neukirch A, Stoll M, Stock C, Obradovic M, Kovar KA (2005) Psychological effects of (S)-ketamine and N,N-dimethyltryptamine (DMT): a double-blind, cross-over study in healthy volunteers. Pharmacopsychiatry 38: 301-11

Gouzoulis-Mayfrank E, Thelen B, Habermeyer E, Kunert H, Kovar K, Lindenblatt H, Hermle L, Spitzer M, Sass H (1999a) Psychopathological, neuroendocrine and autonomic effects of 3,4-methylenedioxyethylamphetamine (MDE), psilocybin and d-methamphetamine in healthy volunteers. Psychopharmacol 142: 41-50

Gouzoulis-Mayfrank E, Thelen B, Habermeyer E, Kunert HJ, Kovar KA, Lindenblatt H, Hermle L, Spitzer M, Sass H (1999b) Psychopathological, neuroendocrine and autonomic effects of 3,4-methylenedioxyethylamphetamine (MDE), psilocybin and d-methamphetamine in healthy volunteers. Results of an experimental double-blind placebo-controlled study. Psychopharmacol (Berl) 142: 41-50

Gouzoulis E, Steiger A, Ensslin M, Kovar A, Hermle L (1992) Sleep EEG effects of 3,4-methylenedioxyethamphetamine (MDE; "eve") in healthy volunteers. 32: 1108-1117

Greer G (2007) Email correspondence to L Jerome concerning the MDMA research story

Greer G, Tolbert R (1986) Subjective reports of the effects of MDMA in a clinical setting. J Psychoactive Drugs 18: 319-27

Griffiths RR, Richards WA, McCann U, Jesse R (2006) Psilocybin can occasion mystical-type experiences having substantial and sustained personal meaning and spiritual significance. Psychopharmacol (Berl) 187: 268-83; discussion 284-92

Grob CS (2005) Psilocybin research in advanced-stage cancer patients. MAPS Bulletin 15: 8

Grob CS (2007) Email correspondence to L Jerome concerning relevance of Dr. Grof to inspiration of psilocybin/cancer anxiety study

Grob CS, Poland RE, Chang L, Ernst T (1996) Psychobiologic effects of 3,4-methylene-dioxymethamphetamine in humans: methodological considerations and preliminary observations. Behav Brain Res 73: 103-7

Grof S, Goodman LE, Richards WA, Kurland AA (1973) LSD-assisted psychotherapy in patients with terminal cancer. Int Pharmacopsychiatry 8: 129-44

Halpern JH (2006) Update on the MDMA-assisted psychotherapy study for treatment-resistant anxiety disorders secondary to advanced stage cancer. MAPS Bulletin 16: 16

Hanes KR (1996) Serotonin, psilocybin, and body dysmorphic disorder: a case report. J Clin Psychopharmacol 16: 188-9

Harris DS, Baggott M, Mendelson JH, Mendelson JE, Jones RT (2002) Subjective and hormonal effects of 3,4-methylenedioxymethamphetamine (MDMA) in humans. Psychopharmacol (Berl) 162: 396-405

Hasler F, Bourquin D, Brenneisen R, Bar T, Vollenweider FX (1997) Determination of psilocin and 4-hydroxyindole-3-acetic acid in plasma by HPLC-ECD and pharmacokinetic profiles of oral and intravenous psilocybin in man. Pharm Acta Helv 72: 175-84

Hasler F, Grimberg U, Benz MA, Huber T, Vollenweider FX (2004) Acute psychological and physiological effects of psilocybin in healthy humans: a double-blind, placebo-controlled dose-effect study. Psychopharmacol (Berl) 172: 145-56

Heekeren K, Neukirch A, Daumann J, Stoll M, Obradovic M, Kovar KA, Geyer MA, Gouzoulis-Mayfrank E (2007) Prepulse inhibition of the startle reflex and its attentional modulation in the human S-ketamine and N,N-dimethyltryptamine (DMT) models of psychosis. J Psychopharmacol 21: 312-20

Kast E (1967) Attenuation of anticipation: a therapeutic use of lysergic acid diethylamide. Psychiat Quart 4: 646-57

Kast E, Collins V (1964) Study of lysergic acid diethylamide as an analgesic agent. Anesth Analg 43: 285-91

Krupitsky E, Burakov A, Romanova T, Dunaevsky I, Strassman R, Grinenko A (2002) Ketamine psychotherapy for heroin addiction: immediate effects and two-year follow-up. 23: 273-283

Krupitsky EM, Burakov AM, Romanova TN, Grinenko NI, Grinenko AY, Fletcher J, Petrakis IL, Krystal JH (2001) Attenuation of ketamine effects by nimodipine pretreatment in recovering ethanol dependent men: psychopharmacologic implications of the interaction of NMDA and L-type calcium channel antagonists. Neuropsychopharmacol 25: 936-47

Krupitsky EM, Grinenko AY (1997) Ketamine psychedelic therapy (KPT): a review of the results of ten years of research. J Psychoactive Drugs 29: 165-83

Kuypers KP, Ramaekers JG (2005) Transient memory impairment after acute dose of 75mg 3,4-Methylene-dioxymethamphetamine. J Psychopharmacol 19: 633-9

Kuypers KP, Ramaekers JG (2007) Acute dose of MDMA (75 mg) impairs spatial memory for location but leaves contextual processing of visuospatial information unaffected. Psychopharmacol (Berl) 189: 557-63

Kuypers KP, Wingen M, Samyn N, Limbert N, Ramaekers JG (2007) Acute effects of nocturnal doses of MDMA on measures of impulsivity and psychomotor performance throughout the night. Psychopharmacol (Berl) 192: 111-9

Leonard HL, Rapoport JL (1987) Relief of obsessive-compulsive symptoms by LSD and psilocin [letter]. 144: 1239-40

Lester SJ, Baggott M, Welm S, Schiller NB, Jones RT, Foster E, Mendelson J (2000) Cardiovascular effects of 3,4-methylenedioxymethamphetamine. A double-blind, placebo-controlled trial. 133: 969-73

Liechti ME, Gamma A, Vollenweider FX (2001) Gender differences in the subjective effects of MDMA. Psychopharmacol (Berl) 154: 161-8.

Liechti ME, Vollenweider FX (2001) Which neuroreceptors mediate the subjective effects of MDMA in humans? A summary of mechanistic studies. Hum Psychopharmacol 16: 589-98

Mas M, Farre M, de la Torre R, Roset PN, Ortuno J, Segura J, Cami J (1999) Cardiovascular and neuroendocrine effects and pharmacokinetics of 3,4-methylenedioxymeth-amphetamine in humans. J Pharmacol Exp Ther 290: 136-45

Mithoefer M (2004) MDMA-assisted psychotherapy in the treatment of Posttraumatic Stress Disorder. MAPS Bulletin 14: 3-4

Mithoefer M (2006) MDMA-assisted psychotherapy in the treatment of posttraumatic stress disorder (PTSD): ninth update on study progress. MAPS Bulletin 16: 14-15

Mojeiko V (2006) Israel MDMA/PTSD research project. MAPS Bulletin 16: 10

Moreno FA, Delgado PL (1997) Hallucinogen-induced relief of obsessions and compulsions. 154: 1037-38

Moreno FA, Wiegand CB, Taitano EK, Delgado PL (2006) Safety, tolerability and efficacy of psilocybin in 9 patients with Obsessive-Compulsive Disorder. J Clin Psychiatry 67: 735-40

Oehen P (2006) MDMA/PTSD psychotherapy study in Switzerland launched. MAPS Bulletin 16: 15

Pahnke WN, Kurland AA, Unger S, Savage C, Grof S (1971) The experimental use of psychedelic (LSD) psychotherapy. Int Z Klin Pharmakol Ther Toxikol 4: 446-54

Ramaekers JG, Kuypers KP (2006) Acute effects of 3,4-methylenedioxymethamphetamine (MDMA) on behavioral measures of impulsivity: alone and in combination with alcohol. Neuropsychopharmacol 31: 1048-55

Riba J, Anderer P, Jane F, Saletu B, Barbanoj MJ (2004) Effects of the South American psychoactive beverage ayahuasca on regional brain electrical activity in humans: a functional neuroimaging study using low-resolution electromagnetic tomography. Neuropsychobiol 50: 89-101

Riba J, Anderer P, Morte A, Urbano G, Jane F, Saletu B, Barbanoj MJ (2002a) Topographic pharmaco-EEG mapping of the effects of the South American psychoactive beverage ayahuasca in healthy volunteers. Br J Clin Pharmacol 53: 613-28

Riba J, Rodriguez-Fornells A, Barbanoj MJ (2002b) Effects of ayahuasca on sensory and sensorimotor gating in humans as measured by P50 suppression and prepulse inhibition of the startle reflex, respectively. Psychopharmacol (Berlin) 165: 18-28

Riba J, Rodriguez-Fornells A, Urbano G, Morte A, Antonijoan R, Montero M, Callaway JC, Barbanoj MJ (2001) Subjective effects and tolerability of the South American psychoactive beverage Ayahuasca in healthy volunteers. Psychopharmacol (Berlin) 154: 85-95

Sewell RA, Halpern JH, Pope HG, Jr. (2006) Response of cluster headache to psilocybin and LSD. Neurology 66: 1920-2

Spitzer M, Thimm M, Hermle L, Holzmann P, Kovar KA, Heimann H, Gouzoulis-Mayfrank E, Kischka U, Schneider F (1996) Increased activation of indirect semantic associations under psilocybin. Biol Psychiatry 39: 1055-7

Strassman RJ (1994) Human hallucinogenic drug research: regulatory, clinical, and scientific issues. NIDA Res Monogr 146: 92-123

Strassman RJ (1996) Human psychopharmacology of N,N-dimethyltryptamine. 73: 121-24

Strassman RJ, Qualls C (1994) Dose-response study of N,N-dimethyltryptamine in humans. I. Neuroendocrine, autonomic, and cardiovascular effects. Arch Gen Psychiatry 51: 85-97

Tancer M, Johanson C (2003) Reinforcing, subjective, and physiological effects of MDMA in humans: a comparison with d-amphetamine and mCPP. Drug Alcohol Depend 72: 33-44

Tancer ME, Johanson CE (2001) The subjective effects of MDMA and mCPP in moderate MDMA users. Drug Alcohol Depend 65: 97-101.

Umbricht D, Vollenweider FX, Schmid L, Grubel C, Skrabo A, Huber T, Koller R (2003) Effects of the 5-HT2A agonist psilocybin on mismatch negativity generation and AX-continuous performance task: implications for the neuropharmacology of cognitive deficits in schizophrenia. Neuropsychopharmacol 28: 170-81

Vollenweider FX, Gamma A, Liechti M, Huber T (1998a) Psychological and cardiovascular effects and short-term sequelae of MDMA ("ecstasy") in MDMA-naive healthy volunteers. Neuropsychopharmacol 19: 241-51

Vollenweider FX, Leenders KL, Scharfetter C, Maguire P, Stadelmann O, Angst J (1997) Positron emission tomography and fluorodeoxyglucose studies of metabolic hyper-frontality and psychopathology in the psilocybin model of psychosis. Neuropsycho-pharmacol 16: 357-72

Vollenweider FX, Vollenweider-Scherpenhuyzen MF, Babler A, Vogel H, Hell D (1998b) Psilocybin induces schizophrenia-like psychosis in humans via a serotonin-2 agonist action. Neuroreport 9: 3897-902

Vollenweider FX, Vontobel P, Hell D, Leenders KL (1999) 5-HT modulation of dopamine release in basal ganglia in psilocybin-induced psychosis in man—a PET study with [11C]raclopride. Neuropsychopharmacol 20: 424-33

WHO Expert Committee on Drug Dependence (1985). Twenty-Second Report-Technical Report Series #729. Geneva, Switzerland.

Wittmann M, Carter O, Hasler F, Cahn BR, Grimberg U, Spring P, Hell D, Flohr H, Vollenweider FX (2007) Effects of psilocybin on time perception and temporal control of behaviour in humans. J Psychopharmacol 21: 50-64

About the Publisher

Founded in 1986, the Multidisciplinary Association for Psychedelic Studies (MAPS) is a membership-based, IRS-approved 501 (c) (3) non-profit research and educational organization. We assist scientists to design, fund, obtain approval for, conduct, and report on studies evaluating the risks and benefits of MDMA, psychedelic drugs, and marijuana. MAPS' mission is to sponsor scientific research designed to develop psychedelics and marijuana into FDA-approved prescription medicines and to educate the public honestly about the risks and benefits of these drugs.

For decades, the government was the biggest obstacle to research. Now that long-awaited research is finally being approved, the formidable challenge is funding it. At present, there is no funding available from governments, pharmaceutical companies, or major foundations. That means, for the time being, the future of psychedelic and marijuana research rests in the hands of people like you.

Can you imagine a cultural reintegration of the use of psychedelics and the states of mind they engender? Please join MAPS in supporting the expansion of scientific knowledge in this promising area. Progress is only possible with the support of individuals who care enough to take individual and collective action.

Since 2000, MAPS has disbursed over four million dollars to worthy research and educational projects.

How MAPS Has Made a Difference

- Sponsored and obtained approval for the first LSD-assisted psychotherapy study in over 35 years. The study is taking place in Switzerland in subjects with anxiety associated with end-of-life issues.

- Sponsored the first US FDA-approved study evaluating MDMA's therapeutic applications, for subjects with chronic posttraumatic stress disorder (PTSD), as well as MDMA/PTSD pilot studies in Switzerland, Israel and Spain.

- Waged a successful lawsuit against DEA in support of Professor Lyle Craker's proposed MAPS-sponsored medical marijuana production facility at the University of Massachusetts-Amherst; led campaigns to gain support from over 50 members of the US House of Representatives.

- Supported long-term follow-up studies of pioneering research with LSD and psilocybin from the 1950s and 1960s.

- Sponsored Dr. Evgeny Krupitsky's pioneering research into the use of ketamine-assisted psychotherapy in the treatment of alcoholism and heroin addiction.

- Assisted Dr. Charles Grob to obtain permission for the first human studies in the United States with MDMA after it was criminalized in 1985.

- Sponsored the first study to analyze the purity and potency of street samples of "Ecstasy" and medical marijuana.

- Funded the successful effort of Dr. Donald Abrams to obtain permission for the first human study into the therapeutic use of marijuana in 15 years, and to secure a $1-million grant from the National Institute on Drug Abuse.

- Obtained orphan-drug designation from the FDA for smoked marijuana in the treatment of AIDS Wasting Syndrome.

- Funded the synthesis of psilocybin for the first FDA-approved study in a patient population in twenty-five years.

- Sponsored "Psychedelic Harm Reduction" programs and services at events, concerts, schools, and churches.

Benefits of MAPS Membership

As a MAPS member, you'll receive the tri-annual *MAPS Bulletin*. In addition to reporting on the latest research in both the U.S. and abroad, the Bulletin includes feature articles, personal accounts, book reviews, and reports on conferences and allied organizations. MAPS members are invited to participate in a vital on-line mailing list and to visit our website, which includes all articles published by MAPS since 1988.

Unless otherwise indicated, your donation will be considered an unrestricted gift to be used to fund high-priority projects. If you wish, however, you may direct contributions to a specific study. Your tax-deductible donations may be made by credit card or check made out to MAPS. Gifts of stock are welcome, as are trust and estate planning options.

The MAPS list is strictly confidential and not available for purchase. The *MAPS Bulletin* is mailed in a plain envelope.

MAPS SUBSCRIPTION RATES
Student/Low income Membership — $20
Basic Membership — $35
Integral Membership — $50 (Includes a complimentary book)
Supporting Membership — $100
Patron Membership — $250+
International members add $15 for postage

MULTIDISCIPLINARY ASSOCIATION FOR PSYCHEDELIC STUDIES
10424 Love Creek Road, Ben Lomond, CA 95005
voice: (831)336-4325 • fax: (831)336-3665
e-mail: askmaps@maps.org
Please visit our website: www.maps.org

Ordering Information

LSD Psychotherapy (ISBN: 0-9798622-0-5) ...$19.95/copy
Shipping and Handling Charges
Domestic book rate (allow 3 weeks): $4.50
Domestic priority mail (allow 7 days): $6.60
($1.00 each additional copy)
Overseas airmail rates (allow 10 days):
Canada/Mexico ($7.00)
Other Countries ($9.00) — Pacific Rim ($10.00)
($1.00 each additional copy)

Methods of Payment
Check or money order in U.S. Dollars,
Mastercard, Visa, American Express

Wholesale Orders Welcome: Discount: 50%

Other ways to order *LSD Psychotherapy*
Via secure credit card transaction at *www.maps.org*
Through your favorite local bookstore

Send Orders to:
MAPS/ *LSD Psychotherapy*
10424 Love Creek Road, Ben Lomond, CA 95005
voice: (831)336-4325 • fax: (831)336-3665
e-mail: askmaps@maps.org • www.maps.org